ECONOMICS
Principles and Practice

Second Edition

Philip Black
Trudi Hartzenberg
Barry Standish

In association with the IMM

INSTITUTE OF
MARKETING
MANAGEMENT

PITMAN PUBLISHING
128 Long Acre, London WC2E 9AN
Tel: +44 (0)171 447 2000
Fax: +44 (0)171 240 5771

A Division of Pearson Professional Limited

First published in Great Britain in 1995
Second edition 1997

© Philip Black, Trudi Hartzenberg and Barry Standish 1997

ISBN 0 273 62813 5

British Library Cataloguing in Publication Data
A CIP catalogue record for this book can be obtained from the British Library.

10 9 8 7 6 5 4 3 2

Typeset by Pantek Arts, Maidstone, Kent, England.
Printed and bound in South Africa.

The Publishers' policy is to use paper manufactured from sustainable forests.

CONTENTS

PREFACE TO FIRST EDITION

This book is aimed at filling an important gap in the economics textbook market. As such we have set ourselves three overriding objectives, all of which are pertinent to Southern African students starting out on a first course in economics.

Our primary focus is the typical small and open economy, because we believe that the problems and challenges faced by such an economy are similar to those experienced by Southern African and many other developing countries. These countries all trade extensively with the rest of the world and are therefore vulnerable to changes in the world economy. The economic survival and prosperity of a small and open economy ultimately depend on its ability to compete in world markets and attract capital investment, technical know-how and particular labour skills from the rest of the world. This ability in turn requires a measure of social and political stability as well as a business environment conducive to profitable enterprise.

A second objective is to reinforce the theoretical sections of the book with examples drawn from developing countries generally and Southern Africa in particular. To this end we have made extensive use of various local sources, including the publications of the South African Reserve Bank and the Central Statistical Services, as well as several World Bank reports.

Our third objective is to provide a sensible integration of the micro and macroeconomic components of the book, and also to introduce the reader to some recent contributions in the literature. These include the notion of contestable markets, seller concentration ratios, the New Classical and Neo-Keynesian approaches to macroeconomic adjustment, the role played by real exchange rates in ensuring balance of payments equilibrium, and the 'conditionality debate' surrounding the involvement of the International Monetary Fund and the World Bank in the economic affairs of developing countries.

The book itself falls into seven major sections. Part I highlights the basic economic problem of relative scarcity and introduces the reader to the basic principles of supply and demand. This is done within the context of the chief markets and institutions that make up a modern economy. Parts II and III constitute the microeconomic components of the book and focus on the behaviour of individual consumers and producers under different market conditions. A distinction is made between the polar cases of perfect competition and monopoly while much of the discussion centres on the more realistic cases of monopolistic competition, oligopoly and game-theoretic behaviour on the part of large enterprises.

Part IV outlines the principles of national accounting and develops a simple macroeconomic model of the economy. We use this model to show how the aggregate level of output and employment and the average price level in an economy are determined, and how they may be affected by changes in the underlying demand and supply conditions. Part V introduces money into our macroeconomic model and emphasises the important role played by interest rates and exchange rates in establishing macroeconomic equilibrium in a small and open economy.

Parts VI and VII are devoted to an analysis of important macroeconomic policy issues. We distinguish between fiscal policy, monetary policy and balance of payments policy and show how these may help the policy-maker to come to grips with the problems of unemployment, inflation and cyclical instability. In the last two chapters we try to pull together the various strands by focusing on the particular problems facing a small and open economy and spelling out the relevant policy implications.

PREFACE TO SECOND EDITION

Although our primary focus and chief objectives remain the same, we have made several important changes to the book in an attempt to add substance to it and make it more reader-friendly. The most important changes can be summarised as follows.

- The new edition contains two new chapters. Chapter 15 – on 'Financial markets and the flow of funds' – gives a detailed account of the financial sector and draws out the important distinction between money markets and capital markets. As such, it provides a broad framework within which the role of money and the conduct of monetary policy can be evaluated. Chapter 24 – on 'Poverty, growth and the role of government' – takes the material covered in Part VII a little further than before, and discusses some of the determinants of poverty and possible solutions to it.

- The chapter on 'Market structure, firm behaviour and public policy' has been expanded and brought forward to the new Chapter 6, while Chapter 10 now deals only with the functional distribution of income and also contains several new sections. Issues surrounding the personal distribution of income are included in the new Chapter 24.

- We have added new sections and sub-sections to many of the chapters, and also updated much of the data contained in Parts IV, V and VI.

- The new edition contains some 30 new 'Illustrative' and 'Case' examples, as well as several 'Exhibits' on famous economists. These examples and exhibits are all aimed at extending material covered in the text, and applying theoretical issues to real-world situations.

- Each chapter now has a 'summary' and a list of 'Questions for review' at the end.

ACKNOWLEDGEMENTS

There are several individuals and institutions to whom we owe a debt of gratitude. They are Mr James McLuckie for his continuous support of the project, Mr Brian Collings for assistance rendered during the initial stage, Mr Andrew Mendelson and Ms Laura Halton for important contributions made to several chapters, Ms Linda Foulkes for her efficient typing, and the staff of Pitman Publishing for their encouragement and cooperation.

As far as the second edition of the book is concerned, we would like to thank the following individuals for their valuable contributions: David Mahadea of the University of Transkei, Tony Leiman of the University of Cape Town, Steven Hosking of the University of Port Elizabeth, and several anonymous reviewers.

PART I

Introduction

Part I of the book gives an overview of the fundamental principles according to which a typical modern economy operates. These principles apply to all individuals and households, whether rich or poor, and also bear upon all known economies, irrespective of whether they are driven by markets or whether they contain elements of central planning.

Chapter 1 looks at the basic problem of relative scarcity and discusses the core principles whereby individuals, institutions and countries respond to this problem. Included among these principles are the notions of opportunity cost and comparative advantage, and in Chapter 1 we show how individual persons can improve their own material well-being by trading with one another on the basis of the principle of comparative advantage.

Chapter 2 introduces some of the analytical tools used by economists when studying the real world. Here we consider the production possibilities frontier and show how a small open economy may achieve a higher level of material well-being by trading with other countries. Chapters 1 and 2 are both concerned with the question of how the problem of relative scarcity may be overcome through a process of economic exchange, or trading.

Chapter 3 provides a bird's eye view of the major components of a typical market economy. This is done by expanding gradually the so-called circular flow diagram and spelling out the interrelationships between the various components. Chapter 3 forms the basis of all subsequent chapters and can be regarded as a 'map' through which we explore the workings of a modern economy.

CHAPTER 1

The foundations of economics: scarcity and the gains from trade

In this chapter we shall examine the basic economic problem and show how people respond to it by engaging in various forms of economic exchange. It will be shown that the basic economic problem is that of relative scarcity coupled with the need to choose among scarce resources. From this we develop the concepts of opportunity cost and comparative advantage. Finally by making use of the concept of comparative advantage we can illustrate why people trade and what the gains from trade are.

1.1 The basic economic problem

The world often seems like a very complex place. With hundreds of nations, millions of businesses and billions of people doing different things all the time, it is a great challenge to sort out the issues that really matter, and to identify the factors that are common to us all.

One of the virtues of economics as a science is its ability to simplify the real world. Economics tries to strip aside the detail in order to lay bare the underlying structure of the economic world. Economists attempt to understand those forces which motivate Man as an 'economic animal', and to spell out the implications of these forces. There are many ways in which we can simplify the real world. We could look at an abstract economy with, for example, only two people in it. We could, if you like, choose a very cold island in the North Atlantic, or a small land-locked country in Africa. But if we do have to choose a place in which to conduct our experiments, why not select one of the most beautiful places on earth?

Like pearls scattered across a blue landscape, the many thousands of islands of the South Pacific continue to be one of the great treasures of the world. This patchwork of atolls, islands and archipelagos is perfect too for the understanding of economics. Some of these islands are entirely isolated while others are crowded together and have set up their own economic communities. Many of these islands are rich but, unfortunately, many are also very poor.

For the purposes of this chapter we shall examine two remote islands in the Central Pacific Basin – the islands of Utopia and Famine.

Seen from a distance the island of Utopia is a shimmering green gem surrounded by coral reefs and platinum beaches. Fruits and vegetables grow in abundance in the deep valleys of the rain forest. The fish are so copious in the shallows that Utopians have no need to venture into deep waters. The only boat on the island is the Ceremonial Vessel – used only by the Elders.

The islanders of Famine on the other hand are an unlucky lot. Placed at the confluence of tide and wind, hurricanes and tornadoes occur on a regular basis. What little soil remains after the storms is poor and prospects for fishing in shallow waters are bleak. As a result Faminers have developed a strong maritime tradition and sail far and wide in search of food from the ocean and from other islands.

Both our islands face the same basic economic problem – that of a *scarcity of resources and unlimited wants*. Faminers work hard to eke out an existence from the barren landscape. Scarcity here is self-evident: people lack basic goods like vegetables, fruit and clothing.

Utopia also suffers from a scarcity of resources, even though its citizens are not as poor as those of Famine. Here the scarcity is not for basic goods, however. Rather it is for those luxuries which grow only very high up in the forests and for the young abalone which live well below the tidal zone. There is also a scarcity of fine garments and hurricane-proof housing (even Utopia has a storm or two).

It is evident that the basic economic problem in Utopia is not simply that of a scarcity of goods and services, but rather scarcity as the result of unlimited wants. Here the unlimited wants is what really creates the scarcity and, as a result, the basic economic problem.

On the islands of both Utopia and Famine there is a relative scarcity, albeit a scarcity of different goods and services. In consequence both Faminers and Utopians have to choose between their various wants. On Famine the choice is fairly straightforward: one can either go fishing in the deep waters or go hungry. In Utopia the choice is not between food and no food but rather about what kinds of food to gather and what kinds of materials to collect for house-building. While food is in abundance in Utopia, the most desirable types of food are those that are difficult to collect, e.g. bird eggs and deep sea fish.

> **Basic economic problem.** *The basic economic problem is that of scarcity as a result of unlimited wants. As a consequence choices have to be made.*

1.2 Opportunity cost

We have seen that as scarcity exists choices have to be made. One of the important contributions of economics is the idea that it is more useful to consider costs in terms of opportunities foregone than to do so in simple monetary terms. (Such monetary assessments are impossible on Utopia and Famine anyway as they currently use some very complicated barter system.)

> **Opportunity cost.** *Opportunity cost is the cost of the next best alternative foregone when a choice is made.*

On Famine the choice made, as seen above, is between deep sea fishing and going hungry. But hunger *per se* is *not* the opportunity cost of fishing: it is merely the *consequence* of not fishing. Rather the opportunity cost of fishing is the next best alternative to fishing. This may include the repair of boats and fishing gear, or the building of new boats, or it may involve resting and recuperating or having wild and extravagant parties.

If Faminers spend too much time partying they will forfeit the opportunity of catching enough fish or working on their boats and, as a consequence, go hungry. Conversely, if they spend too much time fishing they may not have enough time left for resting and recuperating, in which case their quality of life is bound to suffer – notwithstanding an abundance of fish.

Utopians too have to choose between gathering basic vegetables and fruits and collecting the more exotic foods, or engaging in leisure activities. If they spend too much time gathering basic foods, they may have to forfeit leisure time and go without bird eggs.

In today's world opportunity cost is used whenever individuals make purchases. While most people will consider the price of a good or service before purchasing it, the decision to purchase it is made less as a result of its price and more by considering what else the money could be spent on.

1.3 Economic interaction – the gains from trade

There is a commonly held notion that when there is trade (between people or between countries) one of the parties involved is being exploited. If somebody is gaining then somebody else must be losing. This section sets out to show that, not only is this an incorrect notion, and that people do benefit from trade, but that the potential benefits can be enormous.

To illustrate the principles involved we return to our island of Utopia. But now we return to a very early part of the island's history – *a time when people did not trade*. There was a folklore, buried in the history of time, that people who were very good at doing things (what we today would call highly productive) would have little incentive to trade with people who were not that good at doing things. It was also believed that if there was trade the less productive person was going to be exploited.

Now the problem with such beliefs was that they resulted in widespread dissatisfaction on the island – the type of dissatisfaction that happens if there is no change. For you or me the island of Utopia probably looks like a paradise. For the Utopians it was distinctly boring – nothing changed. Year after year things stayed exactly the same. Life became no worse but also it became no better. The Utopians had come to believe that the principle of absolute advantage was the principle which dominated trade.

> **Absolute advantage.** *An absolute advantage exists where an individual can produce a good or service with less effort (resources) than some other individual.*

One day this tedium was broken. There was a storm and a book written by a man called A. Smith was washed up on the beach. The words in the book had a galvanising effect on the Elders of the island. With time for reflection and debate, and considerable difference of opinion, some consensus was reached that the principles outlined in the book should at least be given a fair chance. The book was, of course, *The Wealth of Nations*. In it are outlined the gains to be had from trade and also the means of harnessing them to achieve a higher quality of life. What Adam Smith advocated was that an individual (or country) can gain from trading with other individuals (or countries) as a result of differences in opportunity costs. Economists refer to this phenomenon as the principle of comparative advantage.

> **Comparative advantage.** *A comparative advantage exists where an individual (or country) has a lower opportunity cost in the production of some good or service than does some other individual (or country).*

Finally we are able to understand how gains from trade can be achieved.

> **Gains from trade.** *Gains from trade can be achieved when an individual produces those goods or services for which he or she has the lowest opportunity cost relative to other individuals.*

Returning now to Utopia, we see these principles being applied, at least at a relatively simple level. The most obvious change is a clear division of labour into different tasks along the lines of comparative advantage. Those who are fleet of foot exploit the higher reaches of the mountains while the very strong collect copious amounts of the more common fruits. One Utopian family, the Aquarians, have even ventured into the deeper parts of the lagoon in search of marine delicacies. At the end of each day all the collectors come together and exchange goods. This is then followed by a night of feasting and festivities. To the Utopians the gains from trade are evident. Their nightly orgies have risen to such heights of opulence as to far outweigh even the 'Great Time of Abundance'. For Utopians the quality of life has never been so good.

Faminers too have had ample time to think about their economic problem. Although they did not have the benefit of Adam Smith's book, they had enough common sense to realise that certain gains could be had from a system of labour division based on the principle of comparative advantage. Some of them soon became master anglers while others became master boat-builders. Some Faminers even became master story-tellers who would exchange their stories for fresh fish.

1.4 Terms of trade

Returning to the island of Utopia, there was one question that continued to vex the Utopian economists (even here there were those with a comparative advantage in economics). After a long day of theorising and forecasting the economists also gathered at the market-place. As they watched the Gatherers bargain and barter, their main concern was over how barter rates were established. What they did note was that these rates were not static but changed over time. To further complicate matters each Gatherer appeared to have some minimum rate at which there was no trade.

How is the rate of exchange determined? What makes each individual Gatherer stop trading? The answer, as we will see, lies in the principles of opportunity cost and comparative advantage.

Let us consider the situation of two of the Gatherers. The first, Nimbus, gathers bird eggs from the highest reaches of the rain forest. These are considered a great delicacy. In a normal day she can gather 20 eggs. The other Gatherer is Mammoth. He is enormously strong and ideally suited to digging and carrying root vegetables. Mammoth usually brings 20 root vegetables to the market each day. On the other hand when Nimbus turns her hand to digging, she can usually bring only two roots to the market. Mammoth, when he doesn't actually fall from the trees, can collect two eggs during a full day's work. The position is presented in Table 1.1.

Table 1.1 Eggs or roots collected in a single day

	Nimbus	Mammoth
Eggs	20	2
Roots	2	20

Nimbus can collect 20 eggs or two roots in a day while Mammoth can collect two eggs or 20 roots. Why should the Gatherers trade? When will they not trade?

The reason why the Gatherers trade is that they will each gain from this trade. Imagine that our Gatherers do not trade but wish to eat both eggs and roots each day. Without trade Nimbus must collect at least one root. As this takes half a day she ends up with ten eggs and one root. By the same reasoning Mammoth has one egg and ten roots. Now consider the case where the two Gatherers are prepared to swap eggs for roots in the ratio of 1:1 (i.e. one egg for one root). It is likely that Nimbus will collect only eggs and Mammoth only roots. If each swaps half of his or her daily collection both Nimbus and Mammoth will end up with ten eggs and ten roots. Both Gatherers have gained from trade.

Where do the absolute and comparative advantages lie? Bearing in mind the above definitions, it is obvious that Nimbus has the absolute advantage in collecting eggs and Mammoth in digging roots. Who has the comparative advantage? To identify comparative advantage we need to calculate the opportunity costs.

For Nimbus the opportunity cost of one root is ten eggs (she gives up ten eggs to collect one root) while the opportunity cost of one egg is $\frac{1}{10}$ root, i.e. 0.1 root. For Mammoth the reverse is true. These ratios are shown in Table 1.2.

Table 1.2 Opportunity costs

Nimbus	$1r = 10e$ and $1e = 0.1r$
Mammoth	$1e = 10r$ and $1r = 0.1e$

The comparative advantage in eggs lies clearly with Nimbus – she has the lowest opportunity cost in the collection of eggs; while the comparative advantage in roots lies with Mammoth.

The final issue we need to consider here are the circumstances under which our Gatherers will not be willing to trade. In order to do this we need to calculate the ratios within which the Gatherers are willing to trade.

Given the data in Table 1.2, Nimbus is willing to trade up to ten eggs for a single root. Likewise Mammoth is willing to take as little as 0.1 egg for a root. We are therefore in a position to state the exchange boundaries for roots and eggs:

$$0.1e < 1r < 10e$$

$$0.1r < 1e < 10r$$

In other words one root can be traded for between 0.1 eggs and ten eggs and one egg for between 0.1 root and ten roots. Should either party attempt to exchange outside of these boundaries no trade will take place (for example, one egg for 15 roots).

Paying attention to the definition of the terms of trade above, i.e. the price of one good in terms of the other, what will be the terms of trade? In other words, at what ratio will the goods actually be exchanged? Here it is not possible to say. Certainly we know that the terms of trade must lie within the trade boundaries. Where they will actually settle depends on the relative bargaining strengths of the two Gatherers and just how desperately each wants eggs and roots each day.

EXHIBIT

Smith and Ricardo

Adam Smith is generally considered to be the founding father of modern economics. His *Wealth of Nations*, published in 1776, was the first major treatise on economics, and has been widely quoted by economists past and present. In it he argued that the wealth of a nation depends on whether its people are able to engage in specialised work and trade in free and competitive markets. He is perhaps best known for coining the phrase, 'the invisible hand'.

According to Smith, an 'invisible hand' would see to it that the wealth and well-being of a nation is maximised when each of its members are given the freedom to pursue his or her own happiness in a way that he or she sees fit. This was one of the first attempts to acknowledge the virtues of the free market system.

▶

Exhibit
continued

Smith's theory of specialisation is of some relevance to our book. He argued that when workers become specialised in performing specific tasks, rather than undertake many tasks at once, they can collectively produce more with the same effort. For this to be possible, however, they must be furnished with specialised tools and equipment, which can only be accomplished by means of a process of capital investment. Such a process, in turn, requires an adequate volume of savings and a market that is sufficiently large to absorb the total product. The theory thus envisages a kind of virtuous circle of continuous economic progress.

David Ricardo, together with Smith, Thomas Malthus and John Stuart Mill, was one of the most prominent members of the so-called 'Classical school'. He was a highly successful business person before he published his major work, *Principles of Political Economy*, in 1817. He is famous for his theory of comparative advantage as applied to international trade. In the original version of the theory, he used the example of two countries, England and Portugal, and explained why both will be better off if England exported wool to Portugal and imported wine in return – even though both goods could be produced more cheaply in Portugal! Although his theory has been much refined over the years, it is still valid today, and it is largely for this reason that we discuss it in some detail in the next chapter.

Summary

- The basic economic problem is one of relative scarcity, i.e. the co-existence of a scarcity of resources and unlimited wants. This is true of poor and rich people alike.

- All people must therefore make choices, e.g. of how to use their weekly salary in such a way as to fulfil their most important needs. In making such a choice, each person must consider the opportunity cost of his or her action, i.e. the cost of the next best alternative foregone when a choice is made.

- The concept of opportunity cost is crucial to all forms of exchange between people. A person can gain from trading a good or service if he or she can produce it at a lower opportunity cost than other individuals. Such a person is said to have a comparative advantage in the production of the particular good or service.

- Likewise, the terms of trade, or the price of a good in terms of other goods foregone, depend on differences in the opportunity costs of individuals engaged in trade.

Questions for review

1. Discuss the 'basic economic problem' and explain why it applies to all countries, rich and poor.

2. What are the opportunity costs of enrolling for a first course in economics? Or of participating in an all-night party?

3. Why do individuals trade with one another? What is the connection between the gains from trade and the principle of opportunity cost?

4. Consider Tables 1.3 to 1.5 and establish for each case who has the absolute advantage, the comparative advantage and what the trade boundaries are. In one of these situations there will be no trade. Which one? Why?

Table 1.3 Eggs or roots collected in a single day: case 1

	Nimbus	Mammoth
Eggs	20	20
Roots	2	1

Table 1.4 Eggs or roots collected in a single day: case 2

	Nimbus	Mammoth
Eggs	60	5
Roots	10	40

Table 1.5 Eggs or roots collected in a single day: case 3

	Nimbus	Mammoth
Eggs	20	40
Roots	2	3

CHAPTER 2

Production, prices and trade

In this chapter we shall re-examine the basic principles established in Chapter 1 by developing a simple model of the economy. Although this is a highly abstract model which only begins to describe the complexities of the real world, it does at least give a framework within which to understand the basic principles of opportunity cost, comparative advantage and economic exchange.

When economists look at a real-world problem, they try to simplify it by formulating a theoretical model aimed at enhancing our understanding of the relevant issues. The process involves making simplifying assumptions about the problem under investigation, building a logically consistent model, and testing it empirically. This last stage entails a comparison of the conclusions or predictions of the model with what actually happens in the real world. Ultimately the model will stand or fall by its ability to explain and predict accurately.

If the conclusions of the model are not borne out in the real world it is usually the model that is at fault. Here one needs to go back to the proverbial drawing board and re-examine the basic assumptions as well as the logical deductions that were made. Economic analysis is really an endless process of challenging existing models, accepting or rejecting them and, where necessary, improving them in such a way as to provide a better understanding of the real world.

This methodology will be used throughout the book, and its meaning will become clear as we consider the notions of supply and demand and focus on some of the more lively debates in economics.

2.1 The production possibilities frontier (PPF)

Chapter 1 outlined the basic economic problem – scarcity and choice – and showed how this accounts for the existence of trade between people. We will now use the simple model of the production possibilities frontier (PPF) to further illustrate this point.

Our model assumes there are only two goods, say vegetables and garments, both of which are produced by means of a fixed quantity of inputs, or factors of production, and with a given technology. The factors of production may include a given tract of arable land, and a certain number of labourers and machines used in the production of both goods. By technology we mean the actual methods used in the production of vegetables and garments, which we assume to remain the same for the time being.

The factors of production

When we produce goods and services we use a wide variety of physical and human resources – collectively known as factors of production. There are four broad categories of production factors:

- **Land.** This is made up of the physical land around us as well as all natural resources. Hence the gold which is underground, the rivers that flow across our land, and the forests which grow next to the rivers are all part of this factor of production.

- **Labour.** Naturally enough this is made up of people who are willing and able to work, and is ultimately determined by the number of hours worked and the intensity with which people work. When people improve their ability to work, for example by going to college, this is said to be adding to human capital.

- **Capital.** This is usually taken to mean the physical capital of a country. Roads, bridges, factories and machinery are all part of the capital stock. It is what some people refer to as the 'means of production'. Capital actually comes from the savings of ordinary people. From whom do firms borrow the money they need to build factories and buy machinery? From the people!

- **Entrepreneurship.** An entrepreneur is someone with the ability or experience to identify and utilise a profitable opportunity in the market, and take on the risk of doing so. Without entrepreneurs there would be no economic activity, and indeed no economics!

Linear PPFs

Figure 2.1 illustrates the simplest possible model of the basic economic problem. The vertical axis shows the quantity of garments that can be produced in the economy within a given period of time. If all resources were employed in the making of garments, for example, an amount OC of garments could be produced. Likewise, if all resources were used in the production of vegetables only, an amount OD of vegetables could be produced.

The line joining points C and D represents the production possibilities of choices between garments and vegetables. For instance, if the country chooses to be at point E then an amount OF of garments and OG of vegetables will be produced with the given quantity of production factors. Alternatively, if production occurs at point H, then OI garments and OJ vegetables will be produced.

What we have done here is to establish a graphical model of the basic economic problem. We are now able to see positions of unlimited wants (any position to the right of the PPF) and scarcity (as illustrated by the PPF itself). Furthermore, we can now also illustrate graphically the concept of opportunity cost. What is the opportunity cost of moving from position E to position H,

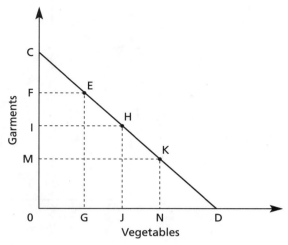

Fig. 2.1 A linear PPF

or increasing production of vegetables from OG to OJ? As noted in Chapter 1, the answer lies in the next best alternative foregone, that is, the amount OF – OI of garments.

The PPF shown in Fig. 2.1 is obviously a straight line. Consider for example points E, H and K. These points were chosen to ensure that a movement from E to H and one from H to K imply equal decreases in the quantity of garments produced, that is:

$$OF - OI = OI - OM.$$

What is immediately obvious is that the corresponding increases in vegetable production are also equal, that is:

$$OJ - OG = ON - OJ.$$

In other words, a linear PPF implies equal proportional changes in production.

What would these proportional changes mean in the real world? It means that factors of production are equally as productive in the making of garments as they are in the production of vegetables. This is clearly a most unlikely situation when it comes to the production of goods as dissimilar as garments and vegetables. It suggests that a vegetable farmer is as efficient at supplying vegetables as he or she is at making garments. Likewise, a garment maker is also an expert at producing vegetables.

Non-linear PPFs

In contrast to linear PPFs, real-world conditions will be more accurately reflected by a non-linear PPF. In the case shown in Fig. 2.2, the PPF is non-linear and is said to be concave from the origin.

The concave PPF in Fig. 2.2 can be interpreted in the same way as a linear PPF, i.e. we can produce OC garments or OD vegetables, or some combination

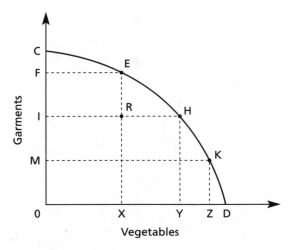

Fig. 2.2 A non-linear PPF

along the PPF, with our given resources. However, what this PPF shows is the more realistic situation where factors of production are not fully substitutable between the two sectors. For example, if the economy moves from E to H to K in Fig. 2.2, then, as we give up equal amounts of garments (OF – OI = OI – OM), the increases in vegetable production occur at a decreasing rate (OY – OX > OZ – OY).

2.2 The PPF and economic efficiency

Economic efficiency is conventionally defined in terms of both *productive efficiency* and *allocative efficiency*. These concepts refer to the allocation of a country's given resources at a particular point in time, and must be distinguished from the notion of *economic growth* – sometimes referred to as dynamic efficiency.

Productive efficiency

Sometimes called X-efficiency or 'organisational slack', productive efficiency refers to a situation in which the existing resources of a country are utilised in the most efficient manner. Productive efficiency occurs when a country finds itself on its PPF, e.g. points E or H on the PPF shown in Fig. 2.2.

Conversely, any output combination lying inside the PPF, such as point R in Fig. 2.2, indicates the presence of X-inefficiency insofar as the available resources can be used to produce more of one or both goods, e.g. the combinations lying between points E and H. X-inefficiency may result from a lack of motivation on the part of productive agents, and from a lack of knowledge about supply and demand conditions in the market-place. In essence, productive inefficiency means that the available resources of a country are not being fully utilised.

Allocative efficiency

Allocative efficiency refers to the actual position on the PPF. It reflects an efficient allocation of resources among alternative uses giving rise to production of the *optimal mix of commodities*. The latter is determined by the relative preferences of consumers as reflected in the market prices of the two goods. For example, if the consuming public had a strong preference for garments relative to vegetables, it can be expected that the demand for garments, and hence also its supply, will be large relative to the demand for and supply of vegetables. Under these conditions an efficient economy is likely to operate at a point such as E on the PPF in Fig. 2.2. Such an economy can be said to be efficient in both the productive and allocative sense of the word.

Economic growth

Economic growth implies an increase in the quantity of goods and services produced over time. There are essentially two reasons why an economy may grow: namely, an increase in the *productivity* of the *existing* factors of production, for example because of technological progress, and an *increase* in the quantity of the factors of production.

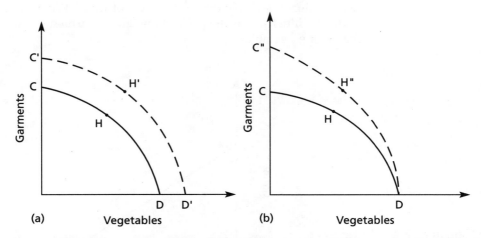

Fig. 2.3 (a) Economic growth; (b) Technological progress in the garments sector

In terms of the model developed in this chapter, economic growth can be shown as an outward shift of the entire PPF, e.g. from CD to C'D' in Fig. 2.3(a). Several factors may be responsible for such shifts:

- *The more productive use of the existing factors of production.* Here we assume that technological change, e.g. computerisation, enables both sectors to produce more with their given resources, e.g. point H' compared to H in Fig. 2.3(a). Alternatively, if technological progress should benefit one sector only, e.g. the garments sector, the PPF might undergo a rotational shift from CD to C"D in Fig. 2.3(b).

In both cases illustrated in Fig. 2.3, technological progress enables the economy to produce more of both goods with its given resources. This is illustrated by a movement from point H to points H′ and H″.

- *Increases in the quantity of land and labour.* While there is clearly a limit to the amount of land available for production purposes, the labour force may grow as a result of natural population growth or a net immigration of workers.

- *Increases in the quantity of machines, tools and other equipment.* These are referred to as capital goods which are produced or acquired through a process of investment. In a closed economy the source of investment is domestic savings while in an open economy investment may be funded either from domestic or foreign sources.

2.3 Prices and the PPF

At the moment we have yet to examine the meaning and formation of prices in a monetary economy. However, it is possible within the context of the PPF to examine relative prices (which, from an opportunity cost perspective, is exactly what prices are). Figure 2.4 establishes a so-called price line, MN. We refer to this line as the domestic terms of trade. What the domestic terms of trade line illustrates is the price of one good (garments in this case) in terms of the other (vegetables).

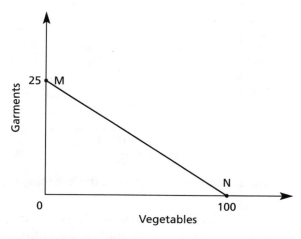

Fig. 2.4 The domestic terms of trade line (or price line)

A simple way of understanding the construction of a terms of trade line is to allow the two goods to have monetary prices (as we understand them in the real world) and for there to be a so-called budget limit. In Fig. 2.4, for example, it is assumed that the total budget available to consumers is R500. Consumers can buy either 25 garments at point M, or 100 kilograms of vegetables at point N, or some combination of the two goods. Garments therefore cost R20 each while vegetables cost R5 per kilogram. It follows that the slope of our price line shows the relative prices of the two goods. In absolute terms the slope of MN is $\frac{1}{4}$ and we can therefore say that one garment effectively equals 4 kilograms of vegetables.

If the income of consumers were to increase, say from R500 to R1000, but the prices of the two goods remained the same, our price line will undergo a parallel outward shift, e.g. from MN to M'N' in Fig. 2.5(a). Consumers are now able to purchase 50 garments at R20 each at point M', or 200 kilograms of vegetables at R5 each at point N', or some combination of the two goods along M'N'. It is important to note that in this example the domestic terms of trade have remained unchanged.

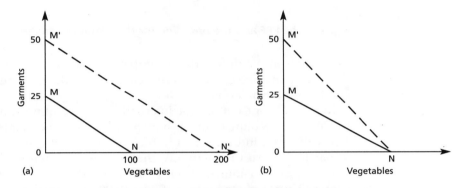

Fig. 2.5 (a) Increase in consumers' income; (b) Fall in the price of garments

Alternatively, if the price of garments were to fall, from R20 to R10 for example, the slope of the price line is bound to increase. This is illustrated in Fig. 2.5(b) by the rotational shift in the price line from MN to M'N. It is clear that consumers now have a choice of either buying 50 garments at R10 each, or 100 kilograms of vegetables at R5, or some combination of the two goods. In this instance the terms of trade can be said to have moved in favour of garments.

2.4 Gains from trade

We are now in a position to demonstrate the gains from trade between two countries, and for this purpose we return to our two island economies, Utopia and Famine. Figure 2.6 shows the PPF for Famine where, at point E, it is producing and consuming two goods, fruit and fish products. It has achieved allocative and productive efficiency at point E where its domestic price line, MN, is tangent to the PPF. At point E the country is utilising all its resources to produce and consume OF kilograms of fruit and OG kilograms of fish.

Now, remember our earlier discussion where we showed that for trade to occur between two individuals there had to be a corresponding difference in comparative advantage. The same is also true of countries. Here the condition

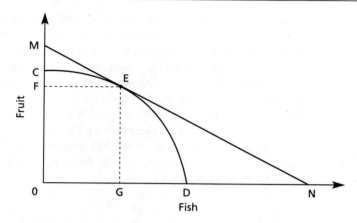

Fig. 2.6 The PPF and the price line for the island of Famine

for trade is also a difference in comparative advantage which, from the point of view of any one country, is reflected in the difference between its domestic and international terms of trade.

In Fig. 2.7, for example, the international terms of trade line is given by VW. Its slope (in absolute terms) is higher than that of the domestic price line, MN. This difference indicates that in the world economy generally, and in Utopia in particular, fruit is relatively cheaper and fish relatively more expensive than they are in Famine. This is easily verified by assuming that consumers in Famine have a given budget of, say, R500. At prevailing world prices, given by the slope of VW, they can evidently acquire more fruit and fewer kilograms of fish than they can in the domestic economy.

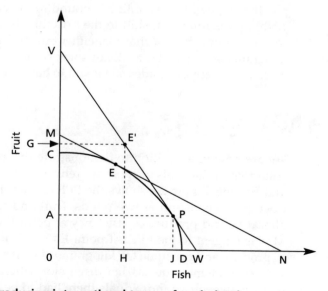

Fig. 2.7 Introducing international terms of trade (VW)

Famine evidently has a comparative advantage in the production of fish while Utopia has a comparative advantage in the production of fruit. It would therefore pay Famine to export fish and import fruit: it gets more for its fish on world markets and pays less for fruit than it does domestically.

Now, if Famine specialises according to its comparative advantage, i.e. fish, it will change the proportion of fish and fruit produced according to world prices rather than domestic prices. (At the same time any difference which might have existed between relative prices inside and outside Famine will disappear, i.e. MN no longer exists.) Production changes to point P and, depending on domestic demand, consumption after trade may occur at a point such as E'.

At points P and E', Famine produces OJ kilograms of fish of which OJ – OH are exported to Utopia and OH kilograms are consumed by Faminers. Similarly, Faminers consume OG kilograms of fruit of which OG – OA are imported and OA kilograms are locally produced. Famine therefore exports the good in which it has a comparative advantage, i.e. fish, while Utopia likewise specialises in the good in which its own comparative advantage lies, i.e. fruit.

What is important about point E' is that it lies both to the right and above the position that Famine was in before trade – E. In other words, after specialisation and trade Faminers are able to consume more of both goods than they did before trade.

CASE EXAMPLE

South Africa's trade with other countries

Table 2.1 South Africa's top 20 trading partners

	1994		1995		1995
COUNTRY	RANK	TOTAL TRADE Rbn	RANK	TOTAL TRADE Rbn	TRADE BALANCE Rbn
GERMANY	1	16.68	1	20.58	–11.48
UK	2	14.9	2	19.04	–2.47
USA	3	12.96	3	16.34	–6.66
JAPAN	4	12.05	4	14.99	–4.77
ITALY	6	4.75	5	6.42	–1.6
SWITZERLAND	5	8	6	6.04	1.28
CHINA/TAIWAN	7	4.42	7	5.77	–0.68
ZIMBABWE	11	3.48	8	5.51	3.58
BELGIUM	8	4.34	9	5.36	1.11
THE NETHERLANDS	9	4	10	5.36	0.76
FRANCE	10	3.71	11	4.99	–2.51
IRAN	47	0.22	12	4.52	–4.23
HONG KONG	12	2.96	13	3.58	0.33
SOUTH KOREA	13	2.82	14	3.54	0.55

▶

Case example
continued

Table 2.1 Continued

COUNTRY	1994			1995		1995
	RANK	TOTAL TRADE Rbn	RANK	TOTAL TRADE Rbn	TRADE BALANCE Rbn	
PEOPLE'S REP. OF CHINA	14	1.37	15	2.89	−0.8	
AUSTRALIA	15	1.74	16	2.58	−0.63	
SPAIN	16	1.72	17	2.6	1.04	
MOZAMBIQUE	21	1.49	18	2.35	2.12	
SINGAPORE	22	1.45	19	2.3	−0.51	
ISRAEL	17	1.68	20	2.01	0.78	

Source: Department of Trade and Industry Republic of South Africa

From Table 2.1 it is clear that South Africa's top four trading partners have not changed. Of significance is the move by Zimbabwe from 11th place in 1994 to 8th in 1995, and by Mozambique from 21st to 18th. The table highlights the continued importance of Europe, the USA and Japan in South African trade.

Table 2.2 South Africa's market share in Africa, based on 1992 and 1993 export figures

Country	% share
Swaziland	46
Namibia	75
Lesotho	92
Botswana	78
SADC	30
Comesa	12
Sub-saharan Africa	5.20
N Africa	5
Africa	3

Source: Global Strategy Project, Trade Policy Monitoring Unit & DTI, March 1996, University of Cape Town

Table 2.2 shows clearly that South Africa is an important trading partner for other African countries, accounting for 30 per cent of the market for SADC countries. Of South Africa's exports to Africa, Southern Africa absorbs 70 per cent. SACU countries account for 60 per cent of South Africa's exports to Africa, with a further 20 per cent going to Zimbabwe, Zambia, Mozambique and Malawi.

Summary

- The production possibilities frontier (PPF) is a heuristic device indicating the maximum quantities of two goods that a country can produce with its given resources. While there are many combinations of the two goods from which to choose, the country will always strive to reach a combination that lies on its PPF.

- Any point on the PPF represents a state of *productive* efficiency, while points lying below it are productively inefficient. Likewise *allocative* efficiency refers to production of the optimal mix of commodities. Economic growth – or *dynamic* efficiency – is shown by an outward shift in the PPF, and results from increases in the quantity or productivity of a country's resources.

- The domestic terms of trade refer to the relative prices of goods produced within a country, e.g. the price of one good in terms of the other. Both the position and the slope of the domestic price line will determine the exact position on the PPF where an economy will produce. At this point the price line will be tangent to the PPF, and the economy will have achieved both allocative and productive efficiency.

- The gains from trade between two countries stem from the difference in their respective comparative advantages. For any one country the latter difference is reflected in the difference between its domestic and international terms of trade. Such a country will gain from trade by producing and consuming in accordance with its international price line: it will specialise in the production of the good in which it has a comparative advantage, export some of it in exchange for imports of the other good, and end up consuming more of both goods than it would have done in the absence of trade.

Questions for review

1. Consider a typical production possibilities frontier (PPF) indicating the choice between producing two goods, guns and butter. Explain (a) why the community might decide to produce more guns relative to butter, and (b) what the opportunity cost of such a decision will be.

2. Using the concept of a PPF, distinguish between 'productive' and 'allocative' efficiency. Do you think the countries of southern Africa, or any other country for that matter, are ever likely to be efficient, in the productive and allocative sense of the word? Why?

3. Why does a country stand to 'gain' by trading with other countries?

CHAPTER 3

A bird's eye view of the economy: circular flows, prices and markets

This chapter provides a broad overview of the chief components comprising a typical modern economy. Its main purpose is to highlight the interrelationships that exist between the various components, as it is these interrelationships that will be further explored in the microeconomic and macroeconomic sections of the book.

We start by introducing a circular flow diagram showing the functional relationships between two of the most important institutions, i.e. households and firms. This is followed by a section dealing with the basic concepts of supply and demand, and the determination of prices, which can be viewed as the economic link between households and firms. In the remaining sections we gradually expand our circular flow diagram by introducing other important institutions, such as the financial sector, foreign markets and the government.

3.1 Households and firms

In this section we shall assume that households own all the factors of production. In addition to land, capital and labour, they also own entrepreneurial services which they are able to sell to firms. Firms in turn use the factors of production to produce goods and services which they sell to households.

Figure 3.1 provides a simple illustration of a circular flow diagram. The left-hand side of the diagram indicates the process by which households supply production factors to firms in exchange for money income. For example, the owners of land receive a rental from tenants, capital owners receive dividends or interest payments from borrowers, labourers receive wages and salaries for labour services rendered, and entrepreneurs receive profits in return for combining land, capital and labour into profitable ventures. These incomes are collectively known as *national income* – shown by the heavy flow line in Fig. 3.1.

Firms use the factors of production to produce a variety of goods and services and offer them for sale to households. The supply of goods and services is shown as the thin line on the right hand side of Fig. 3.1. The amounts spent by households, or *national expenditure*, are shown as the heavy line. These lines complete our circular flow diagram.

According to Fig. 3.1, firms purchase factors of production which generate income to households. Households in turn use this income to buy the goods and services which firms produce. As firms receive this expenditure they are

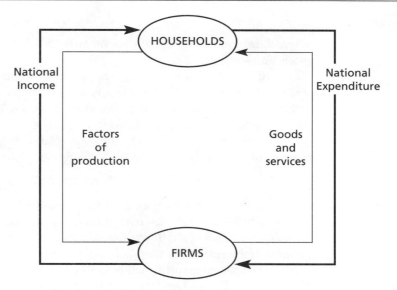

Fig. 3.1 Circular flow diagram

able to utilise more factors of production, generate more income and therefore more expenditure. What one sees in practice is therefore a circular flow of income and expenditure. This simple circular flow can be regarded as the driving force in the economy – the 'engine of growth'.

3.2 A digression: introducing markets

Our exploration of a typical modern economy requires us to digress slightly from our building of the circular flow model. We do this in order to explore further the relationship between households and firms.

Prices play a pivotal role in the functioning of all market economies. They are formed by the forces of demand and supply, and ultimately determine the quantity of goods and services produced by firms and consumed by households.

The national or total expenditure by households gives rise to the *aggregate demand* while the total quantity of goods or services produced by firms constitutes *aggregate supply*. These aggregates are linked by the average price level, which is simply a weighted average of all prices in the economy.

The demand function

As far as the demand side is concerned, we can state that national expenditure determines the actual quantity of goods and services demanded by households, that is:

$$E \rightarrow D$$

where E represents national expenditure and D the quantity demanded of goods and services.

One of the fundamental hypotheses in economics is the so-called *law of demand*. According to this law the quantity demanded of any good or service will be larger the lower is its price, and *vice versa*. Thus the demand for the good or service is inversely related to its price.

The same law also applies to the aggregate demand. But here we assume demand to be inversely related to the (weighted) average price level, P, that is:

$$D = f(P) \ ceteris \ paribus$$

where the term *ceteris paribus* implies that all influences other than price are temporarily held constant. These influences may include the incomes of consumers and, as we shall see below, taxes, government expenditure and incomes in the rest of the world.

An aggregate demand function is illustrated in Fig. 3.2 where the relationship between demand and the average price level is assumed to be an inverse one. At an average price of R10 for example, the quantity demanded by households equals 1000 units. However, if the average price should fall to R8, the quantity demanded will increase to 1100 units of output.

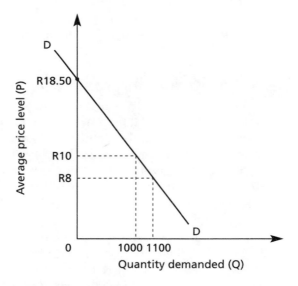

Fig. 3.2 An aggregate demand function

It should be noted that the demand curve can be either linear or non-linear and, as will be illustrated later in the book, can have virtually any shape. An example of a linear consumption function is:

$$D = 18.50 - 1.2P$$

where the first term on the right-hand side of the equation represents the *position* of the function, or its intercept with the vertical axis, and the coefficient of the second term (i.e. 1.2) represents the *slope* of the function. The latter indicates the extent to which quantity demanded will change in response to a given change in the average price.

The position of the demand function will change if we relax our *ceteris paribus* assumption and introduce a so-called *exogenous* change. For example, an increase in the incomes of households will cause an outward shift in the demand function from DD to D'D' in Fig. 3.3, implying that at an average price of R10 households are now able and willing to purchase 1300 units of output.

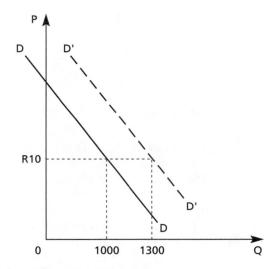

Fig. 3.3 An outward shift in the demand function

The supply function

Turning now to the supply side, economists usually assume that the quantity supplied of a good or service is positively related to its price. This *law of supply* is also true of the aggregate supply of goods and services. For example:

$$S = g(P) \text{ ceteris paribus}$$

where S is the aggregate quantity of goods and services supplied, P is the average price level and the term *ceteris paribus* has the same meaning as before. The factors held constant here may include the prevailing technology and the costs of the factors of production, e.g. the price of labour or the prices of imported materials.

Figure 3.4 illustrates a typical aggregate supply function. At an average price of R8, for example, the aggregate supply of goods and services equals 900. But if the aggregate price increases to R10, aggregate supply will rise to 1000 units. Here it is assumed that with no change in production costs, firms would want to boost their profits by expanding output at the higher price.

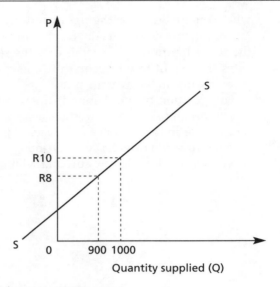

Fig. 3.4 An aggregate supply function

The position of the aggregate supply function will change if we relax our *ceteris paribus* assumption. If firms were suddenly faced with an increase in production costs, for example a higher wage bill, they are likely to cut back production at the given average price level. This is shown in Fig. 3.5 by an inward shift of the supply function from SS to S'S', indicating that at a price of R10 firms now produce only 800 units of output.

Conversely, a sudden improvement in climatic conditions may boost agricultural output and shift the supply function in Fig. 3.5 from SS to S"S". Firms are now able to supply 1200 units at the given average price of R10.

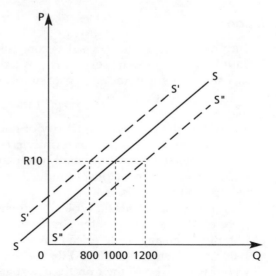

Fig. 3.5 Shifts in the supply function

The equilibrium concept

The final step in our analysis of markets is quite straightforward: we merely bring together the aggregate demand and supply functions to derive the so-called *equilibrium price level*. This is done in Fig. 3.6 where the earlier aggregate demand and supply functions are reproduced. The equilibrium combination of price and quantity occurs at point E where the two curves intersect, because that is the only point where quantity demanded equals quantity supplied.

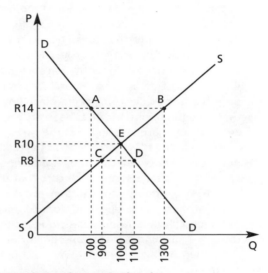

Fig. 3.6 Equilibrium price and quantity level

The concept of equilibrium can be explained by introducing a situation of disequilibrium into our model. At a price of R14 in Fig. 3.6, for example, quantity supplied equals 1300 units and demand is 700 units. There is therefore an excess supply equal to 600 units, i.e. the distance AB in Fig. 3.6. Firms who are unable to sell their output will now be forced to lower their price so as to encourage households to expand their purchases. As the price begins to fall from R14 to R13 and below, demand will start to increase *along* the demand curve and supply will contract *along* the supply curve. This process will continue until point E is reached, where demand equals supply at the equilibrium price of R10.

Conversely, if the price was initially R8, demand would exceed supply by the distance CD in Fig. 3.6. Competition among households will thus force the price upwards so that supply will increase along the supply curve, and demand will decrease along the demand curve, until the market equilibrium is reached at point E. It is only at the equilibrium price and quantity that the economy will achieve stability under the prevailing demand and supply conditions.

It is a relatively simple matter to show how exogenous changes may affect the equilibrium price and quantity. For example, an outward shift in the aggregate demand function will bring about an increase in both the equilibrium price and the equilibrium quantity, *ceteris paribus*; and similarly, an inward shift in the supply function will cause an increase in the equilibrium level of output. These issues will be further explored in Parts II and III of the book.

ILLUSTRATIVE
EXAMPLE

Real-world markets

In this chapter we have introduced the notion of a 'market equilibrium', or a situation in which supply equals the quantity demanded of a good. We also assumed, implicitly, that consumers and producers will reach a *stable* equilibrium fairly quickly and costlessly, and that they will only start trading once the equilibrium price and quantity have been established. The process is thus similar to that of an auction, where an auctioneer calls out different prices but prohibits any trade from taking place until such time as he or she is satisfied that an equilibrium price has been agreed upon. At that price both the seller and the buyer are satisfied that they are getting the best possible deal.

We all know that markets do not actually behave in this manner: buyers do not usually know whether they are buying the best good at the lowest possible price, and sellers cannot be sure that they are getting the highest possible price for their goods; nor can they ever be certain that they do. Most markets therefore operate under conditions of uncertainty, and never actually reach a stable equilibrium. Nonetheless, they generally do behave in an *equilibrating* fashion – 'groping towards an equilibrium' – in the sense that prices tend to rise when there is excess demand and fall when there is an excess supply of the good.

People's expectations also play an important role in this equilibrating process. In the agricultural sector, for example, where the future is notoriously uncertain, farmers often base their decisions on how much to produce on what they expect the future price to be. The latter price is usually based on the current or most recent price, with some allowance being made for past mistakes, i.e. the extent to which past expectations have deviated from actual prices. We are talking here of what is generally referred to as 'adaptive expectations' – an issue to which we return in Chapter 14 below.

Most prices and quantities in the real world do not change on a daily or even weekly basis. They are often fixed contractually by mutual agreement, for a limited period, and as we shall see in Chapter 14, there are good reasons why buyers and sellers may prefer such contractual arrangements.

3.3 Circular flow with product and factor markets

We are now in a position to return to our circular flow diagram. We do this by introducing markets into our model.

When households make purchases from firms they do so in what is called the *product market*. In Fig. 3.7 household purchases are reflected in the aggregate demand function, DD, while the aggregate supply is shown as SS. The equilibrium price is given by P_e and the equilibrium level of output by Q_e.

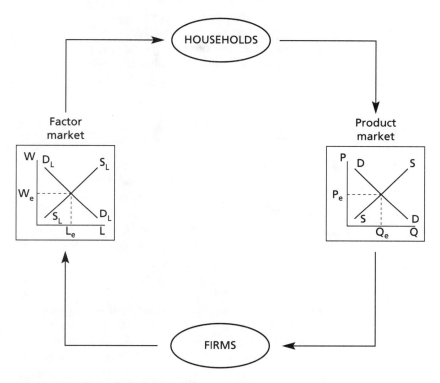

Fig. 3.7 Circular flow diagram with factor and product markets

Also shown in Fig. 3.7 is the factor market where firms buy factors of production from households. Although there are several production factors involved, Fig. 3.7 shows the market for only one such factor, i.e. labour. Like all other demand curves, the demand for labour, $D_L D_L$, is inversely related to its price, the wage rate. It is therefore assumed that the demand for labour by firms will be greater the lower is the wage rate, and *vice versa*. While it is important also to distinguish between the slope and the position of the labour demand function, we shall do so in more detail in Chapter 5. Suffice it to mention here that the labour demand function in Fig. 3.7 will shift outwards (inwards) if firms experienced an increase (decrease) in the demand for their products or if the productivity of labour were to increase (decrease).

The supply of labour by households is assumed to be positively related to the wage rate – indicated by the positively sloped labour supply function, $S_L S_L$, in Fig. 3.7. The position of $S_L S_L$, as is the case with all other supply functions, is determined by certain exogenous factors. A sudden outflow of migrant workers, for example, will shift the labour supply function to the left and *vice versa*.

Equilibrium in the labour market occurs where the labour demand and supply functions intersect, thus yielding an equilibrium wage rate, W_e, and an equilibrium level of employment, L_e, in Fig. 3.7. An exogenous change affecting the labour demand or supply functions will also change the equilibrium wage rate and level of employment.

It is important to note that the heavy lines in Fig. 3.7 indicate the direction of the flows of money. Households receive factor incomes from firms while firms receive revenue from the sale of goods and services to households.

3.4 Financial markets

There are other important markets which we would like to include in our circular flow diagram. The first of these is the financial markets.

Included in the financial markets are the commercial and other types of banks, collectively known as deposit-taking institutions, mutual fund and assurance companies, and the stock exchange. These are but a few examples of what has become a vast and highly complex sector in the modern economy, and in Chapter 15 we shall look at this sector in more detail.

As is evident from Fig. 3.8, the financial sector channels non-consumed income, or household *savings*, back into the economy. This flow of funds from households is in practice a net flow of savings as households also borrow on financial markets by way of personal overdrafts and housing bonds. Figure 3.8 also shows how firms borrow funds from the financial markets. They do so for many reasons, but the most important one, at least from an economic perspective, is their need for funds to expand their productive capacity. We call this *investment expenditure*.

As we have done for the product and factor markets, we may also introduce the concept of a price in financial markets. The most important financial price is the *interest rate* which is determined by the supply of funds, or household savings, and the demand for funds, or investment expenditure undertaken by firms.

The amount of money that households choose not to spend on consumption, or savings, is assumed to be positively related to the interest rate. In other words, an increase in the interest rate will raise the opportunity cost of consumption, or of *not* saving, and thus give rise to an increase in household savings. The savings function, shown as SS in the middle block of Fig. 3.8, is really a supply function whose position may change when relevant factors other than the interest rate undergo change. For example, an increase in household incomes will shift the savings function to the right, thus indicating that households are now prepared to save more than before at the given interest rate.

The investment function, II in Fig. 3.8, represents the firms' demand for loanable funds. Like all other demand functions, it shows an inverse relationship between price and quantity demanded; or in this case, between the

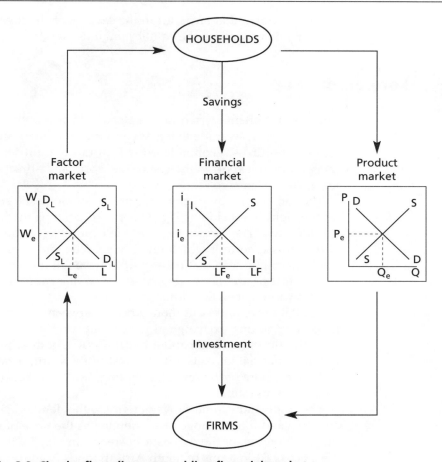

Fig. 3.8 Circular flow diagram – adding financial markets

interest rate and the demand for loanable funds. In other words, as the interest rate falls firms tend to borrow more, and *vice versa*. It is important to note that this relationship holds not only for funds which firms may borrow from financial markets, but also for their own funds, e.g. retained profits.

The position of the investment function is determined by several exogenous factors, the most important of which are the expectations that firms hold about the future. If firms expect the economy to grow more rapidly in future, they may well expect their profits to be higher as well. They may therefore decide to expand their productive capacity by undertaking a new investment project, in which case the investment function in Fig. 3.8 is bound to shift to the right.

Investment expenditure plays a critical role in fostering economic growth in the world today: it is the vehicle through which the expectations of firms are fulfilled.

Equilibrium is established where demand equals supply, i.e. at the interest rate, i_e, in Fig. 3.8. While the latter equilibrium represents a stable situation, it should be noted that any shift in the savings or the investment function will bring about a change in the equilibrium interest rate.

3.5 Foreign markets

The world is often referred to as a global village and the reason is not difficult to find. Countries trade extensively with each other and benefit from each other's resources. Economic growth in most countries depends in part on their ability to export to the rest of the world and attract capital and technical know-how from abroad.

The role played by foreign markets in the domestic economy is illustrated on the right-hand side of Fig. 3.9. A distinction is made between trade and capital flows. The former refers to the exports (X) and imports (M) of goods and services, both of which link households and firms with the rest of the world. It can be seen that the export flows point into the country – indicating that while certain goods and services leave the country the amounts paid for them (by foreigners) flow into the country.

Capital flows represent money flows between countries for which there is no corresponding exchange of goods and services. We distinguish between capital inflows (K_i) and capital outflows (K_o), both of which are assumed to link the financial markets with the rest of the world. Examples of these flows include offshore borrowing and lending, IMF and World Bank loans and foreign direct investment.

The trade and capital flows determine the demand and supply of foreign currency and the exchange rate – defined as the price of foreign currency, e.g. dollars, in terms of the domestic currency. In Fig. 3.9 the vertical axis shows the price of $1 in terms of South African rands (e.g. $1=R4.20), while the horizontal axis represents the quantity of dollars. Also shown are the South African demand for dollars, D_fD_f, and the foreign supply of dollars, S_fS_f. Like all other markets, the foreign exchange market in Fig. 3.9 is characterised by a demand and supply function, and by a price (called the exchange rate).

South Africans demand dollars basically for two reasons, namely, to pay for imports and to invest abroad or repay foreign loans. It is suggested that the demand function, D_fD_f, is downward sloping because as the rand price of a dollar increases, i.e. the rand depreciates, imports become more expensive. South Africans are therefore likely to demand less foreign exchange as they cut back on their imports and their investments abroad.

Likewise, foreigners supply dollars to the domestic market in order to acquire South African rands. They do so for basically two reasons, namely, to pay for South African exports and to invest in the domestic economy. The supply function, S_fS_f, is assumed to be upward sloping since a rise in the price of a dollar (or depreciation of the rand) will make South African exports cheaper in dollar terms. Foreigners are therefore likely to supply more dollars in order to acquire more South African exports and increase their investments in South African financial markets.

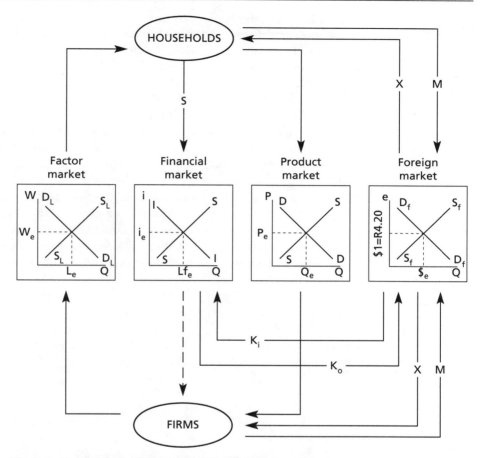

Fig. 3.9 Circular flow diagram – adding foreign markets

There is nothing peculiar about the equilibrium price and quantity in a foreign exchange market. Equilibrium is reached when the demand for foreign currency equals the supply, e.g. at an exchange rate of $1=R4.20 in Fig. 3.9. It should be noted that the positions of D_fD_f and S_fS_f, and hence the exchange rate, may change for several reasons, but these will be discussed in Chapter 18.

3.6 The government sector

The final component of the modern economy is the government sector. Government deals in three types of financial flow – current revenue (T) and expenditure (G), and government debt. Both are shown on the left-hand side of Fig. 3.10. Government receives revenue from firms in the form of company tax and VAT contributions, and from households in the form of income tax, VAT, customs and excise, fuel tax, and various forms of licensing. These revenues should ideally cover the government's *current* or *consumption* expenditure on households and firms. The former takes the form of civil servant salaries and pensions of various types, while the bulk of expenditure going to firms takes the form of payments for goods and services and subsidies paid to farmers, educational institutions and the health sector.

Government *capital* or *investment* expenditure benefits both households and firms and includes the provision of roads, harbours, school buildings and other physical infrastructural services. These expenditures are generally financed through loans provided by local financial institutions. It is therefore usually the case that total government expenditure, including both the consumption and capital components, exceeds tax receipts and that this difference is made good by an increase in the public or government debt.

In South Africa the public debt has been growing rapidly over the past few years, and although this issue will be considered in more detail later in the book, it is generally accepted that the problem of public indebtedness has become the rule rather than the exception throughout the world.

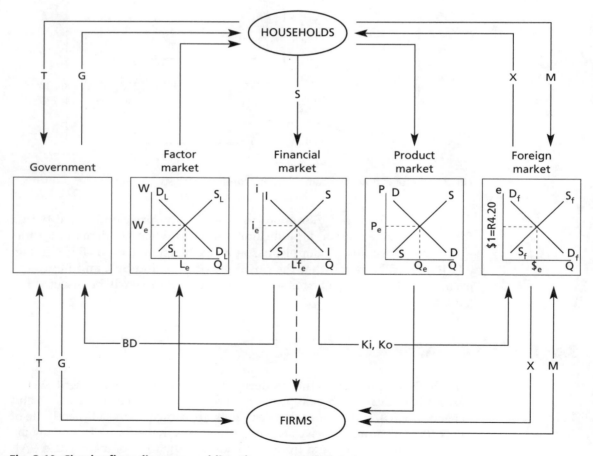

Fig. 3.10 Circular flow diagram – adding the government sector

The budget (BD) deficit can be funded by means of borrowing on the domestic financial markets – shown by the flow *BD* in Fig. 3.10. When the government borrows domestically it is in effect competing with the private sector, i.e. households and firms, for the savings that are available in the economy. The latter may be limited, however, either because households do not save enough or because foreigners do not invest in the domestic economy. Under these conditions the government may come to play a dominant role in the financial markets and limit the availability of loanable funds to the private sector. We return to this point in Part VI of the book.

3.7 Equilibrium in the circular flow

Understanding equilibrium in the circular flow is the same as coming to grips with the concept of macroeconomic equilibrium. We saw earlier in this chapter that equilibrium in any particular market can be seen as a situation when the market clears and there are no forces acting to change price or quantity. Macroeconomic equilibrium is similar in concept. The only difference is that in microeconomics it is the equilibrium of a single market that is of concern, while in macroeconomics it is the equilibrium of the economy as a whole.

The easiest way of visualising macroeconomic equilibrium is by means of the circular flow diagram and a summary of the circular flow. What should we take as the most important parts of the circular flow concept? The engine of the economy, i.e. the relationship between national expenditure and national income, as demonstrated in Fig. 3.1, is arguably the most important part of of the macroeconomy. Hence this is the basis of a summarised version of the circular flow. All other flows in the circular flow are considered to be either withdrawals from the circular flow or injections into the circular flow. The summarised version of the circular flow model is shown in Fig. 3.11.

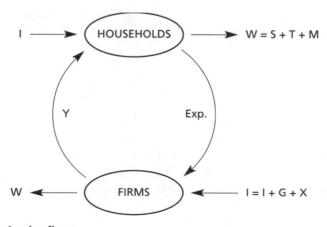

Fig. 3.11 Summary of circular flow

The summarised circular flow has reduced all the flows of the full model into four types of flows. The first two are those which we have referred to as the engine of the economy – national income (summarised here as 'Y') and national expenditure (Exp.). All other flows are shown either as withdrawals (W) or injections (J). Withdrawals are those flows of funds which leave the engine of the economy. These are savings (S), taxes (T) and imports (M). Such withdrawals occur from both households and firms. Injections are those funds which come into the engine of the economy but from outside of the circular flow. These are investment (I), government expenditure (G) and exports (X). Again there are injections into households and into firms.

Macroeconomic equilibrium exists when the economy is in some kind of steady state. In other words, output and production are neither increasing nor decreasing and there is no pressure which could bring about such changes. In consequence there are two conditions for macroeconomic equilibrium:

- National income must equal national expenditure.
- Withdrawals must equal injections.

The condition for equilibrium is that there should be no forces for change. This requires that income be equal to expenditure. Should income not equal expenditure then the economy will either become larger or smaller (depending on the situation). If income is equal to expenditure, then the only way in which they will continue to remain in equilibrium is if the total amount of funds being withdrawn from the economy is equal to the amount which is coming in from outside sources – withdrawals must be equal to injections.

It is important to appreciate the importance of equilibrium in both micro and macroeconomic contexts. The concept of equilibrium is important not because equilibrium is some kind of 'holy grail'. Equilibrium is not a particularly desirable state and economists are not concerned with ensuring that markets remain in equilibrium. Rather equilibrium is important because it allows us to understand the forces which act to bring about a change in equilibrium, or there understand the process – the sequence of events – which will result from a change in a market. (If exports increase, what happens next?; if interest rates decline, how does the economy respond?)

3.8 Conclusion

The discussion and illustrations presented in this chapter indicate the important allocative role played by several important markets in the economy. We have merely given a bird's eye view of the demand and supply sides of these markets, and of the respective equilibria, and it is now time for a more detailed look at them. We do so first by considering each market in isolation before returning, in Parts IV to VII, to the broader macroeconomic view.

Summary

- In a typical modern economy households supply factor services to firms and receive a reward in the form of factor incomes. These incomes are then spent on acquiring goods and services that are produced by firms with the aid of the selfsame factors of production originally supplied by households. There are two types of market involved here, i.e. factor markets and product markets, each of which is characterised by a demand and a supply function and a corresponding equilibrium price and quantity.

- The modern economy can be represented in the form of a circular flow diagram depicting the interaction between different markets. In addition to the factor and product markets, it is important also to consider financial markets, foreign markets and the government sector.

- Household savings constitute the supply of loanable funds in the financial sector, and are positively related to the interest rate. The demand for loanable funds, or investment, comes from firms, and is inversely related to the interest rate. These funds are ultimately transformed into (physical) capital for production purposes.

- In foreign markets the price, or exchange rate, is determined by the demand for foreign exchange and by the corresponding supply. The former arises from imports and capital outflows, while the supply of foreign exchange comes from exports and capital inflows.

- The government sector has an important effect on all other markets and institutions. Its income consists of taxes paid by households and firms, and the money it borrows on financial markets. Government spending benefits both households and firms, and consists mainly of salaries, transfer payments and capital investment in the infrastructure of the economy.

Questions for review

1. When a market is said to be 'in equilibrium', it means that the supply of the good or service equals the demand for it. What factors could give rise to a change in this equilibrium?

2. In today's world, with its sophisticated financial markets, most investors can shift their investments between countries at very short notice. How would the sudden withdrawal of foreign investment from a country affect its 'foreign sector'?

3. By making use of a full circular flow model examine the impact of the events listed below on each of the markets and on the economy as a whole:

   a) A very severe drought.

   b) A major shock to business confidence.

   c) A significant increase in the international price of a country's most important export (in South Africa the price of gold doubles; Zimbabwe – tobacco; Zambia – copper, Namibia – diamonds).

4. Making use of the summarised version of the circular flow (Fig. 3.11), assume that of any income received people spend 80 per cent and save the rest. There is an increase in investment of R1000m which is a grant from a foreign donor. Calculate the total change in national income.

PART II

Consumer and producer behaviour

We are now in a position to expand our analysis of demand, supply, prices and markets. We do so in Chapters 4 and 5 where the focus will fall on the demand and the supply sides of markets, respectively. In Chapter 4 we consider the determinants of the individual consumer's demand and the market demand, and also introduce the market supply in order to derive the equilibrium price and quantity. Chapter 5 looks at production and the costs of production, both of which ultimately determine the individual firm's supply and the market supply of a good or service.

CHAPTER 4

Demand, supply and prices

A concept central to our study of markets is *equilibrium*. Equilibrium is a state in which opposing forces balance each other out and no individual can do better given the actions of others and the resource constraints they face. In product markets the equilibrium price and quantity occur where the quantity supplied of a good is equal to the quantity demanded. At the equilibrium price all consumers can make their planned purchases and producers can make their sales. At this price everyone is happy!

4.1 The individual consumer's demand

This section examines the individual consumer's demand for a product. The consumer derives satisfaction (or utility) from the consumption of goods and services. How much utility the individual derives from the consumption of a particular good depends on the individual's *preferences* or *tastes*.

Suppose we observe an individual's consumption of chocolate bars over a particular period of time, say a day. The sum of the utilities derived from all units consumed is the *total utility*.

Table 4.1 shows the total utility derived from chocolate consumption. Initially, as consumption of chocolates increases total utility rises. However, it reaches a maximum when four chocolate bars are consumed, and if five bars of chocolate are consumed total utility remains unchanged. The fifth chocolate does not add to or detract from total utility: the consumer has reached *the point of satiety*. Consuming more than five units leads to a decrease in total utility. The sixth chocolate does not go down so well: the consumer experiences *disutility* from the consumption of chocolates.

Table 4.1 Total and marginal utility

Quantity/day	Total utility	Marginal utility
0	0	–
1	10	10
2	16	6
3	20	4
4	22	2
5	22	0
6	20	–2

It is useful also to refer to the additional utility that the consumer derives from the consumption of each extra unit of the good. This is known as the *marginal utility* (MU), and is shown in the last column of Table 4.1. In general, marginal utility decreases as more of the good is consumed over a given period of time. This general principle has been formalised as the *law of diminishing marginal utility*.

The law of diminishing marginal utility states that, given the consumer's tastes or preferences, each additional unit of a good consumed will add less utility than the unit consumed immediately before it, over a given period of time. Figure 4.1 shows the total utility associated with the consumption of chocolate bars (a) and the corresponding marginal utility (b).

When we examine individual consumer behaviour we are assuming that the consumer is a *rational* individual. This means that the consumer will want to maximise utility. The consumer's selection of goods takes place within a *framework of constraints*, however. These constraints include the consumer's budget or income and the market prices of the goods and services on which the budget is spent. The consumer is thus faced with a constrained choice: having more of one good necessarily means having less of another. This problem of choice is common to all economic decisions and refers to the familiar concept of opportunity cost.

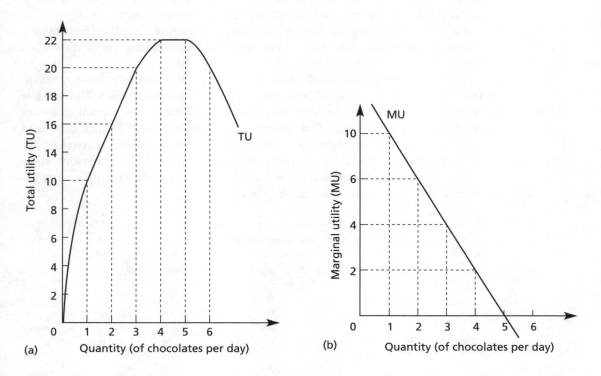

Fig. 4.1 (a) The individual's total utility curve; (b) The individual's marginal utility curve

The utility-maximising combination of goods

Consider a consumer who has a daily budget of R10 and wants to spend it on two goods, applies (A) and oranges (R). The consumer's preferences are reflected in the utility derived from consumption, as shown in Table 4.2.

Table 4.2 Marginal utility of A and R

Q_a	MU_a	$\dfrac{MU_a}{P_a=R2}$	Q_r	MU_r	$\dfrac{MU_r}{P_r=R1}$
1	10	5	4	4	4
2	6	3	5	3.5	3.5
3	4	2	6	3	3
4	3	1.5	7	2	2
5	2	1	8	1	1
6	1	0.5	9	0	0

What would be the best way of spending the budget of R10? In order to maximise total utility the consumer must allocate his or her budget between the two different goods such that the marginal utility from the last rand spent is equal for both goods. This is known as the *principle of equimarginal satisfaction*, and requires that we calculate the ratio, MU/price, for each good – as is done in the third and sixth columns of Table 4.2. If the price of good A is R2 and the price of good R is R1, the ratio MU/price will be equalised when two units of good A and six units of good R are bought. The consumer will thus maximise utility subject to his or her budget constraint of R10. In other words:

$$MU_a/P_a = MU_r/P_r$$

If the ratio MU/price is greater for good R than for good A, the consumer can increase total utility by spending more on R and less on A. In this way the MU from R will decrease while the MU for A will increase, until the last rand spent on each yields exactly the same amount of utility. The consumer is then in equilibrium or has maximised utility from consumption.

Why does a demand curve slope downwards?

In order to derive the individual's demand curve for a good, we ask what happens when the price of the good changes, *ceteris paribus*. To do this we use the expression:

$$\frac{MU_a}{Pa} = \frac{MU_r}{P_r}$$

Now we ask what will happen if the price of apples rises. This price increase disturbs the equilibrium condition, so that:

$$\frac{MU_a}{P_a} < \frac{MU_r}{P_r}$$

The common-sense conclusion is that when the price of apples rises, the marginal utility per rand spent on apples falls. So, the consumer should buy fewer apples (and more oranges) until the *MU* of apples has risen (according to the law of diminishing marginal utility) and the *MU* of oranges has fallen, until equilibrium is restored. From this we can conclude that a rise in the price of a good, *ceteris paribus*, will lead to a decrease in the quantity of the good demanded by the consumer. This shows that the consumer's demand curve is downward sloping.

This explanation for a downward-sloping demand curve has relied on the concept of marginal utility. A different explanation for the downward sloping demand curve can also be considered. If the price of apples rises while the prices of other goods do not change, then apples become relatively more expensive. The relative price of apples (P_a/P_r) increases. It makes sense then to substitute good R (i.e. oranges) for apples. This process of finding substitutes for apples, called the *substitution effect* of the price change, implies that as the price of the good rises, less of it will be bought. This effect is always the same for all goods, irrespective of how we classify them.

The increase in the price of apples has a second effect which depends on the type of good we consider. If the consumer's income is fixed, then a price increase means a decrease in real income or purchasing power. The effect of this lower real income will depend on the income elasticity of the good we're looking at. If the good is normal (with a positive income elasticity, and we assume that apples are normal goods), then the *income effect* will mean that less apples are bought. We say that the income effect then reinforces the substitution effect. The substitution effect and the income effect both lead to fewer apples being bought.

If the good is inferior, then the income effect will lead to more of the good being bought when its price rises (it has a negative income elasticity). In this case the substitution effect and the income effect work in opposite directions. Usually though, the substitution effect will be stronger, so that overall if we add together the income and substitution effects, the effect of a price increase is to decrease the quantity demanded, so that the demand curve is downward sloping. For some inferior goods, the income effect will be larger than the substitution effect so that when price increases, more of the good will be demanded; the demand curve will thus be upward sloping, as for Giffen goods which, as already indicated, are very rare indeed.

From individual demand to market demand

We already know that the market demand curve is downward sloping, and we can now verify this by deriving the market demand curve from individual demand curves. If each consumer's demand is independent of the demand of other consumers, then diagrammatically market demand is derived by horizontal summation of the individual demand curves. This is done in Fig. 4.2.

Assuming that there are only two consumers, I and II, Fig. 4.2 shows the quantities of the good that each demands at a price of R1. These are then added and plotted on the market demand curve. If this summation is done for all other prices, the market demand curve is derived and, as expected, depicts an inverse relationship between price and quantity demanded.

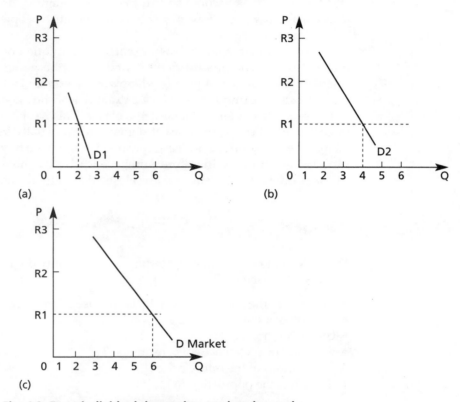

Fig. 4.2 From individual demand to market demand

4.2 Bandwagon and snob effects

So far we have considered an individual's demand for a good to be independent from the quantities demanded by other consumers. This allowed us simply to add together the individual demand curves in order to derive the market demand curve.

For some goods, however, an individual's demand for a particular good may be affected by the number of other consumers who have purchased the same good. This could mean that the individual's demand is influenced by a desire to be in style or in fashion – to have a good because almost everyone else has it. We refer to this as the *bandwagon effect*. This effect is often observed with children's toys such as Ninja Turtles and Barbie dolls. Creating the bandwagon effect is a major objective in the advertising of such toys and is also a key to success in selling clothing – something that our forward-looking marketer in Utopia will be well aware of!

The bandwagon effect makes the demand for a good more elastic than it would otherwise be. This is because as the price drops we observe an increase in quantity demanded not only because of the effect of the lower price, but also because it has become stylish to own it. Quantity demanded may thus increase because of the lower price and also because people want to jump on a particular bandwagon!

Some consumers want to own exclusive or unique goods – referred to as the *snob effect*. The quantity demanded of a snob good will be higher the smaller is the number of people who own it. Designer clothing, rare works of art and exclusive imported goods are examples of snob goods.

The snob effect makes demand less elastic. This happens because when the price of a good drops the market demand for it usually increases. This good therefore has less appeal to these consumers who were buying it purely for its snob value, and they therefore purchase less of it. The market demand for such a good would therefore be less elastic than if there were no snob effect.

4.3 Market demand

There are many factors that can influence the quantity demanded of a particular product. These include:

- the price of the good itself (e.g. P_x in the case of good X)
- the prices of other goods (e.g. P_y and P_z)
- consumer income (Y)
- the tastes or preferences of consumers (T)
- expectations of the future price (E)
- the size of the population (N).

All this can be summarised in the *demand function*:

$$Q_{dx} = f(P_x, P_y, P_z, Y, T, E, N)$$

which simply says that the quantity demanded of good X (Q_{dx}) depends on or is a function of the price of good X, the prices of other goods, consumers' income and tastes, their expectations about the future price, and the population size. This is quite a complex relationship, so to start with, we focus on the relationship between the quantity demanded and the price of good X, assuming for convenience that all other factors remain unchanged. We thus invoke the so-called *ceteris paribus* – a Latin phrase meaning all other factors remain constant – because it helps us to simplify complex relations and to focus on the essence of the argument.

We can illustrate this relationship between price and quantity by considering the daily demand for chocolate bars on the island of Utopia. If chocolate bars are too expensive, Utopians will surely buy other sweets, or even fresh fruit, instead. If chocolates are too cheap, however, those Utopians with foresight may decide to stock up to ensure they have enough chocolates during times of shortages.

In Table 4.3 we give an example of a *market demand schedule* which shows how many chocolate bars will be demanded at different prices.

Table 4.3 Market demand schedule for chocolates

Price	Quantity demanded
R2.00	200 000
R1.50	250 000
R1.00	300 000
R0.50	400 000

This information can also be shown in the form of a diagram. Figure 4.3 shows the market demand curve for chocolate bars, with the quantity plotted along the horizontal axis and price along the vertical axis.

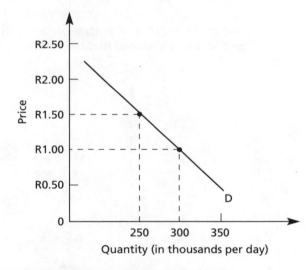

Fig. 4.3 The market demand curve for chocolate bars

The market demand curve slopes downward from left to right. It illustrates the *inverse relationship* between price and quantity and is referred to as the *law of demand* (see Chapter 3). If price changes from R1.00 to R1.50 per chocolate bar, the *quantity demanded* will decrease from 300 000 to 250 000. This is shown by a movement along the demand curve. A change in the price of the good is the only factor that can cause such a movement along the demand curve and is referred to as a *change in quantity demanded*.

Changes in demand

Several factors could cause the market demand to change its position. If, for example, one of Utopia's bright young researchers provided proof that chocolate consumption is beneficial to consumers' health, it can be expected that more chocolate bars would be demanded at every price. This would be shown as a rightward shift of the entire market demand curve, as indicated in Fig. 4.4, and we would describe it as an *increase in demand*.

Let us consider some other factors that may cause a change in demand for a product:

- *A change in real income.* When consumers receive a salary or wage increase, their real income or purchasing power increases so that they can afford more chocolates. The resultant increase in the demand for chocolates will cause a rightward shift in the market demand curve.
- *A change in the price of other products.* If chocolates have a close substitute, such as fruit gums, then if the price of fruit gums should fall people will buy them rather than chocolate bars. Thus the demand for chocolate bars will decrease.

Similarly, if products are complementary (used together in consumption), a change in the price of one good will have an effect on the demand for the other. A fall in the price of cars will result in more cars being purchased and will also lead to more tyres and petrol being demanded.

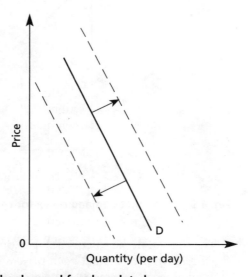

Fig. 4.4 Changes in the demand for chocolate bars

- *A change in tastes or preferences.* If a forward-looking Utopian marketer should launch an advertising campaign promoting the health benefits of chocolates, it may well lead to an increase in the demand for chocolate bars; a campaign highlighting the health risks of chocolates will decrease it.
- *Expectations of future price changes.* If the price of chocolate bars is expected to rise due to a shortage of cocoa beans, the demand for chocolate bars is likely to increase almost immediately.

● *A change in the size of the population.* Additional people coming into the market, especially if chocolate features prominently in their diet, will increase market demand.

4.4 Price elasticity of demand

Economists have developed various measures to quantify the responsiveness of consumer demand to changes in the factors that we have included in the demand function. It is interesting to note that, usually, consumers can respond almost instantaneously to changes in these factors. We say that demand is responsive to changes in price for example. When we consider the supply side of the market a bit later, we will find that the response of the producers or suppliers often takes much longer or takes place with a *lag*.

The price elasticity of demand measures the responsiveness of quantity demanded to a change in the price of the good itself. In order to calculate the elasticity numerically we divide the percentage change in the quantity demanded of a good by the percentage change in its price. The formula used for determining the degree of elasticity is:

$$E_d = \frac{\% \text{ change in } D}{\% \text{ change in } P}$$

$$= \frac{\Delta D / D}{\Delta P / P}$$

where D represents the quantity demanded and P the price.

The price elasticity of demand is always a negative number due to the inverse relationship between quantity demanded and price. Economists often omit the minus sign for simplicity, but the negative relationship still holds, since a positive sign would imply that the demand curve slopes upwards. This is a very rare phenomenon. Sir Robert Giffen once described the case of a positive relationship between price and quantity, and consequently a good with a positive price elasticity is referred to as a *Giffen good*.

When the demand elasticity is high (–5 would be considered high), the quantity demanded is very sensitive to a change in price; and likewise, when the elasticity is low (for example –0.1), the quantity demanded is relatively insensitive to a change in price. Thus a demand elasticity of zero implies that the product is entirely insensitive to any change in price, or perfectly inelastic. A demand elasticity between zero and one (if we ignore the negative sign) indicates relative inelasticity, whereas demand elasticities between one and infinity imply relative elasticity.

Why is price elasticity of demand important to producers?

For an individual firm the total revenue from the sale of its product is found by multiplying the quantity sold by the price charged per unit. If a firm knew how people would respond when the price of its product changed, it would be able to predict what would happen to its sales revenue. Price elasticity of demand can help the producer to make such predictions.

If buyers of a particular product are very price sensitive (i.e. demand is elastic) then even if the price increased by a relatively small amount, demand for the product would drop significantly. The producer would then find that its sales revenue has decreased (i.e. there would be less money in the till at the end of the day). Conversely, if buyers are not very price sensitive or demand is inelastic, then, when price increases, demand will decrease, but only slightly. The producer will thus find that its sales revenue increases at the end of the day.

By looking at the factors that influence price elasticity of demand, we would be able to predict the price elasticity of demand for a product.

- *Availability of substitutes and complements.* The most important factor determining the elasticity of demand for a good is the availability of substitutes (or complements). If a consumer can buy something else that will serve the same purpose, a very small change in price may result in a large change in the quantity purchased. Thus an increase in the price of butter will lead to a relatively large drop in quantity demanded as consumers redirect their purchases to a close substitute such as margarine. Conversely, if the product has no substitutes, a large change in price will result in only a small change in quantity demanded. Goods with few substitutes include salt, insulin, specific medication and so on. For these items demand is said to be relatively inelastic.
- *Necessities and luxuries.* Some goods and services are necessary to life and thus the quantity demanded may be relatively insensitive to price changes. However, consumers can do without luxuries and easily replace them with necessary goods should the former become more expensive. Thus the demand for necessities is relatively price inelastic while the demand for luxury goods tends to be relatively elastic.
- *Relative importance in consumer's budget.* The proportion of income spent on a good will also influence the elasticity for that good. Price elasticity of demand for a good is directly related to the portion of the consumer's income spent on it. If the price of a cheap product, such as a box of matches, should increase by, say, 50 per cent, demand is unlikely to fall by much since the effect of the price rise on consumer budgets will be negligible. However, if the price of an expensive product increased by 50 per cent, sales would be reduced drastically thus indicating a relatively high price elasticity of demand.

4.5 Income elasticity of demand

We have seen that besides price there are other factors that may cause consumers to adjust their demand for a good or service. Elasticities may also be calculated to show the responsiveness of consumer demand to changes in these factors. One such example is the income elasticity of demand, the formula for which is similar to that for price elasticity, namely:

$$E_y = \frac{\% \text{ change in } D}{\% \text{ change in } Y}$$

$$= \frac{\Delta D / D}{\Delta Y / Y}$$

where Y represents income.

Rising consumer incomes will lead to an increase in the demand for most goods and services. They have positive income elasticities and are referred to as normal goods, including both luxury goods and necessities. In the case of luxury goods, a given increase in income will lead to a proportionately larger increase in quantity demanded. Examples are champagne, leather jackets and fancy sports cars whose income elasticities all exceed one. Conversely, the income elasticity for most other goods is smaller than one, and they are usually referred to as necessary goods. Inferior goods can be defined as those whose purchases decline as incomes rise. Potatoes and public transportation are examples of inferior goods and the income elasticity for such goods is negative.

Income elasticities are useful in assessing actual or potential opportunities in the market place. They are key sources of information when forecasting the pattern of consumer demand as the economy grows or contracts. As real income increases or decreases, the demand for most products increases or decreases respectively. But the effect of an income change will differ from product to product, from country to country and also over time. For example, aggregate income on the island of Famine is relatively low, so that increases in that income are bound to be directed at the consumption of basic products. In a more developed economy like that of Utopia, however, the increased income will be channelled towards more luxurious goods.

Such patterns of consumer behaviour have distinct consequences for an entrepreneurial supplier wanting to enter the market. In a growing economy the producer will be more inclined to supply products with relatively high income elasticities, while during periods of economic decline more resources will be allocated to the production of goods with low income elasticities. Thus the entrepreneur should consider both the actual level of income in the country and the future direction and extent of economic growth.

4.6 Cross-elasticity of demand

A different type of elasticity involves the demand for two related products. Cameras and film can illustrate the point. If the price of cameras increases consumers will demand fewer cameras and also cut back their purchases of film. The demand curve for film will thus move inwards and bring about a decrease in quantity demanded at the given price.

The cross-elasticity of demand can be defined as the percentage change in the demand for one good relative to the percentage change in the price of another. Hence, we have the following formula:

$$E_c = \frac{\% \text{ change in } D_f}{\% \text{ change in } P_c}$$

$$= \frac{\Delta D_f / D_f}{\Delta P_c / P_c}$$

where D_f represents the amount of film demanded and P_c the price of cameras.

In the above example of two complementary products it can be expected that the cross-elasticity of demand will be negative; that is, the increase in camera prices will lead to a decrease in demand for film. However, the cross-elasticity of demand need not always be negative. Margarine and butter are normally substitutes and therefore an increase in the price of margarine may lead to increased demand for butter. As the price for one product increases, so the demand for the substitute increases and hence a positive cross-elasticity of demand exists. In summary, therefore, complementary products have a negative cross-elasticity of demand and substitutes a positive one.

Cross-elasticities of demand are important to the business community as they provide a useful measure of the relationship between goods. A high positive or negative cross-elasticity indicates a close relationship between goods; that is, a change in the price of one good has a significant effect on the demand for the other good. Moreover, if the cross-elasticity of two goods is zero, it implies there is absolutely no relationship between the goods.

ILLUSTRATIVE EXAMPLE

Classification of goods

We can summarise the classification of goods according to elasticities as follows:

- According to price elasticity:
    normal good: $E_d < 0$
    Giffen good: $E_d > 0$

Usually we take the absolute value of the elasticity coefficient, i.e. drop the minus sign, because most of the goods we deal with are normal, thus:

    luxury good: $E_d > 1$
    necessity: $0 < E_d < 1$

- According to the income elasticity of demand:
    normal good: $E_y > 0$
    inferior good: $E_y < 0$

- According to cross-elasticity of demand:
    substitutes: $E_c > 0$
    complements: $E_c < 0$

curves have identical shapes. Since $TC = TVC + TFC$, the TC curve is simply the TVC curve that has been shifted upwards by the amount of fixed costs; the two curves are therefore parallel.

Figure 5.3(a) also indicates that both the total variable and the total costs of the firm increase only gradually when output is expanded up to the level of four chairs, after which they both begin to increase at a progressively faster rate. The principle involved here is, of course, the law of diminishing marginal returns: beyond the level of four chairs, further increases in output require progressively larger quantities of labour (and other variable inputs). The cost implications are straightforward: if labour is available at a constant wage, as we have assumed, then it must follow that the expansion of output will ultimately entail progressively larger increases in the variable and total costs of production.

Figure 5.3(b) depicts the firm's average and marginal cost curves. Average cost is simply the total cost per unit of output, or

$$AC = \frac{TC}{Q}$$

and is measured by the slope of a ray drawn from the origin to the relevant point on the TC curve (in Fig. 5.3 (a)). Likewise, marginal cost refers to the change in total cost resulting from a small change in output; that is, it represents the extra cost of producing an extra chair. Algebraically:

$$MC = \frac{\Delta TC}{\Delta Q}$$

and is measured by the slope of a tangent drawn to the relevant point on the TC curve (in Fig. 5.3(a)).

The shape of the MC curve is also explained by the principle of diminishing marginal returns. Figure 5.3(b) shows that marginal cost decreases up to the level of four chairs and then starts to rise at an increasing rate. In other words, as the firm expands output beyond the level of four chairs, it will require progressively larger quantities of labour. This must perforce imply correspondingly larger additions to the firm's total cost.

Marginal cost plays a pivotal role in the firm's output decision, particularly in the short run, even though the actual producer in Famine may not be aware of it. As explained in section 5.2, the firm decides whether to produce an additional unit of output by comparing the cost of producing that unit, i.e. MC, with the additional revenue received from the sale of that unit. In the next chapter we shall show that MC is in fact an important determinant of the firm's supply curve.

5.4 Costs of production in the long run

Remember that, in the short run, some factors of production are assumed to be fixed. For example, a firm cannot increase its plant size in a short period of time. In the long run, however, the firm can vary the quantity of *all* its factors of production. The distinction between fixed and variable factors thus disappears, and so does the distinction between fixed and variable costs.

A firm can change its plant size in the long run to meet its production requirements. Each possible plant size can be represented by its own short run ATC curve. Consider the case of a firm which has the choice of three different plant sizes. In Fig. 5.4 the smallest plant is indicated by ATC_1, the medium sized plant by ATC_2, and the largest plant by ATC_3. If the firm plans to produce 700 units of output it will choose the small plant. However, if it expects 1800 units to be a more profitable level of output it will choose the medium-sized plant, and so on.

If the firm initially chooses the smaller plant to produce 700 units of output, but then finds that demand is growing rapidly, it may eventually wish to expand output to 1800 units. It is possible to produce 1800 units with the existing plant at an average cost of OC_2. This would be the situation in the short run when plant size is fixed. In the long run, however, the firm can replace the existing plant with the medium-sized plant, and produce 1800 units at a much lower cost than before, i.e. OC_1 in Fig. 5.4.

The *long-run ATC* curve, sometimes called the firm's planning curve, shows the lowest per unit cost at which it is possible to produce a given level of output when there is enough time for the firm to adjust its plant size. In Fig. 5.4 the long-run ATC curve consists of the segment of plant 1's ATC up to point a, the segment of plant 2's ATC curve between a and b, and the segment of the ATC curve of plant 3 from point b. If we assume that instead of merely three plant sizes, there are many possible plant sizes, the points of intersection will increase resulting in a continuous curve, which is the long-run average cost curve (LAC) of the firm. Each point on the LAC shows the minimum cost of producing a specific level of output. The LAC curve is U-shaped and is often called the envelope curve because it envelopes the short-run ATC curves. The producer will select the plant size by reference to this curve, and in doing so will choose that short run plant which yields the least unit cost of producing the output it anticipates.

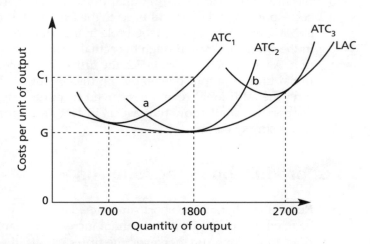

Fig. 5.4 The long-run average total cost curve

Economies and diseconomies of scale

The *U*-shape of the *LAC* curve is accounted for by *economies* and *diseconomies of scale*. Economies of scale are factors that account for decreases in long-run *ATC* that occur when the firm's plant size increases. These include:

- *Specialisation of factors of production*. In a small firm workers will be performing a number of different tasks. As the firm expands workers are able to specialise in particular functions and hence their efficiency increases, thereby reducing the costs per unit of output.
- *Bulk discounts on the prices of raw materials and other inputs*. Suppliers of raw materials and other inputs will often charge a lower price if bulk purchases are made. When a firm produces high output levels, it requires larger volumes of inputs, and can thus take advantage of the associated price discounts to reduce its unit costs.
- *Economic use of by-products*. The production of many types of goods gives rise to by-products that also have economic value. Large-scale firms are often able to recycle 'waste' products in ways which would be uneconomical for smaller firms. For example, a small saw mill may simply throw away sawdust, but a large wood processing plant may find the volume of such a waste product large enough to sell it as a sweeping compound for cleaning floors.

Diseconomies of scale refer to increases in the long-run average cost of production, represented by the rising portion of the *LAC* curve. These result from the difficulties involved in managing and co-ordinating production activities in a large enterprise. These include:

- *Management of the firm*. Once the firm grows beyond a certain size, problems of co-ordinating a large number of plants and diverse operations become more complex. Central management must communicate with many more areas of the firm and process a much larger volume of information in order to operate efficiently. Often this involves more delegation of authority to middle and lower management levels. Co-ordination of decision making at the different levels and the necessity of monitoring all operations may result in inefficiencies that cause the cost per unit of output to rise.
- *Over-specialisation*. When the firm grows beyond a certain size, the efficiency of workers declines. The production process becomes divided into a series of insubstantial and unchallenging tasks. With the reduction of hours worked due to automation, productivity naturally declines, causing cost per unit of output to rise.

Technological progress

While we have focused here on the shape of the short and long run cost curves, it is important also to consider their *position*, and in particular the factors that might bring about a reduction in production costs – or a downward shift in the cost curves. This brings us to the crucial issue of factor productivity.

There are presumably many factors that determine the productivity of workers. Apart from their innate abilities, cultural background and levels of education and training, technology – in the form of new machines and new production techniques – plays a pivotal role in utilising existing skills and honing new ones. Technology enables a firm to produce the same output with fewer inputs, or a larger output with the same inputs – which is another way of saying that it lowers production costs and boosts the profits of firms.

Technological progress is, of course, related to the level of education of a country's population, and in particular to the number of people trained in engineering and the natural sciences. Thus, if the people of Utopia are better educated than their counterparts in Famine, they will also be better able to develop and utilise new technologies and get even further ahead of Faminers.

There is little doubt that technology has played an important role in the post-war development of Europe and North America, and more recently in the growth of South East Asia, and in the accompanying box we elaborate further on this point.

CASE EXAMPLE

Technology and economic growth

Neoclassical economics assumes that it is the economic factors of production – natural resources, labour and capital – which drive economic growth. Countries are assumed to have the same technology, but differing factor endowments, and it is these endowments which allow a nation to be competitive in the global market. In other words, a nation's competitiveness hinges on its comparative advantage.

Modern economic theory recognises the critical role played by factors such as education (human capital formation), scientific endeavour and technology. The productivity of the factors of production, and their ability to add economic value, is determined by technology. Advances in science and technology spawn new knowledge, new production capabilities and methods, new products and new demands. Innovation gives rise to new industries and new sources of competitive advantage. Michael Porter maintains that the ability of a nation to innovate and to use technology is a key explanatory factor in the competitiveness of nations. Although government policies can create the environment in which technological transfer can take place, they are not a sufficient condition. Managers and technicians within firms receiving foreign technology must be able to assimilate and adapt that technology to domestic conditions and needs.

Numerous studies have shown that human capital plays a vital role in technological development. However, education itself does not ensure that a nation will successfully implement technology. The type of skills are important – the East Asian countries not only had high levels of enrolment in secondary and tertiary education, but also a higher proportion of students studying sciences and engineering than other countries. African countries appear to be at a disadvantage here, since the proportion of science and engineering graduates is extremely low.

Technological progress is not a costless process, nor can it simply be

Case example
continued equated to the passing of ideas from one firm or country to another. Firms or nations which develop a near technology are often reluctant to part with it freely, given the time and money they have invested. Secondly, a significant part of technological knowledge is often embodied in 'doing' – the skill has to be honed by doing, rather than learning by instruction. In addition, technological knowledge requires a supportive environment, including institutions and societal norms, in order to flourish.

Nations can follow a three phase development plan: select strategic industries, search for appropriate technologies and adapt and assimilate the technologies. Implementation of such a three phase strategy was central to Korea's success. A problem in South Africa, common to many developing countries, is the reluctance of the private sector to engage in scientific and technological development. In South Africa the bulk of these activities are carried out by government institutions, with the private sector having very low levels of investment in research and development.

It would seem that a mutually reinforcing relationship exists between capital accumulation (both human and physical) and technological progress. Just as a high rate of capital formation and a well-educated workforce spur technological change, so technological change, by raising incomes, stimulates the acquisition of skills. It is the interaction between trade (based on the principle of comparative advantage), technological progress and international competitiveness which drives economic growth.

Summary

- Production is the process during which factors of production are used to produce goods and services. These factors include natural resources, labour of different skills, capital or man-made machines and tools, and entrepreneurship.

- Capital is assumed to be fixed in the short run, while labour is variable. Each producer is subject to the law of diminishing marginal returns – as reflected in the downwardly sloped marginal product curve. This simply means that the increase in total output becomes smaller and smaller as more labour is added to the fixed factor.

- The demand for a factor of production is similar to that for a good or service: it shows an inverse relationship between price and the quantity demanded. The demand for labour is thus inversely related to the wage rate. A firm demands labour in accordance with its marginal revenue product (MRP), which is found by multiplying the marginal product of labour by the product price. This is the firm's demand curve for labour, and if it is one of many firms demanding labour in the labour market, its optimal employment level will be where MRP equals the given wage rate.

- Short-run costs consist of total fixed and total variable costs. Average cost is simply the total cost per unit of output, while marginal cost (MC) refers to the change in total cost resulting from a small change in output. Both the total cost and the *MC* curves embody the principle of diminishing marginal returns, i.e. beyond a certain level of output, each one increases at a progressive rate.

● As far as the long run is concerned, all factors of production are variable. The firm can adjust its plant size – given by its short-run *ATC* curve – to meet new production targets. Its long-run average cost curve (*LAC*) is an envelope of all its short-run *ATC* curves, and is often referred to as the envelope or planning curve. The *LAC* is U-shaped as it embodies the effect of economies and diseconomies of scale.

● Both the short- and long-run cost curves may undergo parametric shifts as a result of new technologies that change the productivity of the factors of production.

Questions for review

1. Explain (using diagrams in the process) how the law of diminishing marginal returns influences the shape of the firm's short-run cost curves.

2. How does the firm decide how many workers to hire?

3. Explain why the firm's long-run cost curve may be U-shaped.

4. Distinguish between 'economies of scale' and technological progress.

PART III

Market forms:
a microeconomic analysis

The preceding chapters have shown how the supply and demand functions together determine the equilibrium price and quantity of a good or service. But the precise nature of the equilibrium depends on the type of market within which the transactions are assumed to take place. This section therefore distinguishes between several product and factor market forms ranging between the two polar cases of perfect competition and monopoly.

We begin this section with a chapter giving a broad overview of the determinants of market structure, such as the degree of seller concentration, barriers to entry and product differentiation. The polar cases of perfect competition and monopoly are considered in Chapters 7 and 8, respectively, providing a useful benchmark against which to assess the more realistic markets discussed in Chapter 9. In the latter chapter we first focus on the monopolistically competitive market which, as the name suggests, contains elements of both competition and monopoly and takes cognizance of the real-world phenomena of product differentiation and advertising. This is followed by a discussion of oligopolistic markets in which a few large sellers may either compete with each other or enter into a co-operative cartel. Chapter 10 deals with the functional distribution of income and shows how wages, rental income, interest payments, dividends and profits all contribute to the national income of a country.

CHAPTER 6

Market structure and firm behaviour

We have so far looked at how the firm makes its production decision. This involves deciding which factors of production to use and how to combine them in the production process in order to produce efficiently. The firm goes to the factor markets to select factors of production and decides on the production technique it will use. It is also important for the firm to take into account the conditions of the product market where it will sell its output. It has to take into account the number of competitors it has. For example, if it has no competition it would be operating in a monopoly situation. In such a situation the firm will have much more independence in its decision making. If it has a very large number of competitors, it would be operating in a perfectly competitive market. In such a situation the firm has to take careful account of the behaviour of its competitors.

Most markets in the real world fall between the two extremes of monopoly and perfect competition. They are described as oligopolies and monopolistically competitive markets. An oligopoly is a market in which there are a small number of sellers or producers. A monopolistically competitive market (not to be confused with monopoly) consists of a large number of producers, but not as many as in a perfectly competitive market.

For convenience we make a distinction between perfectly competitive markets and imperfectly competitive markets (which includes monopolies, oligopolies, and monopolistically competitive markets).

Firms also have to take into account potential new entrants to the market. These potential entrants could pose a threat to firms in the market. The threat of potential competition therefore acts as a disciplining device on the behaviour of firms in the market. In South Africa (as in many other countries) the threat of new competition is indeed very real as the process of trade liberalisation gathers momentum. Given the conclusion to the Uruguay Round of negotiations on the General Agreements on Tariffs and Trade (GATT), which has led to the establishment of the World Trade Organisation (WTO), countries like South Africa have to reduce their trade barriers, such as tariffs. These protective measures had created effective barriers to international competition and protected domestic firms from the threat of potential competition. As these barriers are removed, domestic firms, for example in the clothing and textile industry, are facing increased competition from producers in countries like China and South Korea.

6.1 Competitive versus imperfectly competitive markets

We usually distinguish competitive markets (perfect competition) from imperfectly competitive markets (i.e. monopoly, oligopoly and monopolistic competition). The classification is made according to the number of competitors and other important distinguishing characteristics. What follows here is a brief summary only, as we will consider each market in much more detail in the chapters that follow.

Perfect competition

This is the most efficient market form (we will discuss the concept of economic efficiency in the chapter dealing with perfect competition). Such a market consists of a very large number of small firms or production units. No single firm can have any marked influence on the market. There are no barriers to entry into the market, so that new firms may enter as they wish in response to market signals, or may leave if they decide to. All market participants have perfect knowledge of conditions within the market – producers know what consumers would like to consume, or what the best technique is to use in the production process. All firms will produce exactly the same product using the same technique of production. All factors of production are perfectly mobile, meaning that, for example, if workers would like to change jobs, they are free to do so. There is also no interference with the operation of market forces. Price is determined by demand and supply (as we have seen in Chapter 4), and the phenomenon of one product-one price holds. Each firm is merely a price-taker – it cannot deviate from the market-determined price.

As we will discuss later, this is clearly a situation that we are unlikely to find in the real world. Some real-world markets do have some of these characteristics though. For example, in many African countries we find craft markets where wooden and stone carvings, basketware and other crafts are sold. There are few, if any, barriers to entry into such craft markets and there are many sellers of such (often very similar) products. The level of competition in such craft markets is usually very high as sellers try to attract customers. It is also interesting to note that very often the prices charged by sellers are very similar.

Monopoly

This market form is found at the opposite extreme from perfect competition. Instead of a very large number of competitors, there is only one seller or producer and there are no close substitutes for the product. Free entry into the market does not exist, as significant barriers prevent other firms from entering the market. Consequently there is no threat of potential competition for the monopoly firm. We will consider later the factors which may constitute barriers to entry into the market. The characteristics of a monopoly mean that the firm has market power to influence what happens in this market. And as we will see, it means that there are implications for the level of efficiency in the market too. The existence of market power in a monopoly situation means that regulation may be introduced to influence the behaviour of the monopoly.

In the South African beer market, South African Breweries (SAB) has an effective monopoly. It controls virtually all beer production (although some small independent breweries do exist) and has been able to take over breweries that appeared likely to offer any serious competition to it (for example, Inter-Continental Breweries, some years ago).

Oligopoly

An oligopoly consists of a few producers – this could mean that there are only two producers (a duopoly) or a small number of producers. There may be barriers to entry into the market and firms may all produce the same product (such as cement) or they may produce differentiated products (such as cars). Since the number of producers is small, these firms are interdependent – they have to take into account the behaviour of their competitors. This results in a range of behaviour patterns in oligopoly – firms may compete with one another or co-operate with one another. Co-operation may be explicit (with a formal agreement in place) or implicit (where no written agreement exists, but definite co-ordination of activities takes place).

The South African cement market offers a good example of an oligopoly situation with explicit co-operation among firms in the market (in Chapter 9 we examine the cement cartel in some detail). The motor industry offers an example of an oligopoly where competition among firms is active. Two leading producers of luxury cars (Mercedes Benz and BMW) are constantly competing for customers in the high-priced segment of the car market – as we can see from their extensive and expensive advertising campaigns! More recently, the car market has faced international competition from a producer in South Korea. This new competitor in the domestic market led to even greater competition among existing domestic producers, and the resulting lower prices have been welcomed by consumers!

Monopolistic competition

A monopolistically competitive market consists of a large number of firms, but not as many as in a perfectly competitive market. Firms produce differentiated products – so we find many brands of toothpaste, for example. Such product differentiation means that firms will try to persuade consumers that their brand of the product is the best. Advertising (and other forms of non-price competition, such as after-sales service) are very common in this market. The aim of advertising is to increase the demand for the product and also to make consumers less price sensitive, so that when price rises, they do not cut back the quantity that they buy significantly (in economic jargon, the aim is to reduce the price elasticity of demand).

6.2 Elements of market structure: seller concentration

Factors such as the number of competitors and the extent of potential competition describe the structure of the market within which the firm operates and will clearly influence how the firm behaves. The firm's behaviour includes its choice of technology, its pricing policy, its decisions on advertising, and a range of other strategic variables.

We should also note, however, that the firm's behaviour may influence the structure of the market. If two firms decide to merge or if one firm is taken over by another, then the number of competitors changes. If a firm obtains a patent (legal right to be the sole producer of a product or the only producer having the right to use a particular production technique), then this may create a barrier to entry into that industry. Again the structure of the market is influenced by firm behaviour.

Perhaps the most important distinguishing characteristics of a market are the degree of seller concentration, the conditions of entry into the market (or barriers to entry) and the degree of product differentiation.

The degree of seller concentration refers to the extent to which activity in the market is dominated by a few large firms. Extreme concentration is found in the case of monopoly and no concentration is evident in a perfectly competitive market. Concern about concentration stems from the perception that high levels of concentration will be associated with monopoly-like behaviour on the part of the firms. High levels of concentration are linked to behaviour that differs markedly from the ideal of perfect competition, where efficiency (price equals marginal cost) is achieved.

Various attempts have been made to quantify the extent of concentration in the market. One of the most common measures of concentration is the *Gini coefficient*. This measure is derived from the *Lorenz curve*, illustrated in Fig. 6.1.

The lengths of the horizontal and vertical axes are the same in the diagram, and the units of measurement are percentages. Along the horizontal axis we measure the cumulative percentage of firms from the smallest to the largest. We start with the smallest 20 per cent of firms, add to that the next 20 per cent of firms and so on, until the largest firms have also been accounted for. Along the vertical axis we indicate the percentage of total output that each consecutive group of firms produces.

If all firms are of exactly equal size, then the lowest 20 per cent of firms would produce 20 per cent of total output, the lowest 40 per cent of firms, 40 per cent of total output, and so on. The Lorenz curve which joins these points

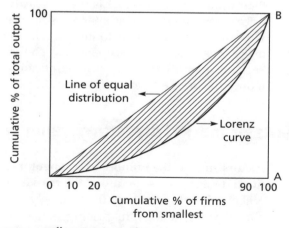

Fig. 6.1 Lorenz curve – seller concentration

would then be a straight line from bottom left-hand corner to top right-hand corner. This would indicate zero concentration in the industry and the Lorenz curve would be a line of perfect equality in size distribution.

If there exists seller concentration, the Lorenz curve will lie below the line of perfect equality. The further away it is from this diagonal the higher is the level of seller concentration.

The Gini coefficient is derived from this diagram. It is determined by the ratio of the shaded area between the line of equality and the Lorenz curve, to the area of triangle OAB. If no concentration exists, the Gini coefficient is equal to zero. The higher the level of concentration the closer it will be to one: in the monopoly situation it will be equal to one.

In the South African manufacturing sector fairly high levels of concentration are evident, as can be seen in Table 6.1 where the estimated Gini coefficients are all relatively high.

Table 6.1 Concentration levels in South African Manufacturing – Gini coefficients 1985

Sector	Gross output			
	Gilbert 1993	Smith 1991	Leach 1992	Fourie & Smith 1992
Food	0.856	0.857	0.873	0.857
Beverages	0.775	0.789	0.826	0.789
Tobacco products	0.422	–	–	–
Textiles	0.780	0.817	0.827	0.817
Furniture and fixtures	0.710	0.779	0.754	0.779
Paper/Paper products	0.815	0.850	0.868	0.850
Wearing apparel	0.743	0.789	0.788	0.789
Leather/Leather products	0.739	0.781	0.782	0.781
Printing/Publishing	0.750	0.804	0.797	0.804
Industrial chemicals	0.805	–	0.854	0.763
Other chemical products	0.825	0.818	0.880	0.810
Rubber products	0.797	0.845	0.851	0.845
Plastic products	0.701	0.738	0.742	0.738
Pottery/China and earthenware	0.793	–	0.844	0.853
Glass/Glass products	0.747	–	0.850	0.788
Other non-metallic mineral products	0.821	0.878	0.875	0.878
Fabricated metal products	0.770	0.828	0.823	0.828
Machinery	0.748	0.796	0.795	0.796
Iron and steel	0.838	0.832	0.893	0.832
Non-ferrous basic industries	0.803	0.777	0.853	0.777
Electrical machinery	0.795	0.842	0.845	0.842
Motor vehicles	0.845	0.903	0.902	0.903
Transport equipment	0.807	0.863	0.860	0.863
Professional/Scientific equipment	0.770	0.816	0.819	0.816
Other manufacturing industries	0.763	0.880	0.811	0.880
Footwear	0.699	0.738	0.740	0.738
Wood and cork products	0.774	0.827	0.823	0.827
Total – Manufacturing	0.823	0.819	–	–

Data from *Census of Manufacturing* 1985, Central Statistical Service (Republic of South Africa).
Source: Concentration and Competition, E. S. Gilbert. Unpublished dissertation, UCT 1993.

6.3 Elements of market structure: barriers to entry

Barriers to entry have an important role in protecting firms within a market from potential competition. Firms in the market are shielded by these barriers from the threat of competition by potential entrants. A long list of factors may constitute barriers to entry. A firm may control the total supply of an important raw material required for production and so no other firms may be able to produce this product. De Beers in South Africa controls virtually all diamond production as a result of the control of the areas where diamonds are mined. Another factor which may be a barrier to entry is patent protection or licensing. This means that a producer has the sole right to produce a product. When we discuss the monopoly situation, we will consider other barriers to entry.

This threat of competition arises when prices and profits rise too much, as is argued by proponents of the theory of *contestable markets*. The theory postulates that even industries with few firms and no actual entry may keep prices and profits low because of the threat of potential entry. The threat of potential entry disciplines incumbent firms provided entry is easy and firms in the industry take potential entry into account when determining price and output levels.

An example of a contestable market that is often cited is the airline industry. It is argued that it costs little to move planes to contest alternative air routes. The airline serving a particular route has an incentive to keep fares and profits low if it is aware that another airline could be attracted, at relatively low cost, to the route and compete away high profits. The South African domestic airline industry was for a long time dominated by South African Airways (SAA). More recently the monopoly power of SAA has been challenged by a number of smaller airline companies, such as Sun Air and Comair. Comair has been extending its coverage of domestic airline routes, as moving into new routes is fairly easy if the aircraft are available, since this would be the most costly part of the process.

6.4 Elements of market structure: product differentiation

Product differentiation is defined from the consumer's perspective. Two products are defined as differentiated if the consumer believes they are different. From a technical perspective (in terms of factors related to the production process and the inputs used) there may be no substantial difference between two products, yet the packaging may be different, and if the consumer views the two products as different, we refer to this perception and describe them as differentiated.

The degree of product differentiation forms a basis for both price and non-price competition among firms. As such it may stimulate product development and innovation. Product differentiation has implications for the elasticity of demand for the product. The greater the degree of product differentiation, the less the possibilities for substitution and hence, *ceteris paribus*, the less elastic the demand will be. Therefore, under perfect competition where there is no product differentiation (all firms produce exactly the same product), the demand for the product will be perfectly elastic. As we move through the range of market forms towards monopoly where there is much greater product differentiation (there is only one firm producing the product and there are no close substitutes for the product), the elasticity of demand will be quite low. This means that even with substantial price increases, consumers do not cut back significantly on the quantity that they buy.

6.5 Objectives of the firm

As we have seen from our discussion here, the structure of the market within which the firm operates clearly has an important influence on how the firm behaves (and the behaviour of the firm will also influence the structure of the market). The behaviour of the firm will also be strongly influenced by the objective it chooses to pursue. In fact, all decisions that the firm makes will be focused on the overall objective of the firm. Before we examine the firms' objectives, it will be useful to focus on exactly what we mean by the term 'the firm'.

Not all firms are of the one-person or one-household kind that used to inhabit the islands of Famine and Utopia during the early stages of their development. We often use the terms 'firm', 'producer' and 'seller' interchangeably in this text. We should be aware that there are in fact differences in the use of these terms. For our purposes, we will define the 'firm' as an entity that produces and sells a product. This means that it is a group of individuals that comes together (on the initiative of the entrepreneur), decides which product or service to produce, chooses a technique of production and the required factors of production, co-ordinates the production process and sells the product to consumers (which involves marketing and distributing the product). All these activities are undertaken by the firm. This is a very broad definition and therefore can include very small and medium-sized firms, large-scale enterprises and conglomerates.

Many different objectives are pursued by firms. A firm may select a single objective or have multiple objectives. As economists we often focus on profit as the most important objective that firms have. Profit is what remains from the firm's total revenue (income from sales) after it has covered all its costs (including normal profit, i.e. the remuneration accruing to the entrepreneur). In this sense we are referring to abnormal or economic profit when we discuss the firm's objective. The pursuit of profit remains one of the important motivating factors for entrepreneurs as they establish firms – it is the return to the entrepreneur for initiating the production of goods and services and for taking the risks that are associated with the process.

Firms may also pursue other objectives such as sales revenue maximisation. In the modern firm, where there is a separation of ownership and control, this is a very realistic objective. In such a firm a manager or group of managers would be responsible for the day-to-day business activities, while the firm is actually owned by shareholders. The shareholders would like a return on their shares, and this comes in the form of dividends. Dividends to shareholders are paid from profit and therefore shareholders would be interested in profit maximisation for the firm. However, managers may receive incentives related to the sales performance of the firm, and they would therefore pursue an objective of sales revenue maximisation. Some potential for conflict between shareholders and owners may therefore exist, especially in typically large firms.

Other firms may set themselves a target market share to achieve or a certain growth rate to attain. Whichever objective or objectives are pursued will influence the behaviour of the firm. If the firm is hoping to increase its market share it may lower its price and advertise its product, whereas if the firm wants to maximise profit it may cut back its advertising expenditure, for example. Firm behaviour is therefore a very complex process, dependent on the structure of the market within which the firm operates, its objectives, and changes in the broader economic environment such as changes in tax policy.

6.6 The role of competition policy

Competition policy (or antitrust legislation) is formulated in order to maintain and promote competition, especially in markets where there may be a tendency for monopolistic practices or collusive activity to develop.

Policy focuses on the acquisition and exercise of market power. A dominant firm may result from the acquisition by one firm of the shares or assets of another firm. Dominance may also be achieved as a result of the merger of existing firms. A *horizontal merger* is a merger of two firms selling the same or a similar product. A *vertical merger* is a result of the merger of a supplier and its customer. An example would be where an oil company and a petrol station merge. A *conglomerate merger* is a merger of companies in unrelated markets producing largely unrelated products. Another means of acquiring and exercising market power is *predatory pricing*. A firm would sell at prices below cost so as to oust smaller competitors and thus obtain a monopoly position in the market. Manufacturers may also enter into *exclusive dealing agreements* with retailers that restrict the sale or use of competing products.

These methods of achieving and exercising market power are examples of *restrictive practices*, and competition legislation attempts to prevent such interference with the competitive forces of the market.

Important to any decision taken within the framework of competition policy, is the definition of the relevant market. Clearly the greater the number of substitute goods included in the definition of the market, or the greater the geographic area, the smaller will be the market share of any single firm; and consequently, the less likely it will be that the firm will be deemed to have abused a dominant position.

Broadly speaking two approaches to competition policy may be identified. On the one hand there is the approach which contends that the market, if left to its own devices, will produce an efficient outcome. This 'hands-off' approach makes no presumption about firm size. It holds that if an oligopoly or monopoly emerges without interference then this is the most efficient means of producing a particular product.

The second approach, adopting an interventionist perspective, takes the view that the market cannot always be relied upon to produce an efficient outcome. This view holds that concentrations of market power may develop and interfere with the operation of competitive forces in the market and hence inefficiencies may result. Consequently some intervention to prevent inefficient outcomes is necessary.

CASE EXAMPLE

South African competition policy

The Maintenance and Promotion of Competition Act, number 96 of 1979, prescribes South Africa's competition policy. This policy is currently under review, and although discussion documents have been drafted, the Act of 1979 is still in force as is the institutional framework which gives effect to the policy. Following the enactment of this legislation, the Competition Board was established. It, together with the Directorate of Investigations, is responsible for initiating investigations into firm behaviour and making recommendations to the Minister of Trade and Industry. The Competition Board has no power to implement the recommendations that it makes; it being the responsibility of the Minister.

The basic areas of importance with regard to South Africa's competition policy are:

1. **Public interest.** This is the final criterion which is used to judge firm behaviour. The Act does not, however, define the public interest. This criterion has to be interpreted by the Competition Board. If firm behaviour can be shown to be against the public interest then the Competition Board may recommend that the firm be forced to cease that activity, and this recommendation may be implemented by the Minister. The fact that the public interest is not defined means that there is some flexibility and discretion involved in decisions by the Competition Board. However, it also brings the possibility of inconsistencies.

2. **Restrictive practices.** These are any act or omission that may restrict the free operation of market forces. While some restrictive practices, such as resale price maintenance, are specifically outlawed, the Act does not contain a comprehensive list and description of such practices.

3. **Competition.** The virtues of competition are lauded in the Act, yet competition is not clearly defined. It appears that competition refers to the day-to-day interactions among firms as they attempt to get an edge on other firms in the same market.

4. **The role of the market.** The Competition Act appears to favour market forces over intervention, yet the specific role of the market and that of government are not clearly delineated.

▶

Case example
continued

Current discussions on competition policy suggest that the institutional frame-work is likely to be enhanced, and perhaps a Competition Court established. The independence and power of the Competition Board is likely to be extended too. The proposed legislation will perhaps focus more clearly on the impact of market dominance by a firm, and define more closely restrictive practices.

Summary

- In this chapter we distinguished between perfectly competitive and imperfectly competitive markets. This distinction can be made on the basis of the number of competitors participating in the market, the ability of new firms to enter the market (or the presence of entry barriers), and the type of product being produced.

- A perfectly competitive market is characterised by a large number of competitors, free entry, and a homogeneous product. Conversely, a monopoly consists of one firm only (but many demanders), with no entry being possible or legally permitted. Oligopolies fall between these polar cases, while the characteristic feature of a monopolistically competitive market is product differentiation.

- The type of market, or market structure, within which a firm operates may determine its own behaviour, while the firm itself may also exert some influence on market structure. But the most important determinants of market structure are the degree of seller concentration, the conditions of entry, and the extent to which product differentiation is possible.

- The degree of seller concentration – measured by the so-called Gini coefficient – refers to the extent to which a market is dominated by a few large firms, and depends on whether the financial and legal systems allow for large-scale acquisitions and take-overs. Likewise, entry barriers can be either of a technical nature – e.g. producing at low unit cost or controlling an important raw material – or can be legally enforced in the form of patent protection and licensing. Product differentiation is technically possible in most industries – e.g. automobiles, toothpaste, beers and breakfast foods – and usually gives rise to both price and non-price competition among firms.

- The single firm may have many different objectives. It may pursue the single objective of profit maximisation, or have multiple objectives. Large firms are characterised by a separation of ownership and control, with shareholders being the owners and managers being in charge of day-to-day operations. While the owners usually want to maximise profits (and hence dividends), managers may prefer to maximise sales or boost the market share of the business.

- Competition policy is aimed at maintaining and promoting competition, or at least limiting the concentration of market power, because this is deemed to be in the best interests of the consuming public.

Questions for review

1. What is seller concentration, how can we measure it, and what are the implications if a market is highly concentrated?

2. What are some of the shortcomings of South African competition policy?

3. Examine some of the possible objectives that a firm may have.

CHAPTER 7

Perfect competition

A world dominated by perfect competition is the ideal state for anti-monopoly crusaders – or so the caricature goes. True perfect competition, just like pure monopoly, is an economic state which is rarely found in the real world – save perhaps on our idyllic islands of Utopia and Famine! Why the notion of perfect competition is important in economics is that it provides a bench-mark (and a simple one at that) against which to analyse and judge other types of markets.

The characteristics of a perfectly competitive market are:

- *Free entry and exit*. Any firm wishing to enter the market can gain access to finance, factors of production, and the necessary technical information to start production in this market. Firms wishing to leave the market face no obstacles either.

- *All firms produce an identical product*. There are no brand names (product differentiation) that can distinguish the product of any firm from any other. Consumers will therefore choose between the products of the various firms solely on the basis of price.

- *There are many producers and consumers*. This means that any single market participant is too small to influence prices and quantities prevailing in the market in any way – no one has any market power.

- *All producers and consumers have perfect knowledge*. Consumers have perfect information about the prices charged by different firms and producers have perfect knowledge about technology and consumer preferences.

The requirements for a perfectly competitive market are clearly very stringent, but at least the model does not assume that the earth is flat! The perfectly competitive model does provide a useful standard against which to compare other market forms, since it is the most efficiently functioning market structure.

7.1 Market demand and the firm's demand curve

Figure 7.1(a) shows the downward sloping market demand curve and the upward sloping market supply curve as well as the equilibrium price, P_e. We have assumed that no producer can affect market price, because of its insignificant size relative to the market as a whole. Therefore the demand curve for the individual firm's output is horizontal or *perfectly elastic* as shown in Figure 7.1(b). Perfect elasticity of the firm's demand curve occurs for two reasons:

- Its product is identical to that of its competitors. Thus if the firm were to raise its price above P_e, it would sell nothing because consumers could get exactly the same good from any other firm at price P_e.
- Since the firm's output is extremely small compared to that of the entire industry, it can sell all that it wishes at price P_e, the market equilibrium price, without disturbing this equilibrium price.

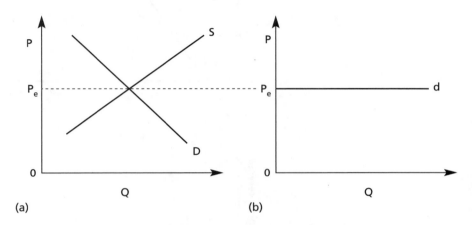

Fig. 7.1 (a) Perfectly competitive market (b) Perfectly competitive firm

Total, average and marginal revenue for a perfectly competitive firm

A demand curve may be viewed from two different perspectives. On the one hand, it shows the quantity of a good that consumers are willing and able to purchase over a period of time at different prices. On the other hand, it shows the revenue per unit that a seller can receive for different quantities of the good sold per period of time. We will focus on the second interpretation here.

If the price determined by the market is equal to R10, the firm can sell all it produces at this price and total revenue is equal to the quantity produced multiplied by R10. Note that whether the firm sells 50 units or 500, the price per unit remains R10. The *average revenue* (*AR*) is determined by taking the total revenue (*TR*) and dividing by the quantity sold. Thus we see that the price of the product is always equal to the firm's average revenue, or $P_e = AR$.

The contribution to total revenue when an extra unit of the product is sold is called *marginal revenue* (*MR*). Since the perfectly competitive firm sells every unit at exactly the same price, P_e, marginal revenue will also be equal to the price of the product; or $P_e = AR = MR$.

Figure 7.2(a) depicts the firm's total revenue curve. The change in total revenue, as an extra unit is sold, is R10; in other words, marginal revenue is R10. By definition marginal revenue represents the slope (gradient) of the total revenue curve. Under perfect competition, the total revenue curve is a straight line through the origin, since revenue is directly proportional to output sold.

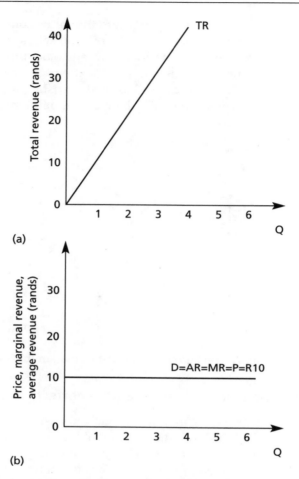

Fig. 7.2 The firm's total revenue curve, marginal revenue curve and demand curve

In Fig. 7.2(b), the horizontal demand curve is also equal to the average and marginal revenue curves: $DD = P = MR = AR$ at all output levels under conditions of perfect competition.

7.2 The perfectly competitive firm in the short run

The perfectly competitive firm's plant size is fixed in the short run. Thus it can only change its output level by changing its variable inputs: the amount of raw materials, labour, and energy inputs.

In order to determine whether the firm is making a profit or a loss, or is just breaking even, we need to compare its total cost (TC) with its total revenue (TR). We've seen that total revenue is found by multiplying the product price (P) by the quantity sold (Q). The firm's total cost (TC) consists of the cost of its fixed factors (fixed costs), variable factors (variable costs) and also its *normal profit*. Normal profit is the return which is necessary to keep the entrepreneur and the resources he or she owns in this firm. We could say that normal profit is the return to self-owned, self-employed resources.

The firm may find itself in one of the following three situations:

1. Total revenue from the sale of output may exceed total cost ($TR > TC$) and the firm earns an economic profit.
2. The firm's total revenue may exceed its total variable cost ($TR > TVC$), and cover some of its fixed cost. Since the firm has to cover its fixed costs in the short run, whether it is producing or not, the loss incurred is thus smaller than it would be if no production were undertaken.
3. The firm's total revenue may not be sufficient to cover its total variable cost of production ($TR < TVC$). In this case the loss (equal to fixed cost) of remaining idle is less than it would be if production were undertaken, and the firm will choose not to produce any output.

Maximising profit

We have assumed that the objective of the firm is to maximise profit. To find the level of output that the firm should produce to meet this objective we can follow either of two approaches. Firstly, we can compare the firm's total revenue with its total cost. Secondly, we can follow the marginal cost–marginal revenue approach. Both will give us the same result.

Table 7.1 contains the total, average and marginal cost data, as well as price, total revenue and marginal revenue data, for a firm in a perfectly competitive market. All data are measured per period of time, such as monthly.

Table 7.1 Cost and revenue data in rands

Output (Q)	Total cost (TC)	Marginal cost (MC)	Average cost (AC)	Price (P=MR)	Total revenue (TR)	Total profit
0	800		–	8	0	–800
100	2000	2	20	8	800	–1200
200	2300	3	11.50	8	1600	–700
300	2400	1	8	8	2400	0
400	2524	1.25	6.31	8	3200	676
500	2775	2.5	5.55	8	4000	1225
600	3200	4.25	5.33	8	4800	1600
650	3600	8	5.40	8	5200	1690
700	4200	12	5.71	8	5600	1600
800	6400	22	8.00	8	6400	0

Total cost–total revenue approach

The firm's total cost data, and its associated output levels, appear in Table 7.1. The price p at which the firm can sell its output is always R8 per unit. The firm's total revenue (TR) from sales at each output level is determined by multiplying this price by the quantity produced (we assume that all output is sold). Profit or loss equals the difference between total revenue and total cost. From the data in Table 7.1, and specifically from the profit data, we can see that the firm should produce 650 units of output to maximise profit. This equilibrium situation is illustrated in Fig. 7.3. At each output level the vertical distance between TR and TC show the loss or profit. We can see from this diagram that at an output level of 650 units, the vertical distance between TR and TC is at a maximum, and hence profit is maximised.

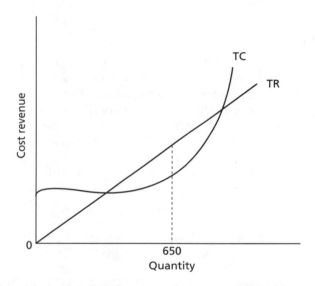

Fig. 7.3 Profit maximisation (total cost–total revenue approach)

Marginal cost–marginal revenue approach

An alternative approach compares the marginal cost (addition to total cost) with the marginal revenue (addition to total revenue) from the sale of an extra unit.

If $MC < MR$, the marginal unit adds less to total cost than it does to total revenue; thus it makes sense to produce this unit. The excess of marginal revenue over marginal cost adds to profit, and so the firm should increase its production as long as marginal revenue exceeds marginal cost.

If, however, $MC > MR$, the firm should cut back its output level because it is making a loss on the production of the marginal unit. This adjustment process continues until MR equals MC, which will ensure that profit is maximised.

Figure 7.4 shows the marginal cost–marginal revenue approach. The *MC* curve is plotted from data in Table 7.1. Note that *MC* refers to the change in *TC* divided by the change in output. The firm's demand curve is perfectly elastic (horizontal) at the price *p* = *MR* = R8. We identify the output level where *MR* = *MC*. In our example this occurs at the output level of 650 units. This confirms the profit-maximising output level that we found using the *TR–TC* approach.

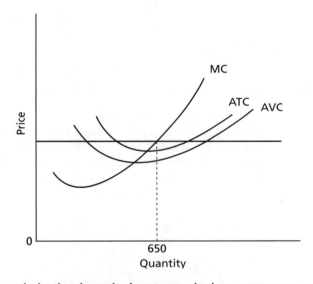

Fig. 7.4 Profit maximisation (marginal cost–marginal revenue approach)

Minimising losses

If the firm's total revenue covers its total variable costs, but not all its fixed costs, then *TR* < *TC*. The firm then has to determine its output level so that it minimises its loss. It focuses on its *TR* and *TVC* curves and finds the output level where total revenue exceeds total variable costs by the largest amount. This excess of *TR* over *TVC* will contribute to covering the firm's fixed costs. Figure 7.5(a) shows this firm's cost and revenue curves. The output level at which the distance between *TR* and *TVC* is a maximum (note that this is a vertical distance on the diagram) will be the firm's loss minimising point.

Using the *MR–MC* approach, we can see that where *MR* = *MC*, the firm's *ATC* is greater than the product price (in Fig. 7.5(b)). This means that the price per unit (or average revenue) is not sufficient to cover the cost per unit (*ATC*), but price is still greater than *AVC*. The firm is making a loss per unit and the challenge is to minimise this loss. The fact that *MR* = *MC* guarantees this.

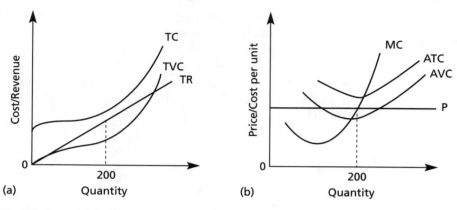

Fig. 7.5 Loss minimisation

Shut-down position

When the firm's total revenue is not even sufficient to cover its total variable cost, it will minimise its losses by producing nothing at all. Its loss will then be equal to its total fixed cost. Note that in the short run this does not mean that the firm goes out of business, but simply that the plant remains idle. In the long run all factors are variable, and therefore also all costs. A firm may be able to become profitable by switching to a different plant size in the long run, or if demand conditions improve. If the sea around the island of Famine ran dry of fish, it may be better for the fishing population to hold on to their boats and nets and hope for better times, at least in the short run.

The shut-down case is depicted in Fig. 7.6.

In Fig. 7.6(a), *TC* lies everywhere above *TR*, and Fig. 7.6(b) shows that *MR* lies everywhere below *AVC*. Using either the *TC–TR* approach or the *MC–MR* approach, we can see that no production is better than any level of production.

To summarise, if price exceeds average variable cost, the perfectly competitive firm should produce that output level where $MR(= p) = MC$ in order to maximise profit or minimise losses. If price is less than average variable cost, it will minimise its loss by producing no output.

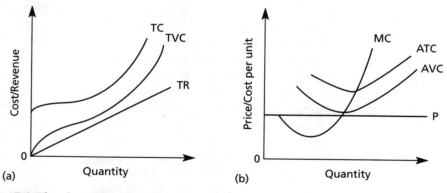

Fig. 7.6 The shut-down case

7.3 The short-run supply curve

The firm maximises profit or minimises losses by adjusting its production to that level where marginal cost equals marginal revenue. As long as price is equal to or greater than average variable cost, the perfectly competitive firm adjusts its output by moving along that part of its marginal cost curve that lies above its average variable cost curve. This part of the MC curve coincides exactly with the definition of a supply curve: the supply curve indicates the amount of a good that the producer is willing and able to provide to the market at different prices.

The relationship between the supply curve and the marginal cost curve for the perfectly competitive firm is illustrated in Fig. 7.7(a). At a price of P_1 the firm is just able to cover its average variable cost: this marks the starting point of the firm's supply curve. With higher and higher prices (such as P_2 and P_3) larger quantities of output would be produced. The equilibrium output is indicated by the point of intersection between the firm's MC curve and each price line (or MR curve). That part of the perfectly competitive firm's MC curve that lies above its average variable cost curve is thus its short-run supply curve.

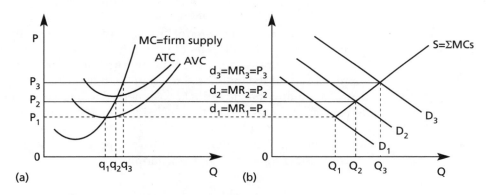

Fig. 7.7 Deriving the industry's short-run supply curve

The supply curve of the industry

Suppose there are 1000 firms, such as that in Fig. 7.7(a), which together make up the perfectly competitive industry. At each price level the industry supply curve is indicated by the horizontal summation of the quantities each individual firm will supply, as indicated by its marginal cost curve above the AVC curve.

In Fig. 7.7(b) the industry supply curve is arrived at by taking the quantity that the individual firm supplies and multiplying it by 1000 (since there are 1000 such firms), and plotting that amount against the relevant price. At a price below P_1, firms are not able to cover their average variable costs and therefore will produce nothing. Hence the industry will supply nothing at a price below P_1, as indicated by the fact that the industry supply curve in Fig. 7.7(b) does not extend below this level.

We know from earlier chapters that market demand and supply determine equilibrium price and quantity for the industry. The individual firm, however, contributes such a small portion of total market supply that it cannot affect the market price. The perfectly competitive firm's demand curve is therefore perfectly elastic (horizontal). Combining these considerations with the perfectly competitive firm's cost curves and the industry supply curve, we can examine the relationship between the industry equilibrium and the firm's equilibrium in the short run. Parts (a) and (b) of Fig. 7.7 are used for this purpose.

When the market demand for the industry's output is D_1 in part (b), its intersection with the industry supply curve, S, determines the equilibrium price level, P_1. A typical firm therefore faces the horizontal demand curve d_1 at the price level P_1 and supplies q_1 units of output.

The firm is just covering its AVC at price P_1, i.e. the demand curve d_1 is tangent to the AVC curve at its lowest point. If the industry demand curve were to shift to a position lower than D_1, and price dropped to below P_1, firms would produce nothing at all. If the industry demand curve shifted to D_2 in part (b), the typical firm would now face a demand curve d_2. It would still not be able to cover its total cost because d_2 lies below the ATC curve. The output of the firm would be q_2. A demand curve of D_3 would imply that the industry is making profits rather than losses, with the typical firm producing q_3 units of output.

Thus as the price of the product rises, so each firm will supply more output, since the higher price offers an opportunity to make more profit, *ceteris paribus*. The industry supply curve is found by the horizontal summation of all the supply curves of the individual firms in the industry. This process is similar to that of summing the individual consumers' demand curves to find the market demand for a product which we considered in Chapter 4. Since all the supply curves of the individual firms are upward sloping the process of horizontal summation will ensure that the industry supply curve will be upward sloping as well – as described by the law of supply.

7.4 The perfectly competitive firm and industry in the long run

In the long run, the firm has enough time to adjust its plant size, and consequently all factor inputs are variable. The elasticity of supply is much greater in the long run than in the short run, because of the flexibility of firms' production schedules in the long run.

Demand increases: new firms enter the industry

Initially the demand and supply curves for a perfectly competitive industry are given by D_1 and S_1 in Fig. 7.8(b). Suppose that there are initially 1000 firms, each like the one represented in Fig. 7.8(a). The supply curve S_1 is the short-run industry supply curve and represents the sum of the marginal cost curves of each of the 1000 firms. Likewise, the market demand curve D, is the sum of all the individual demand curves.

The firm's demand curve is d_1, given the equilibrium price P_1, and its profit maximising output (where $MC = MR$) is 50 units. In this situation the firm is just earning a normal profit ($ATC = p$).

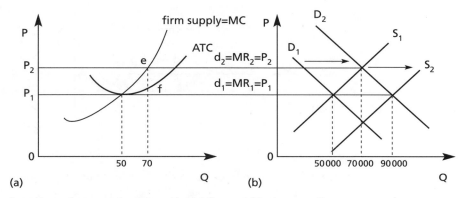

Fig. 7.8 An increase in demand and firm and industry adjustment

Now suppose that an increase in market demand shifts the demand curve from D_1 to D_2, as shown in Fig. 7.8(b). Initially price rises to P_2 and each firm responds by setting this new price (= $MR_2 = d_2$) equal to MC, thus producing 70 units and making a unit profit equal to the distance ef, i.e. the difference between price and ATC.

The long-run response will be a reallocation of resources, as new firms enter this industry in an attempt to capture some of the economic profits. So resources in the economy will be allocated away from other less profitable industries to this one.

Entry by new firms is reflected in Fig. 7.8(b) by the rightward shift of the short-run industry supply curve. As long as excess profits are made, new firms will continue to enter the industry, since in the long run all factors of production are variable. The short-run supply curve will continue to shift rightward until it reaches S_2 and price is back at the initial level P_1. Each firm's demand curve will be back at the initial position d_1, with all firms making normal profits, thus restoring stability to the industry.

Firms leave the industry

Consider the same initial equilibrium as in Fig. 7.8. In Fig. 7.9 industry demand decreases, as shown by the leftward shift of the demand curve from D_1 to D_3. For the individual firm this means that its demand curve falls from d_1 to d_3 (in part (a)), causing a reduction in output (the firm will move down the MC curve until $MC = MR$). Since P_3 lies below the ATC curve, the representative firm is incurring a loss, and some firms will inevitably go out of business. This is an important difference between the short and long run: in the short run, firms may continue production even if they are making a loss as long as *TR* is sufficient to cover *TVC*. However, no firm can sustain losses indefinitely, and thus, in the long run, loss-making firms will leave the industry.

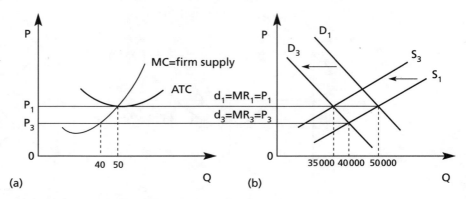

Fig. 7.9 A decrease in demand and firm and industry adjustment

As firms leave the industry, the short-run industry supply curve will shift leftward to position S_3. Price P_1 is restored at the intersection of D_3 and S_3 (Fig. 7.9(b)). The individual firm once again faces demand curve d_1 (where $d_1 = MR_1 = P_1$). At this price, each firm just covers total costs ($p = ATC$) and therefore earns a normal profit. A smaller number of firms (say 700) now make up the market, together producing 35 000 units.

To summarise, the perfectly competitive firm will be in long-run equilibrium when price equals marginal cost equals marginal revenue equals average total cost ($p = MR = MC = ATC$).

In long-run equilibrium the individual firm just earns a *normal profit* but *zero economic profit*. An increase in demand causes an increase in price, which leads to excess profits. This acts as an incentive to new firms to enter the industry, causing the short-run supply curve to shift rightward until price falls back to the level of minimum average total cost. Each firm then operates once again at the minimum point of its average total cost curve, earning only a normal profit. Equilibrium is thus restored in the market.

A decrease in demand causes price to fall, and the firms to incur losses. Some firms will leave the industry, causing the short-run supply curve to shift leftward until price settles at the level of minimum average total cost for those firms remaining in the industry. The remaining firms are then again only making a normal profit, and the market is once again back in equilibrium.

The long-run industry supply curve

The supply curves S_1, S_2 and S_3 in Figs 7.8 and 7.9 are short-run industry supply curves. Along any one of them the number of firms in the industry is assumed constant. In order to say something about the *long-run* industry supply curve we must consider three possible scenarios – one in which costs are constant, one in which costs are increasing, and one in which costs are decreasing.

The constant cost case

So far we have assumed that the prices of factors of production are constant, whatever the level of output produced. This means that even when new firms enter the industry or existing ones leave, the ATC and MC curves of all firms remain at exactly the same level.

We considered three possible positions of the market demand curve, D_1, D_2 and D_3 in Figs 7.8(b) and 7.9(b), each of which has an associated long-run equilibrium. Although the number of firms in the industry associated with each long-run equilibrium varies, the long-run equilibrium position of every firm in the industry is always the same. Every firm will produce at the lowest point on its ATC curve, where its MC curve intersects its demand curve.

If we consider all other possible positions of the market demand curve, then in each case after the long-run adjustment, there would be just enough firms in the industry so that total industry supply would equal industry demand at price P_1. The long-run industry supply curve in the constant cost case is therefore just a horizontal line at the equilibrium price level P_1, as shown in Fig. 7.10(a).

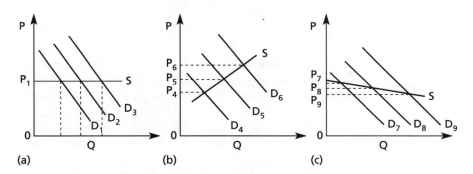

Fig. 7.10 Long-run supply curves for a perfectly competitive industry.
(a) Constant-cost situation; (b) Increasing-cost situation; (c) Decreasing-cost situation

The increasing-cost case

The prices of resources used by the competitive industry may rise as the industry purchases more of them. This will happen if the industry's demand for its factors of production constitutes a large enough proportion of the total supply of such resources. Conversely, if the industry reduces its level of production, the reduction in demand for such resources may lead to a fall in their prices.

For each individual firm in the industry, a rise in the prices of its inputs, and hence its unit costs, will be reflected in an upward shift in its ATC and

MC curves. Similarly, a decline in factor prices, and hence unit costs, will be reflected in a downward shift in the ATC and MC curves. Suppose that successively higher levels of industry demand are considered, as represented by rightward shifts of the market demand curve to positions such as D_4, D_5 and D_6 in Fig. 7.10(b).

When the demand curve shifts from D_4 to D_5, new firms will enter the industry in response to the economic profits that are initially realised. With the entry of such firms, excess profits will be eliminated. First, profits will fall as a result of the fall in price that occurs during the adjustment process because of the expanding level of industry output. Second, excess profits will be reduced by the upward shift of the individual firms' ATC and MC curves, which results from the rise in the price of inputs as industry expansion increases the demand for them.

Once the excess profits have been eliminated by these twin processes, the industry will attain a new long-run equilibrium position, with a larger output level and more firms. Each firm will be operating at the minimum point of its ATC curve, and the ATC curve will be higher than before. Hence the higher level of industry output is supplied at a higher price.

Thus, in the increasing cost case, the long-run perfectly competitive industry supply curve is upward sloping, as shown in Fig. 7.10(b). The long-run equilibrium price associated with higher levels of demand, represented by D_4, D_5 and D_6, is successively higher.

The decreasing-cost case

A perfectly competitive industry may also find that factor prices, and hence its per unit costs of production, may decline as production expands. This could occur, for example, if the suppliers of the inputs to this industry experience economies of scale as they increase their production. The consequent reduction in costs of production might be passed on to this perfectly competitive industry in the form of lower input prices. This will cause the long-run supply curve of the perfectly competitive industry to slope downwards, as in Fig. 7.10(c). For higher levels of demand, D_7, D_8 and D_9, the long-run equilibrium prices are lower at P_7, P_8 and P_9 respectively.

7.5 Perfect competition and resource allocation

When the perfectly competitive industry is in long run equilibrium, competition ensures that every firm uses the technology that yields the lowest possible ATC curve, and produces at the minimum point on the ATC curve; consumers are also charged a price equal to marginal cost. If any firm charges a higher price, consumers will buy from other firms, instantly reducing the sales of that firm to zero (remember that we assumed no product differentiation and perfect information). Each firm is therefore forced to produce at minimum ATC if it wants to stay in business.

The perfectly competitive industry therefore produces at the lowest possible price and distributes it to consumers at a price that just covers the cost of production. The consumer pays for the last unit purchased exactly what it cost the firm to produce that unit. When *all* industries in an economy have reached a perfectly competitive equilibrium, each will produce exactly the quantity at which price equals marginal cost. Finally, because of freedom of entry into and exit from perfectly competitive industries, a perfectly competitive economy will quickly reallocate resources to meet changing consumer preferences or supply conditions.

Thus, in a perfectly competitive equilibrium, there will be no misallocation of resources between the production of different goods, and consumer satisfaction will be maximised. In terms of our earlier example, the island of Famine will have achieved allocative efficiency by producing the optimal combination of fish and garments, and operating on a point on its PPF.

7.6 The perfectly competitive labour market

Factor markets can also be perfectly competitive provided that all the requirements for perfect competition are met. For the labour market this means that there must be a very large number of workers supplying labour services and a very large number of firms hiring workers. Thus no individual market participant will be able to influence the market in any way.

Supply of labour services by the individual

The individual plays a dual role in the economy. In the product markets he or she demands goods and services, while in the factor markets he or she supplies labour or capital services. We will focus here on the labour market, where the individual supplies labour services.

The reward for working consists of the job satisfaction derived from working and from the income earned. Generally the more hours worked, the higher will be the income earned. This provides an incentive to work more, or supply a greater quantity of labour. Time spent not working, however, also has some value (or utility) for the individual. We all need some time off from work to recuperate and to enjoy leisure activities. We will refer to time not spent working as *leisure*.

Clearly we would like to enjoy both leisure and income (derived from work). There is therefore a trade-off: the more time we spend working, the less time we have for leisure. Working thus involves an *opportunity cost*. The *opportunity cost of working* is the amount of leisure time that must be given up. On the other hand the *opportunity cost of leisure* is the amount of income that could have been earned during leisure time.

This trade-off is reflected in the individual's *labour supply curve*. This curve shows the number of hours that the individual is prepared to work at different wage rates (or in the terminology of markets, how much labour he or she would be willing to supply at each price). As we work more hours, our leisure time becomes more scarce and therefore more valuable. We could say that the *marginal utility of leisure* increases as we work more. This means that higher wages are required to compensate for the higher opportunity cost of work; we will supply more hours of labour *only* if offered a higher wage rate.

Our most important motive for working is probably the income we can earn. The first few rands we earn are valued very highly – they have to cover the bills and the necessities of life. As we work and earn more, we discover that our most urgent needs have been met. The additional income we earn is therefore valued less highly. We say that the *marginal utility of income* declines as we earn more. Therefore we may not be willing to work more hours unless we are offered a higher wage rate.

The marginal utility of income, being derived from the goods and services that wages can buy, induces individuals to supply more labour. Higher wages thus encourage the substitution of labour for leisure. This is the *substitution effect* of wages: an increased wage rate encourages people to work more hours.

At some point, when the individual is already working long hours, additional goods and services will have little value. Individuals with very high incomes already enjoy high consumption levels. If they are offered a higher wage rate, they may reduce the number of hours worked in order to have more leisure time and still enjoy a high income level. This negative response to higher wage rates is referred to as the *income effect* of a wage increase. The income effect enables an individual to reduce the number of hours worked without sacrificing income.

The substitution effect of high wages encourages individuals to work more hours. The income effect allows them to work fewer hours without losing income. If the substitution effect dominates, the labour supply curve will be upward sloping. If the income effect is the stronger, the individual will supply less labour at higher wages. This conflict between the two effects is illustrated in the backward-bending labour supply curve, as shown in Fig. 7.11.

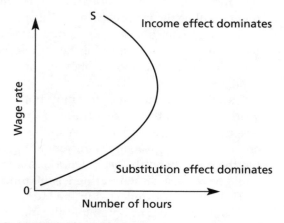

Fig. 7.11 The individual's labour supply curve

At relatively low wage rates, the substitution effect tends to dominate, so that more hours of work will be supplied as the wage rate increases. After some income level is reached, it is reasonable to suppose that higher wage rates will result in fewer hours worked. The income effect then dominates and the labour supply curve bends backwards. The exact point at which the supply curve will bend backwards depends on the value that the individual places on additional income relative to additional leisure. This is the situation of the individual worker. What can we say about the market supply of labour?

The market supply of labour

The market supply of labour represents the total quantity of labour that workers are willing and able to supply at different wage rates in a given period of time. In order to derive the market supply curve of labour, we would use the same process of horizontal summation that we used to aggregate individual demand curves to arrive at market demand. For most industries, we can assume that the substitution effect tends to outweigh the income effect in the aggregate, and hence the market supply curve will be upward sloping.

Determination of the wage rate

The wage rate is the price of labour – it is the price that the individual will be paid, per period of time, for the supply of labour services. All firms have downward sloping demand curves for all their variable factors of production, as we found in Chapter 5. By the same process of horizontal summation used to arrive at market demand from individual consumer demand, the market demand curve for a variable factor of production can be obtained. The market demand curve for labour therefore obeys the law of demand, as explained in Chapters 3 and 4. This is shown in Fig. 7.12.

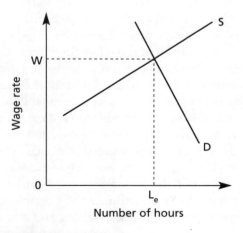

Fig. 7.12 Determination of the wage rate

It is worth adding that the prices of other factors of production, such as land and buildings, can be determined in a similar way. The determination of factor prices in terms of demand and supply curves is generally known as the *marginal productivity theory of factor pricing*.

The demand for a factor of production is a *derived demand*, since it reflects what happens in the market for the product produced by the factor. Factor demand therefore depends on the demand for products. As the demand for the product increases, so the demand curve for that factor will shift to the right. For example, if the demand for Chinese food increases, so will the demand for chefs with appropriate culinary skills.

The interaction of labour supply and labour demand curves will then determine the wage rate as in Fig. 7.12. At the wage rate, W, the number of labour hours supplied will be exactly equal to the number of labour hours demanded. The labour market will clear at this wage rate: all workers who would like to be employed at the wage rate W will find work. If the labour market is perfectly free to adjust, any unemployment will be voluntary, as some workers will choose not to offer their labour services at the prevailing wage rate.

In the real world, however, such a simplistic view of unemployment is clearly inadequate. Unemployment (involuntary as opposed to voluntary) is perhaps one of the most serious challenges facing economists and policy makers today. This is true of developing countries such as those in the Southern African region, but also of developed countries such as those belonging to the European Union. What has become clear is that the problem of unemployment is a persistent problem – often described as a structural problem. This means that those individuals who are unemployed may need to be retrained for new jobs (reskilling) in different industries or trained for jobs still to be created. The process of job creation is certainly much discussed in developed and developing countries as a means of, for example, relieving the burden on the government to provide basic goods such as housing, and reducing income inequality. Intervention in the labour market may therefore be necessary because the smooth process of adjustment described by Adam Smith, and which operates in a perfectly competitive market, cannot be relied upon.

In South Africa, the Labour Market Commission which has been investigating labour market conditions and making policy recommendations, has recently delivered its final report (June 1996). It found that unemployment was worst in rural areas, yet most jobs are created in urban areas. It has recommended that some intervention, in the form of incentives to create jobs in rural agriculture, for example, may therefore be necessary. The Commission did not call for a national minimum wage, but indicated that certain sectors, such as agriculture and domestic service which are particularly low-wage sectors of the economy, could perhaps benefit from a target wage level. Especially in agriculture, the Commission argues, such a policy could lead to more productive use of labour and also increased employment.

7.7 What is wrong with perfect competition?

While the above analysis may suggest that perfect competition is the optimal market structure, there are a few caveats. In a perfectly competitive world, information about technology is readily available to all. As a result, a firm cannot expect to gain much competitive advantage over other firms by developing new technology. Higher than normal profits would be competed away as other firms adopt the new technique. There is, therefore, little incentive to develop new technologies. Since technological innovation is considered essential for economic growth, a perfectly competitive world, while promoting allocative efficiency, may well retard growth (or dynamic efficiency).

Because all firms in a perfectly competitive market produce identical products, a perfectly competitive world could be a very dull one. While this may be true, few of us would argue in favour of attempts to create differences between the products of firms when in fact there is no distinction to be made. For example, advertising may try to persuade us that petrol from Shell is different from that of Caltex. However, petrol is essentially a homogeneous product; such advertising simply raises costs which are ultimately passed on to the consumer in the form of higher prices.

Furthermore, it must be noted that a perfectly competitive world provides for an efficient allocation of resources, *given* the existing distribution of wealth and income among members of the society. What society regards as an equitable *distribution* of income may not be necessarily the same as that associated with a perfectly competitive world. While resources are allocated most efficiently under conditions of perfect competition, this does not mean that they are necessarily allocated in the most equitable way. The *distribution* of income between members of a society is clearly a matter of great concern, and we shall return to this issue in the last chapter of the book.

Perhaps the greatest shortcoming of competitive (and all other markets) is the fact that market values are based on the *private* costs and benefits associated with the actions of individual consumers and producers. They thus fail to capture the external costs and benefits of production and consumption. This is generally referred to as a case of 'market failure', as the next section shows.

7.8 Market failure and the role of government

We have seen earlier that perfect competition leads to maximum economic efficiency. This is however only true in the absence of market failures. Market failures arise from the existence of externalities and public goods, among others.

Externalities

During the production and consumption of some products, harmful or beneficial side effects arise that are borne by firms and people not directly involved in the production and consumption processes. These are called externalities and referred to as *external costs* when they are harmful, and *external benefits* when they are beneficial.

An example of an external cost is air pollution that may result from a production process. The production of garments may, for example, pollute the air and rivers on Utopia, thus causing illness and discomfort among the rest of the population, who may have to bear the resultant costs themselves. An example of an external benefit is the reduced chance of spreading a communicable disease when an individual is inoculated against it.

In the absence of externalities, perfect competition leads to an efficient outcome. This is true only when the *private costs* (i.e. the explicit and implicit opportunity costs incurred by individuals and firms in the production process) are equal to the *social costs* (the costs incurred by society as a whole). Social costs are higher than private costs when firms are able to escape some of the economic costs of production. A firm dumping untreated waste into the air imposes a cost on society for which it does not pay. These costs may include higher cleaning costs and respiratory ailments, and are not reflected in the costs of the firm and therefore not in the industry supply curve.

Consider Fig. 7.13 where the market demand and industry supply curves intersect at the equilibrium output level, Q_n, and the associated price P_n. This equilibrium does not take into account external costs. If firms in the industry were required to pay some or all of the environmental clean-up costs associated with the production process, these additional production costs would be reflected in the market supply curve S_i, which lies above S_n. The equilibrium quantity sold would then be Q_i and the price P_i. In this case the cost of pollution would be borne by the buyers and sellers of this product – not by non-consenting third parties.

The new equilibrium is optimal from society's perspective. This is so because the existence of external costs leads to the production of additional units of the good (equal to $Q_n - Q_i$) that are not valued as much as the cost of producing them. This is evident from the fact that the industry supply curve S_i (which includes all costs) lies above the demand curve D, for all units from

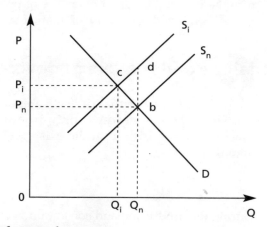

Fig. 7.13 Effects of external costs

Q_i to Q_n. The money value of this excess of costs over value is given by area bcd. It represents society's loss due to external costs when Q_n is produced.

The existence of *external benefits*, on the other hand, means that society suffers a loss due to missed opportunities. The market demand curve for measles inoculations affects the value to the people who pay for them. Benefits, however, accrue to other people who are as a result less likely to contract measles, but who do not pay for the inoculation. These people would gladly pay in order to ensure that other people in their vicinity do not carry the virus, but the market mechanism does not provide for such payments.

Because the market demand curve for goods and services providing external benefits does not reflect the full benefit thereof, it must lie below the demand curve that includes them. Figure 7.14 shows the demand curve D_n and supply curve for a good conferring external benefits on third parties.

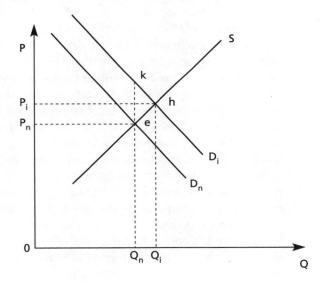

Fig. 7.14 Effects of external benefits

Market equilibrium is determined at quantity Q_n and price P_n. If the value of external benefits to society from this product are added to the demand curve D_n, we would arrive at demand curve D_i. Since D_i includes all benefits it will lie above D_n. Hence the true equilibrium output would be Q_i and the price P_i, thus indicating a larger output and a higher price than before.

With the existence of external benefits, the production of the product will be insufficient from society's perspective. When Q_n units are produced, society forgoes a quantity (Q_nQ_i) that it values more than the cost of producing them. This is seen in the fact that the demand curve D_i lies above the supply curve S between quantities Q_n and Q_i. The money value of the benefits to society of this additional output is represented by area $Q_nQ_i$hk. The cost of the resources required to produce the additional output is given by the area $Q_nQ_i$he. Total benefits therefore exceed additional costs by area ehk. This indicates society's loss due to the missed opportunity of not having the additional output.

Where external costs exist, the market mechanism encourages over-production. Conversely, where external benefits exist, under-production results, or the failure to provide goods even though the value of their benefits exceeds their costs.

Public goods

If the consumption of a product by one individual does not reduce the amount available for consumption by others, we refer to the product as a *public good*. Examples of public goods are national defence, law enforcement and street lighting. The most important characteristic of public goods is *non-rival consumption*. When one individual watches television, for example, it does not interfere with the reception of others. Public goods are also not subject to the *exclusion principle*. A good will be subject to the exclusion principle if its benefits accrued only to those who purchase it.

When the exclusion principle does not apply, there is a tendency for consumers to be *free riders*. A free rider problem arises because each consumer believes that the product will be provided anyway, whether he or she contributes to its payment or not. Each individual believes that because there are so many people sharing the cost of providing the public good, withdrawing his or her financial support will not be noticed, and hence not affect the provision of the good. The problem is that there are often many free riders so that less than the optimal amount of the public good will be provided.

In general, as group size increases, the free rider problem becomes more prominent. It is usually overcome by governments taxing the general public in order to pay for the public good. A further problem, not easily solved, arises because no individual has an incentive to reveal his or her preferences for the public good. It is, therefore, almost impossible for the government to determine the optimal provision of the public good or to induce the private sector to provide it.

CASE EXAMPLE

'Technological' versus pecuniary externalities – the case of electricity

Following on from our discussion in the text, we can distinguish between so-called 'technological' and pecuniary externalities. The former refers to changes in the real consumption or production possibilities of recipients, and can originate on either the demand or supply side of the market. For example, smokers impose negative externalities on people around them, through second-hand smoke. Another example is immunisation, which can slow the spread of contagious diseases, thus preventing third parties from having to pay for medical care.

Pecuniary externalities refer to changes in the conditions of demand or supply facing recipients. For example, if the European Union voted for a common currency and the trade activities of one country were sufficient to

▶

Case example continued

cause a depreciation of the common currency, all other members of the Union would be affected. Although pecuniary externalities tend to change the unit cost of production, they are often not realised due to a lack of information about the potential benefits.

The distinction between the two types of externalities can be shown by means of an example. Consider first the technological advantages of supplying electricity to underdeveloped regions. In a survey conducted in Venda, for example, it was found that the provision of street lighting reduced the crime rate, and stimulated social activities in the community centre at night because lighting made evening functions easier, and safer, to attend. Electricity further improved the quality of social activities, as a television set provided new entertainment for both family and friends.

Pecuniary benefits include increases in demand for electrical appliances, the subsequent demand for resources to produce those items, and improved business opportunities. In the first two cases, the pecuniary benefits, unlike technological benefits, are unlikely to accrue to the community in which they are generated. For example, manufacturers of electrical appliances are likely to be located in industrial areas in the main cities. The increased revenue is likely to be spent in these main cities. Labour and other resources necessary to meet the increased demand are also likely to be drawn from the cities. However, some business opportunities are likely to be created in the underdeveloped region itself, which will supply job opportunities for the local community. For example, electricity may allow some businesses to stay open later, or open up new areas of business.

Electricity provision in South Africa also introduces social costs. Electricity in South Africa is the cheapest in the world, but this private monetary gain is bought at a high social price. Part of the reason for its low cost is that it is generated by burning low-grade coal. The latter releases more pollutants into the atmosphere than does the burning of higher grade coal. In addition, the low price of electricity encourages producers to use more energy intensive methods of production, instead of using more labour, or devising new technologies which use less energy, or alternative sources of energy.

Source: Black, P. A. and Themeli, T. B., 'On the social costs and benefits of electricity supply in a developing region', *Development Southern Africa*, Vol. 7, No. 3, September 1990

Summary

- In a perfectly competitive market there are many individual demanders and suppliers, each of whom is too small to manipulate the price of the good in question. The competitive price is determined by the *market* demand and supply curves, and each individual competitor must accept this price as a fixed parameter.

- The individual firm in a perfectly competitive market will maximise profit by maximising the difference between total revenue and total cost, or by producing the output level for which marginal revenue (*MR*) equals marginal cost (*MC*); and since *MR* equals price under perfect competition, the firm will wish to equate its *MC* with the given price.

- A competitive firm will either maximise its profit or minimise losses, but it will not produce if it cannot even cover its total variable cost. In this case it will 'shut down' its operation. Its short-run supply curve is thus given by that portion of its *MC* curve that lies above the average variable cost curve. Likewise, the market or industry supply curve is simply the horizontal summation of all the individual short-run supply curves.

- In the long run, all resources are variable. Individual firms can adjust their plants, or leave the industry, while new firms can enter it. But competition will ensure that each remaining firm will end up making only a normal profit (i.e. zero economic profit), so that the long-run equilibrium of the firm occurs when price or marginal revenue equals both its MC and average total cost.

- The long-run industry supply curve is derived from the short-run industry supply curves. Its shape depends on whether production costs are constant over time, or changing. In the constant cost case it is simply a horizontal line equal to the equilibrium price, while in the increasing-cost case it has a positive slope and in the decreasing-cost case a negative slope.

- Factor markets can also be perfectly competitive, and the equilibrium price and quantity are determined by the interaction of the relevant demand and supply curves. In the labour market, for example, supply is determined by individual preferences, while the demand for labour is a derived demand, reflecting what happens in the market for the product produced by it.

- Perfectly competitive markets are not necessarily 'perfect' in every sense of the word. They may help to allocate resources most efficiently, but do not always produce the most preferred distribution of those resources. Likewise, competitive markets often 'fail' in the sense that they cannot supply important public goods, or capture the so-called 'technological' external costs and benefits associated with production and consumption.

Questions for review

1. Derive the perfectly competitive firm's supply curve.

2. What should the firm do in order to maximise profit?

3. How does the industry adjust when new firms enter the market? How does the individual firm adjust with the entry of new firms into the market?

4. Discuss the concept of 'externality' and distinguish between 'technological' and 'pecuniary' externalities.

CHAPTER 8

Monopoly

Picture the man – rotund, cigar-smoking, bowler-hatted and beady-eyed. Who is he? A Monopolist! Compared to the good, tidy and clean living people of the perfectly competitive world, he is a veritable monstrosity. However, this is just as much an illusion as the world of perfect competition. There are very few true monopolies. Where they do exist they are usually owned or controlled by government.

Monopoly is a market situation in which a single seller supplies the entire market for a good or service. This complete dominance of the market means that the firm is not subject to competition from rival firms and it is said to have market power. Monopoly is therefore at the very opposite extreme from perfect competition where intense competition between firms exists.

There is a general concern that, because monopoly lacks the desirable characteristics of perfect competition, it should be carefully scrutinised and, as in most countries, regulated. However, just as a perfectly competitive market is a rare phenomenon, so a pure monopoly is difficult to find in the real world. The concept of monopoly is therefore used as a bench-mark against which real world markets may be compared.

8.1 Reasons for monopoly

There are basically three sets of circumstances which can give rise to a situation where a firm has total control of an entire industry, i.e. where it supplies the entire market.

Exclusive control of a factor of production

When a firm owns and controls one of its crucial inputs it will also have monopolistic control over the market for its output. DeBeers in South Africa controls almost all diamond production in the country while the Aluminium Company of America has a monopoly position in the aluminium market because it controls most of the reserves of bauxite, a key input in the production of aluminium.

CASE EXAMPLE

The Zambian copper mines

Copper mining is the mainstay of the Zambian economy, accounting for approximately 90 per cent of Zambia's foreign exchange earnings. The mines were nationalised by President Kaunda in 1969. In the 1980s two government

▶

Case example
continued mining companies merged to form the Zambian Consolidated Copper Mines (ZCCM) – effectively becoming a monopoly. By controlling the mines, the government controlled the entire copper industry. During the 1980s production fell, owing to mismanagement, the use of expensive equipment, poor maintenance and equipment breakdowns. The Chiluba administration has now undertaken to privatise the industry to improve performance.

Economies of scale

Where a particular production technology gives rise to economies of scale, the long-run average cost curve may exhibit decreasing unit costs over the entire range of industry demand. In such a case the firm that gets in ahead of others has a competitive advantage. The lower cost per unit at higher levels of output allows it to charge a price lower than the average cost pertaining at lower levels of output. This firm can therefore meet the entire market demand at prices below those of new rival firms entering the market. The established firm can therefore keep potential entrants out of the market and maintain a monopoly position.

Such a situation is referred to as *natural monopoly* and usually occurs in the production of, for example, electricity, water, roads and railroads. Other industries where economies of scale may result in the domination of the market by a few firms include steel and automobile production.

Government-created monopoly

The government can grant the exclusive right to production to a particular firm and in this way create a *secure monopoly*. It can do this by issuing patents, copyrights, or exclusive franchises.

Patents may be used as a means of stimulating innovation and invention. The patent will last for a specific number of years during which time the firm will enjoy a monopoly position. A patent offers protection and allows the firm to reap the benefits of the innovation or invention. Producers of certain drugs, for example, often benefit from patent protection.

Patent protection has been a topic of serious debate for a long time. During the Uruguay Round of General Agreement on Tariffs and Trade (GATT), developed countries, where most of the world's research and development takes place, sought to extend patent rights to other countries. They say that without patent protection the incentive to develop new products and new production processes will be weakened. The developing countries argue that weaker or even non-existent patent laws will allow them to produce new products under more competitive conditions and therefore avoid paying monopoly profits to the original patent holders in developed countries.

The government may also grant copyright to writers and composers. A copyright is similar to a patent in that it gives exclusive legal control over the production and reproduction of work for a certain period of time.

National, regional and local governments may grant licences to firms to operate a particular type of business. While such licences do not generally bestow true monopoly power, they do limit the number of producers in those areas where licences are enforced. To operate a radio or television station, for example, it is necessary to obtain a licence. If only one licence is issued, it grants monopoly power on broadcast advertising in that area – a very profitable situation.

When economies of scale are significant enough to lead to a natural monopoly, the firm that gains control over output is often able to charge a high price and reap large profits. From the perspective of consumer welfare, such a situation is often considered to be undesirable thus calling for some form of government regulation or control. The government may grant a natural monopoly the exclusive right to supply its good or service in a particular country or region, in return for which the monopolist agrees to a government regulatory body controlling its price and monitoring its operations. We shall return to this issue below.

The above cases are all examples of *barriers to entry* which ensure the existence of monopoly. Other barriers to entry may limit the number of firms in an industry and thus reduce competition. On reflection it is clear that a firm already established in an industry has an advantage over those attempting to gain entry into it. Accumulated know-how, a labour force with the requisite experience, and a well established management organisation all contribute to giving the existing firm an advantage over potential newcomers to the industry. An existing firm's performance record and established lines of credit make it easier for it to get loans from financial institutions. Consumer familiarity with the firm's product resulting from past advertising also has benefits for the existing firm. All these factors give existing firms a distinct advantage over potential entrants into the industry.

8.2 Profit maximisation by a monopolist

The distinguishing characteristic of a monopoly is its potential to earn economic profit almost indefinitely. We examine how the monopolist decides what quantity to produce and what price to charge.

Demand, total revenue and marginal revenue

Since the monopolist is the only firm in the industry, it faces the industry or market demand for its product or service. In other words, the industry demand curve is also the monopolist's demand curve. This means that the monopolist's demand curve slopes downward from left to right and that the monopolist has control over its price and output. This characteristic is, however, not unique to the monopolist. As long as a firm has the ability to change its price by changing its output level, it will be faced with a downward sloping demand curve.

Table 8.1 contains data on demand and revenue for a typical monopolist. Note that a larger quantity can only be sold if the price (or average revenue) is lowered. Total revenue equals price multiplied by quantity. Starting from a zero output level, total revenue rises, reaches a maximum when six units are sold at R7 or when seven units are sold at R6, and declines thereafter. This reflects an important characteristic of a downward sloping demand curve, as explained in earlier chapters. It means that there exists a trade-off. More units of the product can only be sold if the price is lowered. This is the essence of the law of demand.

Table 8.1 Demand and revenue data for a monopolist (rands)

Quantity of output (Q)	Price = Average revenue (p = AR)	Total revenue (TR) (TR = p × Q)	Marginal revenue (MR)
0	13	0	–
1	12	12	12
2	11	22	10
3	10	30	8
4	9	36	6
5	8	40	4
6	7	42	2
7	6	42	0
8	5	40	–2

An important difference between a monopoly and a perfectly competitive firm concerns marginal revenue. A perfectly competitive firm can sell as much as it likes at the same price because its demand curve is perfectly horizontal. Therefore, marginal revenue is always equal to price for a perfectly competitive firm. This is not true for a monopolist because its demand curve is downward sloping.

To sell an extra unit of output the monopolist must lower price. Furthermore, the monopolist must not only accept a lower price for the extra unit sold, but for all units sold. Therefore the marginal revenue, for the monopolist, is less than the price at every level of output except when only one unit of output is produced. This results from the fact that when price is lowered to sell an extra unit of output, the resulting change in total revenue consists of two parts. One part is the increase in total revenue equal to the price received for the extra unit sold. The other part refers to the decrease in total revenue due to the reduction in price on all other units sold (that was necessary to sell the extra unit). For the monopolist, therefore, marginal revenue equals the price of the extra unit, less the extent of the price reduction on other units multiplied by the quantity of the other units.

Marginal revenue is less than price at every level of output except for the first unit. It therefore follows that since price declines as output increases (because the demand curve is downward sloping), marginal revenue must also decline as output increases. This relationship between price, marginal revenue and total revenue can be seen from the data in Table 8.1 and is illustrated in Fig. 8.1.

For each output level in Table 8.1, the related price is plotted to give the demand curve in Fig. 8.1(b) and (c). Total revenue from Table 8.1 is plotted in Fig. 8.1(a).

From parts (a) and (b) it is clear that total revenue reaches a maximum at an output level of six units, and a price of R7 per unit. Note in Table 8.1 that as price is reduced from R7 to R6, the quantity sold increases from six to seven units, but total revenue remains at R42. This is because when price is lowered there is a loss of revenue which is exactly offset by the gain in total revenue from the sale of the extra output. Putting this another way; the marginal revenue associated with the sale of the seventh unit of output is zero. This is shown in Fig. 8.1(c) where the marginal revenue curve crosses the horizontal axis at between six and seven units of output. (The marginal revenue data is plotted at the midpoints of the units on the horizontal axis so that the MR curve actually intersects at six units.)

It is important to remember that the monopolist is not able to sell a given output at *any* desired price. The downward-sloping demand curve does imply that the monopolist can affect price by changing output or that the monopolist affects output by changing price. The level of one automatically determines the level of the other because of the shape of the demand curve. The monopolist is therefore still subject to the constraint that selling more means accepting a lower price, or stated differently, that selling a certain level of output means charging no more than a certain price.

Costs, revenue and pricing

The monopolist needs to know both its revenue and production costs to determine what output level to produce and what price to charge (see Table 8.2).

Table 8.2 Output, revenue and costs for a monopolist (rands)

Quantity of output (Q)	Price= Average revenue (p = AR)	Total revenue TR = pQ	Marginal revenue (MR)	Average total cost (ATC)	Total cost/loss (−) (TC)	Marginal cost (MC)	Profit (+) TR − TLC
0	13	0		10			−10
1	12	12	12	16	16	6	−4
2	11	22	10	10	20	4	2
3	10	30	8	8	24	4	2
4	9	36	6	7.25	29	5	7
5	8	40	4	7.20	36	7	4
6	7	42	2	7.83	47	11	−5
7	6	42	0	10.00	70	23	−28

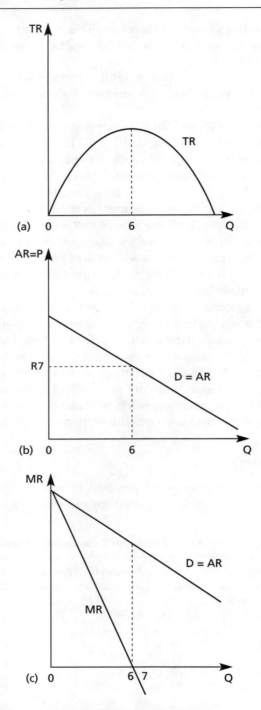

Fig. 8.1 Price, marginal revenue and total revenue

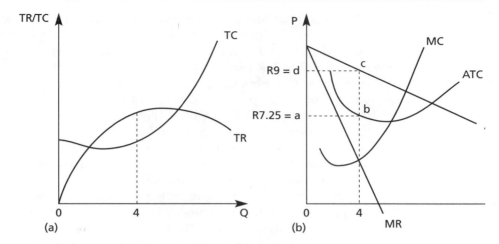

Fig. 8.2 Profit maximisation

By subtracting total cost (*TC*) from total revenue (*TR*) at every level of output, we can determine that output level which would yield maximum profit. We can see that a maximum profit of R7 will be made when four units of output are produced and sold at R9 per unit. This is represented graphically in Fig. 8.2(a). The maximum vertical distance by which *TR* exceeds *TC* indicates the maximum total profit. In our example, at an output level of four units a maximum profit of R7 will be made.

The basic principle used to determine the profit-maximising output level for the monopolist is exactly the same as that described in the case of the perfectly competitive firm. The monopolist will also continue to expand output as long as the marginal cost of producing an additional unit is less than the marginal revenue associated with its sale. This means that the monopolist will produce up to that point where the marginal cost of the last unit produced is just covered by, or is just equal to, its marginal revenue.

It is important to note, however, that the case of the monopolist differs from that of the perfectly competitive firm in two respects. First, for the monopolist marginal revenue is always less than price (except for the first unit). Marginal revenue and price are exactly the same for the perfectly competitive firm. Second, marginal revenue falls as output is increased for the monopolist. For the perfectly competitive firm marginal revenue remains the same at all output levels.

A comparison of the marginal cost (*MC*) data with the marginal revenue (*MR*) data in Table 8.2, indicates that *MR* exceeds *MC* at all output levels up to and including four units. When a fifth unit is produced the *MR*, R4, is less than the *MC* of R7. *MR* therefore exceeds *MC* at all output levels up to and including four units, and is smaller than *MC* at all levels in excess of four units. Profit will thus be maximised when four units are produced and sold at a price of R9. Using the marginal cost–marginal revenue approach therefore yields the same profit maximising output level as the total cost–total revenue approach.

The marginal cost–marginal revenue approach is illustrated in Fig. 8.2(b). The *ATC* and *MC* curves are plotted from the data provided in Table 8.2. The demand curve and its associated *MR* curve are likewise plotted from the data provided. The *MR* curve lies above the *MC* curve up to the output level of four units. Therefore up to this point it is profitable to increase output. In order to maximise profit the monopolist should produce four units of output and charge a price of R9 per unit. The profit-maximising price is identified at the point on the demand curve that lies directly above the intersection of the *MR* and *MC* curves (point c on the diagram). The profit-maximising output level of four units is the point on the horizontal axis that lies directly below the intersection of the *MC* and *MR* curves.

The vertical distance ad = bc, in Fig. 8.2, which is equal to R1.75, is the average profit, so that four units times R1.75 yields a total profit of R7. This is shown by the rectangular area abcd. The latter represents economic profit which is, of course, larger than normal profit. An important distinction between earning economic profit under monopolistic and perfectly competitive conditions is that under perfect competition new firms would be attracted into the industry in the long run. The competitive industry's output will thus expand while rivalry among firms will cause price to fall until only normal profit is made by all firms. In the case of monopoly, however, various barriers will prevent entry by new firms, and the monopolist will be able to earn a monopoly profit *almost* indefinitely. But even the monopolist is not sheltered from advances in technology and changes in consumer demand. Research and changing technology, the development of substitute products, and the expiration of patents and sources of raw materials can all contribute to a weakening of monopoly power.

Monopoly losses

Monopolists may also make losses, in which case they would strive to *minimise* their losses. Consider Fig. 8.3, for example, where the intersection of *MC* and *MR* occurs at output level Q_1. This is evidently a loss-minimising situation. It is not possible for the monopolist to cover all costs at any output level since the *ATC* curve lies everywhere above the demand curve. Producing an output of Q_1 units and selling it at a price of P_1, the monopolist will incur a loss per unit equal to the vertical distance ab. The total loss is indicated by the shaded rectangular area.

The monopolist shown in Fig. 8.3 will only be willing to operate at a loss in the short run, and then only if it is able to cover its average variable cost. This requirement is met in Fig. 8.3 because P_1 lies above the *AVC* curve at the output level Q_1.

8.3 Monopoly or perfect competition?

When we examined perfect competition in the previous chapter, we focused on issues such as efficient resource allocation, incentives for innovation and

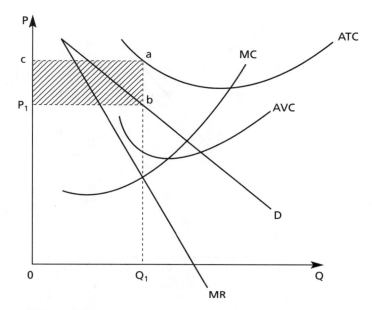

Fig. 8.3 Loss minimisation

technological change, and the implications for income distribution. Since perfect competition provides a useful standard for comparison, it seems appropriate to consider the monopoly case within this context.

In Fig. 8.4(a) we reproduce the equilibrium for a perfectly competitive industry. The industry demand curve D and the short-run supply curve S_c determine the equilibrium price P_c and quantity Q_c. Remember that the perfectly competitive industry's short-run supply curve represents the sum of the marginal cost curves of all the individual firms in the industry.

A single firm now buys up all the firms in the competitive industry without affecting the cost curves of any of them. This single firm is now a monopoly, and its marginal cost curve, in Fig. 8.4(b), is exactly the same as that of the perfectly competitive industry. The industry demand curve is unchanged as well, but the monopolist's view of the demand curve differs from that of the perfectly competitive firms, each of which is assumed to be a price taker. The monopolist knows that when it changes its output level, price will also change. Hence, the monopolist will use the *MR* curve to determine its equilibrium price and output level, as shown in Fig. 8.4(b).

Under conditions of monopoly consumers therefore pay a higher price for a smaller quantity of the product than under perfect competition.

Under perfect competition, output is produced up to the level Q_c, where the price P_c paid for the last unit produced is just equal to the cost of producing that last unit. In this situation price per unit is equal to marginal cost. In a perfectly competitive market, every consumer who is willing to pay a price sufficient to cover the marginal cost of producing the good, will be able to purchase some of the good.

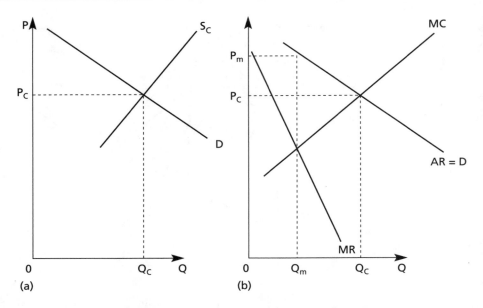

Fig. 8.4 (a) Equilibrium for a perfectly competitive industry; (b) Equilibrium for a monopoly

However, if the market is a monopoly, the section of the demand curve covering the range Q_m to Q_c lies above the *MC* curve. This means that there are consumers who are willing to pay a price for units of output from Q_m to Q_c that exceeds the marginal cost of producing them, but are also unable to do so because the monopolist will not produce and sell them at such a price.

In a monopoly market, therefore, there will be consumers who are willing to pay a price that equals the marginal cost of producing the good, but who will not be able to purchase any of the good at that price. This situation represents an inefficient allocation of resources.

Market structure and costs

So far we have assumed that costs are not affected when a perfectly competitive industry becomes a monopoly. However, it may well be that organisational and technological efficiencies are realised when all perfectly competitive firms are combined to form a monopoly. In such a case the monopolist's *MC* curve will not be the same as that of the perfectly competitive industry.

This situation is illustrated in Fig. 8.5. When all the perfectly competitive firms are combined to form a monopoly, we assume that the greater efficiencies of operation result in a lowering of the average and marginal costs of production. If the cost reductions are large enough the monopolist's equilibrium price, P_m, may be lower than P_c and its equilibrium output, Q_m, greater than Q_c. If the cost reduction is not large enough, however, monopolisation of the industry will result in a higher price and smaller quantity than under perfect competition.

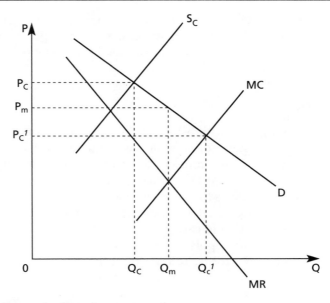

Fig. 8.5 Cost reductions in a monopoly

Note that, even though the profit-maximising monopolist may provide consumers with more output at a lower price, there will still be consumers who are willing to pay a price for the good greater than the marginal cost of producing it. This is illustrated by the section of the demand curve over the range Q_m to Q_c^1 which lies above the *MC* curve. It is for this reason that public policy, or regulation, may be needed to promote a situation where output Q_c^1 is produced and sold at a price P_c^1.

Monopoly and innovation

The incentive for a perfectly competitive firm to innovate is slight because the prospect of reaping above-normal profits from such activity for any length of time is small. Both new and existing firms in the industry will readily adopt the innovation, thus eliminating any competitive advantage otherwise realised by the innovating firm.

For a monopoly the situation is different. With innovation the monopolist faces the prospect of making an above-normal profit for a prolonged, possibly indefinite, period of time. Furthermore, the existence of such profits provides the monopolist with a source of funds to finance technological change and innovation, a source not available to the perfectly competitive firm.

It could however be argued that because the monopolist does not face the threat of competition by rival firms, it may be tempted simply to extract the profits for purposes other than research and development. The monopolist may also protect its existing monopoly situation from the threat of new products and technological change introduced by potential rivals. It may do so by buying up and stockpiling patents and thus effectively stopping technological change and product innovation.

Monopolies may therefore either promote or inhibit product innovation and technological advancement. Public policy, in particular competition policy, is based on the assumption that monopolies are more likely to inhibit such change.

Income distribution

In long-run equilibrium under perfect competition a large number of firms earn normal profits while the payments to factors of production, including labour, are just sufficient to cover their opportunity costs. Monopoly, by contrast, gives rise to a much greater concentration of economic power. The potential exists for super-normal profit over a long period of time. The owners of a monopoly are in a position to earn much more than their time and financial capital could earn in their next best alternative use.

If the monopoly is a corporation, its shareholders will also share in the monopoly profits. To the extent that such shareholders are middle to upper income earners, the distribution of monopoly profit among shareholders will widen the gap between them and lower-income groups.

8.4 Regulation of natural monopolies

We have already referred to the case of a natural monopoly, and indicated that the government may be tempted to regulate its price so as to enable consumers to benefit from the scale economies associated with increased output. Such regulated monopolies, or public utilities, are usually involved in the production and sale of electricity, water, telephone services and some transportation services.

Figure 8.6 illustrates the cost and demand curves of a new electricity supplier on the island of Utopia. The firm's average total cost (ATC) and marginal cost (MC) curves are both negatively sloped over the range of output covered by the market demand curve D. As long as the ATC is falling, MC must lie below it.

The most efficient allocation of resources – that which maximises consumer satisfaction – occurs where price equals marginal cost. It is most efficient in the sense that output is produced up to the point where the price paid for the last unit produced just covers the cost of producing it. For the natural monopolist represented in Fig. 8.6, this occurs where the MC curve intersects the D curve at point b, or at price P_c and output level Q_c.

But will the Utopian supplier produce at point b? No chance! He or she is in the business to make the maximum profit and will want to produce Q_m at price P_m, as indicated by the intersection of the MC and MR curves.

If forced to produce the amount Q_c at price P_c, the monopolist would incur a loss because the cost per unit of output sold will be greater than the price per unit, i.e. a loss equal to area abcd in Fig. 8.6. If Utopia's regulators therefore insist on marginal cost pricing, it will be necessary to

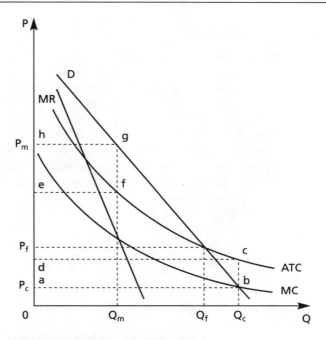

Fig. 8.6 The regulation of a natural monopoly

subsidise the monopolist to prevent it from going out of business. Alternatively, the government may decide to nationalise the natural monopoly – as has happened in many countries – and supply the good at the subsidised price.

Average cost pricing may be viewed as a compromise between the profit-maximising solution chosen by the unregulated monopolist and the marginal-cost-equals-price solution. The average cost pricing solution lies between these two extremes. The producer is allowed to charge a price sufficient to cover all costs of production, including a normal profit, and the consumer is able to benefit from the lower cost per unit made possible by the scale economies of the natural monopoly. The average-cost pricing solution is given by the intersection of the *ATC* curve with the demand curve D in Fig. 8.6, thus indicating an output of Q_f and a price of P_f. This price is just sufficient to cover the average total cost, which includes a normal profit or fair return on capital.

In the long-run competitive equilibrium, price will also equal average total cost. Despite this similarity of the average cost pricing solution to the perfectly competitive outcome, it differs in that price is not equal to marginal cost as in perfect competition. This means that there will still be consumers who would be willing to pay a price greater than marginal cost for additional units of output.

CASE EXAMPLE

Privatisation

Since 1980 more than 2000 State Owned Enterprises (SOEs) have been privatised in developing countries, and 6800 world-wide. Of this figure, 66 per cent have taken place in the former German Democratic Republic, 12 per cent each in Latin America and Eastern Europe, 5 per cent in Sub-Saharan Africa, 2 per cent in OECD countries, and only 1 per cent in the Middle East and North Africa. During the 1990s both the incidence of privatisation and the size of enterprise privatised have tended to increase. In 1992 alone SOEs worth $69 billion were privatised in 50 different countries.

Privatisation can take one of three forms, namely the sale of public sector assets to the private sector, the subcontracting of public services to private agents, and deregulation to allow competition, although the first type is the most prevalent.

The economic argument for privatisation is essentially twofold, i.e. that it will bring certain efficiency gains and, secondly, that it will alleviate fiscal pressures on the State.

Efficiency benefits stem from the principal-agent relationship inherent in contestable markets. In private enterprise, shareholders have a direct interest in maintaining operational efficiency by ensuring that management has the right incentives to minimise costs, invest in research and development, and monitor productivity at all levels of the organisation. When a market is contestable, firms face the constant threat of a take-over or of being eliminated from the market by more efficient firms. By contrast, within a public enterprise, which can rely on financial assistance from the State, there is little incentive to be profitable. Rather, there is an incentive to make maximum use of available subsidies, and so to avoid having them cut in future budgets. In addition, public enterprises may have a social dimension to their objective function which private enterprises do not. For example, the State may wish to subsidise certain services to make them affordable for all sectors of the population, while private enterprises often seek to maximise profit. Realising efficiency gains, however, requires a contestable market – a privately owned monopoly may be as inefficient as a public monopoly.

The potential financial gains from privatisation stem from three sources:

- The immediate proceeds from the sale of assets can be used to retire public debt, or to fund social programmes, the development of infrastructure or other programmes.
- Privatisation broadens the tax base, since public enterprises do not pay tax. Furthermore, if efficiency gains are realised and competition stimulates productivity in other sectors of the economy, further increases in tax revenue may be induced.
- Privatisation reduces the drain on the fiscus from subsidising inefficient, loss-making public enterprises. The funds released can be diverted to other programmes.

Privatisation can provide an opportunity for foreign investment, primarily through strategic partnerships with domestic firms. In the current South

Case example
continued

African context, privatisation plays a critical role in restoring confidence, both locally and abroad, as a sign that the government is committed to economic reform, and has made a significant shift towards a market-friendly economy. Privatisation is not a straightforward issue – potential gains have been outlined above, but these need to be weighed against potential losses. For example, COSATU (The Congress of South African Trade Unions) has opposed efforts at privatisation in South Africa, on the grounds of job losses. Low income consumers may suffer disproportionately if public enterprises were supplying services at below marginal cost and the private firm raises prices. Public ownership of key areas of economic activity can have an important political dimension, particularly in Africa with its colonial history, and in countries where private ownership is not a feature of the dominant culture. For example, in Zambia, the nationalisation of the copper mines became a symbol of freedom from colonial rule, and the Chiluba government's decision to privatise had to be carefully negotiated.

In South Africa to date the only privatisations that have occurred have been ISCOR (1989), National Sorghum Breweries (1991), and the recent (1997) sale of 30 per cent of TELKOM's assets to two foreign companies. It has also been suggested that, following extensive restructuring (possibly in response to the threat of privatisation), it may not be necessary or desirable to privatise ESCOM. The government has contracted an international firm of consultants to assist them in identifying enterprises for privatisation.

8.5 A price-discriminating monopolist

Our analysis has shown that a monopolist may be able to earn more than normal profit. Under certain circumstances a monopolist may practise price discrimination and in this way earn even a greater profit. Firms that are not monopolists may also be able to practise price discrimination, but often a monopolist is in a better position to do so because it is the only supplier of a particular product.

Price discrimination means that the same good or service is sold at different prices when there are no cost differences to justify this. Price discrimination is a fairly common practice. Examples include movie theatres charging different prices to adults and pensioners, or utility companies charging different rates for businesses and residences.

The conditions for successful price discrimination include:

- *The market for the good or service must consist of clearly identifiable segments.* For example, it is relatively easy to charge one price to adults and one to children. Often a monopoly can sell its product in one country at a particular price and charge a different price in another country. It is also possible to segment a market according to which unit of output is sold. An electricity utility keeps track of the amount of electricity customers use and can charge different rates for different levels of use.

- *The different groups of consumers in the identifiable market segments should have different elasticities of demand for the product.* The elasticity of demand is an indicator of a market segment's sensitivity to price changes. When a market can be segmented according to differing demand elasticities, price discrimination will yield greater sales revenue than if a uniform price is charged.
- *The good or service in question should not be resaleable,* or the firm should be able to prevent the resale of its product.

An international monopolist: dumping and price discrimination

Consider a firm that is a monopolist in its home country and is protected from foreign competition by tariffs and other import restrictions. Suppose that there are no export restrictions so that the firm could, if it wanted to, also sell the good on the world market. On the world market it would be a price taker; it would operate in a perfectly competitive market for the good.

Figure 8.7 illustrates this case. Part (a) represents the firm's domestic monopoly situation. The firm faces a downward sloping demand curve, AR_1, and its associated marginal revenue curve, MR_1. The world market as it pertains to this firm is shown in part (b), where the competitive price is P_c. Since the firm is a price taker in the world market, this price line is also the firm's marginal revenue curve *vis-à-vis* the world market.

In order to maximise profit the firm will ensure that marginal cost equals marginal revenue in both the domestic and international markets. Since the marginal cost of producing the output is the same irrespective of where it is sold, this means that marginal revenue in the domestic and international markets will have to be equal.

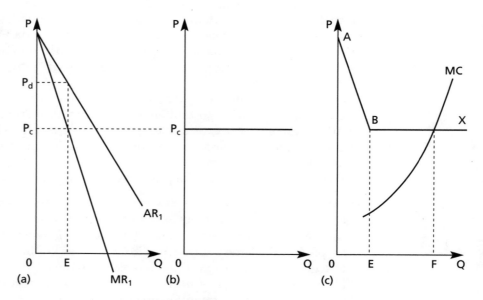

Fig. 8.7 Monopoly and price discrimination

The horizontal sum of MR_1 and P_c is shown in part (c) of Fig. 8.7. The downward-sloping segment AB corresponds to the segment of MR_1 that lies above the world price. If output OE or less is produced it will all be sold on the domestic market. For outputs larger than OE, the relevant marginal revenue is the world price P_c. This is shown by the segment BX. The explanation of this horizontal segment is intuitively clear; for outputs larger than OE, the world price exceeds marginal revenue in the domestic market. The addition to the firm's total revenue will therefore be larger if it sells all units in excess of OE on the world market.

To determine the profit-maximising output level, we find that point where marginal cost intersects the combined marginal revenue curve, i.e. output level OF in part (c). Since this output level is greater than OE, some of the good will be exported. From our discussion we know that quantity OE will be sold on the domestic market and the remaining EF units will be exported. The domestic sales will occur at price P_d (part (a)) while the foreign sales will be made at the competitive world price P_c.

The domestic price exceeds the world price because the firm is a price-discriminating monopolist. It is able to practise price discrimination in this instance because it faces two market segments with different price elasticities of demand. It is also worth noting that the monopolist charges the higher price in the domestic market where demand is relatively less elastic than in the world market.

A government may sometimes want to encourage exports in order to improve the balance of trade or to acquire foreign exchange. To encourage exports it may offer an export subsidy, i.e. a bonus payment to the firm for every unit exported. The effect of an export subsidy of s per unit will be to raise the world price by s. Applying the same analysis as before, it is easy to see that the effect of the subsidy will be to increase total output beyond OF, increase the quantity of exports, and to raise the domestic price above P_d.

CASE EXAMPLE

Price discrimination in telecommunications

The telecommunications industry world-wide has been undergoing fundamental change during the past decade. Advances in analogue and digital technology, increasing sophistication and power in computer hardware and software, and the move to a global economy have changed the way people communicate and exchange information. The traditional view has been that telecommunications, like other infrastructure and utilities, is a public good and, therefore, society is best served by making it a responsibility of the state. Consequently, telecommunications has been a state monopoly in most countries, and often linked to the postal service. A number of countries have elected to separate the two services, and privatise telecommunications. South Africa has undergone the first phase, whereby the Department of Posts and Telecommunications was split into TELKOM and the Post Office, while it has also recently begun to practise TELKOM.

▶

Case example
continued

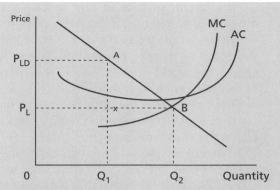

Fig. 8.8 How price discrimination can increase revenue

Telecommunications has long been considered a natural monopoly owing to large set-up costs, such as the physical network of cables or fibre optic lines, exchanges and terminals. Once these are in place, average cost declines sharply and the marginal cost of a call is minimal. Despite the low marginal cost, TELKOM has long practised price discrimination in the form of differential rates per call unit depending on distance, and lower rates during off-peak hours. Thus, the requirements for effective discrimination, namely separable markets and the impossibility of resale between markets, are met. Higher charges are levied on long-distance calls, and the profits are used to subsidise local calls. This policy raises revenue, as is illustrated in Fig. 8.8.

In Fig. 8.8, TELKOM can charge long-distance callers a price of P_{LD}, in exchange for quantity OQ_1 of the service. Local callers will pay only P_L per unit, and use Q_1Q_2 call units. It can be seen that, if all calls were charged at P_L, the company would be making losses, since $P = MC < AC$. Price discrimination results in total revenue ($P_{LD}AQ_1O + XBQ_2Q_1$), which exceeds non-discrimination revenue of P_LBQ_2O. The profit on long-distance calls more than compensates for the loss on local calls.

However, the profits realised from such a strategy can be eliminated by changes in the conditions of supply and demand. On the supply side, operational inefficiencies, restrictive labour agreements, spiralling costs of imported equipment and a lack of innovation have tended to reduce TELKOM's profitability. On the demand side, the emergence of close substitutes are leading to an inward shift of the demand curve. Private cellular telephone providers are the prime source of competition. The rising popularity of the Internet is also squeezing profits because, although communication and data exchange via the Internet still require the telephone line, it is usually cheaper and more efficient to use than fax or a standard telephone call. Furthermore, TELKOM is under considerable political pressure to expand its networks and services to previously disadvantaged and rural communities, without increasing user charges to cover the cost.

Source: Black, P. A., Orgell Baird, P. and Heese, A., 'Ownership and competition in telecommunications: the case of South Africa', *South African Journal of Economics*, Vol. 66, No. 2, 1997

8.6 Contestable markets

The theory of contestable markets (mentioned briefly in Chapter 6 in connection with barriers to entry) was developed by William Baumol, and some of his colleagues in the early 1980s. It was presented as a new theory of industry structure – and it would show that under certain circumstances monopoly is more efficient than perfect competition. Contestable market theory focuses on the impact of potential competition in the market. Provided there are no barriers to entry and that exit from the market is costless (there are no sunk or irrecoverable costs) then the threat of potential competition will ensure that firms in a market behave efficiently. The theory goes further to argue that if the relationship between market demand and the most efficient-sized firm is such that a large-scale firm is more efficient than a smaller firm, then a monopoly may be the most efficient market structure, provided a credible threat of potential competition for the monopolist exists. The focus on the role of potential competition in contestable market theory contrasts with the neo-classical theory of market structure, which we follow almost exclusively in this text, and its focus on actual competition (the number of firms in the market). According to Baumol and his colleagues, any market structure may be optimal. Optimal market structure depends on the nature and extent of market demand and also on the technology used in production. If small-scale production is efficient, then the market will consist of many small firms; by contrast, if economies of scale are important in production then fewer large-scale firms will be found in the industry.

CASE EXAMPLE

The South African beer market

South African Breweries (SAB) closely approximates a monopoly in the market for clear beer. SAB does not have exclusive access to natural resources, or government support, but its size and financial strength have allowed it to dominate the market. Furthermore, the high profile of its brand names in the market, significant influence with distributors assisted by SAB's shareholdings in the retail and hotel industries, a well established distribution network, and accumulated production and marketing experience, all represent considerable barriers to entry.

SAB was the subject of a controversial judgement by the Competition Board in 1982. The Board held that the acquisition by SAB of the only other independent beer producer, Inter-Continental Breweries (ICB), was against the public interest but maintained that little could be done to dismantle the monopoly. SAB faces limited competition in the clear beer market from Mitchells Breweries, and in the broader beer market from National Sorghum Breweries (NSB), but neither is a substantial competitive threat. An attempt by NSB to challenge SAB in the clear beer market in 1994 failed, and SAB maintains its effective monopoly position in the market.

Summary

- A monopolist is a single seller supplying the entire market for a good or service. This may be due to the fact that the firm is experiencing decreasing average costs, or because of government protection in the form of patents, licenses, copyrights and exclusive franchises.

- Since a monopolist faces the market demand curve for its product, its marginal revenue (*MR*) curve is also negatively sloped. It maximises profit by setting *MC* equal to *MR*, and determining the corresponding price on the basis of its (market) demand curve. At this price, which is always higher than its *MC*, it can make a positive economic profit and, given the absence of entry by new firms, continue to do so for a long time.

- Keeping other things constant, equilibrium price under monopoly is higher than under perfect competition, and output lower, so that consumers would presumably prefer the competitive option. But monopolies do have a dynamic edge over their perfectly competitive counterparts. They can spend part of their profits on R&D to develop new technologies that reduce their costs of production and ultimately also their price.

- An important special case is that of the natural monopoly. It is special because the firm experiences decreasing unit costs over the entire range of market demand. Under these conditions perfect competition is not possible, since marginal cost pricing will entail substantial losses. The market thus lends itself to monopoly pricing. But if the good or service is deemed to be of strategic importance, or in the public interest, the authorities may decide to regulate it – as has indeed happened with the provision of electricity, telecommunications, water and transportation services. In such cases, the government may either nationalise the monopolist, or force it to set price equal to average cost or *MC*, in which case it may have to compensate it by means of an appropriate subsidy.

- Monopolies can boost their profits by practising price discrimination, i.e. charging different prices to different groups of consumers. A necessary condition for price discrimination is that the market should consist of clearly identifiable segments, or groups of consumers, that differ in respect of their price elasticities of demand.

- Some monopolies operate in what is known as contestable markets. These are markets in which there are no barriers to entry, so that the incumbent firm operates under the constant threat of *potential* competition. The net effect is that the monopolist has little choice but to behave like a perfectly competitive firm and charge a price equal to *MC*, or very close to it.

Questions for review

1. Compare the equilibrium of the perfectly competitive firm with that of the monopolist.

2. Examine the relationship between marginal revenue, price, total revenue and price elasticity of demand for the monopolist.

3. What conditions are necessary for successful price discrimination?

4. Should natural monopolies (with decreasing unit cost of production) be owned or controlled by government?

CHAPTER 9

Imperfectly competitive markets

In the last two chapters we have indulged in a bit of normative economics. Perfectly competitive markets do not actually exist and pure monopolies are very rare. Why they are important is that they allow us to establish the outer parameters within which real markets exist.

Now, at last, we come to the real world. In the real world most markets are either oligopolistic or monopolistically competitive.

9.1 Monopolistic competition

Monopolistic competition has four distinctive characteristics:

- There is a very large number of firms.
- Each firm's product is slightly differentiated from those of its competitors.
- Firms are free to enter or leave the industry.
- Firms engage in non-price competition such as advertising.

A large number of firms

There are many firms in a monopolistically competitive industry, but not as many as in a perfectly competitive industry. Thus no firm is large enough to dominate the market. Monopolistically competitive markets include hairdressers, pharmacies and restaurants in a typical large city.

Product differentiation

Each firm's product in a monopolistically competitive market is slightly different from those of other firms, in terms of product characteristics, service, packaging and advertising. Product differentiation is perhaps the factor that distinguishes this market most from perfect competition. Under perfect competition, where products are homogeneous, each firm faces a horizontal demand curve, indicating that each firm's product is a perfect substitute for that of every other firm.

With product differentiation, under monopolistic competition, each firm's demand curve is slightly downward sloping. The determination of the equilibrium price and output level will be examined in section 9.2.

Freedom of entry and exit

As in perfect competition, monopolistically competitive firms have the freedom to enter or leave the industry. Freedom of entry and exit means that there are no barriers to competition in a monopolistically competitive industry: the threat of new firms coming into the industry encourages competition among incumbent firms, and those that are not able to compete effectively will leave the industry. In the long run this means that monopolistically competitive firms, like their perfectly competitive counterparts, make only a normal profit.

Non-price competition

Since each firm produces a similar yet differentiated product, it will attempt to emphasise the differences in its product in order to increase demand. We refer to this as non-price competition and it can take many forms, of which advertising and after-sales service are two examples.

In a perfectly competitive market there is no incentive for firms to engage in non-price competition because all firms' products are identical and all consumers have perfect knowledge about products. Non-price competition flourishes under monopolistic competition where firms try to emphasise differences which may be real (e.g. differences in product characteristics) or perceived (better or more attractive packaging). Product differentiation, which forms the basis for non-price competition, is defined from the consumer's perspective; if the consumer believes that two products are different, they are indeed differentiated products.

9.2 Equilibrium in monopolistic competition

When we examine monopolistic competition carefully we find that product differentiation is the factor that most distinguishes this market from perfect competition. Product differentiation is reflected in the demand curve: with no product differentiation under perfect competition, the demand curve is perfectly elastic. At the other extreme, under monopoly, the demand curve is much less elastic because the product has no close substitutes (extreme product differentiation exists).

Product differentiation is therefore associated with substitutability: less product differentiation implies greater substitutability, and therefore a higher elasticity of demand. Similarly, more product differentiation means less possibility of substitution and therefore a lower elasticity of demand.

Facing a downward sloping demand curve, a monopolistically competitive firm is only able to change its level of sales by changing its price. This is similar to the situation under monopoly. The monopolistically competitive firm is aware that in order to increase sales it must lower its price. Thus, as under monopoly, but unlike perfect competition, at any output level price is always greater than marginal revenue, and thus the monopolistically competitive firm's demand curve lies above its marginal revenue curve.

Short-run equilibrium

The short-run equilibrium of the monopolistically competitive firm looks like that of the monopolist except that the former's demand curve is more elastic.

Figure 9.1 shows a profit-making situation (part (a)) and a loss-making situation (part (c)) for a monopolistically competitive firm. The firm will always adjust its price and output level so that MR equals MC (assuming that it can cover its average variable costs). In part (a), the firm's demand curve is such that it produces Q_1, at price P_1. The resulting profit is shown by the shaded area. In part (c) the demand for the firm's product is weak; the entire demand curve lies below its ATC curve. Assuming that it can cover its AVC, the best the firm can do is to produce Q_2 and charge a price P_2. In this way it minimises its losses, which are represented by the shaded area.

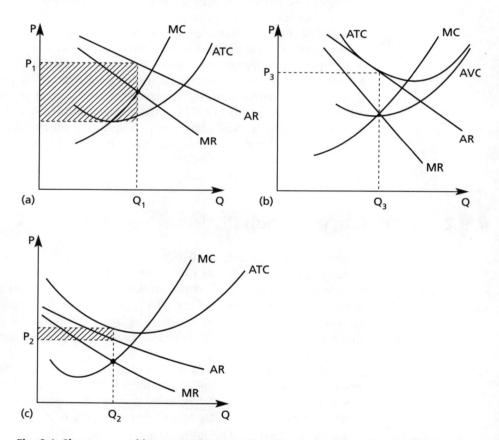

Fig. 9.1 Short-run and long-run situations for the monopolistically competitive firm

Long-run equilibrium

For the monopolistically competitive firm Fig. 9.1(a) can only represent a short-run situation, since there are no barriers to entry and new firms will enter the market, attracted by the prospect of making a profit. As new firms introduce new brands into the industry, the market has to be shared by more and more firms, and thus each firm's market share is reduced. This implies that the individual firm's demand curve and associated marginal revenue curve will shift leftward. New firms will continue to enter the market as long as abnormal profits exist, shifting the demand curves of firms leftward until the abnormal profits of each have been eliminated.

The monopolistically competitive firm will finally be in long-run equilibrium in the situation depicted in Fig. 9.1(b). It will produce output Q_3 and charge a price P_3, as determined by the intersection of MR and MC. The price P_3 is just equal to the average total cost at this point. Therefore the firm's total revenue is just equal to its total cost (which includes a normal profit). There is no more incentive for new firms to enter the industry, the typical firm's ATC curve is tangent to the demand curve and thus firms are only making normal profits.

Alternatively, each of the many firms could be making a loss, as shown in Fig. 9.1(c). If, in the long run, a firm continues to make a loss, it will leave the industry and the share of the market of the remaining firms will grow. Their demand curves and associated marginal revenue curves will thus shift to the right. This process will continue until enough firms have left the industry so that those remaining are just able to cover costs (including a normal profit). The industry is then once again in long-run equilibrium, as in Fig. 9.1(b).

CASE EXAMPLE

The South African motor industry

The motor industry in South Africa – valued at R17.1 billion in 1994 – is a good example of a monopolistically competitive market. While each firm has monopolistic control over its own model(s) and make(s), it faces intense competition from other manufacturers. South African car manufacturers include Delta (which manufacture Isuzu and Opel), Samcor (which manufacture Mazda and Ford), Volkswagen, BMW, Mercedes Benz and Automakers (which manufacture Nissan vehicles and Fiat Unos, and have recently begun importing Alphas). Although the number of manufacturers is relatively small, the large number of distributors and range of models creates significant competition. There is also competition from foreign manufacturers such as Hyundai, Daewoo and Subaru.

The manufacturers do not own the distributors, so although there may be a number of BMW showrooms, they are all independently owned. This generates substantial competition, not only between make of vehicle, but also between distributors of the same make. All distributors will pay the same price to the manufacturer, who has a list price for each model. Distributors compete by offering a range of discounts on the list price, but more so through services, such as service contracts, the quality of after-sales service, and so on. Some of the distributors of upmarket vehicles even offer the customer a trial period, where they may drive the vehicle for a week before making a decision.

In 1995, passenger vehicle sales rose 22.9 per cent, while commercial vehicle sales rose 26.3 per cent, despite an average price increase of 8 per cent during the year. The growth in sales was not matched by growth in domestic manufacturing, which highlights the importance of vehicle imports. However, the growth in sales did stimulate activity in the broader industry (including parts and accessories), which experienced 16.5 per cent growth, following growth of 6.2 per cent in 1994 and only 5.2 per cent in 1993.

Source: DPRU, UCT

9.3 Economic evaluation of monopolistic competition

We now examine monopolistically competitive markets using the same criteria that were used to evaluate perfect competition and monopoly.

Monopolistic competition and resource allocation

We could argue that monopolistic competition is wasteful because too many firms operate at excess capacity. Excess capacity means that the firm is producing less output than is required to attain minimum ATC (see Fig. 9.1(b)). It may be argued that consumers' needs would be better served (i.e. they would have a larger output at a lower price) if fewer firms each produced a larger output level.

In long-run equilibrium, the monopolistically competitive firm produces output Q_3 and charges a price P_3, as in Fig. 9.1(b). To the right of this equilibrium point, there is a section of the demand curve that still lies above the marginal cost curve. There are thus consumers willing to pay a price for the product that exceeds the marginal cost of producing it, but are unable to obtain the product at such a price. This stems from the fact that, for a monopolistically competitive firm, the long-run equilibrium price is above marginal cost.

Clearly if perfect competition in long-run equilibrium is taken as the ideal of economic efficiency, then monopolistic competition falls short of this ideal.

Economic efficiency and product differentiation

Unlike perfect competition, monopolistically competitive markets offer consumers a choice of products on the basis of quality, service, product image, and other aspects of non-price competition. The consumer, however, pays for the advantage of product variety. The question of whether product differentiation is more or less desirable than product homogeneity (at a lower price) is essentially a normative issue. The reader may wish to consider various markets, and decide whether differentiation is justified or desirable in each.

Advertising

Advertising can provide the consumer with information about differences among products. Such information is provided in order to increase the demand for the product and lower the consumers' elasticity of demand (to make them less price sensitive) by engendering brand loyalty.

However, advertising may go beyond the simple provision of information and attempt to tailor consumer demand to goods. It is often difficult to distinguish informative advertising from that which encourages consumers to buy for reasons only superficially related to the product, or on the basis of claims which may be entirely false. Brand loyalty is often the result of an image projected by an advertising campaign, rather than any intrinsic characteristics of the product.

The question thus arises as to whether scarce resources should be spent on advertising. Some advertising provides information about product prices, quality and substitutes, and therefore provides the consumer with a saving in terms of resources allocated to searching and shopping. Shoppers' guides and newspaper advertising provide this kind of information.

Television and cinema advertising, on the other hand, are examples of relatively non-informative advertising. Cigarette adverts are also a good example. They often attempt to portray smoking as a vital adjunct to a sophisticated, carefree lifestyle, while providing little or no factual information to the potential consumer. Of course, our earlier Utopian marketer might well argue that Utopia is a free country and that no one is forcing smokers to buy cigarettes. If cigarette smoking is indeed harmful, either to smokers or non-smokers, then the question is: who should bear the responsibility to inform the public? The Utopian marketer, or the Utopian government? Or perhaps the Utopian consumers themselves?

Is advertising wasteful?

Much advertising that is aimed at improving the firm's competitive position, is not informative. It makes claims that brand X is better than brand Y on the basis of dubious allegations and meaningless comparisons. In order to protect its market share, the producer of brand Y will respond with a similar campaign.

Consequently, such competitive advertising may not lead to an increase in market demand. Even individual firms may not experience an increase in their demand as their efforts merely offset one another. But *ATC* curves will be unequivocally higher, reflecting the addition of advertising costs.

Despite this wastefulness, such advertising may persuade consumers to try different products, allowing them to directly acquire information regarding the true characteristics of these products.

It is important to remember that, irrespective of what kind of non-price competition monopolistically competitive firms engage in, in the long run they will all only make a normal profit. The competitive advantage that may result from advertising will only exist in the short run.

Monopolistic competition, innovation and technical change

The long-run equilibrium situation under monopolistic competition shares important characteristics with perfect competition. Free entry into and exit from the industry ensure that firms in both market situations will make only a normal profit in the long run. Under perfect competition, we found that there was consequently little incentive to innovate. Is the situation similar in a monopolistically competitive market?

Product differentiation and the advantages of having a niche in the market may act as a spur to innovation for monopolistically competitive firms. Non-price competition may encourage further product differentiation via product development. Short-run abnormal profits may facilitate innovative activity, but since these do not extend to the long run, the incentive to innovate may also be limited. It may therefore be argued that innovation in monopolistically competitive markets is often perceived rather than real. This may result in the development of more attractive packaging, rather than substantial product improvement, for example.

Monopolistic competition and income distribution

Since only normal profits are being made in the long run, as in perfect competition, the implications for income distribution under monopolistic competition are similar for the two market forms. All factors of production will be earning their opportunity costs, and since a large number of firms exist under monopolistic competition, the benefits are spread widely. Hence, it may be argued that monopolistic competition favours a relatively equal distribution of income.

9.4 Oligopolies

An oligopoly is an industry consisting of a few large sellers. Some oligopolies produce homogeneous or undifferentiated products; examples of these are cement and steel producers. Other oligopolies produce differentiated products; examples of these are producers of automobiles and electrical appliances.

Perhaps the most important distinguishing characteristic of an oligopoly is the recognised interdependence among firms. This *interdependence* leads to a range of behaviour patterns on the part of firms. At one extreme they may engage in fierce competition, while at the other extreme they may explicitly co-operate. Consequently, there is no single model of oligopoly behaviour, but a range of models to explain different types of behaviour.

An oligopoly market may consist of only two firms (a duopoly), or of many small firms dominated by a few large firms, or of several large firms.

Price and output determination

Each firm knows that any price change it makes will affect the sales of other firms to the industry. If a firm lowers its price, it will attract customers from

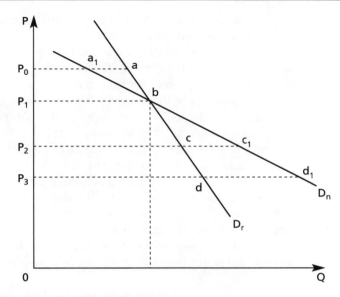

Fig. 9.2 The oligopolist's demand curve

other firms and if it raises its price, it will lose some customers to rival firms. In order to predict the effect of any price change on its sales, the firm has to be able to predict the reactions of its competitors. Such reactions will be reflected in the firm's demand and marginal revenue curves.

Fig. 9.2 shows the oligopolist's demand curve D_n, if it expects no reaction from its rivals when it changes its price. Demand curve D_r incorporates some reaction from the firm's rivals.

If price is initially P_1, the firm is at point b on its demand curve. If price is lowered to P_2 and the firm's rivals do not respond by reducing their prices, then the relevant demand curve is D_n and the firm will move to point c_1 on this demand curve.

If, on the other hand, rival firms do react by cutting their prices, the relevant demand curve is D_r, and the firm will move to point c as price is reduced from P_1 to P_2. The increase in sales is smaller in this case indicating that its rivals have matched the firm's price decrease and therefore have not lost customers to it. The firm has experienced an increase in demand: this is because the industry as a whole is now offering a lower price relative to substitute industries.

Conversely, if the firm were to raise its price from P_1 to P_0 and other firms do not follow suit, then the firm will lose customers and be at point a_1 on D_n. If other firms also raise their price, the firm will move to point a on D_r and will not lose customers. Its loss will be to other industries that produce substitute products.

The oligopolist's kinked demand curve

If the firm is initially at point b in Fig. 9.2, it is reasonable to assume that its demand curve for price decreases will be D_r. This indicates that rival firms, observing the firm's price decrease, will fear losing customers and hence follow with price decreases of their own. On the other hand when the firm raises its price, rival firms are unlikely to follow suit, because customers would respond to the firm's price increase by buying from other firms. Hence the firm's demand curve for price increases is likely to be D_n.

Note that each of the demand curves D_r and D_n would have its own marginal revenue curve. The combined demand curve $D_n D_r$ would then have a marginal revenue curve with a gap, as in Fig. 9.3.

This kinked demand curve offers an explanation as to why prices in oligopolistic markets are slow to change or 'sticky.' If the existing price is P_1, the firm may be reluctant to lower its price, because it knows that its rivals will also lower their prices. Consequently the demand curve below this price is likely to be inelastic – any price decrease would lead to a fall in total revenue. The firm may also be reluctant to increase its price, since if it raises its price above P_1, it will lose many customers to firms who do not follow suit. Thus the segment of the firm's demand curve above P_1 will be elastic.

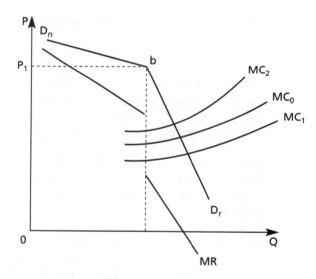

Fig. 9.3 The oligopolist's kinked demand curve

Another reason why price may be 'sticky' at P_1 concerns the vertical segment (or gap) in the firm's marginal revenue curve. Assume that price P_1 was arrived at by equating MR and MC and that the marginal cost curve is MC_0, as in Fig. 9.3. Suppose that production costs rise (in particular, the firm's variable costs), so that marginal cost would shift upward to MC_2. Or suppose that production costs decrease, then the marginal cost curve would shift downward to MC_1. In both cases, applying the $MC = MR$ principle leaves price unchanged at P_1. Therefore, as long as MC lies within the gap in the MR curve, the firm will not change its selling price.

The kinked demand curve thus provides one possible explanation as to why firms in an oligopoly are reluctant to change an existing price.

Explicit collusion: the cartel

A cartel is a combination of firms whose aim is to limit the scope of competitive forces within a market. The firms usually enter into an agreement pertaining to price and output levels. In most countries, however, cartels are now illegal. Perhaps the best known contemporary cartel is the Organisation of Petroleum Exporting Countries (OPEC), which determines a price at which it will sell oil to the rest of the world.

CASE EXAMPLE

The OPEC cartel

OPEC was formed in 1960. In 1973 members of the cartel cut output and prices of crude oil tripled. By the mid-1980s, however, there was a surplus of oil on the market and prices fell. Why was OPEC unable to keep prices high?

1. OPEC never established a barrier to entry. When prices rose, non-cartel members increased production, and put downward pressure on prices.
2. Since 1970 demand for oil became more elastic as substitutes were developed for petroleum products. In response to OPEC's initial production cutbacks, consumers developed more energy-efficient technologies.

In the 1980s OPEC tried to raise prices by reducing production, and met with short-term success. The price increases may have been caused by other factors, such as an increased demand resulting from the Iran–Iraq war. Members of OPEC were also in disagreement over quotas. By 1989 cheating among member nations was rampant, and production exceeded the total quota, putting pressure downward on prices. The disagreement over quotas and subsequent cheating destroys the cartel's ability to maintain high prices.

Suppose that a group of firms, producing a homogeneous product, forms a cartel. A central management body is appointed and its function is to determine the uniform cartel price. Its first task is to estimate the market demand for the product. Once it has determined this demand curve, e.g. D in Fig. 9.4, it can derive the associated marginal revenue curve *MR*. Assuming that all member firms purchase their inputs in perfectly competitive markets, the cartel *MC* curve can be determined by horizontal summation of the member firms' *MC* curves. Having determined the cartel *MC* curve, the management body will determine the cartel price which will maximise the joint profit of the member firms.

The price which will be charged by all firms (P_e) is determined by the intersection of *MR* and *MC* in Fig. 9.4(c). This point of intersection also determines the collective output of the cartel (Q_T). How will this output be distributed among the individual firms?

Applying the profit-maximising principle, the MC of each firm will have to be equated with the cartel MR. Assuming that the cartel consists of two firms only with MC curves MC_1 and MC_2 in Fig. 9.4(a) and (b), equating the cartel MR to MC_1 and MC_2 will allocate the cartel output between the two firms so as to maximise joint profit. Note that OQ_1 and OQ_2 add up to the total output OQ_T.

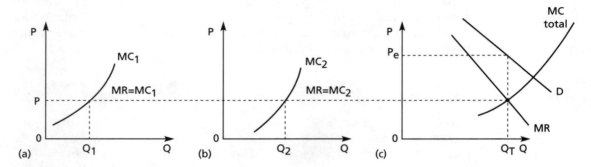

Fig. 9.4 The profit-maximising cartel

There are a number of factors that make a cartel prone to instability:

1. *The management body has to estimate the market demand curve.* This, in itself, is a difficult task, but is further complicated by the fact that negotiations within the cartel may take a long time. By the time agreement has been reached, the market demand curve may have changed.
2. *Cost estimates have to be submitted by the member firms.* These are likely to change over the duration of the agreement, and high cost firms, which could distort cartel costs, may be asked to shut down in return for a share of profit.
3. *There is an incentive to cheat.* Firms could increase their market share beyond that allotted to them by the cartel, e.g. by undercutting the cartel price. These firms are referred to as price chisellers.

Given that explicit collusion is illegal in most countries, firms may seek other means to co-ordinate their activities.

Price leadership

A fairly common form of implicit collusion is price leadership. Consider a situation where one firm is recognised as the dominant firm in the market. It may be a large firm or have been in the market for some time. It will set its price so as to maximise profit and the other firms, the followers, will adopt this price and adjust their output accordingly.

The price leader effectively behaves like a monopolist. The leader firm begins by estimating the market demand for the product, as shown in Fig. 9.5. It then

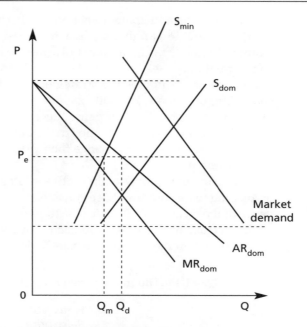

Fig. 9.5 Price leadership in an oligopoly market

estimates how much the group of follower or minor firms would supply at different prices – this is their supply curve, S_{min} in Fig. 9.5. The dominant firm then determines its demand curve for the product by deducting the quantity that the group of minor firms would supply at each price (which we read off from the curve S_{min}), from the quantity that the market would demand at the same price (which we read off from the market demand curve). This series of calculations provides the points on the dominant firm's demand curve, AR_{dom} in Fig. 9.5. The dominant firm then derives its marginal revenue curve, MR_{dom}, from its demand curve. It then calculates its marginal cost curve which, as we have seen, is the same as its supply curve, S_{dom}, and by equating *MR* and *MC*, it derives the profit-maximising output and price levels, Q_d and P_e.

The minor firms, relying on the dominant firm to interpret market conditions, act as price takers (similar to perfectly competitive firms) and determine their profit-maximising output level where price equals marginal cost – given by S_{min} in Fig. 9.5. They therefore collectively produce an output level Q_m. Total output in the industry is therefore equal to the quantity produced by the dominant firm (Q_d) plus that produced by the minor firms as a group (Q_m). This total supply is exactly equal to the market demand at the equilibrium price, P_e.

Price leadership is quite common in oligopoly market situations such as those for steel, cigarettes, retail groceries and coal.

Games oligopolies play

Given the interdependence among firms in an oligopoly, the individual firm knows that the decisions of other firms will affect its profit. Hence it will take into account the anticipated reactions of its rivals when changing its price or another strategic variable such as advertising expenditure. The strategies adopted by the firms in an oligopoly may be analysed within the context of a game situation.

Game theory examines the strategies of individuals or organisations with conflicting objectives. We will examine an oligopoly with two firms (a duopoly) using the principles of game theory. The game is therefore played in a market and the players are the firms, Firm I and Firm II. Their strategies describe their decisions to change their price or output levels. The payoffs are the resulting profits.

Each firm considers two alternative strategies: raising price by 10 per cent or keeping price constant. Each considers two possible reactions on the part of its rival: the rival raises its price by 10 per cent or does not raise its price. The profit increase or decrease from each move for each possible reaction by the rival is shown in the payoff matrix in Table 9.1.

Table 9.1 Payoffs for duopolists from price changes (R millions)

| | | Firm II's strategies | | |
		Raise price by 10%	Keep price constant	Firm I's maximum loss
Firm I's strategies	Raise price by 10%	I's profit down R9 II's profit down R9	I's profit up R6 II's profit down R15	R9
	Keep price constant	I's profit down R15 II's profit up R6	I's profit no change II's profit no change	R15
	Firm II's maximum loss	R9	R15	

Each firm will take into account the reaction of its rival when deciding on a pricing strategy. If Firm I raises its price, it could increase its profits by R6 million, or decrease them by R9 million, depending on the reaction of Firm II. If it keeps its price constant it could potentially lose R15 million! Since Firm I cannot control the actions of Firm II, it would be prudent to adopt the strategy that potentially incurs the minimum loss, rather than leaving the fate of the firm to chance by wagering on compliant behaviour from Firm II.

Hence it makes sense to select the strategy that results in the minimum loss of profit, i.e. raise price by 10 per cent. Similarly, if Firm II raises its price it could lose R9 million (if Firm I raises its price), whereas if it keeps its price constant it could lose R15 million if Firm I raises its price by 10 per cent. Firm II therefore chooses to raise its price by 10 per cent and suffers a decrease in profit of R9 million as opposed to the alternative of a R15 million decrease.

Each firm will select that strategy which yields the 'better' of the bad outcomes. Firm I chooses to raise its price by 10 per cent as does firm II. In Table 9.1 this corresponds to examining Firm I's maximum loss, and choosing the strategy which minimises this loss. For Firm II, the final row indicating its possible maximum loss is examined, and the strategy which minimises this loss is selected. This is known as the *maximin strategy*.

Close examination of Table 9.1 indicates, however, that by retaining their current prices, neither firm would suffer any decrease in profit. If both firms recognise this and agree to co-operate (collude!) then neither would lose any profits. There is however an incentive to cheat, as the potential increase in profits in Table 9.1 indicates. Firm I could increase its profit by R6 million by cheating, as could Firm II if it did not stick to the price agreement. The delicate stability of any collusive agreement is thus always in jeopardy; the incentive to cheat and reap a short-term profit gain is very great.

9.5 Economic evaluation of oligopoly

Oligopoly and economic efficiency

An oligopoly firm cannot, given its downward sloping demand curve, produce at the point where *ATC* is at a minimum. By this criterion, oligopoly is not efficient.

It may be the case, however, that oligopoly firms experience significant economies of scale. If such an oligopoly were reorganised to become a perfectly competitive industry, it could transpire that per unit costs of production would be higher for the larger number of small firms than it would be for the larger firms in an oligopoly.

Innovation and technological change

It may be argued that technological change and innovation are fostered in an oligopoly environment which brings together elements of competition and monopoly. The possibility of abnormal profits, behind sometimes substantial barriers to entry, encourages innovation and provides a source of finance for research and development. This is similar to the situation of a monopoly. The existence of rival firms, however, will act as an additional spur to engage in non-price competition in the form of product development and innovation. The pressures of competition encourage technological development, and this is boosted by the profit incentive.

A counter-argument is that collusion may encourage a cosy 'live and let live' approach among oligopolists. Consequently, less progressive and innovative behaviour may result. If this is the case then oligopoly will be very much like monopoly in this area.

Advertising and profits

Advertising may contribute to abnormal profits because it encourages product differentiation and proliferation. Product differentiation and proliferation may constitute powerful barriers to entry and thereby protect incumbent firms from potential competition. This helps firms to charge higher prices and thereby realise monopoly profits.

Empirical evidence

The real world is populated by many oligopoly industries; what is their performance record? Empirical studies indicate that industries dominated by a small number of large firms have higher profit rates than more competitive industries. These studies also indicate that the larger firm size tends not to be a result of economies of scale. This seems to suggest some production and distribution inefficiencies.

CASE EXAMPLE

The cement cartel

In South Africa the cement industry is dominated by three producers – Pretoria Portland Cement, Anglo-Alpha and Blue Circle. In 1988 the Competition Board granted them an exemption to continue operating as a cartel (cartels are illegal in South Africa). At the time this decision drew much criticism. However, the Competition Board concluded that the producers should be allowed to fix prices and control production of a product which requires high capital inputs and large production volumes to ensure a constant supply of cement at affordable prices.

The cartel, in terms of its exemption, determines prices at the manufacturing level and decides on a return on investment for the industry. Cement producers argue that the cartel ensures efficiencies through economies of scale.

A recent investigation has lead to the exemption being rescinded. The important question now is what the impact of this decision by the Competition Board will be. Will we see active competition among the formerly colluding firms and will cement prices fall?

9.6 Imperfectly competitive factor markets

The structure of the product market plays an important role in the determination of the equilibrium quantity and price of a product. We have seen that output levels and prices vary considerably across the range of market forms from perfect competition, through monopolistic competition and oligopoly to monopoly. In a similar way the structure of a market will affect the level of employment of a production factor as well as its price. We will examine the determination of price and employment in imperfectly competitive labour markets.

Workers in a perfectly competitive labour market (as described in Chapter 7) compete with one another for jobs, and each will deal with his or her employer concerning conditions and terms of employment. Workers may, however, band together to act collectively in a labour market. A *union* (trade or labour) is an organisation of workers that represents them collectively in bargaining with employers on matters such as wages and terms of employment. Perhaps the most important objective of the union is to secure higher wages for its members. There are a number of ways in which this objective may be pursued. While analysing these, we assume that there is a large number of employers competing with one another to hire labour.

Restriction of supply

Certain jobs require specific skills, training or education, and it is therefore possible to restrict the supply of such labour. In this way wages may be raised. In labour markets for unskilled workers, this is much more difficult, because the barriers to entry, in terms of skill or educational requirements, are much lower. Workers can fairly easily enter such markets to compete for jobs.

Workers in skilled trades such as plumbers or electricians band together to form *craft unions*. By controlling the length of apprenticeship programmes and restricting membership, a union can control the supply of labour in these trades. The more effectively they do this, the easier it is to force the employers to hire only union members. This further strengthens the craft union's ability to restrict the labour supply.

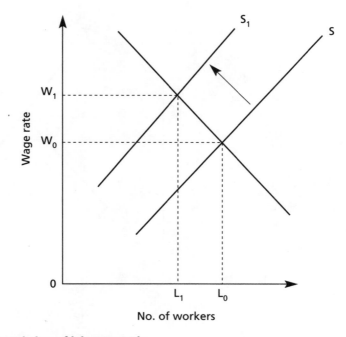

Fig. 9.6 Restriction of labour supply

A number of professions require a licence to practise. The medical and legal professions are good examples. Extensive training and testing of individuals is required before they are allowed to practise, and this restricts the supply of these services. It is often argued that these measures are implemented in the 'public interest' – as a guarantee of quality services.

Unions also support legislation that restricts the supply of labour generally. Such legislation includes child-labour laws, immigration quotas, compulsory retirement at a certain age and a shorter working week. The effect of all these measures is to increase the wage rate. Fig. 9.6 indicates that a reduction of supply (a leftward shift of the supply curve to S_1) will lead to a higher wage (W_1), but there is a cost associated with this in that fewer workers are employed (i.e. the employment level decreases from L_0 to L_1). A trade-off between wages and employment therefore exists.

Wage setting

Industrial unions organise all workers, skilled and unskilled, in a particular industry. Such unions derive strength from numbers, and therefore aim to maximise membership. An industrial union forces firms in the industry to bargain exclusively with the union over wages and other conditions of employment. Firms unwilling to reach agreement with the union face the threat of a *strike* – the cessation of their labour supply – at least until some agreement is concluded.

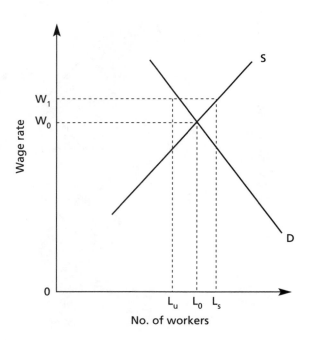

Fig. 9.7 Wage setting

This bargaining power enables the union to obtain wages for its members above the level that would pertain in a perfectly competitive market. This is illustrated in Fig. 9.7, where W_0 would be the perfectly competitive wage, with corresponding employment level L_0. Using its bargaining power, the union pushes up the wage to W_1; given a downward sloping demand curve the employment level decreases to L_u. This leads to an excess supply of labour ($L_s - L_u$) – these workers are willing to work in the industry but cannot find jobs, and are thus *involuntarily unemployed*.

CASE EXAMPLE

Wage rigidity and the teaching profession

The South African teaching profession is facing a serious shortage of maths and science teachers, and it is possible to look at this crisis, or at least parts of it, from a labour market perspective. The problem is in fact more complicated than it might seem: not only is there a shortage of maths and science (M & S) teachers, but there is also a surplus of arts teachers – all of whom are working for the same uniform wage!

The shortage of M & S teachers is illustrated in Fig. 9.8, where the relevant demand and supply curves are given by $D_{m\&s}$ and $S_{m\&s}$, respectively. At the fixed wage, $\overline{w}$, the shortage of M & S teachers equals AB (which could get worse in the long run as some teachers leave the industry and the supply curve shifts inwards).

In practice, it would seem, the shortage of M & S teachers has been artificially eliminated by a process of 'inferior substitution'. Many schools have been using surplus arts teachers or temporary substitutes from outside, with limited training or experience in the field, to teach M & S courses at all levels. In terms of Fig. 9.8, this stop-gap policy would have shifted the supply curve outwards to $S'_{m\&s}$, but because of the lower productivity, the demand (or marginal productivity) curve may well have shifted inwards – e.g. to $D'_{m\&s}$. Although there is no shortage at point F, the output of matric equivalents, or the quality of school leavers – not shown in the diagram – is now appreciably lower than it would have been at point E.

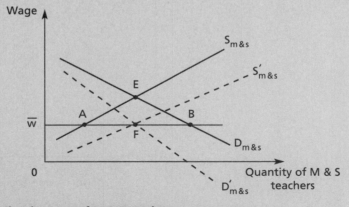

Fig. 9.8 The shortage of M & S teachers

Case example
continued

The problem sketched in Fig. 9.8 could get worse if M & S teachers, or 'inferior' substitutes, became demotivated and frustrated, and rationally decided to shirk. In this case the marginal (physical) productivity of M & S teachers will be even lower than before.

Increasing labour demand

When unions raise wages in the labour market, either by restricting labour supply or by direct bargaining, the employment level decreases. There is thus a trade-off between the higher wage and a lower level of employment. If it is possible to increase the demand for labour then a higher wage and a higher level of employment would be the result. Figure 9.9 illustrates that, with an outward shift of the demand curve from D_0 to D_1, the wage increases from W_0 to W_1 and employment rises from L_0 to L_1.

The marginal productivity theory of labour demand indicates that any factor that increases labour productivity will shift the labour demand curve to the right. Trade unions may support, or even conduct, training courses to increase productivity and therefore the demand for labour. Another means of increasing labour demand in specific industries is to put tariffs and quotas on imported goods that compete with domestically produced goods, thereby raising the price of imports. This will tend to increase the demand for domestically produced goods which are substituted for the more expensive imported goods. The demand for labour used to produce the domestic goods is thus increased. Labour unions therefore have an interest in supporting employers in lobbying for tariff legislation that protects their industry from import competition.

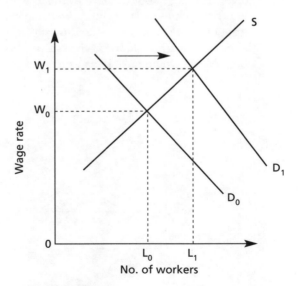

Fig. 9.9 Increasing labour demand

Monopsony

A monopsony is a market where one buyer purchases a product or factor of production from many sellers. It is, in a sense, the opposite of monopoly, where there is one seller of a product or factor. A labour market where one employer, the monopsonist, confronts a non-unionised group of workers competing for jobs, is a monopsony.

Table 9.2 and its graphical representation in Fig. 9.10 indicate how wages and employment are determined in a monopsonistic still labour market. As the only employer of labour, the monopsonistic has to pay a higher wage in order to attract more labour. This is reflected in the first two columns of Table 9.2 and by the upward sloping supply curve in Fig. 9.10.

The higher wage (or average cost of labour) must be paid to all workers already employed, not only to the last worker hired. If this were not done, workers already employed would be unhappy, leave and have to be rehired at the higher wage paid to the last worker hired. Therefore the marginal cost (i.e. the additional cost of hiring the last worker) includes not only his or her wage, but the increases in the wage that must be paid to all previously hired workers in order to raise their wage to the level of the last worker. This is equivalent to the increase in the firm's total cost of labour, i.e. the addition to total cost resulting from the employment of one more worker. Figure 9.10 shows clearly that the marginal cost of labour rises faster than the average cost (the supply curve).

Table 9.2 Wage and employment determination in a monopsony labour market

No. of workers employed (L)	Wage rate = Average cost of labour (W = AC_L)	Total labour cost (TC_L)	Marginal cost of labour (MC_L)	Marginal revenue product of labour (MRP_L)
1	3	3	3	15
2	4	8	5	13
3	5	15	7	11
4	6	24	9	9
5	7	35	11	7
6	8	48	13	5

According to the marginal productivity theory of factor demand, the firm will hire labour up to that point where the marginal cost of the factor equals its marginal revenue product ($MC_L = MRP_L$). From Table 9.2, we see that the optimal number of workers to hire is four, where both the marginal cost of labour and its marginal revenue product are equal to R9. This is shown by the intersection of the MC_L and MRP curves in Fig. 9.10. The wage is determined from the supply curve, since a point on the supply curve indicates the wage

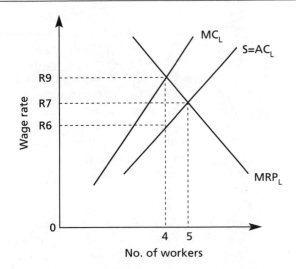

Fig. 9.10 A monopsonistic labour market

for which workers are willing to supply their labour services. Hence, the wage will be R6 per worker.

By comparison, if the labour market was perfectly competitive, the equilibrium would be determined where supply equals demand. Since the *MRP* curve is the demand curve for labour, the intersection of *MRP* and *S* would indicate that five workers would be employed and the wage would be R7 under conditions of perfect competition.

We can conclude that when workers compete for jobs offered by the monopsonist employer, the equilibrium wage and level of employment will be lower than those that would emerge if the market was perfectly competitive, due to the monopoly power that the monopsonist exerts over the demand for labour.

9.7 Labour market discrimination

Gary Becker (see Exhibit below) was one of the first economists to develop a coherent theory of labour market discrimination. He argued that employers may have a 'taste' for discrimination, in the sense that they dislike associating with members of a particular group. They would thus refrain from employing those individuals, even though they may stand to gain financially from doing so. In other words, firms discriminate against a particular group because they perceive the non-pecuniary benefits from discrimination to be larger than the pecuniary benefits derived from hiring an individual from that group.

In some instances, discrimination is based on the need to reduce information costs, or to compensate for insufficient information. This kind of discrimination is often referred to as 'statistical discrimination'. When a firm is trying to fill a position, it maybe difficult to gauge a candidate's suitability within the time available without some type of screening criteria. Often qualifications are used to discriminate, because they imply something about the skills or abilities of the candidate. Employers tend to view the employment relationship as long term – they want to employ good quality recruits whose skills can be readily upgraded, and who will not leave the firm before the full value of any investment in their training has been recouped by the firm. If there are entrenched beliefs or perceptions, whether these are justified or not, that systematic differences exist between the abilities, job loyalty or other desirable attributes of different categories of people, wage differentials will exist between these groups. The demographic category to which a person belongs serves as a filter – each member is assumed to have the perceived characteristics of that group. Such a model seems to be consistent with observed patterns of discrimination against blacks, women and the disabled.

Discrimination has also been legally enforced in many countries over the years. Legislated discrimination under the apartheid era in South Africa introduced distortions into the labour market primarily through artificial signalling. On the demand side, it provided an artificial demand for less skilled white workers, while the demand for black workers was artificially suppressed. A 'floor' wage for white workers was created, in conjunction with a guaranteed demand for unskilled white workers by the public sector acting as an 'employer of last resort'. On the supply side, further distortions were introduced by differential access to education, based on race. This ensured a steady supply of skilled white workers, and a 'shortage' of skilled black workers. In some instances, legislation resulted in an anomalous situation, whereby a surplus of black labour co-existed with job vacancies having to be filled by imported white workers.

Even with the scrapping of statutory discrimination, racial income differentials tended to persist. This was so because even in a competitive labour market, asymmetric access to education created an advantage for white workers. In other words, racial differences in income are better explained by racial discrimination in the supply of education than by direct racial discrimination in employment. Therefore, in the short term at least, instituting equal opportunity policies is unlikely to rectify racial income differentials – which may suggest that a case can be made for affirmative action (see Chapter 10).

EXHIBIT

Gary Becker

A recent winner of the Nobel Price in Economics, Gary Becker has produced highly original work in several important fields. These include the theory of discrimination, human capital theory, the economics of crime and punishment, and the decision-making behaviour of individual households.

Becker is perhaps best known for his work on discrimination, which started with his doctoral thesis at the University of Chicago and culminated in the publication of *The Economics of Discrimination* in 1957. In it he developed a rigorous theory of racial and gender discrimination, based on neo-classical principles, and showed how the maximising behaviour of individuals may be

▶

Exhibit
continued

affected by a 'taste for discrimination'. As the accompanying example shows, Becker's original theory spawned a whole body of new theories and empirical investigations into discriminatory practices.

In another major work, *Human Capital* (first published in 1964), he set out the principles underlying the individual's decision to become educated and trained. He was also the first to distinguish between 'general' and 'firm-specific' training and to point out the implications of each type of training for the individual and the firm. His 'Crime and Punishment: An Economic Approach', published in the *Journal of Political Economy* in 1968, provided a highly original analysis of the economics of the crime industry, and argued that the decision to enter it was a perfectly rational one, being based on expected benefits and costs and on the associated degree of risk. In his 'A Theory of the Allocation of Time', published in the *Economic Journal* in 1965, and in *The Economic Approach* to *Family Behaviour*, published in 1976, he deals with the question of how decisions are made at the level of the individual family, including decisions about getting married and divorced and about how many children to have.

These seminal works have clearly helped us to understand ourselves better, and if any student wanted to know precisely why he or she is reading this or any other textbook, Gary Becker would be the man to turn to.

Summary

- Monopolistically competitive markets contain elements of both monopoly and perfect competition. The market is characterised by product differentiation, free entry and exit, and a large number of competing firms, each producing a similar yet slightly differentiated product. Examples include the markets for beer, breakfast cereals and toothpaste.

- A monopolistically competitive firm has a monopoly over its own brand, and thus faces a negatively sloped market demand curve which lies above its MR curve. Its short-run equilibrium is similar to that of a monopolist except that its demand curve is much more elastic – due to the presence of many close substitutes. It sets price such that $MC = MR$, and is able to make a positive economic profit in the short run.

- In the long run, however, new firms can enter the market, shifting the demand and MR curves of incumbent firms leftwards, until all abnormal profits have been eliminated from the market. Each firm will charge a price equal to average cost, at an output level representing higher than minimum unit cost – which can be viewed as the price paid by consumers for the advantage of product variety.

- Oligopolistic markets consist of a few large firms that may either compete with each other or enter into an implicit or explicit collusive arrangement.

- An oligopolistic firm's behaviour depends on what it expects its rivals will do. It can be fairly sure that if it lowered its price its rivals will follow suit, while if it raised its price, they will not. It will thus be faced with a kinked demand curve, and a discontinuous *MR* curve, which partly explains why oligopolistic prices tend to be relatively stable.

- Oligopolists may also form cartels aimed at limiting the scope for competition in their market. They may do so either explicitly and end up charging the monopoly price (e.g. the OPEC cartel), or implicitly in the form of a so-called price-leadership cartel (e.g. retail groceries, and steel and coal production). In the latter case the subordinate firms merely accept the price set by the dominant firm, and adjust their output accordingly.

- Cartels are notoriously vulnerable to cheating on the part of individual members. This often takes the form of 'strategic games', according to which a member firm tries to anticipate the reactions of its rivals and act accordingly. Such games may have either stable or unstable outcomes.

- Factor markets may also be imperfectly competitive. There are many variations here. On the supply side, for example, labour unions may set wages above the equilibrium level, or restrict the supply of labour by imposing licensing and other entry requirements; while on the demand side, they may lobby for tariff protection in an attempt to boost the demand for domestic labour.

- A monopsony is really the opposite of monopoly: it is a market in which there is only one firm buying a factor of production, e.g. labour services, from many sellers. In this case the monopsonistic firm will hire labour up to the point where the marginal cost of labour equals its marginal revenue product. Both the equilibrium wage and level of employment will be lower under monopsony than under a perfectly competitive labour market.

Questions for review

1. Explain with the use of a diagram how the dominant firm in a situation of price leadership will determine its equilibrium price and output level.

2. Examine (again with the use of diagrams) the impact of trade unions in the labour market. Relate your discussion to the South African labour market.

3. Monopolistic competition offers the consumer a range of products from which to choose, but the consumer pays for this advantage of choice. Discuss the impact of product differentiation (including the role of advertising by the firm) in this market.

4. A cartel is an inherently unstable organisation. Why is this so?

5. Why do firms discriminate? Can a discriminating firm expect to survive in the long run?

CHAPTER 10

The functional distribution of income

Few topics in economics generate as much controversy as does the distribution of income, since it is here that the rewards conferred on different agents by the economic system can be observed and compared. Households are the ultimate owners and suppliers of the resources used to produce all output in the economy, and thus all income accrues to them. The distribution of income takes us into the field of macroeconomics, since we are examining the distribution of national income or gross domestic product. Yet the principles of analysis that we employ when examining the distribution of income belong to microeconomics.

10.1 Functional versus personal distribution of income

Classical economists such as Adam Smith and David Ricardo focused on the distribution of income among three important social classes, i.e. landowners, capitalists and workers. The factors of production owned by each of these groups were land, capital and labour, respectively, and the reward to each of these factors was assumed to equal the income accruing to each of these social classes. It is for this reason that the theory explaining the determination of factor prices became known as the theory of distribution. Some of the great debates among the classical economists, to which Karl Marx later contributed, centred on the impact of social transformation on the distribution of income among these factors of production. These debates essentially focused on the *functional distribution* of income. Changes in technology and the process of capital accumulation, which Marx considered in much detail, have had a marked effect on the distribution of income among these functional categories over time.

These clear-cut divisions among the social classes, and hence between the categories of production factors, have become somewhat fuzzy in recent times. It is quite common for one individual to receive income from the ownership of more than one factor of production. In South Africa as in other countries, for example, some companies have implemented Employee Share Ownership Programmes (ESOP). This means that some employees in the mining sector and also in retail grocery stores, for example, have become shareholders in the companies to which they supply labour services. In return they receive a share of profit in the form of dividends. Economists have therefore shifted their focus to the *personal distribution* of income.

The personal distribution of income refers to the distribution of income among households and does not focus on the source of the income received.

Clearly the functional distribution and the personal distribution of income are related. The relationship between the two distributions of income is forged by the ownership of factors of production. Ownership of factors of production, such as land or capital, which we can refer to as wealth, increases the income generation potential of the individual. This is one reason why in many developing countries in particular, there are calls for the redistribution of factors of production such as land. In South Africa a process of land redistribution is currently under way and it is expected that its redistribution may have a significant effect on the future distribution of income in South Africa.

In this chapter we will be concerned with the functional distribution of income. Our discussion of the determination of wages, both in perfectly competitive and imperfectly competitive markets (in earlier chapters), has been quite lengthy. Wage income constitutes by far the major component of national income, hence this emphasis is justified. Approximately 70 to 80 per cent of national income accrues to individuals in the form of wage and salary incomes. The remainder is divided among rent, interest, dividends and profits. In the following sections we will therefore examine wage differentials among workers which may exist and persist in the labour market. We then focus on the three other factors of production and examine the determination of the returns to these factors.

10.2 Wage differentials in the labour market

Wage differentials in the labour market tend to persist over long periods of time. This means that they cannot merely be temporary 'disequilibrium differences', which can be eliminated over time, but are in fact 'equilibrium differentials'. We examine the causes of these persistent wage differences here.

Some of the early labour market theories explained these equilibrium wage differences using the idea of segmented labour markets. They argued that labour markets consisted of distinct segments and that it was extremely difficult (and costly) for an individual to move from one segment to another. For example, the labour market segment for opera singers could be entered only by individuals who had the innate ability and had undertaken specialised training. It would be very difficult for someone who does not have the ability or the training to enter that labour market segment. These early theories therefore explained wage differences among non-competing groups in these distinct segments of the labour market in terms of the barriers resulting from human differences.

Over time the wage difference among these groups will change as a result of changes in the demand for and supply of different types of labour. The demand for computer programers has undergone dramatic change over time. About 50 years ago, when the computer industry was in its infancy, the demand for workers with these skills was limited, but with the growth of the computer industry, this demand increased dramatically. More recently, with the general increase in computer literacy, and technological developments in the field, the nature of the skills required in the industry has been changing very rapidly. Time is therefore a very important consideration when we examine wage differentials – the shorter the time period under consideration, the less is the mobility we are likely to observe among the labour market segments.

Some wage differences remain even in the long run because the supply of specific characteristics remains low relative to the demand for them. An important factor is education – many skills are acquired, not innate. The stock of skills that the individual acquires is referred to as *human capital*. Just as capital accumulation by a firm requires investment, so acquisition of human capital requires time, effort and resources. The investment in human capital, which increases the productivity of the individual, is rewarded by a higher wage.

Human capital accumulation takes the form of formal education at school, college, university, or other education institutions. While additional skills are being acquired through the process of formal education, the individual is incurring an opportunity cost. The opportunity cost is the income foregone while studying. The individual, when deciding whether or not to study further, will weigh this cost against the benefit of the higher future income expected after completing the education programme. This 'cost-benefit' analysis is undertaken by all individuals, whether consciously or sub-consciously, and lies at the root of the decision to invest in human capital.

Another means of accumulating human capital is through on-the-job training or education. Wage differentials in most firms reflect differences in human capital acquired on the job. Some firms may run training programmes for their employees to equip them with firm-specific skills, or on the other hand to develop general skills which can be transferred to other jobs. Generally there is a positive relationship between the individual's wage and the length of time spent at a specific firm, which reflects to some extent the value of on-the-job training.

Wage differentials also result from differences in labour market structures. As we saw in earlier chapters the wage determined in a perfectly competitive labour market differed markedly from that in a monopsony. Furthermore, institutions in the labour market, in particular labour unions, could through a range of activities, ranging from bargaining to a restriction of supply, also alter the wage rate from that which would hold in a perfectly competitive market.

CASE EXAMPLE

Minimum wages

Just as labour unions can obtain a higher than equilibrium wage (as under perfect competition), governments can legislate a higher than equilibrium wage, referred to as a *minimum wage*. A minimum wage specifies the lowest wage that may legally be paid. In South Africa (as has been mentioned in Chapter 4) there has been much debate about minimum wages. The Congress of South African Trade Unions (COSATU) launched a campaign during the 1980s in favour of a 'living wage', effectively demanding a minimum wage to ensure a minimum standard of living for workers. A minimum wage (as we

▶

Case example
continued

have seen in our earlier analysis of price controls) effectively sets a price floor below which the wage may not fall. Our analysis indicated that this could result in a surplus of labour (unemployment) – and hence minimum wages are not viewed favourably in some quarters. If a minimum wage policy is effective, it raises the wage of the employed workers. This increases the disparity in the labour market between the 'insiders' (the employed) and the 'outsiders' (the unemployed) – there is thus a cost associated with the implementation of a minimum wage policy.

Labour market statistics reveal that wages also vary with race and sex. Analysis of these wage differences shows that even when differences related to human capital are taken into account, these wage differences persist. These differences are explained in terms of discrimination – as discussed in the previous chapter. Likewise, affirmative action (see Case example below) is an attempt to redress wage differences that have resulted purely from past discriminatory practices.

CASE EXAMPLE

Affirmative action in South Africa

Affirmative action has become endemic to the South African labour market. The speed and spread of implementation has virtually spawned a new industry, with large numbers of personnel consultants specialising in affirmative action recruitment, many others offering services around the design and implementation of affirmative action strategies, and numerous training institutions assisting firms in managing cultural diversity in the workplace.

A question immediately arises as to why employers are suddenly choosing to appoint disadvantaged black candidates to positions for which advantaged white candidates are readily available, at the same or a lower wage. An unlikely answer is that private firms are acting in a socially responsible way, and are taking it upon themselves to correct socio-economic imbalances caused by discriminatory policies of the past. It is more likely that employers perceive the net private benefits of affirmative action to be greater than that of maintaining the status quo. Furthermore, given the high costs of identifying, recruiting and training disadvantaged candidates, employers must be expecting a substantial future stream of benefits.

There is also the issue of an excess demand for, or limited supply of, suitably qualified candidates in certain careers. Given that there is an increasing pressure from organisations such as COSATU and the Black Management Forum on government to institute racial quotas, and that conflicting opinions have emanated from within government, firms may consider it prudent to take action now. Firms which wait may find targets impossible to meet from a shrinking pool of suitable, available candidates. A recent survey reports that approximately 12.5 per cent of the increase in affirmative action programmes can be attributed to the threat of legislation (*Sunday Times*, May 22, 1994).

▶

Fierce wage and benefit competition is already evident within careers such as chartered accountancy, which have significant barriers to entry. The same survey reports that one third of respondents pay a premium of up to 50 per cent in order to attract top calibre black staff.

Firms may well expect a stream of future benefits, because the change in political dispensation has altered the economic environment in which they operate. Government, organised labour, a burgeoning black consumer market and foreign investors are more likely to support firms engaged in affirmative action than those who are not. If, as a result, firms are able to realise reductions in operating costs, and increases in demand, their profits will rise. The image of the firm may be enhanced by practising affirmative action, and previously disadvantaged candidates may bring non-job specific attributes to the position, such as an improved negotiating position with predominantly black factory workers, an innate understanding of the black consumer market, and key contacts within emerging black business circles. Under this scenario, affirmative action forms part of a long-term profit-maximising strategy.

As a counter, if white workers perceive their career prospects to be dampened by affirmative action, they may become disillusioned, resulting in a fall in productivity, which will increase costs. Another danger, realised in the USA, is that affirmative action with an infinite time horizon can create a culture of entitlement. Mamphela Ramphele has cautioned against this, saying that performance must ultimately be the responsibility of the individuals – ' . . . he right to equal opportunities cannot be extended to the right to successful outcomes'.

In South Africa, affirmative action policies focus almost exclusively on black empowerment, yet other groups have been equally discriminated against. The above survey noted that 100 per cent of affirmative action programmes focused on black advancement, 78 per cent included Asian and coloured advancement, 66 per cent took cognisance of gender, and only 31 per cent extended to disabled people. There is clearly a need for a shift in focus here.

Source: Black, P. A., 'Affirmative action: rational response to a changing environment', *South African Journal of Economics*, Vol. 61, No. 4, 1993; 'Affirmative action in South Africa, or rational discrimination a-la Akerlof', *South African Journal of Economics*, Vol. 65, No. 1, 1996

10.3 Rent

Rent is the price paid for the use of land and other natural resources, which are generally fixed in total supply. The fixed level of supply, in particular, distinguishes rent from other forms of factor income, since it is predominantly determined by increases in demand. This is particularly true of small island economies like Utopia and Famine, where owning a piece of land or a natural resource can be a major source of income.

To simplify matters, assume that all land is of equal quality. The productivity of each unit will therefore be the same. Furthermore, we assume that the market for land is perfectly competitive – there are many suppliers and many demanders of land.

Figure 10.1 indicates a fixed supply of land, S, with D_2 the demand curve for the use of that land.

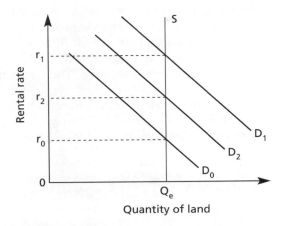

Fig. 10.1 Determination of rent

As with all economic resources, the demand for land is a derived demand. The demand curve slopes downward because of the law of diminishing marginal returns. The supply of land is fixed, or perfectly inelastic. This characteristic of supply means that demand is the active determinant of the price of land. The price of the goods produced on the land, the productivity of land, and the prices of the other factors that are combined with land in production, together will determine the demand for land.

Given the supply of land, S, and demand D_2, the rent would be r_2. Should demand increase to D_1 or decrease to D_0, rent would increase to r_1 or decrease to r_0, respectively. Note that changes in rent do not have any impact on the supply of land.

The perfect inelasticity of the supply of land should be contrasted with the relative elasticity of such property resources as warehouses and apartment buildings. These specific examples of the factor land are not fixed in total supply. A higher price will provide an incentive for entrepreneurs to construct and offer larger quantities of these resources. Similarly a decline in price will lead to existing facilities being denigrated or converted to other purposes. The same general reasoning applies to the total supply of labour. Within limits a higher wage will induce more workers to enter the labour force, and a lower wage will cause them to drop out of the labour force. Therefore the supplies of non-land factors will, in general, be upward sloping. A high price provides an incentive to offer more; a low price to offer less.

This does not apply to the total supply of land. Rent does not serve an incentive function here, because the total supply is fixed. It could, therefore, be eliminated without affecting the productive potential of the economy. For this reason rent is considered to be a surplus, that is a payment that is not necessary to ensure that land will be available to the economy as a whole.

Thus far, we have assumed that all units of land are of the same quality. Differences in quality and location, however, contribute to productivity differences. These differences will be reflected in differences in demand. *Ceteris paribus*, renters will pay more for a unit of land which is strategically located with respect to other factors of production and product markets.

Land also has alternative uses. Although land is a free gift of nature and has no production cost from the perspective of society as a whole, the rental payments of individual producers are costs. The total supply of land is available to society even if no rent is paid, but from the producer's perspective, land has alternative uses, and therefore payments have to be made by specific producers to attract land from those other uses. Such payments are costs, but at a societal level they represent a surplus, since there is no alternative use for them at that level.

10.4 Interest and the return to capital

The rate of interest is the price at which funds can be borrowed. As for other factors of production, the rate of interest is determined by the interaction of demand and supply.

In business, loans of funds are used primarily for investment in productive capacity. The marginal productivity theory of factor demand applies here too. Firms will demand the quantity of borrowed funds that equates the marginal revenue product of the investment financed by the funds with the interest payment charged for borrowing.

In order to determine whether the marginal revenue product (*MRP*) of a capital good is greater than the cost of financing it (i.e. whether the investment is profitable) we need to be able to compare money values received at different times. To make such comparisons a procedure called *discounting* is used. Two important points about discounting need to be noted. First, a sum of money received at a future date is worth less than the same sum received today. Second, the difference in values between money today and money in the future is smaller when the interest rate is higher. This is so, because money you have today can earn interest in the interim. If the annual interest rate is 10 per cent, your R1 will be worth R1.10 one year from now if you lend it to someone. If the annual interest rate is 15 per cent, then that same R1 would be worth R1.15 a year from now, and R1.10 a year from now would be worth less than one rand now.

How is the interest rate determined?

The two characteristics of discounting outlined above are all that is required to explain why the quantity of funds demanded declines when the interest rate rises, that is why the demand curve for funds is downward sloping.

As with other factors of production, the demand for borrowed funds is a derived demand, flowing from the desire to invest in capital goods. As the interest rate rises, future returns from an investment are worth less in today's terms. Consequently, a machine that appears to be a good investment when the rate of interest is 10 per cent may not be when the interest rate is 15 per cent. Therefore, as the interest rate on borrowing rises, more and more investments that previously looked profitable begin to look unprofitable. The demand for borrowing for investment purposes is therefore lower at higher rates of interest.

Similar guidelines apply to the supply side of the market – where the lenders are consumers, banks and other business firms. Loans will look better to lenders when the interest rates are higher, and thus the supply curve for loanable funds is upward sloping.

Figure 10.2 shows the downward sloping demand curve for loans and the upward sloping supply curve. The market determined interest rate is 10 per cent per annum.

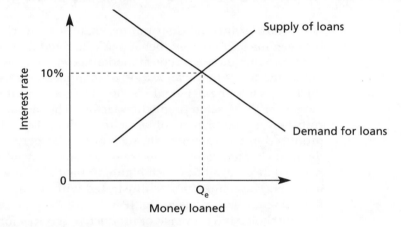

Fig. 10.2 Determination of the interest rate

10.5 Profit

Profit is the prime motivating force in a capitalist-type economy. As such, it influences both the level of resource utilisation and resource allocation. It is the expectation of making a profit that induces firms to innovate, and which in turn leads to investment, and hence to economic growth.

Profit is the return for entrepreneurial ability. It is the reward to the entrepreneur for initiating the productive process, for gathering together the factors of production required and for taking the risks associated with this process.

A part of the entrepreneur's return is a normal profit. This is the minimum return that is necessary to keep the entrepreneur in a specific line of production. By definition the normal profit is a cost. When a firm's total revenue covers all costs (explicit and implicit) and the normal profit, what remains of total revenue is economic profit.

The only certainty regarding the future is that it is always uncertain. Consequently, any entrepreneurial endeavour involves risks. Profits can be seen as a reward for assuming such risks.

Innovations resulting from research and development by the firm may lead to profits. However, there is also uncertainty associated with innovation. The profits from innovation will be temporary, since rival firms will imitate successful innovations and compete away economic profits.

The existence of monopoly is also a source of economic profits. Because of the protection offered by barriers to entry, a monopolist may enjoy economic profits almost indefinitely. The monopolist, behind the barriers to entry, can restrict output and thus increase the price of its product.

10.6 National income and the circular flow diagram

Our study of income distribution enables us to highlight the connection between the *microeconomic* behaviour of individual markets and the *macroeconomic* performance of a typical modern economy. The functional distribution of income refers to the allocation of total income between all factors of production, while the personal distribution tracks that same income to all the owners of those same production factors. The income to which we are referring here is national income, or the value of all the goods and services produced in the economy during a particular period of time, say a year. As the next chapter shows, there are several methods of measuring the value of national income, all of which highlight the links between factor and product markets. These links can be illustrated with the aid of the familiar circular flow diagram, as is done in Fig. 10.3.

Households offer a range of productive services for sale in what is known as factor markets, i.e. the labour market and the markets for land, buildings, financial capital and entrepreneurs – as shown in the middle part of Fig. 10.3. Firms buy or hire these services and reward their owners by paying them wages and salaries, rent, interest and dividends, and profit. These rewards constitute the national income of a country, and are shown in the top left corner of Fig. 10.3. Part of the national income – referred to in Fig. 10.3 as consumption expenditure – is spent on goods and services in so-called product markets, where firms offer their output for sale. The remaining components of national income, i.e. household savings and taxes, are channeled through the financial markets and the government sector, respectively. Household consumption expenditure becomes the revenue of firms which enables them to go back to the factor markets and continue to buy or hire productive services. Thus national income flows in a circular fashion from factor markets to product markets and back again to factor markets.

Figure 10.3 provides the link between the micro and macro sections of this book. In the sections that follow we shall be shifting our focus to an analysis of the determinants of *national* income and expenditure. But to do this in a meaningful way, it is important that we understand and appreciate the *microeconomic*

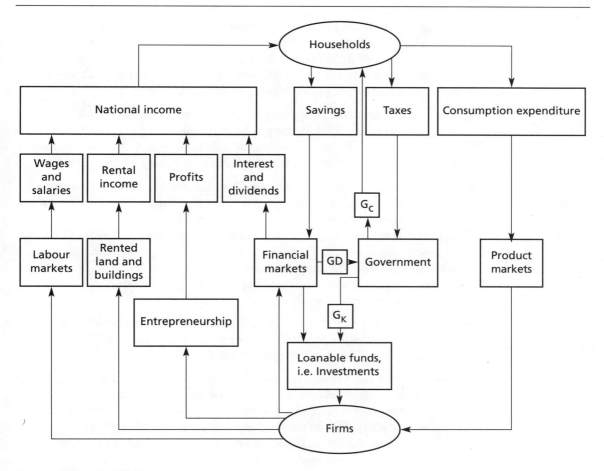

Fig. 10.3 The circular flow diagram

foundations on which a modern economy is built, and it is partly for this reason that we have been focusing here on the behaviour of individual consumers and producers and on the operation of individual product and factor markets.

Summary

- In this chapter we have focused on the functional distribution of income, or the allocation of the national income between the various factors of production. This is different from the personal distribution of income, which tells us very little about the original markets where incomes are earned.

- While wages constitute by far the largest component of national income, it is of interest to note that wage differentials tend to persist for very long periods. This is due to differences in both innate abilities and acquired abilities, i.e. those that are acquired through investment in human capital, e.g. formal and on-the-job education and training. Human capital formation is similar to any other form of investment – it entails an initial cost, e.g. the money spent and time taken educating oneself, which is then expected to yield a return in the form of additional income earned in the workplace.

- Wages also vary with race and sex, and in the South African context this may be largely ascribed to both voluntary acts and past policies of racial discrimination. The recent spate of affirmative action programmes is indeed an attempt to redress wage differentials caused by past policies.

- Both rent and interest are determined in the market-place by their respective demand and supply functions. In the case of rent, however, the supply of land and other natural resources is assumed to be fixed, so that the price, or rental rate, is effectively determined on the demand side. Likewise, interest is earned in the financial sector, where the price, or interest rate, is determined by the demand for loans (on the part of households and businesses) and by the corresponding supply (or the amounts saved by households and institutions).

- Profits are the rewards earned by individual entrepreneurs and by the owners of businesses for the risk they take in providing capital and performing the all-important entrepreneurial function.

- This study of the functional distribution of income, or the allocation of national income between the factors of production, provides the link between the micro and macroeconomic sections of this book – factor incomes are earned in factor markets and either spent in product markets or channeled to the financial sector and the government in the form of savings and taxes, respectively.

Questions for review

1. How can equilibrium wage differentials in the labour market be explained?

2. How is rent determined? Should rent control be permitted?

3. Examine the links between the factor markets and the product market.

PART IV

National income determination and aggregate demand and supply

In Part I of the book we introduced the concept of the circular flow diagram and emphasised the important role played by different individuals and markets in determining the allocation of resources in a modern economy. Parts II and III looked at the individuals and markets in greater detail focusing on the derivation of individual and market demand and supply functions and the determination of the relevant short- and long-run equilibria.

We now turn our attention to the *macroeconomic* aspects of a typical modern economy. Economics is all about demand and supply and in the chapters that follow we shall be chiefly concerned with the aggregate demand for goods and services, or *national expenditure*, and the aggregate supply, or *national income*. The aggregate demand and supply functions are no different from their microeconomic counterparts except that they represent the sum of *all* goods and services demanded and supplied in the country in a particular period of time. Aggregate demand and supply also determine the aggregate level of real output, employment and prices all of which are needed to measure and assess the macroeconomic performance of the economy. This is the subject of national income accounting and is discussed at some length in Chapter 11.

Chapter 12 introduces the Keynesian approach to the determination of national income while Chapter 13 discusses the determinants of aggregate demand and supply and the resultant establishment of the equilibrium price and output. Chapter 14 looks at some modern schools of macroeconomic thought focusing on two important features in the modern economy, i.e. expectations and wage and price contracts, both of which determine the speed with which the economy adjusts to changing circumstances.

CHAPTER 11

National income accounting

This chapter introduces several important macroeconomic aggregates that are widely used to measure the performance of an economy over time. The chapter itself falls into four parts. The first examines the concept of national income and production and outlines the most important measure of the performance of the economy – that of gross domestic product. The second section investigates the general approaches to measuring national production. The third section details several other important measures while the final section considers problems of omission and interpretation.

11.1 Gross domestic product (GDP)

Chapters 1 and 2 explored the economic behaviour of certain islanders in the Central Pacific basin. How did these islanders assess their economic quality of life?

From an economic point of view quality of life means the ability to consume goods and services both now and in the future. To our islanders these were mainly vegetables, fish and boats. In a similar way, economists measure the economic well-being of a country by measuring the value of all the final goods and services produced within a certain time period (e.g. every year or every quarter (three months)).

The most general of all the measures used to assess the economic well-being of a country is the so-called gross domestic product (GDP). For islanders in the Central Pacific the GDP was simply the value of all the food collected, fish caught and other services rendered for final consumption. For more modern economies the principle is the same – we measure the value of final goods and services produced.

> *Gross domestic product*. GDP is the value of final goods and services produced within the boundaries of a country within some specified time period.

CASE EXAMPLE

South Africa's Gross Domestic Product

In 1995 the South African GDP was R485 billion. While such a number does have its uses, and sounds very large, there are other, more useful ways of looking at GDP. The two most important are the rate of change in GDP – which is the rate of economic growth – and the level and rate of change of per capita GDP. Per capita GDP is the total value of GDP divided by the total number of people in the country. This is therefore a good measure of the economic quality of life and changes in this quality over time.

Figure 11.1 shows the rate of change of South African GDP and per capita GDP for the years between 1950 and 1995. These are shown in real values – in other words adjusted to remove the distortionary effects of inflation.

The figure illustrates two distinct phases in the recent economic history of South Africa.

The first is from the years following the end of the Second World War until 1980. The second starts towards the end of 1981 and is yet to end. From the end of the 1940s the South African economy had a time of unprecedented growth. Averaging more than 4 per cent over the whole period, growth rates of 5 per cent and 6 per cent were not uncommon. Since 1981 there has not been a single year where economic growth has reached 4 per cent. These poor economic performances have been reflected even more acutely in the economic quality of life. Per capita GDP increased in every year from 1950 to 1980 (in fact it has increased for most of this century). However, since 1980 economic standards of living have fallen in nearly every year. These have yet to show any promise of improving.

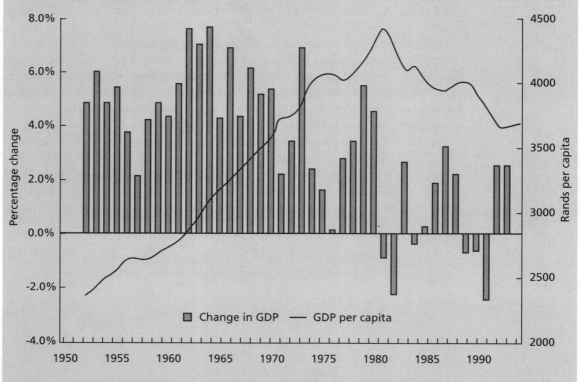

Fig. 11.1 Gross domestic product at 1985 prices – annual change and per capita

11.2 Measuring GDP

Having established what it is we want to measure we can now proceed to consider the actual measurement process. There are three ways in which the final value of production can be measured.

Expenditure approach

The most obvious way of measuring GDP is to measure actual expenditure on final goods and services. In terms of the flow diagrams presented in Chapter 3, we thus have to measure total expenditure by households or consumers (C), investment expenditure by the private sector (I), government consumption and capital expenditure (G) and total exports (X).

The only deduction which needs to be made is for imports. As the value of imported goods (M) is included in the first three items above we have to correct for this by deducting the value of imported goods. This results in a measure called net exports ($X - M$). As a result estimating GDP via total expenditure can be expressed by the following identity:

$$\text{Total expenditure} = C + I + G + (X - M) \qquad [11.1]$$

Income approach

As income is generated in the production of goods and services, GDP is also equal to the value of factors of production used in the production process. This income approach measures the left-hand side of the familiar circular flow. Here we measure the total return to all the owners of factors of production, that is, total remuneration in the form of wages, salaries, interest payments, dividends, rentals and profit. One problem associated with the income approach is the fact that its data source is the receiver of revenue – who may not necessarily have all the required information at his or her disposal!

Value added approach

Within the conceptual framework of the circular flow model, the value added approach to measuring GDP moves away from trying to measure the flows between households and firms. Rather it measures economic activity within firms themselves.

What is measured at the level of the firm is the value which is added by firms at each stage of the production process. Firms buy intermediate goods and services from other firms, add value to these goods and sell them either to consumers or other firms. Value added at the level of the individual firm is measured as the difference between total sales and purchases of intermediate goods from other firms.

Value added is therefore also the total value of factors of production purchased from households by firms (and the government). In consequence just as the total of all income generated is a measure of the value of production so too is the total of all value added.

> *Intermediate goods. Intermediate goods are semi-processed products which are purchased by one firm from another.*

> *Final goods. Final goods are those purchased by the end user. These include: all goods and services purchased by consumers; consumption expenditure by government; and investment expenditure by government and firms.*

In order to clarify the three approaches to measuring national production a simple example is presented in Table 11.1. The example is that of the making of a wire fence.

Table 11.1 Measurement of GDP – individual firm (rands)

	Purchase of semi-processed minerals/ metals used at each stage	Purchases of other inter- mediate goods and services = value added elsewhere	Purchases from households = value added within firm	Total sales value
Mine	0	20	50	70
Steel maker	70	30	20	120
Wire maker	120	20	30	170
Fence maker	170	40	10	220
Total		110	110	

There are four columns in the table. The first two show the value of purchases of intermediate goods and services used at each stage of the production process. The third column shows the value of purchases of production factors from house-holds, that is, the value added by each firm indicated on the left-hand side of Table 11.1. The fourth column gives the total sales value of each of these firms.

The first step in the making of a wire fence is to mine the necessary iron ore (and other raw materials). In this process the iron ore mine buys R20 worth of goods from other firms (e.g. electricity, water, hard hats, overalls, etc.). In addition it pays R50 to households (in the form of wages, interest, rent and profit) and by doing so generates R50 worth of value added. In this case value is added by the fact that iron ore is extracted out of the ground. The iron ore is then sold to a steel maker for R70. In turn the steel maker buys additional intermediate goods and services to the tune of R30 and adds value by pur-chasing production factors from households worth R20. After converting the ore into steel the steel maker sells the steel to the wire maker who adds value and sells wire to the firm responsible for making and erecting the fence. The fence is eventually sold to the end user for R220.

By making use of the expenditure approach we can see that the contribution to GDP is R220, i.e. this is the value of the final good sold to households. But what about the value added and income approaches? The total of column 3 shows only R110. What is missing from this is the total value which was added in the production of all the other intermediate goods listed in column 2. At the level of individual firms considered in Table 11.1, column 2 would not count as value added. However value has been added somewhere in the economy as a result of the production of these intermediate goods and services. Hence the value of national production is the total of the value added by the firms examined in the table as well as the value added in the making of the other intermediate goods. This adds up to a total of R220 and coincides with the expenditure method. As the income generated and value added are always identical the income method also totals to R220.

11.3 Other national accounting measures

Gross domestic product is the most fundamental of all national accounting measures. It is both possible and useful to develop a variety of other measures in addition to that of GDP. Together these form the family of national accounting measures.

Gross national product

The measure of gross national product (GNP) is very similar to that of GDP. It does however differ in one important respect. GDP measures the value of domestic production. In other words it measures the value of production within the boundaries of a country. GNP, on the other hand, measures the value of production of the citizens of the country, e.g. South Africans. The similarity between GDP and GNP is that most South Africans live in South Africa. The difference lies with South Africans who live outside the country and remit income back to South Africa, and with foreigners working in South Africa who remit income and profit out of South Africa.

The correct terminology for these financial transfers are *net foreign factor receipts* – the difference between funds remitted to South Africa and funds leaving the country. The most important component of these foreign factor flows are profits and dividends remitted by subsidiaries of foreign companies. Finally we are able to define GNP:

GNP = GDP – foreign factor payments + foreign factor receipts   [11.2]

Net national product

In national income accounting convention the inclusion of the word 'gross' indicates that the measure includes depreciation of existing capital stock. (Hence GDP, GNP, gross domestic fixed investment, etc., all include the value of depreciation.) It will be realised that the definition of GDP as the market value of final goods and services automatically includes depreciation. This happens because producers make provision for depreciation which is included in the sales price of their goods and services. At its simplest level depreciation can be seen as the value of machinery wearing out during the course of the production process. When producers plan their marketing strategies prices will include not only the returns to factors of production (wages, profits, etc.) but also the cost of new machinery needed to replace worn out machines.

GDP and GNP therefore include not only the returns to the owners of factors of production but also provisions for depreciation. Net national product (NNP) corrects for this by eliminating the provision for depreciation and gives, as a result, a better indication of the return to the owners of factors of production. This is generally considered a superior way of assessing changes in the economic quality of life. NNP can be defined by the following identity:

$$\text{NNP} = \text{GNP} - \text{depreciation} \qquad [11.3]$$

National income

National income (NI) is defined as the net return to the owners of factors of production. It is derived from NNP. There is one essential difference between NNP and NI. NNP is measured in terms of market prices, i.e. at prices at which goods and services are sold, less the provision for depreciation. National income, on the other hand, is the return to the owners of factors of production. What these owners have received is the costs of factors of production. As a result national income is measured in terms of factor cost.

There are two factors which can make a difference between market prices and factor cost:

- *Indirect business taxes*, e.g. customs and excise taxes, *ad valorem* taxes and VAT. These taxes are paid by the producer to the government. While they are part of market prices, they evidently do not form part of factor cost.
- *Subsidies to businesses*, e.g. the bread subsidy and subsidies given to marginal gold mines, farmers, educational institutions and health services. Subsidies work to reduce market prices. In consequence measuring the value of production through market prices understates the return to the owners of factors of production.

So NI can be calculated thus:

$$\text{NI} = \text{NNP} - \text{indirect business taxes} + \text{subsidies to firms} \qquad [11.4]$$

Personal income

Personal income is that part of the return to the owners of factors of production which is actually received by people. Four flows are important here.

- *Company tax.* While actually a return to the owners of factors of production, it is remitted to government directly from the firm.
- *Retained profits.* This increases the wealth of the owners of capital but their income is less.
- *Social security payments,* like unemployment insurance and worker's compensation, are paid by firms to government (or some other institution) on behalf of labour. Actual returns to labour are correspondingly less.
- *Transfer payments,* such as old-age pensions paid by government, government disability pensions, unemployment benefits and government housing subsidies. Many people receive income for which there has been no corresponding exchange of production factors. Such incomes are called transfer payments which must be added to the value of current production in order to arrive at personal income (PI).

This gives us:

$$PI = NI \ less$$

Company tax
Retained profits
Social security payments

plus

Transfer payments [11.5]

Personal disposable income

Personal disposable income (PDI) is that part of personal income which is finally available for spending and is therefore of importance to the business community. The difference between income which people receive and that which they can finally spend is determined by the taxes they have to pay. The two taxes paid out of personal income are income taxes and property taxes. The latter include wealth taxes and capital gains taxes. So PDI can be calculated as follows:

$$PDI = PI \ less$$

Income tax
Property taxes [11.6]

Today it could be argued that, with the existence of the PAYE tax system, income taxes are automatically deducted from PI. Most salaried people do not actually receive PI. Rather their taxes are paid on their behalf by their employers and they only receive their PDI. The reason income tax is deducted from PI is simply that national income accounting convention was established before the general introduction of PAYE as a means of collecting income taxes.

11.4 Problems with national income accounting

There are basically three problems associated with national income accounting that we would like to highlight. These are the problems of data reliability, omission and interpretation.

Data reliability

National income accounting is only as good as the information on which it is based. If the underlying information is inaccurate or the sampling techniques are flawed, it must follow that the estimates of national accounts will not reflect the realities of a country. Information can be less than accurate for a number of reasons. These include, among others, potential errors associated with the particular sampling method used, and the fact that when incomes are measured individuals and companies are often reluctant to disclose the full extent of their income.

Omission

It is possible that a wide variety of real economic activities will be omitted from reported national accounts. Where this happens it results in an understatement of the actual value of goods and services produced. Some of the more important omissions include:

- *Goods and services not for resale.* These include all activities undertaken by households that are not bought or sold, e.g. cleaning and cooking, DIY projects of all sorts and subsistence farming. Reporting agencies do make allowances for such activities when they are believed to be significant. Many countries in Africa, for example, attempt to measure the value of subsistence farming.
- *Informal sector activity.* Here goods and services are offered for resale but cannot be measured in the formal reporting process. The reason is that these activities are often illegal in the sense that informal operators do not as a rule register themselves or pay licensing fees and taxes. Examples include the buying and selling of clothes, motor repairs, drug peddling, the sale of pornographic material, prostitution and abortion. Disregarding the moral issues involved, countries like Columbia with its drug industry and Thailand with its sex industries have far larger GDPs than are reported in official statistics.

  Again, when informal activities are considered to be important, authorities do attempt to estimate their contribution to GDP. In South Africa, for example, the Reserve Bank increased the measured value of output by $5\frac{1}{2}$ per cent from the mid-1980s as a result of the growth of the informal sector since that time.

Interpretation

Even without the data problems outlined above, national income statistics should still not be interpreted at face value. There are essentially two problems of interpretation that must be guarded against at all times – comparison over time and comparison between two countries. Some of the more specific problems of interpretation are briefly discussed below.

- *Purpose of production.* National accounting statistics say nothing about the purpose of production. For example, millions of rands spent on housing will have a different impact on the quality of life than if those same millions of rands were spent on the production of weapons. The immediate change in GDP would be the same, however.
- *Social and environmental effects.* Countries which ignore the social and environmental consequences of production may end up with a high GDP but a poor quality of life. Examples include crime and violence, social alienation, traffic congestion, litter and air and river pollution. These 'external' effects are not normally included in the prices of goods and services and yet they often detract from the quality of life of the community at large.

    National income and prices are usually based on the so-called private or monetary costs and benefits and do not allow for the external effects of individual actions. When an oil company pollutes the air and inflicts an external cost on consumers the resultant damage goes unrecorded as no money would have changed hands in the process. If allowance could be made for such costs, aggregate supply and real national income would be smaller than their recorded values.
- *Distribution of income.* National income statistics are aggregate data and say nothing about the way in which incomes are distributed inside a country. Countries with high per capita GDPs do not necessarily compare favourably with low-income countries in which incomes are more evenly distributed. There are several ways of measuring the distribution of a country's income, e.g. the Lorenz curve and Gini coefficient. Both measures indicate the percentage of GDP accruing to given proportions of the country's population. On the whole, however, it is found that incomes are more evenly distributed in rich countries than in poor countries.

CASE EXAMPLE

GDP and the informal sector

The informal sector is made up of many small-scale enterprises and one-person operators who are actively involved in the buying and selling of basic consumer goods. In the absence of an adequate dole system, the informal sector has become an important source of survival in many developing countries. For our purpose here, however, we shall focus on what is perhaps its distinguishing feature, i.e. its illegal status – most informal operators do not usually comply with the licensing and health requirements laid down by local governments, and do not as a rule pay any taxes. They are therefore excluded from the official databases used in the compilation of a country's national accounts.

▶

The informal sector may be viewed as a distributional link – a kind of middle-person – between wage-earners and suppliers of goods and services in the formal sector. Incomes earned in the formal sector are thus spent on goods and services offered for sale by informal traders, who acquire them in the first instance from formal-sector suppliers. In this case it is only the mark-ups applied by informal traders that are excluded from the official estimate of national income – though they do feature in the estimate of national expenditure. This may be one reason why gross domestic expenditure (GDE) usually exceeds gross domestic product (GDP), and why this difference may provide an indication of the size of the informal sector. South Africa's GDE is almost always greater than its GDP, though this difference tends to vary quite significantly over time, e.g. from 1.9 per cent of GDP in 1990 to 5.4 per cent in 1994.

The latter difference must be viewed as a minimum estimate, as some of the profits and wages earned in the informal sector may well remain within that sector, adding value which is not captured in the official estimates.

Source: South African Reserve Bank, *Quarterly Bulletins*, 1990–94

SUMMARY

- National income accounting is an internationally agreed system of measuring the performance of the macro economy. Such accounting systems are important as they provide a means of determining how well the economy is performing over time and how it compares with other economies around the world.

- The most common measure for determining the performance of the economy is Gross Domestic Product (GDP). GDP is the value of all the final goods and services produced in the economy over some period of time, usually a year.

- GDP can be measured in three ways: first, by adding together all the incomes which have been generated through the production of goods and services – the income approach; second, by adding together all expenditures on final goods and services (with an adjustment for changes in inventories) – the expenditure approach; and third, by adding together all the value which is added to goods and services at each stage of the production process – the value added or output approach.

- Gross National Product (GNP) measures the performance of the nation, rather than that of the domestic economy. GNP is calculated by adding all foreign factor receipts to GDP and subtracting all foreign factor payments. Foreign factor receipts are essentially profits which are remitted to the domestic economy from investments in other countries. Foreign factor payments are largely profits remitted from the domestic economy to the owners of foreign investments in the domestic economy.

- Other important measures include National Income, Personal Income and Personal Disposable income.

- There are many reasons why national income accounting data may not accurately reflect the actual quality of life of people. One refers to the reliability of data – how it is collected, the sampling techniques used, and the extent to which allowance is made for inflationary price rises. Another refers to 'errors of omission'. Various types of productive activity may well be omitted from the data base. These could include goods and services that are produced but not offered for sale in the market place (subsistence farming being an important example), illegal goods and services, and the informal sector. There are also problems of interpretation. We do not know what the purpose of production is, or how it impacts on the environment, while national income data tells us little about the distribution of income.

Questions for review

1. What do we mean by the concept of GDP? Why is GDP important?

2. What is the difference between GDP and GNP?

3. Outline in detail the three ways in which we can measure the value of national production (i.e. GDP) and explain why each method should, at least in theory, give the same value of national production.

4. Examine each of the following economic events. Does it add to GDP? What would you call such a transaction?
   a) A firm buys a new truck to deliver finished goods.
   b) A firm buys its sales representative a new car.
   c) A sales representative buys his daughter a new car.
   d) An impoverished university student buys a very old car from a friend.
   e) An impoverished university student has his very old car stolen.
   f) An impoverished student is paid out by his insurance company.
   g) An impoverished student buys a very old car from a second-hand car dealer, but this time with a very new alarm.
   h) Government taxes people in order to pay the interest on public debt.
   i) A less than impoverished student buys shares in De Beers.
   j) The same student buys shares in a newly listed company.
   k) The father of a prospective university student invests in a 12-month, tax-free fixed deposit.

CHAPTER 12

The Keynesian model of national income determination

The Keynesian revolution did for macroeconomics what Galileo did for the flatness of the world. Both succeeded in turning conventional orthodoxy on its head. This chapter explores the fundamentals of one part of the Keynesian approach to macroeconomics, that which today is called the theory of national income determination.

The heart of any economy lies in its ability to produce goods and services. In Chapter 3 it was seen that the production of goods and services creates income which in turn allows for the consumption of goods and services. One of the major concerns of macroeconomics is this ability to produce and therefore the determination of national income. What Keynes did was to challenge the way economists thought about the process by which income was generated. The policies which emerged from Keynesian thinking came to be in direct contrast to the popular convention of the time.

EXHIBIT

John Maynard Keynes

John Maynard Keynes (1883–1946) was the most significant economist since Adam Smith, and one of the intellectual giants of the first half of the 20th century.

A man of many talents, Keynes studied mathematics at Cambridge, and made significant contributions to philosophy, culminating in his *Treatise on Probability* (1921), before turning his attention wholeheartedly to economics. At various times, he lectured at Cambridge, speculated on the stock market, wrote hundreds of newspaper and magazine articles, and acted as an advisor to numerous national and international institutions.

His denunciation of the Treaty of Versailles, articulated in *The Economic Consequences of the Peace* (1919), first propelled Keynes into the public eye, a position which he never relinquished. He was instrumental in the formation of the International Monetary Fund and World Bank, and in later life served as a patron of the arts in Britain.

However, Keynes is best known for his *General Theory of Employment, Interest and Money*, published in 1936, which rocked the foundations of orthodox economic theory, characterised by a sanguine belief in the power of Say's Law to ensure full employment. Keynes established the possibility of unemployment equilibrium, theorising that an economy could reach a state of rest at an output level below full employment.

▶

Exhibit continued

The conclusions of the *General Theory* rested on three key principles:

1. Keynes introduced the idea of money as an asset, rather than simply a medium of exchange, developing a monetary theory of the rate of interest, wherein the interest rate was determined by individuals' preferences for different classes of assets, rather than adjusting to equalise savings and investment. Rather, income and output would adjust to ensure the equality of savings and investment, thus creating the possibility of an unemployment equilibrium.
2. The multiplier, developed by Richard Kahn, a devoted Keynesian follower, allowed Keynes to quantify changes in output resulting from shifts in aggregate demand.
3. Keynes emphasised the pervasive role of uncertainty in economic affairs. This irreducible uncertainty, as opposed to quantifiable risk, would tend to result in a level of investment insufficient to maintain full employment, and prevent the labour market from clearing.

The *General Theory* is an incredibly rich, dense and often obscure work. The task of popularising Keynes fell to John Hicks, in his 1937 article, 'Mr Keynes and the Classics', which introduced IS–LM analysis (Keynes used no diagrams whatsoever). However, the desire to render Keynes explicable to a wider audience robbed the theory of much of its richness, portraying Keynesian theory as a special case of Classical theory in which unemployment was due to the assumption of labour market rigidities – hardly a revolutionary idea.

Alas, the dominance of Hicks' representation has, in large part, led to a neglect of Keynes' views, which is a great pity, since there is much of value in the voluminous work of this visionary polymath.

This chapter is important for two reasons: first, it outlines the essence of the debate between Keynes and his opponents and, second, it details the rudiments of the basic Keynesian model of national income determination.

12.1 Keynes and the Classics

The Great Depression started in 1929 and, for most of the now industrialised world, lasted until the onset of World War II. The Great Depression had a marked impact on many countries. In the United States of America, for example, GNP fell by 30 per cent between 1929 and 1933. Over the same period industrial production fell by 50 per cent, agricultural prices by 60 per cent and unemployment approached one third of the working population.

Prior to the Great Depression economists had paid little attention to macroeconomics – the study of the economy as an entity. Rather, interest lay more in the study of microeconomics. Unemployment, where it existed, was considered not only temporary in nature but also largely voluntary. Such a view extended even to unemployment which was the result of the Great Depression. Economists with such views would come to be called the Classical school.

Given the circumstances of the time, the so-called Classical view was simply not sustainable. The publication in 1936 of the *General Theory of Employment, Interest and Money* by John Maynard Keynes brought about a revolution in economic thinking and initiated a debate which continues even today.

The purpose of this section is to provide a broad outline of Keynes' ideas concerning the process by which national income is generated. The Keynesian vision is best understood within the context of the simplified version of the familiar circular flow model. This is done in Fig. 12.1 where the terminology has been changed to suit our purpose: the income flow is now called aggregate supply (in the sense that income is generated during the process of production) and the expenditure flow is referred to as aggregate expenditure.

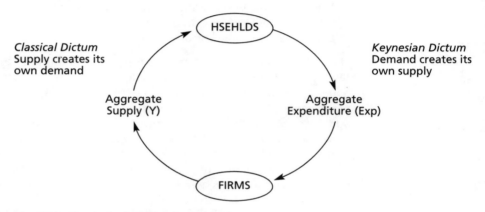

Fig. 12.1 Classical school vs the Keynesians

Now remember the mechanism by which the circular flow works: income is generated as goods and services are produced. In turn this income is used to purchase the goods and services which are produced. In such a process there are two interrelated questions which are really the basis of modern macroeconomics:

- Which of the two events happens first? Does production lead to demand for goods and services because people have income? Alternatively does production take place as a response to demand?
- If the government wanted to stimulate or slow down the economy, which would be the more responsive side of the circular flow to focus on and through the use of what kinds of policy?

As indicated in Fig. 12.1, the Classical school believes that the supply side, or the production process, is the most important feature of the macroeconomy. Supply creates its own demand in the sense that production gives rise to consumption. In today's world the policies which emerge from this basic premise are those that stimulate production, e.g. deregulation, privatisation and tax cuts.

Keynesians, on the other hand, argue that demand, especially from a policy point of view, is more important than supply. Emerging as it did during the Great Depression, the Keynesian view of the world suggests that the appropriate policy response to a recession is to focus on the demand side of the economy. If aggregate demand can be stimulated by means of appropriate policy interventions it can be expected that supply, income and employment will all follow suit. The policies that emerge under this view are changes in government expenditure and taxes, as well as changes in interest rates (and the consequent effect on investment and consumption).

12.2 The Keynesian model: aggregate supply

This and the next two sections lay out the basic structure of the Keynesian model of national income determination. The model is developed here in as simple a way as possible.

Assumptions

- Prices are constant. This is a simplifying assumption which is removed in the next chapter.
- Where people receive income most of it is spent on goods and services produced locally but some will leave the circular flow in the form of savings, taxes and expenditure on imports.
- Producers attempt to keep a constant level of stocks (inventories). Should stock levels fall, production will increase, and if they increase, production will be cut.
- Changes in investment, exports and government expenditure are assumed to be autonomous, that is, not related to changes in national income. This is also a simplifying assumption which is removed in subsequent chapters.

Aggregate supply

Turning first to the supply side of our analysis, it is evident from Fig. 12.1 that the Keynesian model has its roots in the idea of the circular flow. As such the model is developed by using the two most important variables in the circular flow – income and expenditure. Figure 12.2 indicates how these variables are used. Expenditure is presented along the vertical axis of the graph while income is measured on the horizontal axis.

The Keynesian model, developed as it was during the Great Depression, implicitly assumes that the economy is at less than full capacity. What this implicit assumption means is that if there is an increase in expenditure there are sufficient resources available to produce goods and services to satisfy the increased demand. Following from this the aggregate supply function is a line drawn at 45 degrees from the origin. At all points along this aggregate supply function income is equal to expenditure. For example, at levels of expenditure

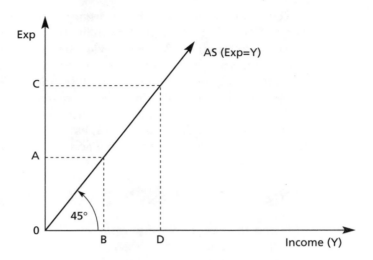

Fig. 12.2 Aggregate supply function in the Keynesian model

OA income is equal to OB. Should expenditure increase to OC, income will increase to OD. What is shown here is that increases in expenditure on goods and services will lead to increases in income as producers demand more factors of production and thereby generate more income.

12.3 The Keynesian model: aggregate expenditure

Following the convention established in Part I we separate aggregate expenditure into its four components – consumption, investment, government expenditure and net exports.

Consumption

While the model of national income determination is largely concerned with short term changes in the economy, it is useful to start with a view of consumption over the long term. We therefore first discuss the long-term consumption function and then develop the short-term consumption function.

Long-term consumption function

From the point of view of the national economy, consumption has two important features:

- Over the long term it is only possible to consume what is produced.
- Not all income is passed through the circular flow as expenditure. Some income leaves the circular flow as taxes, savings or expenditure on imports.

Using these two features as a starting point, the long-term consumption function is plotted on the same set of axes as used for the aggregate supply function. This is presented in Fig. 12.3.

The two features outlined above are evident. First, the long-term consumption function starts at the origin. In other words, if there is no income then there can be no expenditure. Second, the consumption function has a slope which is less than that of the aggregate supply function. What this shows is that not all income is spent in the form of consumption. Imagine a level of income equal to OA. Under the circumstances shown in the figure the resultant consumption expenditure would be an amount OB while an amount of CB would not be spent on locally made goods and services – CB is total withdrawals.

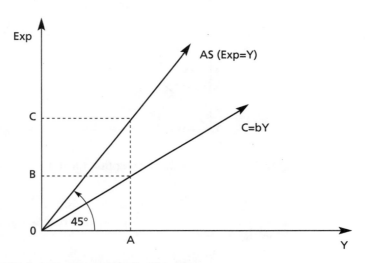

Fig. 12.3 The long-run consumption function

The slope of the consumption function is important. It is equal to the *marginal propensity to consume* (MPC). In Fig. 12.3 the MPC is shown by the symbol *b*. In other words *b* shows the proportion of income which is consumed.

The marginal propensity to consume. The MPC is defined as the change in consumption resulting from a small change in income. Mathematically this is shown as:

$$MPC = \frac{\Delta C}{\Delta Y}$$

Short-term consumption function

The major difference between long-term and short-term consumption is that in the short term it is possible that consumption expenditure can exceed total income. Should this occur the difference is financed from past savings.

The short-term consumption function is shown in Fig. 12.4. Here it is evident that the short-term consumption function starts above the origin. What this means is that when income is zero there will still be some consumption expenditure. This comes from past savings and is called autonomous expenditure. It is shown using the symbol *a*. As with the long-term consumption function the slope of the short-term consumption function is determined by the marginal propensity to consume and represented by the symbol *b*.

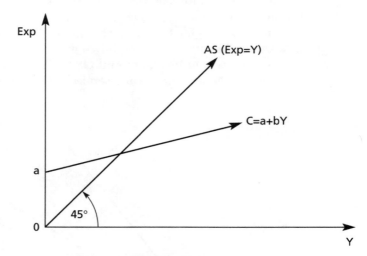

Fig. 12.4 The short-term consumption function

The relationship between savings and income is made clearer in Fig. 12.5. When income is equal to OA, expenditure is equal to OB. As this point also lies on the aggregate supply curve, it means at an income level of OA people are spending all of their income and there is no savings. At other points, OC for example, income is not equal to expenditure. At a level of income OC expenditure exceeds income. It is possible to fund OE expenditure from income but ED expenditure has to come from past savings. Likewise at points to the right of A income exceeds expenditure and there is positive savings.

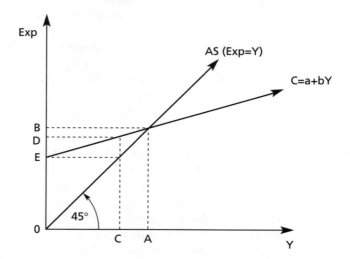

Fig. 12.5 The relationship between savings and income

Investment

True to the assumptions made in the previous section changes in private investment are not related to changes in national income. We simply assume that investment is determined autonomously outside the model, for example, by firms' expectations of the future. Graphically, as indicated in Fig. 12.6, this means that the investment function has a zero slope relative to the income axis. It is simply equal to OI.

Government expenditure

As with investment, government expenditure is assumed to be unrelated to changes in national income. As a result the government expenditure function is also shown as a horizontal line in Fig. 12.6, and the actual amount equals OG.

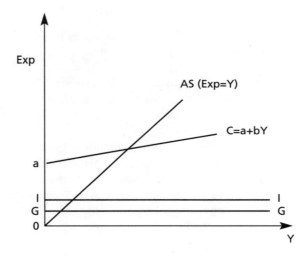

Fig. 12.6 Investment and government expenditure functions

Net exports

Net exports is the difference between exports and imports and is presented in Fig. 12.7. The export function, like government expenditure and investment, is a horizontal line. Unlike government expenditure and investment this is not the result of an assumption but simply due to the fact that exports depend on the incomes of other nations, not our own income. Should the income of our trading partners increase they will buy more goods, including our own goods, and if this happened the export function would shift upwards. In the example in Fig. 12.7, exports equal OX.

Imports, on the other hand, do depend on income inside the country. As income increases so expenditure increases on all goods, including imports. As a result there is a positive relationship between national income and imports.

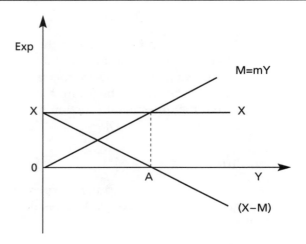

Fig. 12.7 Net export function

The extent of this relationship is given by the symbol m and is called the marginal propensity to import.

> *Marginal propensity to import. The marginal propensity to import is the extent to which imports change as a result of a small change in national income.*

Finally, the net export function is given as the difference between exports and imports. It is therefore a negatively sloped curve which equals total exports when income is zero (assuming there are no imports when income is zero) and declines as income increases. At a level of income OA, net exports are equal to zero (exports equal imports at this point). When income levels exceed OA, imports exceed exports and the net export function becomes negative.

Total aggregate expenditure

The next step is to bring together the various components of aggregate expenditure and show them as a single function. Remember that the aggregate expenditure function is defined as:

$$EXP = C + I + G + (X - M)$$

The final aggregate expenditure function is shown in Fig. 12.8. There are two features of the aggregate expenditure function which must be understood, namely, *the intersection point on the expenditure axis* and *the slope*.

Should national income be zero, the total expenditure which is taking place will consist of autonomous consumption expenditure (a), investment expenditure (I), government expenditure (G), and exports (X). These are summed to give the initial starting point of the aggregate expenditure function when national income is zero, i.e. $a + I + G + X$. In turn the slope is

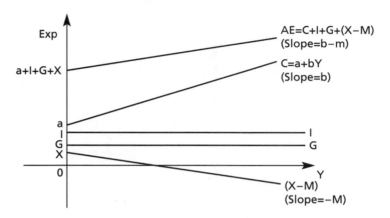

Fig. 12.8 Aggregate expenditure function

determined by the relationship between the various components of aggregate expenditure and income. We know that only consumption and imports are sensitive to changes in income. The slope of the consumption function is given by the marginal propensity to consume (b) and that of imports by the marginal propensity to import (m). As a result the slope of the aggregate expenditure function is the difference between the two ($b - m$).

12.4 Keynesian equilibrium

In the simple Keynesian model equilibrium occurs when aggregate expenditure is equal to aggregate supply. In other words, when expenditure is equal to income. In such a situation the economy is said to be in a 'steady state'. If there are no changes in the value of the components of aggregate expenditure then national income will maintain a constant value over time.

As with many other aspects of economics, one is unlikely ever to see an economy in equilibrium. What is more important, however, is that we understand what is likely to happen when the economy is not in equilibrium. In this model the mechanism which brings about equilibrium is the assumption which was made about how producers respond to changes in stock levels – in particular that they try to maintain a constant level of stocks.

The equilibrium mechanism is best understood with reference to Fig. 12.9. Here equilibrium occurs when national income is valued at OY_2. Aggregate expenditure is equal to aggregate supply – all goods and services produced are sold – and there are no forces to change income or expenditure. On the other hand, when national income is either above or below OY_2 the macro-economy is in disequilibrium and national income, or supply, will change.

Take the situation, for instance, when aggregate expenditure equals BY_1 and aggregate supply is AY_1 in Fig. 12.9; that is, expenditure exceeds supply. What will happen to the level of stocks? The distance AB is the extent to

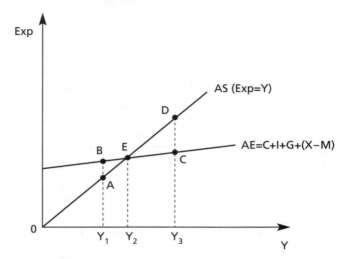

Fig. 12.9 Keynesian equilibrium

which stocks are being depleted. In other words, people are buying more than producers are making, and stocks are being depleted to meet this excess demand.

In turn, producers respond to the falling level of stocks by producing more goods and services. In order to do this, producers demand more factors of production and consequently generate more income. This can be seen in Fig. 12.9. As production increases, aggregate supply increases and producers move from A to E. This generates more income and national income increases from OY_1 to OY_2. The increase in national income raises consumption expenditure so that aggregate expenditure increases from B to E. Once equilibrium is reached there are no internal forces which can bring about any change in income or the equilibrium position.

The reverse of the above process will happen when income exceeds expenditure. As an exercise the reader might describe the forces that will operate when national income equals OY_3.

12.5 Equilibrium and Keynesian unemployment

An important implication of the model of national income determination is the Keynesian notion of unemployment. Classical economists prior to the Keynesian revolution considered unemployment either as frictional or voluntary. It was believed that involuntary unemployment would force down wages and return the labour market to full employment.

Keynes suggested an alternative explanation for unemployment. This explanation is illustrated in Fig. 12.10.

Figure 12.10 introduces a new concept into the Keynesian model – that of full capacity. Ignoring voluntary unemployment, Keynes assumed that the full capacity level of output represents a situation of *full employment*. The latter is shown as the full employment line (fe) and is similar to the production possibility frontier introduced in Part I. What this means is that national income is constrained at a level OY_2. It is only an increase in productive capacity and in the labour force that will allow income to increase beyond OY_2.

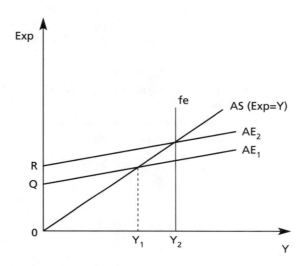

Fig. 12.10 Keynesian unemployment

Keynes explained unemployment in the following way. Imagine a situation as shown in Fig. 12.10 where aggregate expenditure generates national income worth OY_1. In this position the economy is in equilibrium and there are no forces operating to change the position. Yet at the same time national income is less than its full employment level. In this position there are idle factors of production – there is unemployment.

What Keynes therefore suggested was that when the economy found itself in a recession, especially a deep recession like the Great Depression, there were no forces for change that could bring it out of the recession. If these forces existed they appeared to be very weak.

Keynes suggested that, if an economy were in a major recession, aggregate demand type policies – increases in government expenditure, lower taxes and lower interest rate – were the only appropriate policy response. In Fig. 12.10 such a policy is illustrated by a shift in the aggregate expenditure function from AE_1 to AE_2, for example by raising government expenditure and investment by the distance QR. This would bring about the resultant increase in income from OY_1 to OY_2 and eradicate the existing unemployment.

12.6 The multiplier

Keynes' second major contribution to our understanding of the macroeconomy was that of the multiplier. The importance of the multiplier is illustrated in Fig. 12.11. Consider an economy with an initial aggregate expenditure function of AE_1 and national income of OY_1; that is, an initial equilibrium at point E. Suppose also that at point E private investment is zero. If we now introduce new investment equal to OI_1, the aggregate expenditure function will shift to AE_2. What is important here is the extent of the final change in national income. The figure is drawn to show that a relatively small change in aggregate expenditure can lead to a large change in national income. In the figure a relatively small change in investment, OI_1, can lead to an increase in national income, Y_1Y_2, which is much times greater than the initial change in investment.

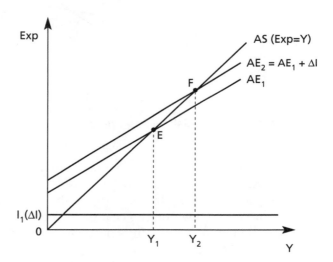

Fig. 12.11 The multiplier

The process by which such apparent good fortune is generated is best understood by a deeper examination of the initial disturbance introduced in Fig. 12.11 – the change in investment. Let us go further and imagine that this is a specific project – for example the expansion of Cape Town's harbour. The total cost of the project is assumed to be R1000m. The marginal propensity to consume is 90 per cent which is another way of saying that the marginal propensity to save (or tax) is 10 per cent. In addition the marginal propensity to import is 10 per cent. In other words when people receive income, 10 per cent will be saved and a further 10 per cent will be spent on imports, leaving 80 per cent to be spent in the domestic economy. In effect, every time someone receives income, 80 per cent of that income will be passed on to create income for somebody else.

This multiplier process is further illustrated in Table 12.1 which shows the initial change in investment and subsequent changes in income, consumption and withdrawals (i.e. savings and imports).

Table 12.1 The multiplier (rands)

ΔI = R1000m
MPS = 0.1
MPM = 0.1
MPW = $MPS + MPM$ = 0.2

	ΔI	ΔY	ΔC	ΔW
	1000m	1000m	800m	200m
		800m	640m	160m
		640m	512m	128m
		512m		
Totals	1000m	5000m	4000m	1000m

The project to expand Cape Town harbour started, as always, with a large press release surrounded by plates of food and a selection of local wines. Waiters, chefs and the wine trade all receive income for their goods and services. The planning and design stage sees increases in income for engineers, architects and ancillary staff. The construction phase sees large construction companies erecting the new breakwaters as the sea is pushed ever further back. When the project is complete the full R1000m has been passed into the hands of individual people. What do these people do with the money? From the stated assumptions they spend 80 per cent of it – R800m. What do they spend it on? On all the goods and services produced by firms.

In turn the firms selling these goods and services now find that their inventories are being depleted. Firms respond by producing more goods and services, thereby generating more income. Eventually the full R800m received by firms is passed on to the owners of factors of production as wages, interest, rent and profit. In turn these people respond in the same way as before – they spend 80 per cent of the income. In this case an amount of R640m.

The process described above repeats itself as people receive and spend proportionately less and less of the initial R1000m change in investment. What is important is that as the initial investment circulates through the economy, the income which is generated via the multiplier process far exceeds the initial investment. In this particular case the R1000m change in investment led to a R5000m change in national income. Consumption expenditure increased by R4000m and withdrawals totalled R1000m.

It is useful to note that total withdrawals equal the initial injection. An analogy to the multiplier process is the role that withdrawals play in the process.

The initial investment started the multiplier process operating and income began to increase. Along with the increase in income goes an increase in withdrawals. Only when an amount equal to the initial change in investment has leaked from the economy is the change in income stabilised.

The value of the multiplier

It is important to be able to calculate the final change in national income resulting from an initial increase in aggregate expenditure. The columns in Table 12.1 were calculated using the readily available formula for calculating the total of a geometric progression. The relevant formula is given as:

$$F = A/(1 - r) \tag{12.1}$$

where F is the final value, A the initial change and r is the value of the progression.

In the terminology we have been using F is the change in national income (ΔY), A is the initial change in investment (ΔI) and r is the proportion of income which is passed on in each round of the multiplier process. Substituting this terminology into the expression above yields:

$$\Delta Y = \Delta I/(1 - MPC) \qquad \text{for a closed economy} \tag{12.2}$$
$$\Delta Y = \Delta I/(1 - (MPC - MPM)) \quad \text{for an open economy} \tag{12.3}$$

where MPC and MPM stand for the marginal propensities to consume and import respectively.

It will be realised that the corresponding multipliers are simply:

$$1/(1 - MPC) \qquad \text{for a closed economy} \tag{12.4}$$
$$1/(1 - (MPC - MPM)) \qquad \text{for an open economy} \tag{12.5}$$

It is finally worth noting that small changes in the marginal propensities to consume and to import can lead to large changes in the value of the multiplier. Some examples are listed in Table 12.2 where it is evident that the multiplier varies significantly with small changes in the MPC and MPM.

Table 12.2 Multiplier values

MPC	MPM	Multiplier
0.9 (90%)	0	10
0.8 (80%)	0	5
0.6 (60%)	0	2.5
0.9 (90%)	0.05 (5%)	6.67
0.8 (80%)	0.1 (10%)	3.33
0.6 (60%)	0.2 (20%)	1.67

Knowledge of the size of these propensities, and hence of the multiplier, is important for policy purposes as they will ultimately determine the efficacy of macroeconomic policies aimed at changing the level of aggregate expenditure.

CASE EXAMPLE

Bidding for the Olympics – role of the multiplier

The city of Cape Town has made a formal bid to host the 2004 Olympics. While the success of this bid will depend on a host of largely unrelated factors, such as weather conditions and the security situation, it is of interest to consider what it might do for the local economy. One approach would be to look into the multiplier effects that the Olympics could have on Cape Town and the rest of the Western Cape region.

Following on from our discussion in the text, let the change in the region's income be given by:

$$Y = kI \left[a(1 - m^*) + (1 - a)\right]$$

where k is the ordinary Keynesian multiplier – as defined in the text; I is the initial autonomous investment in various Olympic facilities and related infrastructural services; a is the temporary or 'once-off' component of the initial investment, consisting of construction expenditure and the wages of temporary workers — assumed to fall away after a certain period; m^* is the initial import leakage, i.e. the proportion of construction expenditure (e.g. steel frames, tiles and state-of-the-art equipment) that is imported from outside *before* the multiplier process is set in motion; and $(1 - a)$ is the permanent proportion of the investment, consisting mostly of the wages of new workers employed on a permanent basis.

Now, it has been estimated that an amount of R9.8 billion will have to be invested to host the Olympics, of which about 28 per cent is of a permanent nature. Cape Town's Bid Committee has itself used a multiplier estimate of 1.6 in its own application to the International Olympic Committee. Thus, if the initial investment leakage is, say, 0.4, then the multiplied increase in Cape Town's income from the initial investment only, i.e. Y, comes to R11.2 billion.

Allowance should also be made for *additional* tourist spending that may result from hosting the Games itself, and from Games-related additions to the infrastructure. This is clearly a difficult call, even for armchair students of economics, but at least the formula is simple and similar to the one used in the text, i.e. $Y = k_t T$, where T represents the value of additional tourist expenditure, and k_t is the tourist multiplier.

It is important to note that some of the import leakages – given by m^* and by the multiplier itself – may well benefit the rest of the country. Investors, tourists and local residents in Cape Town are bound to import (additional) goods and services from regions in the rest of the country, thus setting in motion an export-led multiplier process in those regions.

It is possible also to convert these income multipliers into employment equivalents. All that is needed is an estimate of the number of jobs created per R1 million of investment or tourist expenditure. In the case of construction expenditure, for example, the rate of job creation is estimated at 30 jobs per R1 million, whence it follows that investment in the Olympic Games could give rise to the creation of an additional 336 000 jobs.

Source: (for the multiplier model itself) Black, P. A. and Saxby, G., 'Differential investment multipliers: An application of Weiss and Gooding', *South African Journal of Economics and Management Sciences*, Vol. 9, No. 4, 1996

12.7 Refinements to the model

For certain applications of this model, and for students who wish to continue their study of economics in later years, two additional refinements are needed to the model presented in this chapter. These are the inclusion of the withdrawals and injections into the model and the distinction between planned expenditure and actual expenditure.

Withdrawals and injections

At this stage it is useful to pause and consider what has been examined so far in this chapter. In the context of the circular flow model of Chapter 3 this chapter has examined the relationship between income and expenditure – what we have referred to before as the engine of the economy. We have also come to the conclusion that equilibrium occurs when income equals expenditure.

Doesn't all of this sound very familiar? Refer to Section 3.7 of Chapter 3. What are the conditions for equilibrium in this circular flow? Income equals expenditure, and withdrawals equal injections. The first part of this chapter has demonstrated the first condition. This section shows the latter.

Imagine a very simple economy in which the only component of aggregate expenditure is consumption. The relationship between income, consumption and savings in such a simple economy is shown in Fig. 12.12. The figure shows a single consumption function and the resultant savings function. It was shown earlier that consumption is dependent upon two factors – autonomous consumption, a in the equation, and that part of income which is consumed – the so-called induced consumption, bY in the equation. What is autonomous consumption? It is that part of consumption which is not influenced by current income. Where does it come from? From past savings. Hence if the consumption function starts at a then the savings function starts at $-a$. At a level of income Y_1 all income is being consumed. Hence there are no savings at Y_1. In consequence the savings function starts at $-a$, is zero at Y_1 and has a slope of $(1-b)$. The savings function also fulfils the two conditions for equilibrium. When income is equal to expenditure (in this case consumption) then withdrawals are equal to injections. As there are no injections, savings are zero when the economy is in equilibrium.

Now imagine a simple two-sector economy in which aggregate expenditure is made up of consumption and investment as shown in Fig. 12.13. As with the previous figure equilibrium occurs at Y_1 when consumption is the only component of aggregate expenditure. If we now add investment expenditure to consumption then total aggregate expenditure is AE_2 and equilibrium occurs at Y_2. At this level of income savings equal investment.

This form of analysis can be extended to show that in a multi-sector economy equilibrium occurs when withdrawals (savings plus taxes plus imports) equal injections (investment plus government expenditure plus exports).

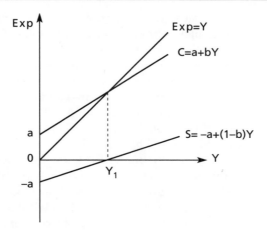

Fig. 12.12 The savings function

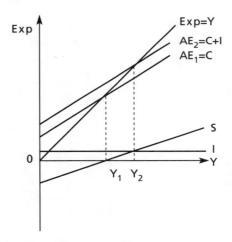

Fig. 12.13 The savings-investment equilibrium

Planned and actual expenditure

It is useful to understand the difference between planned levels of expenditure and actual levels of expenditure. (These are sometimes referred to as desired and actual levels or even *ex ante* and *ex post* – just to really confuse you). The obvious difference between planned and actual expenditure is that planned expenditure is what one sets out to accomplish and actual expenditure is what one ends up accomplishing. The most important component of this is investment expenditure.

Up to this point we have regarded investment as the expenditure used to increase the productive capacity of the economy. It is now necessary to change this definition slightly. Investment expenditure consists of both expenditure on productive capacity as well as any changes in stocks (inventories). It is changes in stocks that are important and that can make a substantial difference between planned and actual levels of expenditure.

Consistent with the assumption made at the beginning of this chapter, producers plan to maintain a certain level of stocks – we made the simplest of all assumptions that producers attempt to maintain a constant level of stocks. If producers do attempt to maintain a constant level of stocks then they plan to make no changes in stock levels. Should actual stock levels diverge from the planned amount then planned and actual expenditure is no longer equal.

Consider the case presented in Fig. 12.14. Equilibrium occurs when planned expenditure equals income; in other words where planned investment equals savings. This will happen when income is Y_1. Now imagine what happens when income is not Y_1, but Y_2. We know from our previous expenditure-income analysis that this is a situation in which expenditure exceeds income, or when stocks are being run down as aggregate expenditure exceeds production and therefore exceeds income. Point f in the figure is the level of planned investment – a certain level of capital expenditure and a constant stock level. But, as we know, because income is less than the equilibrium level of income, levels of stock must be falling. By how much are stocks falling? By an amount ef. The position at e show savings at Y_2 and also shows actual levels of investment. Producers now respond by increasing production. This results in an increase in income. Equilibrium occurs when stock levels are again constant. This can only happen at Y_1 when planned investment is equal to actual investment, and is equal to actual savings.

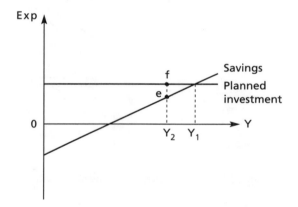

Fig. 12.14 Planned and actual investment

Summary

- Keynes brought about a revolution in macroeconomic thinking when he challenged the classical macroeconomic orthodoxy during the mid-1930s. His work started a debate which continues to this day.

- Prior to Keynes economists believed that the most important part of macroeconomics was the supply side of the economy. Little attention was paid to the flexibility of markets, particularly the labour market. The pervasive unemployment that followed the Great Depression suggested to Keynes that attention also had to be paid to the demand side of the economy.

- The Keynesian model of the macroeconomy is primarily concerned with the demand or expenditure side of the economy. It shows that when an economy is in a recession, increases in aggregate expenditure could help it to break out of that recession. But this Keynesian remedy only works well for an economy that finds itself in a recession, and is of little use to an economy experiencing full employment.

- The Keynesian model breaks aggregate expenditure up into private consumption expenditure, private investment expenditure, government expenditure, and net exports (exports less imports). The relationship between income and consumption is an important one: consumption in the short term partly depends on the current levels of income (induced consumption) and wealth, while it is also partly autonomous, being related to past savings.

- Equilibrium in the model occurs when income (i.e. the value of production) is equal to expenditure (i.e. the total amount spent on goods and services). If production exceeds expenditure, stock levels will increase. Producers will therefore cut production so that incomes will fall until the value of production equals the value of expenditure. If expenditure exceeds production, stocks will fall so that production and incomes will increase.

- Keynes was the first economist to develop a theory explaining the continued existence of unemployment, and also introduced the important concept of the multiplier.

- Keynes showed that total income can equal total expenditure even if the economy is operating below full capacity. At such an equilibrium level of income there will be unemployment and, in the absence of some exogenous change, it will continue to exist unabated. But governments have the power to bring about exogenous change and move the economy to full employment.

- Keynes' second major contribution was his theory of the multiplier: when an economy is operating at less than full employment, it is possible that a small change in expenditure can bring about an increase in total expenditure and income which is larger than the original change in expenditure.

Questions for review

1. Explain the components of the aggregate expenditure function. Which components determine the position of the function on the vertical axis and which determine the slope of the function?

2. What factors determine equilibrium in the simple Keynesian model?

3. What role do savings, planned investment and actual investment play in the equilibrium process?

4. What is the multiplier? How does it work? Why is it important? When does the multiplier not work?

5. What is the Keynesian explanation for unemployment?

CHAPTER 13

Aggregate demand and aggregate supply

The previous chapter examined the relationship between the various components of the demand side of the economy and how they contribute to the determination of national income. In order to expedite the development of the model an assumption of constant prices was made. In this chapter we drop this assumption and add prices to the basic Keynesian model.

Prices are a fact of life and cannot be ignored. This is a message which is of great relevance for students in Africa and those in southern Africa in particular. While many countries of the industrialised world have seen low or even stable levels of inflation since the early 1980s, the same cannot be said of countries in southern Africa.

We develop our macroeconomic model of demand and supply in several stages. First the impact of prices on aggregate expenditure is examined. From this the aggregate demand function is derived. We then examine the impact of prices on aggregate supply and derive both the short- and the long-run aggregate supply functions. Finally the demand and supply sides of the economy are brought together.

It is important to understand what is meant by prices in macroeconomics. Here we take prices to be the price level in the economy – the 'average' price of all goods and services. If prices change the price level changes. The rate of change in prices – the rate of inflation – is not the price level.

This is emphasised as it is often difficult for people who have lived with sustained inflation to distinguish between changes in prices – i.e. the change in the price level – and changes in the rate of inflation.

For the purposes of this chapter the best way to proceed is to make the assumption that there is no inflation – i.e. prices do not change consistently over time. Rather, if there is any change in the price level, then it is a once and for all change.

13.1 Aggregate expenditure and the price level

The major purpose of this section is to examine the relationship that exists between aggregate expenditure and the average price level. In particular our concern lies with what happens to aggregate expenditure if there is a sudden and unexpected change in the price level. What happens to an individual's spending or an economy's aggregate expenditure, if prices suddenly and unexpectedly increase or decrease?

There are a number of reasons why a change in the price level can bring about a change in aggregate expenditure. Some of the changes in aggregate expenditure are permanent while others are only of a short-term nature.

It is useful to distinguish between three ways in which a change in the average price level could bring about changes in the level of aggregate expenditure. These are referred to as the income effect, the wealth effect and the balance of payments effect.

Income effect

Price changes can have short-term effects on income and therefore on aggregate expenditure. For this to happen it is necessary that changes in income lag behind price changes. Imagine a situation in which producers suddenly increase their prices. The immediate effect is that real incomes fall and aggregate expenditure falls. It will be realised that the income effect falls away as soon as producers pay out their higher revenues to themselves and other shareholders, and perhaps also to their workers. Once this happens incomes will increase, as will aggregate expenditure.

Wealth effect

The most important way in which a change in the price level changes aggregate expenditure is through a change in wealth – the so-called wealth effect. It is argued that a change in prices leads to a change in wealth which leads directly to a change in consumption expenditure. It is an inverse relationship so that if the price level rises, wealth decreases and expenditure falls. Similarly, if prices fall both wealth and expenditure will increase.

The inverse relationship between prices and expenditure through the wealth effect can be explained by the simple fact that wealthy people tend to spend more than poor people. A more thorough explanation is given in the accompanying box on the *permanent income hypothesis*.

A change in the price level affects wealth primarily through its impact on the value of certain financial assets. As will be explained in Chapter 15, there are many types of financial assets – money, chequing accounts, stocks, bonds, etc. The financial assets that we are concerned with here are those for which there are no corresponding liabilities. These are called *net financial assets*. In essence net financial assets include money, chequing accounts not in overdraft, savings accounts and certain types of fixed deposits.

What happens to the value of net financial assets when there is a change in the price level? Quite simply, the value of these assets change in the reverse direction. An easy way of understanding this is to consider what happens to the purchasing power of money when the price level changes. When prices of goods and services fall the purchasing power of the money that people are holding increases. In consequence people feel wealthier and spend more. Likewise a price increase erodes the purchasing power of money. People feel poorer and spend less.

The permanent income hypothesis

The Keynesian consumption function posits a stable relationship between consumption and current income, with average and marginal propensities to consume assumed to be roughly constant. These relationships form the basis of the multiplier and thus of Keynesian fine-tuning.

However, this simple theory of consumption has been criticised on the grounds that it lacks adequate microeconomic foundations (i.e. it represents a macroeconomic theory which is not based on the behaviour of rational individuals at a microeconomic level). Furthermore, the results of numerous empirical studies were found to be at variance with predictions of Keynesian theory; in particular, average propensities to consume were found to vary inversely with disposable income.

Such deficiencies led Milton Friedman to propound the permanent income hypothesis (PIH) in his 1957 work, *A Theory of the Consumption Function*. He argued that individuals would base their consumption decisions not on current income, but rather on expected income over a suitably long period, if not a lifetime (hence *permanent* income).

Households with identical permanent incomes and tastes would consume identical bundles of goods and services, regardless of their levels of current income. If individuals experienced an increase in current income, this would only affect consumption plans to the extent that permanent income was raised. If the increase in current income is expected to be temporary, the effect on permanent income, and hence consumption, would be slight.

The PIH is difficult to test empirically, since permanent income, which is a function of individuals' expectations of future earnings, cannot be observed. However, the theory possesses inherent plausibility, and is able to explain certain empirical phenomena better than the Keynesian alternative.

The theory holds potentially serious implications for the effectiveness of discretionary fiscal policy. For example, a temporary tax rebate may not boost aggregate demand in the manner predicted by Keynesian multiplier analysis, since individuals experience a relatively small change in permanent income.

However, many economists would argue that the PIH does not imply such far-reaching results. Such theorists assert that a distinction must be drawn between *consumption expenditure* and *consumption*. In the case of a durable good, individuals consume the benefits of that good over its entire lifetime. If the PIH applied to consumption so defined, rather than the more conventional consumption expenditure, then in the case of the tax rebate considered above, individuals may use the windfall to purchase durable goods, thereby increasing current consumption expenditure without significantly increasing current consumption. If such an interpretation were correct, the tax rebate would have the desired stimulatory effect on aggregate demand.

Balance of payments effect

It is possible that changes in the domestic price level can have long-term effects on the balance of payments and in consequence on aggregate expenditure.

Imagine a situation where prices inside a country suddenly fall. There are two immediate effects on the country's position in international trade. The first is that the price of the country's exports will decline on world markets. More exports will be sold and aggregate expenditure will increase. The second is that as domestic prices have fallen, the relative price of imports have increased and imports will fall. As local people are now buying more domestically produced goods and services, aggregate expenditure increases.

In summary, an increase in prices will result in falling aggregate expenditure as imports increase and exports decline, while a fall in prices causes net exports and therefore aggregate expenditure to increase.

It should be realised that the changes described above are only short term in nature. Reference to the determination of exchange rates in Chapter 3 will show that the described changes will lead to changes in the exchange rate. If the changes in exchange rate exactly offset the changes in domestic prices, there will be no long-term balance of payments effect. Long-term balance of payments effects will happen only if the price changes are permanently larger than the resultant changes in the exchange rate. We shall return to this issue in Chapter 18.

13.2 The aggregate demand curve

In the previous section we showed that there is an inverse relationship between the average price level and aggregate expenditure. What this means is that aggregate expenditure will decline when prices increase, and vice versa.

The inverse relationship between price and aggregate expenditure is further explained with the aid of Fig. 13.1. Imagine an economy with an aggregate expenditure function given by AE_1. The economy is in equilibrium at point A and national income is equal to OY_3. Imagine further that the current price level is OP_1, as indicated by the bracketed term next to AE_1. In consequence point A in the top panel of Fig. 13.1 corresponds with point B in the bottom panel of the same figure.

Now there is a sudden and unexpected increase in the price level, from OP_1 to OP_2 in the bottom panel. In consequence aggregate expenditure falls and the aggregate expenditure function moves to AE_2 (P_2). Producers respond by making fewer goods and services and national income falls. Equilibrium eventually occurs at point C where national income equals OY_2. Point C corresponds with point D in the bottom panel.

Should prices increase again to, say OP_3, the aggregate expenditure function will fall to AE_3 (P_3), income will fall to OY_1 and equilibrium will occur at point E. Again points E and F correspond.

What we have derived here is the aggregate demand curve. All points along a particular aggregate demand curve show the relationship that exists between aggregate expenditure and the average price level. There is an inverse relationship between the price level and aggregate expenditure, and therefore between the price level and the resultant level of national income.

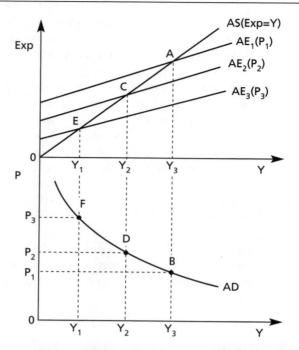

Fig. 13.1 Aggregate expenditure and aggregate demand

Shifts in the aggregate demand curve

As the aggregate demand curve depends entirely on aggregate expenditure, any change in the components of aggregate expenditure will bring about changes in the position of the aggregate demand curve. For example, should investment expenditure or net exports increase the aggregate demand curve will shift to the right. Similarly if there is a fall in government expenditure or an increase in taxes the aggregate demand curve will shift to the left.

This is illustrated in Fig. 13.2 where the initial equilibrium occurs at point E on the aggregate demand curve AD_1, with a price level OP_1 and national income equal to OY_1. Now there is an improvement in business confidence which leads to an increase in investment spending. The consequence is that the aggregate demand curve shifts to AD_2 and, if price remains unchanged at OP_1, the equilibrium moves to point F and national income increases to OY_2.

Slope of the aggregate demand curve

The slope of the aggregate demand curve depends on the strength of the wealth and balance of payments effects resulting from a change in the price level. If these effects are very strong the aggregate demand curve will be relatively flat. This is illustrated by AD_{st} in Fig. 13.3. If these effects are weak, on the other hand, the aggregate demand curve will be relatively steep. This is represented by AD_{lt} in Fig. 13.3.

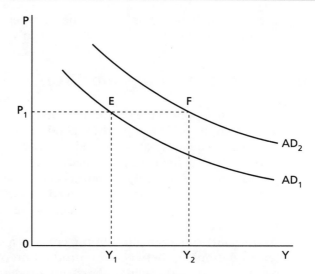

Fig. 13.2 Shifts in the aggregate demand function

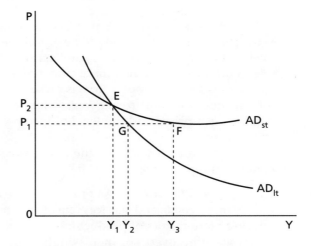

Fig. 13.3 The slope of the aggregate demand curve

Of equal importance, especially for countries with open economies, is the speed of adjustment in aggregate demand following a price change. This is also illustrated in Fig. 13.3. Let the economy be in equilibrium at point E with price level OP_2 and income equal to OY_1. At this point prices now fall to OP_1. The immediate effect is that the country is now more competitive internationally than before so that net exports increase and national income increases to OY_3. The economy thus moves along its short-term aggregate demand curve to point F. However, as the exchange rate begins to appreciate because of the increase in net exports, international competitiveness will decline and income will fall to OY_2. The economy thus moves to point G on its long-run aggregate demand function. In this process the short-term effects on aggregate expenditure of a price change are dissipated and only the long-run effects remain.

13.3 Aggregate supply in the short run

Aggregate supply is the counterpart of aggregate demand. Aggregate supply focuses on the ability to produce goods and services and on the relationship between the quantity of goods and services produced and the price level.

While there have been considerable differences of opinion between Keynesian and Classical economists about the shape of the aggregate supply curve, these have been largely resolved today. A contemporary understanding of aggregate supply demands an examination of aggregate supply in the short run and in the long run.

The short-run aggregate supply curve is a device which shows the short-term relationship between the production of goods and services and the price level. Any particular short-run aggregate supply curve is drawn on the assumption that the costs of production factors remain unchanged. In other words the costs of labour, capital equipment and imported materials remain unchanged.

What this does *not* mean is that the unit cost of output remains unchanged. In the short run there is likely to be a positive relationship between the price level and the quantity of goods and services that producers are willing and able to produce even when input prices remain unchanged. An example of a short-run aggregate supply curve is presented in Fig. 13.4. This illustrates that not only does the short-run aggregate supply curve depict a positive relationship between prices and the level of income, but it also becomes steeper as prices increase.

There are three reasons for the positively sloped nature of the short-run aggregate supply curve:

- *Less productive resources.* As prices increase and producers attempt to produce more goods and services one of the ways in which they respond is by hiring more factors of production. As more and more of the available factors are employed so, increasingly, less productive ones are used. In practice this may mean that fewer suitable workers have to be employed and older machinery and buildings brought into production. As productivity falls so unit cost of production increases.
- *Overtime.* As factories begin to approach full capacity producers may institute overtime work and run their machines for longer periods of time. Overtime work costs more than regular labour time so that unit costs will increase.
- *Diminishing marginal returns.* One of the conclusions of the theory of the firm in microeconomics is that as more and more of a variable factor like labour is added to a fixed factor like machinery, productivity will fall and unit cost of production will increase.

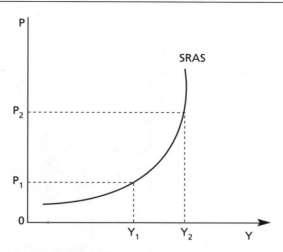

Fig. 13.4 The short-run aggregate supply curve

These effects are illustrated in Fig. 13.4. The economy starts in a position where the price level is OP_1 and income equals OY_1. Price now rises to OP_2. Producers, seeing an opportunity to make increased profits, begin to increase output. If firms had started in positions of less than full capacity then it is a relatively simple matter to scale up to full capacity by employing more workers and using idle plant. From the law of diminishing marginal returns there will be some small decrease in productivity. Hence the increase in output is not directly proportional to the increase in prices. Once full capacity is reached, overtime will start, as well as the employment of less productive labour and older machinery. In consequence output increases but at a decreasing rate. The value of output eventually reaches OY_2.

Shifts in the short-run aggregate supply curve

A short-run aggregate supply curve is drawn for constant input prices. It therefore follows that the short-run aggregate supply curve will shift when input prices change. Such changes are illustrated in Fig. 13.5.

If the cost of the factors of production were to rise, with no change in the price level, producers would supply fewer goods and services. This is shown in Fig. 13.5 as an inward shift in the short-run aggregate supply curve from $SRAS_1$ to $SRAS_2$. If price remains unchanged at OP_1, income will fall from OY_2 to OY_1. Similarly, if the cost of production falls producers could make more profit by producing more goods and services. The short-run aggregate supply curve thus moves to $SRAS_3$ and, at a price level of OP_1, income increases to OY_3.

Changes in production costs occur on a daily basis in most countries. Some of the more important cost items are briefly discussed below.

● *Labour costs.* The cost of labour is the most obvious cost of production and often the most publicised. For labour-intensive firms like clothing and food production labour costs are important. More capital-intensive indus-

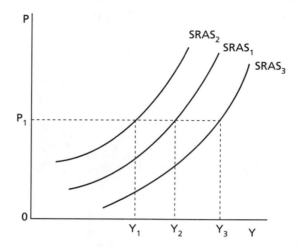

Fig. 13.5 Shifts in the short-run aggregate supply curve

tries, like steel and energy producers, are less sensitive to changes in the cost of labour.

One reason that labour costs are singled out is the fact that wage increases may often lag behind price increases. Where wages are covered by some form of contractual agreement – and most are, even if these are implicit contracts – they tend to lag behind price changes. An unexpected fall in price will cause production and job cuts rather than wage cuts. Only at the next round of wage negotiations might wages be cut which would lead to increased employment and output. Similarly, if prices suddenly increase and wages are constrained by some contractual agreement, producers will respond by producing more goods and services.

- *The cost of imports.* In many small open economies imported goods are a critical part of production. For such countries the most important imports are semi-processed goods (vehicle components, computer parts) or capital goods (machinery). In South Africa, for example, where the sum of imports and exports exceeds 60 per cent of GDP, the bulk of imports are either semi-processed or capital goods. This is important because changes in the cost of imported goods will change the position of the short-run aggregate supply curve.

Many factors can affect the cost of imports. These include:

1. *Exogenous changes in the price of imports.* The emergence of cartels, such as the famous OPEC oil cartel, can lead to increases in import prices. The same would occur when frost destroys the Brazilian coffee crop. Similarly, technological innovation can reduce the cost of imports.
2. *The exchange rate.* Changes in the exchange rate impact directly on the cost of imports and therefore on the position of the short-run aggregate supply curve. Should the domestic currency depreciate, production costs will increase and the short-run aggregate supply curve will shift

inwards, as was illustrated in Fig. 13.5. Alternatively an appreciation of the currency will cause the short-run aggregate supply curve to move to the right.

3. *Import duties.* Any change in import tariffs or customs and excise duties will change the cost of production and change the position of the short-run aggregate supply curve.

- *The cost of domestically produced inputs.* There are many factors which can change the cost of domestically produced inputs. In Africa the most common of these are droughts and floods. In times of droughts less food can be produced and the cost of food increases accordingly. But so too does the price of leather, dyes, cotton, and other agricultural inputs used in production. The result is a leftward shift in the short-run aggregate supply curve.

13.4 Macroeconomic equilibrium in the short run

This section brings together the aggregate demand and short-run aggregate supply curves and also investigates changes in the equilibrium when prices are allowed to vary.

A situation of short-run equilibrium is shown in Fig. 13.6 where the economy finds itself at point A. Given the aggregate demand and short-run aggregate supply curves presented in the figure, the price level, OP_1, equates demand and supply and generates income to the value of OY_2.

To further illustrate why OP_1 and OY_2 represent a unique equilibrium position imagine that the price level is OP_2 and not OP_1. If this were the case the level of income will be OY_3. This would be the result of producers responding to price signals and producing goods and services to the value of OY_3. Aggregate expenditure on the other hand only equals OY_1. In consequence firms are producing more goods and services than are being sold. What firms

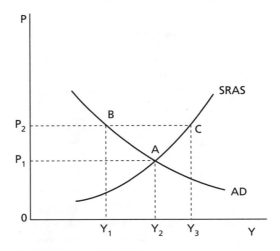

Fig. 13.6 Short-run macroeconomic equilibrium

experience are increases in their stock levels, and they therefore respond in two ways. They cut production so that income falls to OY_2 – this is the same response as in the fixed price model of the previous chapter. They also cut prices. As prices fall aggregate expenditure increases and the value of goods and services sold increases to OY_2. In consequence there has been an automatic adjustment of the economy to an initial disequilibrium situation through changes in prices and incomes.

Changes in equilibrium

Any factor which changes the position of either the aggregate demand or the short-run aggregate supply curves will lead to a change in the short-run equilibrium. Some examples of these changes are illustrated in Fig. 13.7.

Panel (a) of the figure shows the result of a change in aggregate demand. Several factors could account for such a change. One example would be an increase in investment expenditure as a result of improvements in business confidence. This would cause a rightward shift in the aggregate demand curve from AD_1 to AD_2. The increased demand for goods and services leads initially to falling stock levels. Producers respond by increasing output and raising prices. The economy eventually moves to a new equilibrium position at point F where price equals OP_2 and income has increased to OY_2. It is important to note that the increase in aggregate demand has led to increases in both prices and incomes.

Panel (b) illustrates an increase in aggregate supply. This could be the result of improvements in productivity, technological advancement or better weather conditions. As the cost of production falls producers lower prices and therefore produce and sell more goods and services. The economy moves to a new equilibrium position at point F where price equals OP_1 and income OY_2. In this case the increase in aggregate supply has led to an increase in income but to a decrease in the price level.

Short-run equilibrium and the multiplier

As was pointed out in the previous chapter, the multiplier is one of the important features of the basic Keynesian model. This section explores what happens to the multiplier when price changes are taken into account. Figure 13.8 illustrates the point.

The top panel of Fig. 13.8 illustrates the basic Keynesian model. In this model an increase in aggregate expenditure leads to an increase in national income. The increase in income is larger than the initial change in expenditure as a result of the operation of the multiplier. The change in aggregate expenditure from OA to OB results in an increase in income from OY_1 to OY_3.

The bottom panel of the figure shows the corresponding change in aggregate demand. The change in aggregate expenditure indicated in the top panel results in the aggregate demand curve moving from AD_1 to AD_2. However, the increase in income from OY_1 to OY_3 would occur only if there was no change in

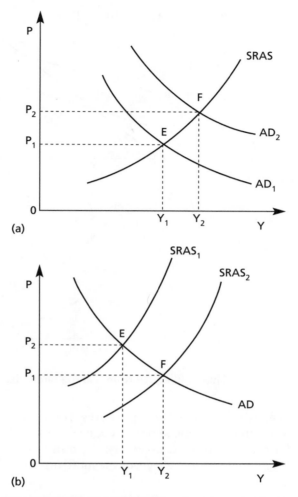

Fig. 13.7 Changes in equilibrium. (a) Increase in aggregate demand; (b) Increase in aggregate supply

the price level. Such a result would only occur if the short-run aggregate supply curve was horizontal over the relevant range. If the short-run aggregate supply curve has a positive slope, as indeed it has, a price increase will be necessary to induce suppliers to produce more goods and services. The result of such a price increase is that it reduces aggregate demand. In consequence we move from point A on aggregate demand curve AD_2 to point B on the same curve. The size of the multiplier has been reduced as a result of the increase in the price level. The final increase in income is therefore smaller, i.e. from OY_1 to OY_2.

Keeping in mind the effect of a price change on the AE curve (*viz* section 13.2 above), the reader might indicate the equivalent to point B in the top panel of Figure 13.8.

It will be realised that the size of the multiplier is now dependent not only on the slope of the aggregate expenditure curve but also on the slope of the

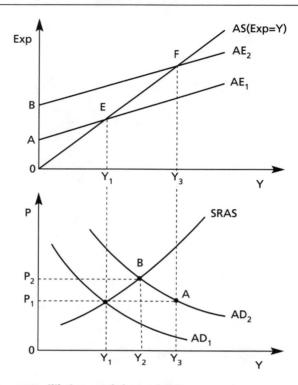

Fig. 13.8 Short-run equilibrium and the multiplier

short-run aggregate supply curve. For any given aggregate expenditure curve, the steeper is the short-run aggregate supply curve, the smaller will be the final multiplier. Conversely, the multiplier will be greater the flatter is the aggregate supply curve, or the more price elastic is aggregate supply.

13.5 Aggregate supply in the long run

The final step in developing our macroeconomic model is the derivation of the long-run aggregate supply curve. In order to do this we shall re-examine the short-run aggregate supply curve over a longer period of time when the costs of production factors are allowed to vary.

Short-run aggregate supply curve in the long run

The previous section presented the short-run aggregate supply curve as an upward sloping function. Each curve was drawn on the assumption that pro-duction costs were fixed. It is important to note that the positive relationship between the price level and supply is only a short-term one. The relationship shown along that short-run curve is unlikely to hold over a longer time period. Figure 13.9 illustrates the principle.

Imagine an economy in equilibrium at point A in the figure with price equal to OP_1 and income OY_1. Further, this is assumed to be a situation of full employment, i.e. everyone who wants a job at the going wage rate is fortunate enough to have one. Now there is a sudden increase in aggregate demand, resulting from an increase in government expenditure, for example. The aggregate demand curve shifts from AD_1 to AD_2, thus raising the average price level to OP_2 and income to OY_2.

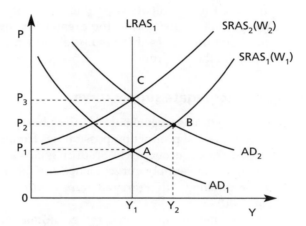

Fig. 13.9 The long-run aggregate supply curve

In order to understand what happens next it is important to realise what has happened in the labour market. The increase in the price level has reduced the purchasing power of wages – the real wage has fallen. People respond to this either by reducing their willingness to work (e.g. lower on-the-job effort, turning down of overtime and weekend work) or by leaving the job market altogether. Now producers face a labour supply problem, and the only solution is to raise wages. As soon as wages increase, the short-run aggregate supply curve moves to the left, from $SRAS_1$ (W_1) to $SRAS_2$ (W_2) in Fig. 13.9. The result is that prices increase yet again and income falls back to OY_1.

Should aggregate demand again shift, the economy will again go through the same motions. Each time the economy will return to the full employment level of national income at OY_1. What this means therefore is that the long-run level of national income is determined by the level of full employment. Full employment of factors implies that factors are used at their *natural* rate (see section 19.1).

As it is the ability to produce and not the price level which determines long-run aggregate supply, the long-run aggregate supply curve is vertical and linear. At some point in time the ability to produce might be seen as $LRAS_1$ in Fig. 13.9. Here the value of real national income is OY_1.

Long-run aggregate supply is reached when all markets are in equilibrium. Consider the situation in which some prices undergo change – a drought causing the price of food to rise, an earthquake forcing up the price of build-ing materials, or technological advances bringing down the prices of televisions and computers. The initial changes to these economic shocks are felt in the most immediate markets – in the case of a drought the markets most immediately impacted include food, fertiliser, water, seed and tractors. Eventually the changes work their way through to other markets – farmers leave the land and force down urban wages, the price of clothes fall as con-sumers are forced to meet the higher food prices, etc. In the long run the constraint on aggregate supply is the ability to produce goods and services. The greater is this ability the greater is long-run aggregate supply. Under these circumstances there is no relationship between prices and aggregate supply in the long run.

Shifts in the long-run aggregate supply curve

The long-run aggregate supply curve has in fact already been encountered in the form of the production possibilities frontier. Just as the PPF represents the capacity of the economy to produce goods and services, so too does the long-run aggregate supply curve. Hence any factor which moves the PPF will also move the long-run aggregate supply curve. Such changes are illustrated in Fig. 13.10.

In the face of an unexpected economic shock – drought, flood, etc. – the ability to produce will be compromised and national income will fall. The long-run aggregate supply will reflect this by moving left to $LRAS_2$. Alternatively, should there be an economic windfall – the discovery of new mineral or oil deposits, technological advances, increases in productivity, etc. – national income will increase and the aggregate supply curve will move right to $LRAS_3$.

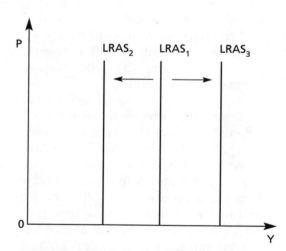

Fig. 13.10 Movements of the long-run aggregate supply curve

13.6 Long-run equilibrium and the speed of adjustment

The previous section showed that in the long run prices do not influence the level of output. It can however happen that, in the short term, the economy is operating off its long-run aggregate supply curve. While it will eventually return to its long-run equilibrium, an important real world issue concerns the length of time it takes for the economy to move back to this equilibrium. This is the so-called *speed of adjustment.*

Consider the length of time it might take to move between points A, B and C in Fig. 13.9 in the previous section. The speed of adjustment between A and B is probably quite rapid. Producers can respond to price changes fairly rapidly by changing production, production mixes or input mixes. This, for some temporary period of time, moves the economy beyond its potential long-run output position – beyond the production possibilities curve.

The movement between B and C may take longer as wage adjustments do not take place as regularly as price adjustments. The fact that there are contractual wage arrangements in the labour market means that producers can hire more labour at the same wage and work more hours at unchanged overtime rates. In any other market the increase in demand would lead to an increase in prices. Wages, on the other hand, only change at the end of the contractual period.

A more serious concern about the speed of adjustment is illustrated in Fig. 13.11. There the economy finds itself in recession at point A with a price level of OP_1 and income equal to OY_1. It can achieve long-run equilibrium by moving either towards point B or to point C. A movement towards point B means that the aggregate demand curve will have to shift from AD_1 to AD_2. However, in the absence of an economic windfall or a change in government policy, the economy would have to move to point C. In order for this to

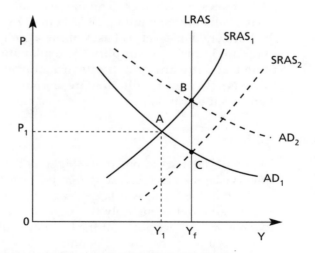

Fig. 13.11 Aggregate supply and the speed of adjustment

happen the short-run aggregate supply curve must move from SRAS$_1$ to SRAS$_2$. In other words, the cost of production, and more specifically wages, will have to fall.

It will now be understood why there is concern about the speed of adjustment. It is difficult to lower wages. In practice, and for a variety of reasons, the inevitable consequence of a recession in the labour market is retrenchment. This immediately results in unemployment. Experience has shown that a deep and prolonged recession is necessary to bring about a drop in wages. What this means is that the movement from point A to point C in Fig. 13.11 will be a difficult and painful experience. Historically, the consequence of this slow speed of adjustment has resulted in political pressure being brought to bear on governments to bring the economy out of recession through the use of fiscal or monetary policy (i.e. increases in government expenditure, tax cuts or a reduction in interest rates). Such changes often, unfortunately, have their own unintended and serious side effects as shown in the next chapter.

13.7 Aggregate demand and supply applied: the South African economy since 1980

The objective of this section is to use the macroeconomic tools developed in the previous sections to provide a broad understanding of the major changes that have occurred in the South African economy since 1980. It will be seen that these tools also provide the means of estimating the future course of prices and income.

The explanation in this section is based on Figs 13.12, 13.13, 13.14 and 13.15. Respectively they show the annual rate of change in GDP and per capita GDP, the BA rate and inflation, the nominal effective rand exchange rate, and the dollar and real rand gold price. (The BA rate is a good indicator of short-term interest rates. *See* Chapter 15 for more detail.)

We shall assume that Fig. 13.12 and 13.13 approximate movements along the horizontal and vertical axes of the aggregate demand–aggregate supply diagram. In order to simplify the explanation, changes in GDP are interpreted as leftward and rightward movements along the income axis. Likewise changes in inflation are shown as upward or downward movements on the price axis.

1980–83: Boom and bust

The year 1980 marked one of the highpoints of the South African macroeconomy. The boom which had started in 1977 reached a climax by 1980 and began to tail off in 1981. This was largely a gold price induced boom. The gold price, which had climbed steadily throughout the 1970s, surged from a monthly average of $250 per ounce at the beginning of 1979 to a monthly average of nearly $700 per ounce by the middle of 1980. These price rises were sustained for nearly a year.

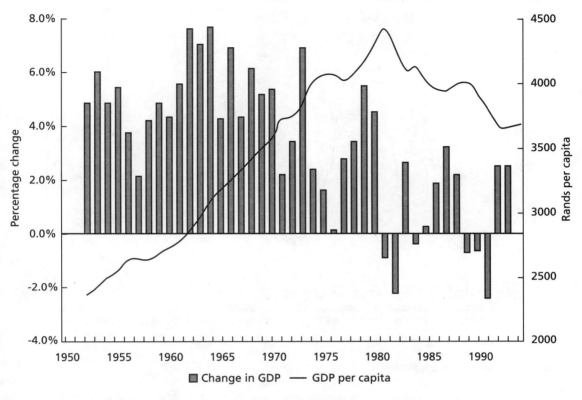

Fig. 13.12 Gross domestic product at 1985 prices – annual change and per capita

The economy responded to this stimulus and a strong economic boom took hold. This is clearly illustrated in Fig. 13.12 where real economic growth is shown to have reached nearly 6 per cent in 1980 and exceeded 5 per cent in 1981. In addition the effective rand exchange rate appreciated from its 1979 level although it did begin to fall again during the course of 1981.

Sadly, it was a situation which did not last. In several of the more important industrialised countries economic conservatism was being championed as a response to the failure of economic policy to address the declining growth and rapid inflation experienced during the 1970s.

There were two important and immediate results of these policy changes:

- The industrialised world went into a major recession.
- World inflation slowed, inflationary expectations were downgraded and, in consequence, the price of gold fell.

There were also some immediate consequences for the South African economy:

- The value of gold exports fell (Fig. 13.15).
- Demand for other exports fell because of the world recession.
- The rand started to depreciate (Fig. 13.14).
- The Reserve Bank increased interest rates (Fig. 13.13).

217

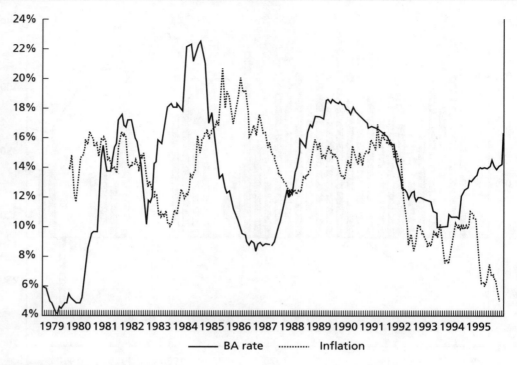

Fig. 13.13 The BA rate and inflation

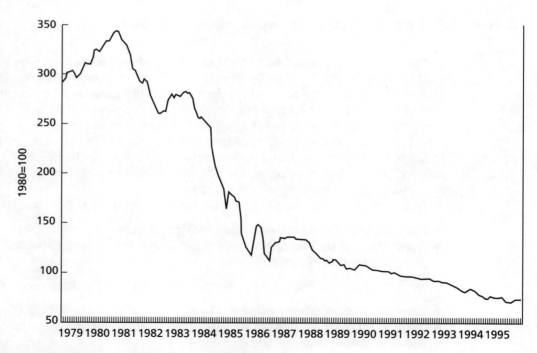

Fig. 13.14 Effective rand exchange rate (nominal rate)

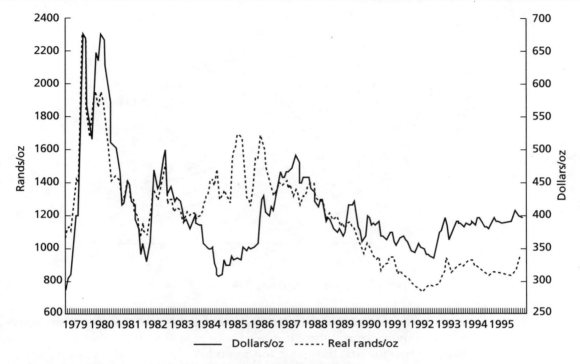

Fig. 13.15 The gold price – monthly averages (dollar and real rand)

- The economy slowed down and by 1983 was in deep recession (Figure 13.12).
- Yet throughout all of this time inflation remained high at between about 14 and 16 per cent (Figure 13.13).

In order to make sense of all this data it is necessary to evaluate what these changes have done to our aggregate demand and aggregate supply curves. This is presented in Fig. 13.16.

The boom of 1980 is shown as point A in Fig. 13.16. The economy was operating at full capacity and experienced equilibrium with aggregate demand equal to (the short-run and long-run) aggregate supply. The changing circumstances between 1980 and 1983 caused both the short-run aggregate supply and aggregate demand curves to shift to the left, i.e. to SRAS$_2$ and AD$_2$ respectively, thus establishing a new equilibrium at point B.

Aggregate demand fell because of lower gold revenues and the fall in other exports. In addition the higher interest rates and lower levels of confidence both served to depress aggregate demand.

Aggregate supply fell, or the cost of production rose, largely as a result of the depreciation of the rand.

The consequence of these two changes was that there was a rapid fall in national income – both changes reinforced this trend – yet the inflation rate was little changed. The changes in aggregate demand and aggregate supply were such that the price level remained unchanged. What these changes did

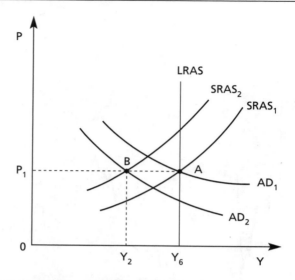

Fig. 13.16 The South African economy 1980–83

conspire to do was move the South African economy off its long-run aggre-gate supply curve and force it into a major recession. (It is of interest to note that this was the first time since the Second World War that the South African economy actually experienced negative growth rates.)

1983–86: Short recovery, continued depression and rising inflation

The South African economy went into recession during 1982 and to all intents and purposes stayed that way until 1987. As is evident from Fig. 13.12 the economy experienced nearly 5 per cent growth in 1984 but underwent con-traction during 1985 and had almost zero growth in 1986. The boom of 1984 was the result of increases in private consumption expenditure (following the low interest rates of 1983) and increases in government consumption expendi-ture. A consumer-led boom cannot be sustained for any length of time and the adverse effects on the balance of payments forced the Reserve Bank to increase interest rates rapidly.

This period was characterised by a dramatic escalation in political violence inside the country, falling levels of foreign confidence in the future of the South African economy and, as a result, the collapse of the rand.

The events described above are interpreted in Fig. 13.17. This period starts at point B (which is the same as point B in Fig. 13.16).

Two factors caused a significant leftward shift in the short-run aggregate supply curve – the collapse of the rand and the beginning of a major drought. The aggregate demand curve also shifted to the left as private and govern-ment consumption expenditure fell.

The relative shifts of the two curves were such that the change in aggregate supply outweighed the change in aggregate demand. As a result the economy

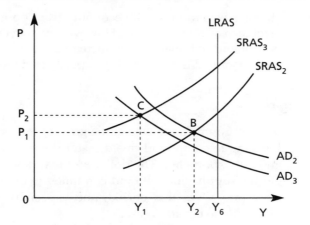

Fig. 13.17 The South African economy 1984–86

moved from point B to point C indicating a further fall in income but with rising prices – a situation referred to as stagflation.

1987–89: Riding the international recovery

In 1986 the world economy entered the recovery phase of what was to prove to be a major international boom. As South Africa is an exporter of primary products it benefited from this boom as net exports increased. On the supply side the collapse of the rand was arrested and widespread unemployment brought pressure to bear on real wages. In addition there was some relief from the drought.

The combination of slightly lower wages, a steady exchange rate and easing of food prices caused the aggregate supply curve to move slightly to the right. The world boom caused the aggregate demand curve also to move to the right. These changes are presented in Fig. 13.18. The result of these two

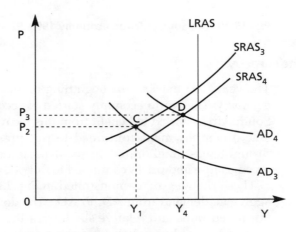

Fig. 13.18 The South African economy 1987–89

changes was to move the economy from point C to point D, with the price level increasing marginally. However the movements reinforced the change in output and national income increased from OY_1 to OY_4. Note, however, that the economy did not reach full capacity as it more or less did in 1980.

1990–92: The big depression

By 1990 South Africa was in the grips of the worst drought in living memory. Working to compound this disaster the world economy went into recession and net exports fell. The dollar and real rand price of gold continued to fall. On the supply side the rand continued to depreciate although at a relatively slow rate. Over this period, and especially towards the end of 1992 the drought also began to ease.

The most significant feature of this period was the fall off in aggregate demand. Aggregate demand moved from AD_4 to AD_5 in Fig. 13.19. With less pressure on the supply side the short-run aggregate supply curve moved marginally to the right. National income fell and inflation slowed.

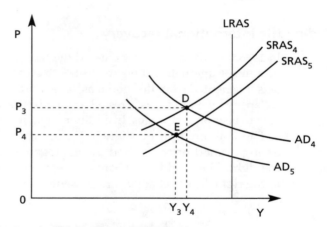

Fig. 13.19 The South African economy 1990–92

1993–95: A short recovery

The year 1993 marked the beginning of a turnaround for the South African economy. The world economy started to recover somewhat during 1992 and South Africa started to benefit from this recovery early in 1993. On the supply side, unemployment continued to put pressure on real wages, while the drought was ameliorated in most parts of the country. In consequence, incomes rose and prices continued to fall.

These changes are demonstrated in Fig. 13.20. The world recovery shifted aggregate demand from AD_5 to AD_6. The downward pressure on real wages, improved rains and relative stability of the rand contained cost increases – shown as a rightward shift of short-run aggregate supply from $SRAS_5$ to

$SRAS_6$. The result was that GDP grew by about 3.5 per cent on average and the inflation rate maintained somewhere in the region of 8 per cent.

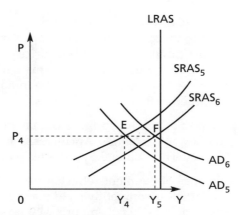

Fig. 13.20 The South African economy 1993–95

From 1996: The beginnings of stagflation

By the beginning of 1996, the recovery of the previous two years was already losing steam. Growth rates were bouyed up by very good rains and abundant agricultural harvests. The industrial sector and other primary sectors show every indication of going into recession. It would appear that this has as much to do with a slowdown in the world economy as with declining levels of domestic business confidence due to social, criminal and political factors. This recession, coupled as it is with a series of political shocks, led to a depreciation of the nominal exchange rate of nearly 30 per cent over the first eight months of 1996. The consequence was that both aggregate demand and aggregate supply moved to the left. A depreciation of this magnitude, unless matched by an equal drop in aggregate demand, will put a significant upward pressure on prices.

Summary

- The simple Keynesian model of the previous chapter has two serious limitations: it ignored both the impact of a change in the price level on levels of expenditure, and the supply side of the economy. The aggregate demand and supply model takes as its starting point the simple Keynesian model of the previous chapter, allows for changes in the price level, and incorporates the supply side of the economy.

- The model has three important features. These are the relationship between expenditure and the price level, which determines the aggregate demand curve; the relationship between the price level and the willingness to supply in the short and the long run; and the familiar concept of equilibrium.

- A change in the price level will affect the level of expenditure in essentially three ways. These are known as the income, wealth and balance of payments effects.

- Income effect: when the price level changes it usually takes some time before wages adjust to the new price level. In that time expenditure will also change. For example, if prices increase expenditure will fall because real wages will have fallen. This will continue until nominal wages have increased by the amount of the initial price increase, and real wages have returned to their previous levels.

- Wealth effect: when there is a change in the price level the real value of money will change. An increase in prices will lower the real value of money. This will make people feel poorer so that they will spend less.

- Balance of payments effect: a rise in the price level will make a country's exports less competitive and make imports more competitive. The result is that exports will fall, imports will increase and total expenditure will be less.

- These three effects all indicate that an increase in the price level will bring about a fall in aggregate expenditure, while a fall in the price level will bring about an increase in expenditure. This inverse relationship between aggregate expenditure and the price level is captured in the so-called aggregate demand curve. A change in the price level will cause a movement along the aggregate demand curve, which may also shift as a result of autonomous changes in expenditure.

- The aggregate supply curve shows a positive relationship between the price level and the quantity of goods and services supplied. A distinction is made between aggregate supply in the short run and aggregate supply in the long run.

- The short run aggregate supply curve is a device which assumes that the costs of the factors of production remain unchanged. It is upward sloping because when production increases, although factor prices remain unchanged, the use of less productive factors, overtime pay and diminishing marginal returns all increase the unit cost of production. The short run aggregate supply curve shifts when factor prices change.

- In the long run the price level cannot affect the level of production because price changes will also be reflected in changes in the cost of production factors. Hence the long run aggregate supply curve is vertical with respect to the average price level. The long run aggregate supply curve will shift when the capacity of the economy to produce goods and services changes.

- Macroeconomic equilibrium occurs when aggregate demand is equal to aggregate supply. Again we make a distinction between the short and long run equilibria.

- In the short run the economy can be in equilibrium either at less than full employment or (for a short period of time) at a level in excess of full employment. Should the economy be in such a short run disequilibrium, however, the price level and aggregate production will adjust in such a way as to return the economy to equilibrium.

- In the long run the economy can only be at equilibrium on the long run aggregate supply curve. If, in the short run, it is operating below full employment, wages and the costs of other factors will fall which will bring the economy back to full employment. Similarly, when the economy is beyond full employment, production costs will increase and the economy will again return to full employment.

- The speed of adjustment is the phrase used to describe the length of time it takes an economy to move from a position of over or under-employment to full employment. The speed of adjustment is usually very rapid when the economy is operating beyond full employment, but rather more tardy when it is experiencing unemployment. When an economy is operating at less than full employment for any length of time it may be appropriate (and politically desirable) for the government to introduce an expansionary policy aimed at bringing it to full employment.

Questions for review

1. What is the aggregate demand curve? How is it derived from the aggregate expenditure function?

2. What determines the position of the aggregate demand curve? What kind of factors will make it move?

3. What determines the slope of the aggregate demand curve? What happens to the slope of the aggregate demand curve if the wealth and balance of payments effects are very small? What would this imply for macroeconomic equilibrium?

4. What is the short-run aggregate supply curve? What determines its position and shape? What will make the curve move?

5. Why is the long-run aggregate supply curve vertical? What will make it move?

6. Which is the most important curve: AD, SRAS or LRAS?

7. Start with a small open economy in long-run macroeconomic equilibrium. Analyse the effects on prices and income of each of the following events. Consider both the short-run and long-run effects.

   a) The international price of the country's most important export doubles.
   b) There is political turbulance and foreign investors take their capital out of the country.
   c) An earthquake devastates the industrial heart of the country.
   d) Workers demand and receive a permanent increase in real wages.

CHAPTER 14

Macroeconomic adjustment: Keynesians and the New Classical school

This chapter will analyse a number of recent developments in macroeconomics within the theoretical framework developed in the previous chapter. The central role of expectations in economics will be examined, along with the contributions of the New Classical and Neo-Keynesian schools.

14.1 Expectations

The role of expectations in economics has long been recognised; it is clear that almost all decisions, both economic and otherwise, are conditioned by people's expectations regarding the future.

For example, consider an individual contemplating the purchase of a car. If she knew that the price of cars would rise next week, she would be more inclined to purchase now, whereas if she knew that the price was set to fall, she would in all likelihood defer her purchase. With import duties on motor vehicles set to fall further over the next few years, South African consumers might well expect prices to fall, or at least to rise less rapidly than before, and defer their purchases accordingly.

The problem, of course, is that knowledge of the future is seldom (if ever) certain, and thus we are forced to rely on our subjective expectations as to the future path of car prices, and act accordingly. Because of the importance of people's expectations, macroeconomic theorists have had to find ways to incorporate these expectations into their models. This is a daunting task, since the processes by which people form their expectations are little understood.

At first, economists settled for treating expectations as exogenous (or static). While this approach allowed economists to analyse the effects that changes in expectations would have on the economy, it is clearly inadequate, as it does not allow for people changing their expectations in the light of unexpected developments.

14.2 Adaptive expectations

The first significant attempt to model expectations endogenously came from Philip Cagan, a Chicago economist under the tutelage of Milton Friedman.

Under Cagan's adaptive expectations model, people adjust their expectations according to their past experience or, more specifically, according to the extent to which they were proved wrong in the past. Intuitively, if yesterday's expectation of today's price turned out to be too low, then today's expectation of tomorrow's price will be adjusted upwards.

This can be expressed algebraically as:

$$E_t(P_{t+1}) = E_{t-1}(P_t) + \alpha[P_t - E_{t-1}(P_t)] \qquad [14.1]$$

$E_t(P_{t+1})$ is the individual's expectation at time t of the price at time $t + 1$; $E_{t-1}(P_t)$ is the expectation at time $t - 1$ of the price at time t; and α is the coefficient of adjustment $(0 < \alpha < 1)$ which determines how quickly expectations adjust in the light of new developments. In other words, people adjust their expectations according to the extent to which their prior expectations were disappointed, i.e. the difference between the *actual* price in period t, P_t, and the price that was previously expected to prevail, $E_{e-1}(P_t)$.

We shall now consider the effects of such expectations within the familiar framework of our model of aggregate demand and supply. We do so by examining Milton Friedman's famous 'fooling' model, which purported to explain short-term fluctuations in the level of aggregate output. Friedman incorporated expectations into his model by assuming that labour supply depended on the *expected* real wage rate (W/P_e), rather than the actual real wage rate (W/P), as had conventionally been assumed. The implications of this assumption for aggregate demand and supply are illustrated in Fig. 14.1.

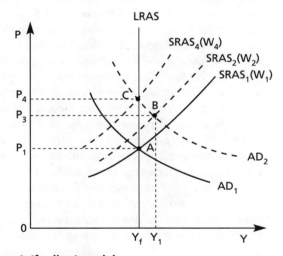

Fig. 14.1 Friedman's 'fooling' model

The economy is assumed to have reached an initial equilibrium at point A where the price level is OP_1 and real income or output is equal to its full capacity level, OY_f. If this equilibrium has prevailed for a long enough period of time, people will expect existing prices to continue into the future. But suppose that aggregate demand expands from AD_1 to AD_2, putting upward pressure on prices, and that employers also raise nominal wages as indicated by the shift in the short-run aggregate supply function from SRAS$_1$ (W$_1$), to SRAS$_2$, (W$_2$). The economy now finds itself at point B – beyond the full employment level of income. It should be noted that the price increase (from OP$_1$ to OP$_3$) exceeds the nominal wage increase (from W$_1$ to W$_2$) so that the real wage, W/P, has actually fallen.

However, workers are 'fooled' into believing that the real wage has increased. The reason is that under adaptive expectations workers' expectations will be based partly on the old price, OP$_1$, and partly on the new price, OP$_3$. Their expectations of future prices will thus be higher than OP$_1$ but lower than OP$_3$. They take into account both the historical trend, i.e. of no change in the price, and the recent price increase.

If workers erroneously believe that the real wage has increased, they will be prepared to supply more labour and help to increase output from OY$_f$ to OY$_1$ in Fig. 14.1. Thus the equilibrium has moved to point B where the economy is now operating beyond its full capacity level of income.

Clearly, this situation cannot endure. Workers will soon realise that the real wage has not in fact risen, and begin to withdraw some of their labour from the market and raise nominal wages. The short-run aggregate supply curve will likewise shift inwards until, eventually, point C on the long-run aggregate supply curve is reached. At point C nominal wages have caught up with prices so that the real wage is back at its original level.

Friedman's model purports to explain fluctuations in aggregate output, as well as showing that, in the long run, output cannot deviate from OY$_f$. This proposition is known as the *natural rate hypothesis*, and is of fundamental importance in macroeconomics, since it implies that Keynesian demand-management policies cannot affect the level of employment in the long run. However, the model is not particularly convincing; it is doubtful that workers can be so easily fooled, or that their folly can persist for any significant period of time.

What eventually led to the demise of adaptive expectations was the realisation that they were irrational under most circumstances. Since rationality lies at the heart of virtually all of economic theory, this turned out to be a fatal critique.

To illustrate, consider the case of a wheat buyer. Clearly, his buying decisions will depend not only on current prices, but on expected future prices. Under adaptive expectations, the buyer would form such expectations on the basis of the historical price of wheat. However, if the wheat buyer had access to climatological forecasts for the following year, it would obviously be irrational not to take such factors into account when forming expectations. Thus was born the *theory of rational expectations*, in which individuals are assumed to consider the effects of *all* relevant variables when forming expectations.

14.3 Rational expectations and the New Classical school

Keynesian orthodoxy prevailed in economics until roughly the end of the 1960s. This entailed a belief in the efficacy of demand management – discretionary monetary and fiscal policies aimed at boosting aggregate demand and curbing unemployment.

New Classical theorists, using the theory of rational expectations, attempted to show in particular that demand management is doomed to failure, and generally that governments have a minimal role to play with regard to the functioning of the macroeconomy.

There are various forms of the *rational expectations (ratex) hypothesis*, which can be divided into two main groups.

The weak form of the ratex hypothesis asserts that individuals will not persist in making expectational errors, but will adjust their expectations accordingly, using all relevant information. Many contend that this form is simply equivalent to the standard economic assumption of rationality.

The strong form of ratex posits that people do not make systematic errors in their expectations. In other words, their expectations are neither consistently higher nor lower than the actual values of the relevant variable. Errors are unavoidable, given the essentially unpredictable nature of the world, but they occur at random. The strong form assumes that people, by observing the workings of the economy over a period of time, will come to understand the relationships between important economic variables (for example, how an increase in the money supply will affect prices and interest rates).

This strong version of ratex appeals strongly to many theorists, since it would seem to carry the standard assumption of rationality through to its logical conclusion. It has been used by New Classical theorists to generate some startling results, the most important of which is the policy ineffectiveness proposition,which states that demand management can have no effect on output or employment, either in the long or the short run.

To illustrate this theory, let us return to the model examined in the previous section. In Fig. 14.2 we consider the case of a rightward shift in the aggregate demand, induced by an increase in the money supply. Under adaptive expectations, we have seen that workers may be temporarily 'fooled', allowing a short-run increase in output, before they gradually adjust their expectations and the economy moves from point B to point C.

However, New Classical man is far more canny than his adaptive counterpart. He understands how an increase in the money supply will translate into a price increase from OP_1 to OP_4, and will immediately demand a corresponding nominal wage increase. Thus, the real wage will remain constant, and the economy will move instantaneously from point A to point C.

In this way, it is theorised that rational expectations on the part of workers will completely negate the effects of government policy. Thus there is no inflation–unemployment trade-off, even in the short run.

It is important to note at this point that New Classical theorists do not reject all kinds of fiscal policy, merely demand management. Many advocate *supply-side* policies, or programmes designed to expand the productive capacity of the economy, i.e. shifting the long-run aggregate supply curve to the right. Supply-side theorists believe that the best way to achieve growth is by creating a favourable business environment, for example, by lowering personal income and corporate tax rates, rather than by any direct governmental involvement in the economy.

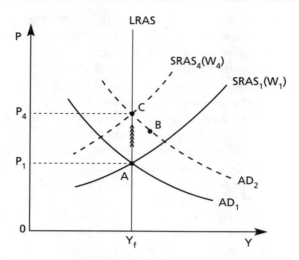

Fig. 14.2 Incorporating rational expectations

New Classical theorists have thus been able to use the Rational Expectations Hypothesis to promote their *laissez-faire* agenda. Unsurprisingly, both Ratex and its policy implications have been extremely controversial. In particular, many critics find the strong version of the Ratex hypothesis to be fundamentally implausible. While it may have some merits in a situation where the economy remains relatively stable over time, it becomes much less tenable where an economy is constantly subjected to external shocks and undergoing structural change.

Ratex and the policy ineffectiveness proposition have also been criticised on empirical grounds. It is extremely difficult to reconcile the reality of persistent business cycles with the predictions of the theory.

However, for all its shortcomings, the 'Ratex revolution' has served to focus economists' attention on the role of expectations, and on the powerful (and perverse) effects that such expectations can have.

EXHIBIT

Robert Lucas

Robert Lucas's name is closely associated with the theory of rational expectations – for which he won the Nobel Prize in Economics in 1995. Most of his pathbreaking work in this field appeared in two books, namely, *Studies in Business-Cycle Theory*, published in 1981, and a two-volume collection entitled *Rational Expectations and Econometric Practice*, co-edited with T. J. Sargent and published in 1982. His basic thesis was that private individuals have the same information as policy-makers and can therefore fully anticipate the effects of monetary, fiscal and exchange rate policies. They will thus take the necessary preventative action and render such policies wholly ineffectual. The only way that governments can change real income in the

Exhibit continued

economy is by doing the unexpected and catching people unawares – but then only for a short time.

Lucas's theory has much in common with Friedman's monetarist approach (see Chapter 17) in that both argue for a non-activist role on the part of government. It is probably fair to say that both have had a profound impact on governments everywhere and are partly responsible for the renewed belief in the efficacy with which free markets operate.

14.4 The Neo-Keynesian school

New Classical macroeconomics launched a strong counterattack against Keynesian orthodoxy, purporting to show how rational behaviour would lead to full-employment market clearing. The problem for Keynesian theory was that it lacked *microeconomic foundations*. In other words, it was not rooted in the rational behaviour of individuals. The central assumption of the Keynesian model (that of sticky wages) was merely that – an assumption, without any theoretical underpinnings.

Neo-Keynesians have sought to revive Keynesian theory by providing it with microeconomic foundations. In particular, they have sought to construct theories to explain how rational behaviour by individuals could lead to inflexible wages and prices. A number of such theories have been developed, and in this section we will review a few of the most important ones.

Implicit contract theory

It has been observed that, contrary to the predictions of classical theory, wages tend not to fluctuate over the business cycle. Neo-Keynesians rationalise this phenomenon by arguing that wage contracts, which stipulate wage conditions and thus impart rigidities to the labour market, are preferred by both employers and workers. These contracts may be of a formal nature, but more often consist of an implicit understanding between management and workers – hence *implicit* contract theory. Wage-stabilising contracts reduce uncertainty and risk to employees effectively granting them insurance against recession, while for employers, they have the advantage of forestalling costly wage negotiations and strikes.

As a result of such contracts, wages will be held above the market-clearing level during a recession. In this way, Neo-Keynesian theorists have been able to justify Keynes' 'arbitrary' assumption in terms of rational maximising behaviour.

Efficiency wage hypothesis

The *efficiency wage hypothesis* provides an alternative explanation for the same phenomenon. It is argued that, since monitoring the performance of workers is costly, firms are willing to pay wages higher than the market-clearing level in order to increase productivity and discourage shirking. Again, in this case, the labour market will fail to clear.

Price contracts

As with wages, there are a number of reasons why prices may not fluctuate freely. In fact, the majority of prices which we encounter on a day-to-day basis are preset, rather than fluctuating in response to changing market conditions.

This has the advantage of saving time and reducing uncertainty for buyers. The reduction in information requirements facilitates purchasing decisions, since the acquisition of information is costly, in terms of both time and money.

Stable prices also hold benefits for firms. It is clear that continually adjusting prices in response to changing market conditions would be a significant drain on a firm's resources. Many firms prefer to set prices according to simple rules of thumb, the most common of which is *mark-up* (or *cost-plus*) *pricing*. Such a policy entails setting price equal to average variable cost plus some mark-up to cover fixed costs and profits. This approach is *efficient*, since it allows management to delegate most pricing decisions to lower-level employees. It is also *equitable*, since it enables consumers to see that price increases are due entirely to cost increases, rather than profiteering.

Now that a theoretical basis for price and wage rigidities has been established, let us examine their effects within our familiar macroeconomic model. This is done in Fig. 14.3 where, for the reasons mentioned above, prices and wages are fixed at OP_1 and W_1 respectively. Thus, in the short run, any quantity of output must be supplied at price OP_1, giving rise to the horizontal short-run aggregate supply curve $SRAS_1$ (W_1).

Let us further suppose that the government implements a contractionary fiscal policy (reducing government expenditure and/or raising taxes), causing

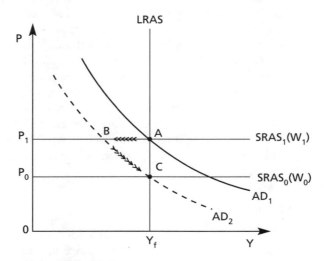

Fig. 14.3 Price and wage rigidities

aggregate demand to shift leftwards from AD_1 to AD_2. Since prices are fixed in the short run, a pure quantity adjustment will occur establishing a new short-run equilibrium at point B, which is a point of less than full employment. This means that the wage is too high to clear the labour market. Of course, since B is a point of long-run disequilibrium, it cannot persist for any great length of time; market forces will eventually dictate a change in wage and price contracts, causing a fall in wages from W_1 to W_0 and in prices from OP_1 to OP_0, until long-run equilibrium is re-established at point C.

As we have seen in section 14.3, New Classical theorists would argue that this adjustment occurs immediately, but we have examined several reasons why this may not be the case. Thus, Neo-Keynesian theorists would seem to have provided Keynesian theory with adequate microeconomic foundations, showing how inflexibilities can hinder adjustment, thus causing persistent business cycles. This has provided some theoretical justification for demand-management policies.

Summary

- One of the major problems with the model developed in the previous chapter is that it ignores the way in which expectations are formed and how expectations affect the macroeconomy. The development of the various theories of expectations represents an attack by members of the old Classical school (now called the New Classical school) on orthodox Keynesian thinking.

- There are two important theories of how expectations are formed and how they affect the macroeconomy – adaptive and rational expectations.

- The theory of adaptive expectations suggests that people form expectations based on past experiences. Expectations about future events are adjusted in accordance with past mistakes. This theory was used by Milton Friedman in his 'fooling' model to show that fluctuations in economic activity would occur only when expectations are not consistent with current events. This would occur, for example, when price increases in the current period are greater or smaller than what was expected previously.

- The theory of rational expectations suggests, correctly so, that people do not form expectations by looking only at past events. Rather, expectations are formed on the basis of all existing knowledge, which includes both past and current events. Hence expectations will be incorrect only if something totally unexpected occurs.

- The expectations revolution was sufficient to undermine the Keynesian theory and the policy recommendations it made – i.e. that governments had a role to play in stabilising the macroeconomy. Rational expectations suggest that such stabilisation policies will be futile.

- There has been a number of Keynesian responses to the New Classical attack under the banner of Neo-Keynesian economies. What Neo-Keynesians have attempted to show is that there are sound microeconomic reasons why the economy might remain at less than full employment even if expectations are formed rationally.

- Implicit contract theory and the efficiency wage hypothesis suggest that, for various reasons, actual wages may be higher than equilibrium wages. Price contract theories suggest that prices and wages may be sticky for contractual reasons. The conclusion of these theories is that there are sound microeconomic reasons why unemployment might persist over time.

Questions for review

1. Should governments intervene in economies operating under adaptive expectations?

2. If the theory of rational expectations held true, would a modern economy always find itself in a state of full-employment equilibrium?

3. How would you explain the Neo-Keynesian proposition that wages and prices tend to be rigid?

PART V

The monetary sector

If people are the life-blood of a nation then the financial sector is the veins and arteries. The most important service provided by the financial sector is the conversion of savings (often short-term savings) into long-term loans. What is important is that the structure of the financial sector is able to cope with rapid changes in the flows of short- and long-term capital. As the economy itself becomes increasingly more complex, so too must the financial sector become increasingly more sophisticated.

If this is not complicated enough in itself, it is also desirable that there be some element of control over the activities of the financial sector. This is so for two reasons. First, control over the supply of money is generally considered desirable as money acts on interest rates, the exchange rate and inflation. The second reason is the need to protect depositors and the economy from bank defaults and insolvency.

The challenge facing the financial authorities essentially amounts to a fine-tuning exercise. While having to control the financial sector in order to achieve their own longer term economic objectives, policy makers must ensure financial markets are sufficiently flexible and resilient to meet future challenges as the economy grows and changes.

Before we turn to such policy issues, however, it is necessary to understand the nature of the monetary sector. This is the purpose of the following four chapters. Chapter 15 provides a broad institutional view of the financial sector. In Chapter 16 we introduce the concept of money and discuss some of the more important banking institutions in the economy; while Chapters 17 and 18 focus on the relationships that exist between money, interest rates, exchange rates and prices.

CHAPTER 15

Financial markets and the flow of funds

Financial markets are one of the most important conduits through which savings and investment are channelled in an economy. Investment – whether in physical or human capital – is an important source of economic growth. Yet without savings there can be no investment. What the financial markets do is provide a means by which borrowers and lenders can come together and buy and sell financial resources.

This chapter examines:

- The general nature of financial transactions and financial institutions.
- The different financial instruments and their pricing.
- The important distinction between capital markets and money markets.

15.1 Lenders and borrowers

In the jargon of economics, people who save, i.e. lenders, are known as surplus units (SUs) while people who borrow are called deficit units (DUs). While people save for many reasons – to travel, for security purposes, to make some large purchase – the bulk of their savings is of an institutional nature; in other words, most people save for the time that they will retire. If, instead of keeping money in a locker or under a mattress, savers lend their money to people who want to borrow, they can charge them an interest. And by charging an interest, savers will see that the value of their money grows a lot faster than if it was simply put under a mattress.

Similarly, people who borrow do so for many reasons. They may borrow money to buy a fancy durable consumer good, or to invest in a profitable commercial enterprise. Consumers are often willing to pay interest on a loan so as to bring the enjoyment of consumption forward in time: they can borrow now to buy that big red sports car they have always wanted, or they can save for it (and run the risk of being too old to enjoy it one day!). Business people borrow money because they want to make a profit on an investment. The profit must be larger than the interest charged, otherwise the project will make a loss. Governments also borrow on the financial markets to make up the difference between government expenditures and tax revenues.

15.2 Direct financial transactions

Financial transactions can take one of two forms, i.e. 'direct' financial and 'indirect' financial transactions.

Direct financial transactions take place either when people are in direct contact with each other – eyeball-to-eyeball – or when they use the services of a neutral third party. In this case the third party does not assume any risk in the transaction – this person merely charges a commission for bringing the two parties together. An example of such a person in the real estate market is the estate agent, while in financial markets direct finance refers to people using the services of a registered stockbroker to buy shares on the Johannesburg Stock Exchange (JSE), or making use of a bond dealer to buy corporate or government bonds. Under direct finance, the financial paper which is issued by the borrower is held as a financial asset by the lender.

Figure 15.1 illustrates the flow of funds which would occur when such direct financial deals are concluded. The diagram assumes that households are net lenders (SUs) and that firms are net borrowers (DUs). It will be immediately apparent that the figure is a more detailed version of Fig. 3.8 of Chapter 3, and it illustrates a demand for (by DUs) and a supply of (by SUs) loanable funds at different interest rates. On the assumption that people save and firms borrow, there will be a flow of funds from households which are called savings. These, after passing through the care of a financial broker, end up as a net flow of funds called investment. DUs will usually offer some form of receipt – what some people would call an IOU – in the form of share certificates, debentures, bonds, treasury bills, BAs, and so on. These flow from DUs (firms and government) to SUs – usually people.

What we are seeing in action is the movement of the resource called 'capital'. Capital is, after all, non-consumed income which is lent out so that other people can put it to use. As capital is a factor of production the use of such capital generates income. For the privilege of using other people's money, DUs are expected to pay a price – interest, dividend payments and profit. There is a second form of income generated here, i.e. the commission charged by brokers – as shown in Fig. 15.1.

15.3 Indirect financial transactions

Indirect financial transactions occurs when SUs and DUs do not come into direct contact with each other, and often do not know who the other parties are. The reason is the existence of a third party who is willing to bear the risk of the financial transactions. The most common example of these third parties are commercial banks, life assurance companies and pension funds. SUs thus exchange their savings for IOUs issued by a financial institution – not those issued by DUs. These take many forms – cheque and savings deposits, assurance policies, retirement annuities, endowment policies and pension funds. The DUs borrow their funds directly from the financial institution and not from the SUs.

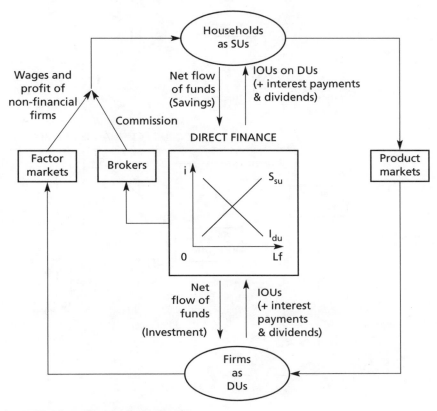

Fig. 15.1 Direct financial transactions

There has been a considerable growth in this form of financial transaction over the latter half of this century. The main benefit has been a major improvement in the efficiency of financial markets. It reduces the risk faced by any individual SU as surplus funds are now spread across a range of different DUs. The result has been a greater mobilisation of savings. It has also made the market more efficient as it allows financial institutions to make available loans of various sizes and different times to maturity. Such flexibility would be very difficult without the existence of financial intermediaries.

The operation of indirect financial markets is represented in Fig. 15.2, where the market for direct finance have been reproduced. In the indirect financial market funds are again supplied by SUs in the form of savings. The supply curve of these funds, S_{su}, indicates that they are positively related to the interest rate. The demand curve for the funds from the SUs, D_{fi}, shows the willingness of financial institutions to borrow at different interest rates. Hence the higher is the interest rate, the more willing people will be to lend and the less willing financial institutions will be to borrow.

In turn, the financial institutions take the funds which they have borrowed and offer them for loan to the DUs. This relationship is illustrated in the second market for indirect finance. Here the financial institutions are the suppliers of funds, hence the supply curve is called S_{fi}. The higher the interest

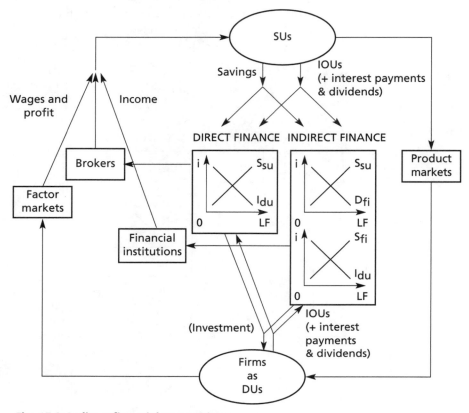

Fig. 15.2 Indirect financial transactions

rate, the more willing financial institutions are to lend out funds; and the lower is the interest rate, the less willing they are to lend out. DUs are the borrowers – whose investment function is given by I_{du}. As before, there is an inverse relationship between interest rates and the willingness to borrow.

The difference between the interest rate which financial institutions charge people they lend to (i.e. DUs) and the people they borrow from (i.e. SUs), is the source of their income. All of this income is remitted back to households in the form of wages, rent, dividends, interest and profit and all of it adds to GDP.

15.4 Financial institutions

There are a myriad of different types of financial institutions which operate in the financial markets. Figure 15.3 lists a few of these within the context of the type of finance each institution deals in. We have already made the distinction between institutions which deal in direct and indirect forms of finance. In South Africa the most common types of institutions engaged in direct financial deals are stockbrokers and bond dealers, of which there are hundreds, and SAFEX (the South African Futures Exchange). SAFEX provides the means by which producers of various commodities (gold, coal, steel, sugar, etc.) are able to sell forward.

What this means is that one agrees today about the price which will be paid some time in the future. It allows producers to hedge (i.e. reduce their own risk) against a variety of factors. The two most important of these are fluctuations in the exchange rate and fluctuations in the international price of a commodity.

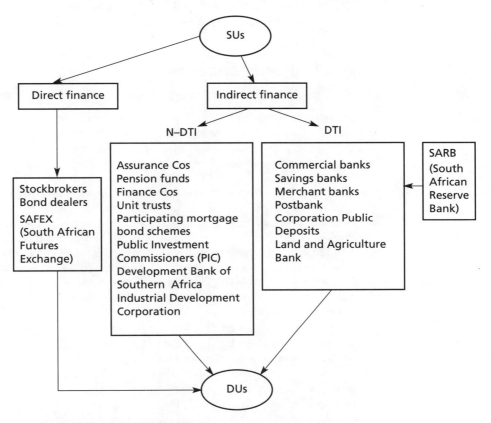

Fig. 15.3 Financial institutions

There is one important distinction to be made within the part of the financial markets which deal in indirect financial transactions. Here we find two general types of firms – those which are classified as deposit-taking institutions (DTIs) and those which are not. DTIs are what we would commonly regard as banks. Hence commercial banks, savings banks, merchant banks, the Post Office Bank, amongst others, are deposit-taking institutions. Those which are not DTIs include the life assurance companies, pension funds, the various finance companies, the Development Bank of Southern Africa (DBSA) and the Industrial Development Corporation (IDC).

15.5 Capital markets and money markets

There is a wide variety of different types of financial instruments. For direct finance these include government bonds, treasury bills, shares in companies, bankers' acceptances (BAs) and hire purchase and leasing contracts. As far as indirect finance is concerned, deposit-taking institutions use such instruments as cheque and saving account deposits. Non-deposit-taking institutions use instruments like life assurance policies, pension contracts and mutual fund certificates. These instruments all have 'prices', or interest rates or yields, some of which are briefly explained in the illustrative example.

<table>
<tr><td>ILLUSTRATIVE
EXAMPLE</td><td>

Pricing of financial instruments

Some of the more important 'prices' can be summarised as follows:

- *Short-term interest rates* on bank deposits and loans. After one year the future value, F, of a deposit, D, is simply $F = D + rD = D(1 + r)$, where r is the short-term interest rate; and after more than one year, it is $F = D(1 + r)^n$ where n is the number of years. The present value of F is simply derived by solving for D.
- *Short-term government bonds*. Here the implied interest rate, or yield, depends on the difference between the face value of the bond (i.e. the maturity value, or the value that appears on the certificate) and its current market price. For example, if a government bond with a face value of R10 000 and a one-year maturity sold for R8750, it would imply an effective interest rate of 14.3 per cent, i.e. if one invested R8750 now, and got paid R10 000 a year later, the interest rate on the investment is 14.3 per cent. The formula is simply $(MV - MP)/MP$, where MV is the maturity value and MP the market price.
- *Long-term government bonds* (of more than a year). These usually pay a fixed amount of interest (or coupon) each year (or every six months) over a period of several years. The implied interest rate, or yield, depends on (the present value of) the amount of interest paid and the face value of the bond, as well as on its current market price. Consider a R10 000 bond paying interest each year of R1000, i.e. a coupon rate of 10 per cent. Now, if the bank rate and other interest rates increased to 11 per cent, this will immediately reduce the price, or capital value, of the bond – from R10 000 to R9091. Why? Because by buying the bond for R9091 and receiving R1000 each year, the buyer will be earning 11% on his or her investment.
- *Equity or shares*. Here the return, or yield, is determined simply by the expected change in the price of the share and the expected dividend payments; or $(SP_{97} - SP_{96} + DP)/SP_{96}$, where SP is the share price (in 1996 or 1997) and DP is the dividend payments.

</td></tr>
</table>

While there are many different financial instruments, one of the most important distinctions we need to make is that between the capital market and the money market.

Capital markets

The capital market is the market for long-term borrowing and lending, i.e. for periods exceeding one year. Institutions such as the government, municipalities, public enterprises and some private companies raise funds on the capital market by selling bonds, stocks and other securities where these will be redeemed some time in the future. Holders of these securities can also sell them on the stock exchange to other investors.

There are two characteristics of capital markets which are important for our purposes:

- The interest rate which is determined in the capital market is a long-term interest rate.
- It is a free market in which nobody interferes or sets the interest rate. The long-term interest rate is therefore a market determined rate.

These characteristics have an important implication. The fact that this is a free market which deals in long-dated stock means that the interest rate in the capital market is the best indicator of future interest rates in other financial markets. In South Africa the most commonly reported long-term securities include the Escom 168 and the RSA 150.

Money markets

In contrast to the capital market, the money market refers to the demand for and supply of money. Just as with the capital market the money market has two important characteristics:

- The interest rates in the money market are short-term interest rates (applicable to periods of up to one year).
- The South African Reserve Bank directly controls the interest rates in the South African money market. In most countries today central banks control money market rates.

The Reserve Bank controls interest rates by means of keeping the banking sector indebted to the Reserve Bank. The extent of this indebtedness is called the money market shortage. By ensuring that there is always a money market shortage, any increased demand for credit in the money market must eventually lead to a larger money market shortage. DTIs who borrow from the Reserve Bank pay an interest rate on this borrowing. This is called the bank rate. The DTIs then take the money and lend it out to people and firms at the bank rate plus a mark-up. The mark-up covers the perceived risk of lending, and generates some profit. Hence when the bank rate changes all interest rates change.

One of the best indicators of expected future changes in the bank rate is the BA rate (bankers' acceptances rate). If the banking sector expects that the bank rate will increase some time over the next 90 days, the BA rate will begin to increase immediately. Similarly if it is thought that the bank rate will fall in the next 90 days, the BA rate will begin to fall immediately.

In coming to grips with interest rates in the money market it is important to take into account those factors which the Reserve Bank has in mind when it chooses a particular bank rate. There are four major factors:

- Inflation
- Money supply
- The state of the economy
- The state of the Balance of Payments

It is too early in this book to begin to explore these factors in detail, but several subsequent chapters are devoted to this. However, two general points should be made.

First, the list of factors is not shown here in any order of preference. In other words, inflation is not the most important factor, or the Balance of Payments the least important. Rather the order of priority changes as circumstances change. In South Africa today the most important factor is the state of the Balance of Payments. In the early 1980s, by contrast, it was inflation, while by the mid-1980s it was first the state of the economy and then the Balance of Payments.

Second, a change in interest rates does not work in the same direction for each of the factors. For example, an increase in interest rates will help to slow down inflation and stabilise the Balance of Payments. It will also slow down the economy. This may be desirable in a boom but would be very dangerous if the economy was in a recession. Similarly, cutting the bank rate will stimulate the economy but it can also result in inflation and in a depreciation of the exchange rate.

Summary

- Financial markets are the means by which savings (non-consumed income) are channelled back into the economy as loanable funds. Two general types of transaction take place in financial markets. These are direct financial deals, where lenders know who the borrowers are (e.g. shares and government bonds) and indirect financial deals, where lenders do not know who the borrowers are (savings accounts and other time deposits).

- One of the more important distinctions within the financial markets is that between capital and money markets.

- Capital markets are the markets for long term borrowing and long term savings – e.g. the markets for long term bonds, certain savings accounts and equity. Capital markets are characterised by their long term nature and the fact that they are relatively free. In other words, nobody can directly interfere and manipulate interest rates in the capital market. Hence interest rates in the capital market (particularly the long bond rate) is one of the best indicators of the market's current expectations about future interest rates.

- The money market is the market for short term borrowing and short term savings. It is also a market where, in South Africa and in many other countries, interest rates are set directly by the central bank. Hence money markets are short term markets where interest rates are not necessarily determined by market forces, but often set by the central bank.

Questions for review

1. Why do some people save and other people borrow?

2. Why do some people both save and borrow?

3. What kind of income is generated (what is the value added) of the financial markets? How do we measure this value added?

4. What are the risks and benefits of being in the direct finance rather than in the indirect finance part of the financial markets? Why do people choose one or the other? Which one would you choose to channel your savings through?

CHAPTER 16

The nature and creation of money

The king was in his counting house counting out his money
The queen was in the parlour eating bread and honey!

Which is really more important: money or bread and honey? This chapter starts by examining why money is important and also why money is not important. It then goes on to address what constitutes money and how different types of money can be created by the banking system. It closes with a discussion of the South African banking sector.

16.1 Why is money important?

Before we address those monetary issues which economists believe to be important, let us pose a more simple question: how important is money to an average person?

Unless one is either extremely wealthy or an aesthetic, one is likely to respond that money is extremely important. This presumably implies that more money makes one happier. In fact, it is not really money that makes people happy. Rather it is the access to goods and services which is provided by money that is important. What is therefore really important to individual people is income and not money. Money is simply the transition between the generation of income and the eventual consumption of goods and services.

Money is important for other reasons, however. One of these reasons is that it overcomes the need to enter into barter trade. Imagine a world in which there is no money. People who sell their factors of production must take some good or service from the buyer. This immediately reduces the opportunities for trade and the subsequent gains from trade. In such a barter economy there must be what is called a *double coincidence of wants* if trade is to take place. In other words, each person involved in trading must have the good or service that others want, otherwise no trade will take place. The existence of some type of medium of exchange overcomes this problem and encourages trade.

Within economic theory there are two conflicting views about the importance of money.

Classical economists of old and today's New Classical economists believe that money is not very important. For these economists money is merely a means by which real transactions and economic activity are facilitated – a 'veil' behind which the real economy operates. They believe in the neutrality of money and argue that an increase in the quantity of money, all other things being equal, will merely lead to a proportional increase in the price level. Changes in the quantity of money therefore have no real impact on the economy.

In contrast to these classical views there are many economists who do not accept the neutrality of money theorem. In addition, central banks worldwide constantly adjust money supply as economic conditions change. Such views suggest that changes in money will have differing effects depending both on the chosen exchange rate regime and the length of time over which the disturbance is considered. In this approach money is important because it can contribute to real income (in the short term), influence interest rates and the exchange rate, contribute to inflation and contribute to the determination of future expectations.

16.2 What is money?

Money can be anything – so long as it is accepted by people as money! Generally, in order to be accepted as money a commodity must exhibit the following three characteristics.

Medium of exchange

For a commodity to be accepted as money it must be recognised by people as a medium of exchange. There must be trust that other people will also accept the commodity in exchange for goods and services. So long as this trust exists the commodity being used as money need have no intrinsic value – the paper money used today is an obvious example. Even historically there are examples – dog teeth were used as money on the Admiralty Isles. On the island of Yap in the South Pacific, for example, limestone discs about 1 metre in diameter served as money. On the other hand, and more commonly, commodity monies also had some intrinsic value – cowrie shells, precious stones and precious metals, especially gold.

In addition to the role which trust plays in making a commodity acceptable as a medium of exchange, it is also desirable that the commodity be easily portable and have a high value relative to its mass.

Store of value

If a commodity is used as money it must maintain its value – it must be a store of value. For this reason perishables and fragile items have little appeal as money. Precious metals, on the other hand, can hold value extremely well. It is almost impossible to destroy metals. They can be cut up, melted and otherwise pulverised without loss of value. This stands in contrast to dog teeth, cowrie shells, precious stones and paper money.

As a store of value, money should ideally maintain a constant purchasing power. Inflation undermines the store of value characteristic as do fluctuations in the price of commodity monies like gold.

Unit of account

A final characteristic of money is that it be a unit of account. To do this the commodity must be divisible while still maintaining the same value. Some commodities immediately lose their appeal – one dog's tooth had value, half a tooth had none. The same holds for cowrie shells, large limestone discs, cows, sheep and precious stones. Of all the commodity monies precious metals are the most easily divisible.

16.3 The evolution of money

Over the centuries gold gradually became the most desirable form of money largely because it was the one commodity which most fulfilled the characteristics of money. It is rare and precious, in that small quantities embody large wealth. It is also highly divisible, unlike dog teeth and precious stones. Gold will not deteriorate over time and is difficult to damage.

By the beginning of the 20th century gold had become the dominant form of money although little gold was actually handled in transactions. The financial system had evolved into the fractionally backed currency system called the Gold Standard at the time. A fractionally backed system refers to a currency which is partially backed by some real commodity like gold.

The Gold Standard had evolved from practices started originally by goldsmiths. As goldsmiths had secure vaults, wealthy people used to store their gold in these vaults. The goldsmith issued receipts against deposits. As these receipts were seen to embody trust they became a means of exchange. They started to circulate as money, in the knowledge that they were fully backed by gold. The next step in the evolution of money was the realisation by goldsmiths that as there were always considerable deposits of gold in their vaults, they could issue loans against such gold and charge interest on the loans. The goldsmiths turned into banks and a fractionally backed currency system evolved.

With the advent of central banking, the right to issue notes was removed from individual commercial banks and vested in the central bank. The monetary system which evolved, little different from the banker–goldsmiths, was a fractionally backed monetary system called the *Gold Standard*.

The Gold Standard contributed to great stability in currencies, prices and exchange rates and was therefore an important contributor to the growing international trade during the late 19th and early 20th centuries. The first major test faced by the Gold Standard was the First World War when it came under pressure. As a result of the war, exchange rates became misaligned relative to their Gold Standard rates. In addition the adjustment mechanisms were both slow and subject to political influence. For the Gold Standard, already under pressure as a result of the war, the Great Depression of 1929 marked the beginning of the end. By 1933 most countries had abandoned the Gold Standard.

Since that time most of the countries in the world have had currencies which are not in any way physically backed by precious commodities. These are called *fiat money*. Fiat money is accepted as money simply because people have trust in it.

16.4 Types of money

As has been suggested above, any commodity can be money so long as people accept it as money. While one might have problems paying for dinner with a dog's tooth in today's world, there are other types of money apart from notes and coins. Some restaurateurs may accept a Swiss watch or an Australian opal as payment for a dinner, or insist that the customer does the washing up at the end of the evening!

One way of coming to grips with the meaning of money is to realise that it can in fact be any commodity which embodies *purchasing power*. A useful way of distinguishing between the various types of money is to do so in terms of the *liquidity* of money. By liquidity we mean the ease with which various types of money can be used to make purchases. Here we distinguish between *transactions money* and *near money*.

Transactions money

Transactions money, often called 'bank money', is made up of the most liquid types of money. The money supply measure of transactions money is called M1 and it consists of items that are actually used for transactions. There are two components:

- Notes and coins which are in circulation outside the banking system. (Money inside banks has no purchasing power until it is withdrawn or loaned out.)
- Demand deposits – accounts from which funds can be withdrawn on demand. Chequing accounts (current accounts) make up the bulk of demand deposits.

Near money

Near money or 'broad money', as it is sometimes called, includes M1 as well as savings accounts and similar financial assets that are very close substitutes for transactions money. Measures of near money are usually called M2 and M3.

Money supply definitions

As a result of different types of financial institutions and the existence of different types of financial products, the actual definitions of the money supply differ from country to country. The South African money supply definitions are presented in Fig. 16.1.

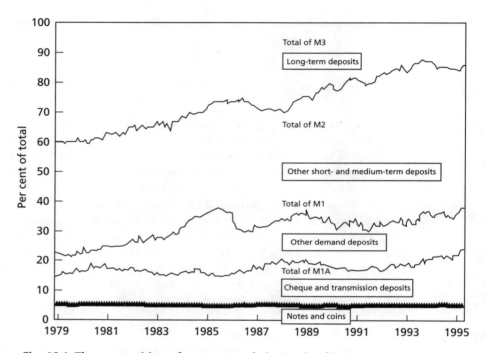

Fig. 16.1 The composition of money supply in South Africa

There are four commonly used measures of money supply in South Africa. These are M1A, M1, M2 and M3:

- M1A is made up of notes and coins (currency) plus cheque and transmission deposits.
- M1 consists of M1A plus demand deposits other than cheque and transmission deposits.
- M2 is made up of M1 plus short- and medium-term deposits.
- M3 is made up of M2 plus long-term deposits.

It is of interest to note two important features of Fig. 16.1. The first is the small size of the currency component compared to other components of the money supply. The second is the relative fall in the importance of long-term deposits in favour of short- and medium-term deposits.

16.5 The money creation process

In our discussion of the different types of money we indicated that demand deposits, or chequing accounts, can be regarded as transactions money. It is important to realise that these deposits include not only those with credit balances but also all overdrafts. A cheque drawn on an overdraft facility has as much purchasing power as that drawn from any other account. It follows from this that if banks issue more loans, such as overdraft facilities, the money supply will increase. It is the issuing of loans by banks that forms the basis of the money creation process.

We have in fact already encountered the money creation process once before in this chapter. Remember the goldsmiths who became bankers? They did this by realising that people rarely withdrew all their funds at the same time. The goldsmiths became bankers by realising that they only needed to hold a portion of any deposit as a reserve against that deposit. The rest could be loaned out – at a profit.

There follows a detailed explanation of the money creation process which is based on a fractional reserve banking system. The example used here is that of a multi-bank system. (The explanation is the same irrespective of the number of banks.) Two simplifying assumptions are made:

● There is a 20 per cent reserve requirement, i.e. for every deposit made with a bank, the bank must hold 20 per cent as a reserve and can lend the rest out.
● There is no cash drain from the system, i.e. people are holding just as much cash as they need for transaction purposes. Should they receive any more money they will deposit it with their bank.

Our example refers to Table 16.1.

Table 16.1 The money creation process in a multi-bank financial system

Bank	New deposit	New loan	Reserve
One	1000	800	200
Two	800	640	160
Three	640	512	128
Four	512	409.6	102.4
Five	409.6	327.7	81.9
Six	327.7	262.2	65.5
All other banks	1310.7	1048.5	262.2
Total for system	5000	4000	1000

A single deposit of R1000 cash is made with one of the banks in the multi-bank system – Bank One. Bank One must now keep R200 as a reserve and can lend the rest out. It does this by making overdraft facilities available to one of its clients. When this R800 is spent it will eventually return to the banking system as a deposit. All of the R800 returns to the banking system because of the assumption made that there is no cash drain.

Bank Two receives the R800. It must now hold 20 per cent as a reserve against the deposit, or R160, and lends out the remaining R640. This is again spent in the economy and eventually returns as a deposit in Bank Three, which again holds 20 per cent as a reserve and lends out the rest.

As the process continues each bank receives less and less of the initial R1000 deposit, holds 20 per cent of each deposit as a reserve, and lends out the rest. The entire money creation process comes to an end when there are no surplus funds left to lend out. In other words, it happens when the total increase in reserves of the banking system equals the initial deposit.

It is crucially important to know exactly by how much the money supply will increase in response to a given change in deposits. This information is given by the *money multiplier*:

Money multiplier = 1/Reserve requirement

In the above example the reserve requirement was 20 per cent. As a result, the money multiplier is 5 and the final increase in the money supply resulting from the initial deposit of R1000 is R5000. This increase is made up of the initial R1000 deposit and the R4000 loans issued by the banks.

Both the assumptions made above can materially affect the money creation process. An increase in the reserve requirement will lower the value of the money multiplier while a cash drain, often resulting from the growth of the informal sector (or underground economy), will reduce the number and value of new deposits made.

Limitations to the money creation process

The above explanation has shown how commercial banks can increase the money supply as a result of an increase in deposits and the issuing of loans as a multiple of their reserve requirements.

There are three limitations on the ability of commercial banks to increase the money supply:

● *No increase in deposits.* If the state of the economy and interest rates remain unchanged, increases in deposits (referred to as high powered money or the monetary base) can only come from the Reserve Bank or through the Balance of Payments accounts (as either a trade surplus or a capital inflow).
● *Lack of willingness to borrow on the part of the public.* If interest rates remain high it is unlikely that households or firms will wish to borrow on a large scale.
● *Lack of willingness to lend on the part of the commercial banks.*

16.6 The South African Banking system

The South African banking system is modelled on that of the United Kingdom, with a central bank, a governor who is appointed by parliament, and a commercial banking industry in which there is a limited number of multi-branch banks.

From a legal point of view there are only two types of banks in South Africa. These are the South African Reserve Bank and deposit-taking institutions (DTIs). Apart from the Reserve Bank, all other banks are DTIs.

South African Reserve Bank

The South African Reserve Bank started operations in 1921 although initially with rather restricted authority. Between the inception of the Reserve Bank and the promulgation of the Reserve Bank Act of 1944, the Bank came to have increasing powers to control and regulate other banks and conduct monetary policy. Today the Reserve Bank has all of the powers normally associated with central banks – with the exception of the public debt (which is the responsibility of the Department of Finance). The Reserve Bank has the power to extend loans and advances, discount and rediscount bills, and invest and trade in bills. In addition, the Bank has the ability to bring about rapid monetary policy adjustments.

The main functions of the Reserve Bank are:

- *Banker to deposit-taking institutions.* In this capacity the Reserve Bank provides a number of services:

  1. It sets the level of required reserves and also holds these reserves.
  2. It provides a safe place for DTIs to deposit excess reserves and other short-term funds.
  3. It provides facilities for the clearing and settlement of interbank claims.
  4. It acts as a *lender of last resort* to DTIs. If DTIs are in an illiquid situation – in other words if they have insufficient funds to cover withdrawals – the Reserve Bank provides a facility by which the bank can borrow the necessary funds. Such borrowing is called *Reserve Bank accommodation* and it takes place through the *accommodation window*. The total Reserve Bank accommodation is referred to as the *money market shortage*. The Reserve Bank charges DTIs for loans made through the accommodation window, and this charge is called the *bank rate*.

- *Control of the money supply.*
- *Banker to the government.* In this regard the Reserve Bank undertakes three tasks:

  1. It holds government funds taken in by the Receiver of Revenue.
  2. It draws on the above funds and issues cheques as government expenditures are made.
  3. Where government expenditures exceed revenues it may sell government stock to the market.

- *Banker to the nation.* As a central banker the Reserve Bank fulfils a number of other important functions:

  1. It issues currency.
  2. It acts as custodian of the country's gold and other foreign reserves.
  3. It collects, processes and interprets economic statistics and other information.
  4. It is responsible for, together with other agencies, the formulation and implementation of monetary and exchange rate policies.

One of the unique features of the South African Reserve Bank is that it is in part privately owned and listed on the Johannesburg Stock Exchange. It has a share capital of R2 million which is held by 750 shareholders. Shareholding is limited to a maximum of R10 000. There are 12 directors of whom six, including the Governor and three Deputy-Governors, are appointed by the State President. The other six are elected by the shareholders.

Deposit-taking institutions

One of the major departures of the South African banking system from the United Kingdom model took place with the promulgation of the Deposit-Taking Institutions Act (DTI) in November 1990. This act brought South Africa into line with the Basle Accord which, since 1988, made international banking the first industry to be truly regulated at international level.

The passing of the DTI Act changed two essential features of the banking system. Prior to the Act there were specific and distinct types of banks. One of these types of banks, the discount houses, played an important role as intermediary between the banking system and the Reserve Bank in maintaining liquidity in the market. In times of financial stringency, for example, banks could discount bills of exchange with the discount houses. The houses themselves had a special relationship with the Reserve Bank, which guaranteed liquidity through accommodation.

Today there is no legal distinction between any of the deposit-taking institutions. They are distinguishable only by the services they offer and, as a result, by their mix of assets and liabilities. Reserve requirements remain part of the legislation but are now applied as a variable determined by the asset mix.

Commercial banks

Commercial banks derive their profit from loan activity and fees charged for the provision of financial services. Commercial banks offer two prime services. They take in deposits which can be withdrawn without notice, i.e. demand deposits or cheque accounts, and also make available credit in the form of overdraft facilities.

Merchant banks

In practice merchant banks offer five types of service:

- Corporate financing, e.g. assessing corporate structure, administering mergers and acquisitions and the placement of share issues;
- Corporate lending;

- Money and capital market investments;
- International services, e.g. trade financing and spot and forward exchange trading;
- Investment management, particularly pension funds and unit trusts.

Building societies

Building societies were originally created as a means of converting savings into loans on immovable property. The first change – the Banks' Act amendments of 1985 – forced building societies to choose between bank or society status. Today there is no legal distinction between building societies and other banks, and there are only two DTIs which still call themselves building societies.

Post Office Savings Bank

The Post Office Savings Bank offers the public the facilities of an over-the-counter savings bank at over 1700 post offices. The important difference between the Post Office Savings Bank and the commercial banks is that post offices can be found in places where there are no banks, especially in rural areas.

Summary

- Money is important because it allows people to break away from a system of barter. Barter is very restrictive because of the need for the double coincidence of wants. Reduction in trade lowers the gains from trade and standards of living. Money is also important because of its effects on interest rates, prices and exchange rates.

- In order for any object or commodity to be accepted as money it must embody three characteristics. It must be a medium of exchange (i.e. it must be readily accepted), a store of value (i.e. it must be reasonably durable) and a unit of account (i.e. it must be divisible into smaller and smaller parts where each part retains its proportional value no matter how small it becomes). Historically the commodities most widely used as money were the precious metals, particularly gold and silver. Paper money evolved under the Gold Standard where all money was fully backed by gold, in other words, gold was the real money while paper money represented a potential claim on that gold. The ending of the Gold Standard during the early 1930s brought about the evolution of modern money. Today's money is not backed by any precious metal and is called fiat money.

- There are various types of money apart from currency. These include demand deposits (e.g. cheque accounts), saving accounts and time deposits. These various types of money are included in the different measures of the money supply.

- The money supply is calculated using measures called M1, M2 and M3. M1 is the most liquid form of money and is made up of currency and demand deposits, M2 includes M1 as well as short and medium term deposits, M3 includes M2 and long term deposits.

- Under certain monetary regimes, commercial banks have the ability to create money by issuing overdraft facilities. This is the so-called money creation process. Banks are able to create overdraft facilities and therefore money because when a deposit is made into a bank, the bank holds back a portion of that deposit and lends out the rest. As the entire banking system will do this a single deposit can result in a multiple expansion of the money supply. The extent to which money supply will increase following a single new deposit is determined by the money multiplier.

- Under South African legislation there are only two types of banks: the South African Reserve Bank and deposit taking institutions.

- The South African Reserve Bank is the regulator of financial markets. Its main functions include being banker to deposit taking institutions; controller of the money supply; banker to the government; and banker to the nation.

- Private sector banks are called deposit taking institutions. These include commercial banks, merchant banks, discount houses, building societies and the Post Office Savings Bank.

Questions for review

1. In today's world, where money is no longer backed by precious metals, why does money have value?

2. Why do gold and diamonds have value?

3. Most people regard money as the thing that you can put into your wallet or purse. Yet central bank measures of money include all sorts of financial paper. Explain.

4. Which is more important: money or income? Explain.

5. Describe the role of central banks like the South African Reserve Bank.

CHAPTER 17

Money, interest rates and prices

Without money there can only be barter trade with all its attendant problems. Once money is introduced, the economy is in a better position to utilise its potential gains from trade through the establishment of a range of prices, including interest rates and the exchange rate.

It is the purpose of this chapter to outline the relationships that exist between interest rates, prices and real income. In order to simplify this task we first deal with these relationships in the context of a predominantly closed economy – one which does not trade with other countries in the world. This will be followed, in Chapter 18, by a similar analysis for a small open economy.

17.1 Money and prices in a closed economy

As no modern economy is fully closed, we return to one of our sun-swept and isolated Pacific islands. This particular island is a closed economy – the island has no economic contact of any nature with other countries in the rest of the world. Each person on the island is 'fully employed', i.e. anyone who wishes to work at the current real wage has a job. The currency on the island is the cowrie shell (CS). Since there are no living cowrie shells on the island the money supply is fixed.

One day, unexpectedly, a yacht appears on the blue horizon, skippered by an errant student of economics. It is the landfall the student has long searched for – a land of plenty and of low prices. In the keel of the yacht is a great stock of cowrie shells; in fact the student has enough cowrie shells to double the money supply on the island!

Over the ensuing months the happy student settles on the island and spends his entire stock of cowrie shells.

Soon after the student's arrival some important changes occur on the island. Apart from the other-worldliness of the student's dress, the islanders notice that prices have been increasing at a rapid rate. As the student uses his last cowrie shell, the island economist announces that the average price level on the island has doubled over the last few months – he blames sun-spots.

The island economist is wrong of course. What has been experienced is the operation of the *Quantity Theory of Money*. This theory is shown in the following identity:

$$MV = PY \qquad [17.1]$$

where

M = Money supply
V = Velocity of circulation (speed of circulation)
P = Price level
Y = Income (GDP)

The Quantity Theory of Money follows directly from the principles of Classical economics. Remember that Classical economists considered money to have little real importance – money was merely a veil behind which the real economy operated. Expression 17.1 is an example of the basic Classical approach to money.

Before coming to grips with the expression itself, let us first examine the meaning of the separate components:

- The money supply, M, consists of the total amount of money available for spending. On our Pacific island this was made up of the total stock of cowrie shells. To Classical economists these shells represent transactions money – M1. In the modern world, M2 and M3 are better measures of the money supply.
- The velocity of circulation, V, is the speed with which money changes hands as a result of economic transactions. Many factors can influence the velocity of circulation, including the time interval over which workers are paid – a country in which the bulk of workers are paid monthly will have a far slower velocity than one in which workers are paid weekly. Expectations of future inflation will also increase the velocity of circulation as more people undertake transactions sooner rather than later. Finally, it is important to realise that the question of the stability and predictability of the velocity of circulation is of major importance to the conduct of monetary policy.
- The price level, P, can be taken as the average price of all goods and services and is measured by the consumer price index (CPI).
- The level of income, Y, is the level of real GDP. In other words it is a measure of the actual quantity of goods and services produced.

When bringing the various components of Expression 17.1 together, it is possible to understand more clearly what happened on the island after the student's arrival. There was an increase in M. If we assume for the moment that V remained constant over the time (with inflationary expectations and institutional changes more or less constant) and remember that the island was at full employment, we can see that an increase in M can lead only to an increase in prices.

Expression 17.1 is important as it shows how money can influence GDP. If the island had not started from a position of full employment, then it is possible that the economy would first have moved to full employment before experiencing a noticeable increase in prices. Here an increase in M would lead to an increase in both P and Y. Alternatively if the economy is at full employment, as Classical economists would suggest, an increase in the money supply will lead to a proportional increase in prices.

It is also useful to analyse the change to our island economy in terms of the macroeconomic model developed in previous chapters. This is done in Fig. 17.1.

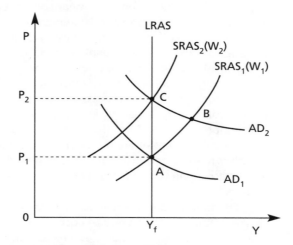

Fig. 17.1 Money and prices in a closed economy

The island economy started in an equilibrium position at full capacity as shown by point A. The errant student's cowrie shells caused an increase in expenditure and moved the aggregate demand from AD_1 to AD_2. Following this change the economy can move either to point B and then to point C or directly to point C. In as small and informal an island as we have in our example it is likely that the increased demand for goods and services will lead to an almost immediate increase in the costs of factors of production, including wages. In consequence aggregate demand and short-run aggregate supply may well move in tandem so that the economy moves directly from point A to C. As was shown by the Quantity Theory of Money, all that happened was an increase in the price level.

EXHIBIT | **Milton Friedman**

Milton Friedman is perhaps the best known living economist in the world today. He has featured prominently in the popular media and has advised many governments across the world. But it is for his many academic contributions, including his pathbreaking work on 'monetarism', that he was awarded the Nobel Prize in Economics in 1976.

Friedman is generally known as the father of monetarism for his many and varied contributions in the field. These include his *Studies in the Quantity Theory of Money*, published in 1956, in which he provided a comprehensive account of the modern quantity theory of money – as discussed in this chapter; *A Theory of the Consumption Function*, published in 1957, in which he developed the now familiar permanent income hypothesis – as discussed in Chapter 13; *A Monetary*

Exhibit continued

History of the United States, co-authored with A. J. Schwartz and published in 1963, in which he argued, *inter alia*, that the Great Depression of 1929–33 was partly caused by monetary mismanagement on the part of the US monetary authorities; and his presidential address to the American Economic Association, entitled 'The Role of Monetary Policy' and published in the *American Economic Review* in 1968, in which he introduced the notion of the 'natural rate of unemployment' – discussed in Chapter 19 below.

Throughout all his work Friedman has consistently argued that 'money matters' in the sense that excessive increases in the money supply will cause inflation and give rise to inflationary expectations (see Chapter 14). Any attempt on the part of governments to stabilise the economy via contractionary or expansionary monetary or fiscal policies will make matters worse rather than better; instead, they should adhere to a so-called 'money-supply rule' according to which the money supply is allowed to grow at the same rate as real GNP.

Friedman also made several other lasting contributions. These included his work on the methodology of economics, the Marshallian demand curve, and on the role of expectations, as well as numerous contributions to our understanding of how free market economies operate.

17.2 Interest rates in a closed economy

On our Pacific island there is no central bank but there is a commercial banker. He uses banking techniques which his ancestors had first learnt from a ship-wrecked goldsmith. He is the island's cowrie shell Custodian.

While cowrie shells are valuable, they are also fragile and subject to the ravages of time. The Custodian has a cool and dark vault rumoured to be somewhere in the west. Over the ages the practice has developed for people to store cowrie shells with the Custodian and use the receipts as currency. Being a good banker the Custodian now lends out money, in the form of cowrie shell receipts, and charges interest on these loans.

What interest rate does he charge?

The Custodian, like all good bankers, is both prudent and profit maximising. He is prudent in that he sets his own reserve requirement at 20 per cent of deposits. In other words, for every cowrie shell in his vault the Custodian can make loans worth another four cowrie shells. He is also a profit maximiser in that he attempts to be fully 'loaned-up', i.e. given his deposits of cowrie shells and the reserve requirement, he maximises his profit when he cannot make any more loans.

If the Custodian is not fully loaned up, what can he do? He must reduce interest rates charged on loans and paid on deposits. Loans will go up, deposits will fall and the Custodian will become fully loaned up. In this sense interest rates are determined by the interaction of the demand for and supply of loanable funds. This in fact is nothing more than was established in the presentation of financial markets in the circular flow model in Chapters 3 and 15, and reproduced in Fig. 17.2.

Figure 17.2 illustrates the positive relationship which exists between people's willingness to save and the interest rate, and the negative relationship between willingness to borrow and the interest rate. The market for loanable funds clears at an interest rate of i_1.

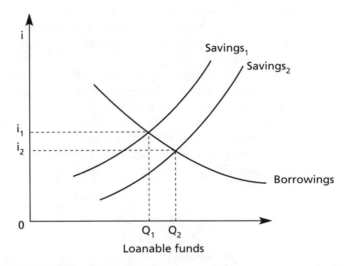

Fig. 17.2 The market for loanable funds

It is now appropriate to examine the impact on the Custodian of the arrival of the wayward student. As the new cowrie shells enter the island economy, so they are deposited with the Custodian. He, in turn, attempts to become fully loaned-up and reduces interest rates. This is illustrated in Figure 17.2. The increase in the deposits of cowrie shells is the real world equivalent of an increase in deposits with banks – an increase in savings. In consequence the savings function moves to the right and the interest rate falls to i_2.

Prices and interest rates

In the above example the drop in the interest rate leads to an increase in loans (from OQ_1 to OQ_2). One would therefore expect an increase in purchasing power putting upward pressure on prices.

Back on the island as time passes and prices increase, the Custodian begins to notice something rather strange. While he has not changed his nominal interest rate since the first decrease, deposits are beginning to fall and there are more and more people wanting to take up loans. This obviously causes the Custodian grave concern as he is moving beyond the limitations of his 20 per cent reserve requirement.

In an attempt to avert a banking disaster the Custodian finally manages to corner the island's financial wizard. She explains to him that it is his own fault that deposits are falling as he has, without knowing, steadily been decreasing his interest rate, long after the first initial decrease. In fact rates have fallen so low that there is little point in keeping cowrie shells with the Custodian. The financial wizard explains that it is obvious to everyone that this is the case by pointing to one of the long-established traditions on the island.

A tradition had developed in which all accumulated interest on deposits were withdrawn every few months and used to fund a wild and extravagant party. The problem for the islanders was that because prices had increased, the cost of the party also increased. As prices increased and nominal interest rates remained unchanged it became increasingly obvious to all that there was not enough money available and that the parties lacked their usual lustre. The Custodian finally acted when the maiden aunts of the island complained that the last party was even worse than those the student held.

The Custodian had discovered *real interest rates*!

It became obvious to the Custodian that he should have considered the after-inflation interest rate – the real interest rate. This is shown in Expression 17.2:

$$\left[\begin{array}{ll} & i = r + P^* \\ \text{or} & r = i - P^* \end{array} \right] \tag{17.2}$$

where r = real interest rate
  i = nominal interest rate
  P^* = expected change in prices

What this expression shows is that nominal interest rates (those rates reported in the press and offered by banks for savings and loans) are made up of two separate components – real interest rates and the expected change in prices. Real interest rates express the after-inflation return people expect on their deposits, and on our island it is the real interest rate that determines the wildness and extravagance of the occasional party.

This is illustrated in Fig. 17.3. If people are concerned about the after-inflation returns to their savings and borrowings, then the vertical axis of the loanable funds market should depict the real interest rate and not the nominal interest rate.

What happened on the island was that while prices increased the Custodian kept the nominal interest rate constant, so that real returns fell. In Fig. 17.3 this is seen as a downward movement along the vertical axis from r_1 to r_0. In other words, because the Custodian did not react to increasing prices and kept the nominal interest rate constant, the real interest rate fell. There was therefore an excess demand for loanable funds equal to the amount $OQ_3 - OQ_1$.

To stop deposits from falling the Custodian has no choice but to increase nominal interest rates in line with inflation in order to keep real interest rates constant.

Precisely the same happens in the real world. As real returns fall, so lenders are less willing to lend. Borrowers on the other hand are more willing to borrow. As this is a disequilibrium situation real interest rates must rise.

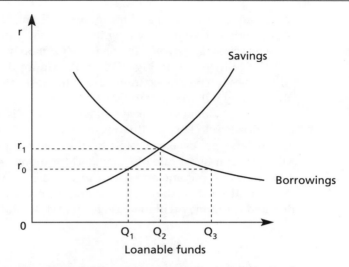

Fig. 17.3 Real interest rates and the market for loanable funds

What we see therefore in the real world is a situation in which the first increase in the money supply leads to falling nominal interest rates. If the resultant increase in loans should lead to price increases, real interest rates will fall. Here the adjustment mechanism is through the nominal interest rate. Nominal rates must increase by the amount of the price increase for real rates to remain constant.

Where inflationary expectations are present in an economy, an increase in money supply will lead directly to increases in nominal interest rates.

17.3 Demand for money

To understand why people demand money it is again necessary to stress that there is an important difference between money and income. People are income maximisers. They do not, on the other hand, attempt to maximise their holdings of money. On the whole people hold money for spending purposes. It therefore follows that the greater is a person's income, the more money he or she will hold for spending purposes, and vice versa. In addition, the greater is the price level for some given level of money income, the more money people will want to hold in order to buy the same amount of goods and services.

Apart from income and prices there is an important relationship between how much money people hold and the interest rate.

People can hold financial assets in a variety of forms. Some of these give a rate of return and some do not. Imagine for the sake of simplicity that people can hold their financial assets either in the form of currency, for which there is no interest rate, or in the form of a government bond which does pay interest. When people choose to hold money rather than the bond they are therefore forgoing the interest on the bond. In other words, the opportunity cost of holding money is the interest rate on bonds. As interest rates increase so the opportunity cost of holding money increases and people will be less willing to hold money.

In consequence the demand for money will fall. Conversely, as the interest rate falls people will be more willing to hold money. What is observed here is a negative relationship between the demand for money and interest rates.

This is illustrated in Fig. 17.4. In the figure the demand for money equals OM_1 when interest rates are i_1, and if interest rates fall to i_0 the willingness to hold money will increase to OM_2.

The money demand curve will shift if there is a change in either income or the price level. This is illustrated in Fig. 17.5. At some particular level of income and prices, e.g. Y_1 and P_1, the demand for money curve is shown as MD_1. At an interest rate of i_1 demand for money equals OM_1. Should there be an increase in income and/or in prices, e.g. to Y_2 or P_2, the money demand curve will shift to the right. If interest rates remain unchanged at i_1, the demand for money will increase from OM_1 to OM_2.

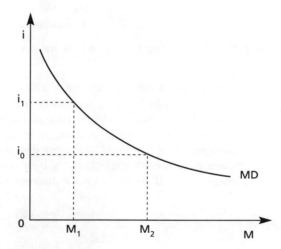

Fig. 17.4 The demand for money curve

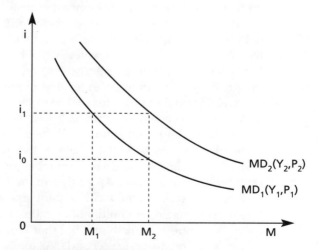

Fig. 17.5 Movements in money demand

Liquidity preference and the speculative demand for money

In the Keynesian view of money there are three reasons why people demand money:

Transactions demand. People hold money for spending. Hence the demand for money is a function of income, prices and the velocity of circulation. You will recognise the classical quantity theory here.

Precautionary demand. People hold a certain amount of money to make up any possible mismatch between expenditures and receipts. Not all people pay bills on time. If you are the person who is owed money you could be a creditor without any money. To avoid such unpleasant effect you would, if possible, hold some money as a precaution against such an outcome.

Speculative demand. Once transactions and precautionary demands are taken care of some people hold money for speculative purposes. The simplest way of understanding how this is done is to imagine that people can hold only two financial assets – money or government stock (i.e. government financial paper as sold on the capital markets). In this approach government stock is a unique investment because it gives a fixed monetary rate of return, for example R10 a year or R10 million a year depending on the value of the stock.

Imagine a simple piece of government stock which pays R10 a year and has a very long time before maturity. What is the value of the government stock if the ruling rate of interest is 10 per cent? This is given by asking how much one would have to save at 10 per cent in order to earn R10. The answer is obviously R100. Now what happens to the value of the government stock if the ruling rate of interest fell to 5 per cent? The value increases to R200! If interest rates increased to 20 per cent your government stock would be worth only R50.

What emerges from this is the principle that there is an inverse relationship between the value of financial paper and the interest rate. Hence high interest rates tend to decrease the value of financial paper and low interest rates increase these values. What is also apparent is that relatively small changes in interest rates can bring about relatively large changes in the capital value of financial assets.

What follows from this is that people who speculate on financial markets are very sensitive to future expected changes in interest rates. Imagine you had a large pile of government stock and you expected interest rates to increase. Would you keep or sell your stock? If you didn't sell it and interest rates did increase, you would have lost a large sum of money.

As a result of expected changes in the future interest rate people have a particular preference for holding a certain amount of money in their asset portfolio. In the jargon of economics people have a certain liquidity preference. When interest rates are very low and the general expectation is that they will increase, speculators prefer to be very liquid – holding as much money and as few stocks as possible. If they were holding stocks the value of these stocks would fall as the interest rate increased. When interest rates are very high there will be a very low demand for money as interest rates are

▶

more likely to fall rather than increase further. Hence speculators will be holding stock in anticipation that it will increase in value.

What this liquidity preference theory reinforces is the inverse relationship which is thought to exist between interest rates and money. This relationship was illustrated in Fig. 17.4.

17.4 Money supply

Chapter 16 focused on the meaning of money, the types of money and the money creation process. In this section we continue in a similar vein by exploring the relationship between money supply and interest rates. In order to do so, we first explore this relationship in terms of our simple island economy. From this we move to a more modern economy where the central bank has as one of its objectives the control of the money supply.

Money supply and interest rates without a central bank

We return once again to the Custodian of the cowrie shells on our Pacific island. It will be recalled that the Custodian is acting as a banker by issuing fractionally backed receipts or currency against the cowrie shells being held as deposits. Imagine now that the demand for loans suddenly increases – possibly to celebrate the departure of the errant student. How does the Custodian banker respond?

As the Custodian is profit motivated, he will issue more loans. What this means is that he is implicitly reducing his own reserve requirement. However as the Custodian is also a prudent banker he will charge more for these loans to compensate for the greater risk which he is taking on by implicitly reducing his reserve requirement. This is illustrated in Fig. 17.6. At an interest rate of i_1 the Custodian is willing to make loans to the extent that the money supply equals OM_1. Should the demand for credit increase he will issue more loans and raise money supply to OM_2. Interest rates are however increased from i_1 to i_2.

The money supply curve will shift if, for some reason, the Custodian is suddenly able to issue more loans. Two factors can cause such a change:

- *An increase in deposits.* The arrival of our errant student on the Pacific Island is one such example. The cowrie shells which the student brought along resulted in an increase in currency. As this was spent and deposited, the Custodian was able to offer increasingly larger loans. Such a change is illustrated in Fig. 17.7. At a constant interest rate of i_1 the Custodian was willing to increase loans to the extent that the money supply curve moved from M^s_1 to M^s_2 and the total money supply on the island increased from OM_1 to OM_2.

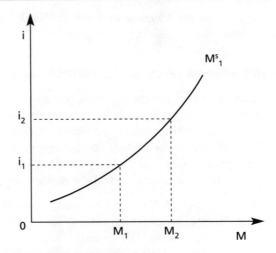

Fig. 17.6 Money supply with no central bank

In the real world such an increase in deposits can result from an increase in the currency itself by the central bank, an inflow of foreign reserves (e.g. the errant student), and by loans made by the central bank either to commercial banks or to the government.

- *Structural changes in a country.* The Custodian, like all prudent bankers, wants to have sufficient reserves on hand to cover potential withdrawals. Should the likelihood of withdrawals fall, the Custodian need hold less reserves and can make more loans, thus boosting the money supply. In today's world an obvious example of such a structural change is the introduction of automatic teller machines. The existence of these machines means that people are able to hold less money for day-to-day transactions,

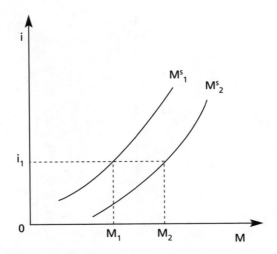

Fig. 17.7 Changes in money supply

and, in the absence of a central bank, commercial banks can reduce their reserves by issuing more loans.

Money supply and interest rates with a central bank

The essential difference between our Custodian banker in the Pacific and bankers in today's world is the existence of central banks and the fact that one of the most important functions of central banks is to control the money supply. While the details of how central banks can control the money supply are given in Chapter 21, we provide the basics here.

Central banks can control the money supply either directly or indirectly:

- *Direct control.* Central banks can control reserve requirements and the liquidity of the banking system. This type of control is illustrated in Fig. 17.8. Here the money supply curve is presented as a vertical line with respect to interest rates. What this means is that the central bank controls the money supply directly. In other words it has full control over the money supply. Should the central bank so wish it can increase money supply either by reducing the reserve requirement or by increasing liquidity in the banking system. Should this happen the money supply curve will move from M^s_1 to M^s_2 in Fig. 17.8.

- *Indirect control.* Central banks can control the money supply indirectly through the setting of interest rates. In today's world it is usually the case that central banks find it simpler and more effective to control money supply indirectly through the control of interest rates. Under this type of monetary regime, which is illustrated in Fig. 17.9, central banks set short-term interest rates in the country. This is done by keeping commercial banks (or deposit-taking institutions) indebted to the central bank, and forcing them to borrow from the central bank through the accommodation window

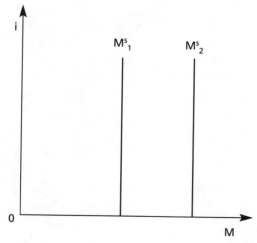

Fig. 17.8 Central bank control over money supply

and pay the bank rate. Commercial banks in turn lend this money out to the public with some mark-up over the bank rate. What this means in practice is that central banks set interest rates and allow people to have as much money as they want at that particular interest rate. The rate i_1 in Fig. 17.9 is a case in point. Should the central bank wish to decrease the money supply it would simply raise the bank rate. In consequence interest rates would increase from i_1 to i_2 and the money supply curve, which is now perfectly elastic with respect to the interest rate, would move from M^s_1 to M^s_2.

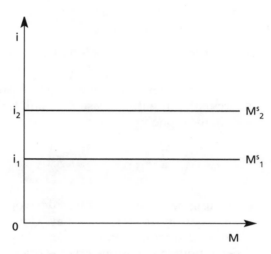

Fig. 17.9 Central bank control over money supply through interest rate control

17.5 Money market equilibrium

Money market equilibrium occurs when money demand is equal to money supply. The nature of the equilibrium will depend on whether their is central bank control and, if so, on whether the central bank controls the money supply directly or indirectly. All three cases are illustrated in Fig. 17.10.

Part (a) of Fig. 17.10 illustrates money market equilibrium in the absence of a central bank. Under these circumstances the interaction of the money demand and money supply curves determines both the interest rate and the total money supply. A shift in either of the curves will change both the interest rate and the amount of money in the economy.

Parts (b) and (c) of Fig. 17.10 illustrate money market equilibrium when a central bank attempts to control the money supply. In the case where the central bank attempts to do so directly, as in panel (b), the variable which is determined in the market is the interest rate. On the other hand, should the central bank attempt to control the money supply indirectly, interest rates will be set and money supply will be determined by the extent of money demand. Should money demand increase, the actual money supply will also

269

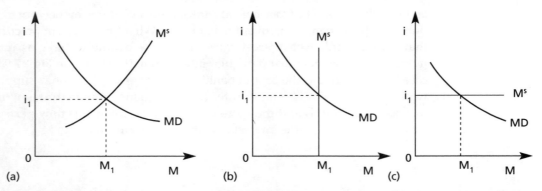

Fig. 17.10 Money market equilibrium. (a) No central bank; (b) Money supply control; (c) Interest rate control

increase; and should the central bank wish to decrease the amount of money in circulation it will increase the bank rate and thereby increase all interest rates in the economy.

Summary

- The original theory of money, developed by the Classical school, is called the Quantity theory of money. Under this theory the total quantity of money (M) multiplied by the speed with which it circulates (V) is equal to real output (Y) multiplied by the price level (P), i.e. MV=PY.

- In a closed economy, i.e. a country which has no commercial dealings with other countries, interest rates are determined by the willingness to lend and the willingness to borrow. Any factors which change the willingness to lend or borrow will change the interest rate. Such factors include changes in income, changes in expectations and changes in the government's budget deficit.

- An important distinction must be made between nominal and real interest rates. When people save what is important to them is their real, after-inflation return. Similarly, when people borrow they are concerned about the real, after-inflation cost. Real interest rates are determined by the real forces underlying the position of the savings and borrowings curves. These include the productivity of capital and the general willingness to save. Nominal interest rates are made up of real interest rates plus the expected future change in the price level. Inflation, which may leave real rates unchanged, has the effect of increasing nominal interest rates by the amount of inflationary expectations.

- Three factors determine the amount of money that people choose to hold, i.e. the demand for money. These are their level of income (wealthy people hold more money than poorer people simply because they buy more goods and services); prices (the higher the prices of goods and services the more money people will need to hold); and the opportunity cost of holding money – the interest rate. Hence the money demand curve is downward sloping with respect to interest rates and will shift if there is any change in incomes or the price level.

● The relationship between money supply and interest rates will depend on the monetary regime and the way in which commercial banks operate. In a country where there is no central bank (or one where the central bank encourages this type of operation) money supply will increase as interest rates increase. Other monetary regimes include those where the central bank sets the total amount of money in the economy and those where the central bank sets interest rates. In the former case demand for money determines interest rates in the money market. In the latter case money demand determines the amount of money in the economy (i.e. the money supply).

Questions for review

1. Imagine an economy which is in some stable long-run equilibrium situation. There is suddenly an unexpected increase in the money supply. What is the likely effect on prices, real GDP, nominal interest rates and real interest rates? (There is no central bank.)

2. Imagine an economy which finds itself in some temporary short-run equilibrium situation and operating at a less-than-full-employment level of output. There is suddenly an unexpected increase in the money supply. What is the likely effect on prices, real GDP, nominal interest rates and real interest rates? (There is no central bank.)

3. Imagine an economy in some temporary short-run equilibrium situation and operating at more than full employment. There is suddenly an unexpected increase in the money supply. What is the likely effect on prices, read GDP, nominal interest rates and real interest rates? (There is no central bank.)

4. Re-analyse questions 1, 2, and 3, on the basis that there is a central bank which:

   a) Attempts to control money supply directly;

   b) Attempts to control money by controlling interest rates.

CHAPTER 18

Exchange rates, interest rates and prices

In the previous chapter we saw how the very existence of money led to the establishment of a range of prices, including the price of money itself, i.e. the interest rate. This chapter introduces yet another price that is related to money. However, unlike interest rates, this price applies to moneys exchanged between different countries – the exchange rate.

Today's world is a global economy and nowhere is this more true than in the field of international finance. In industrialised countries and in many parts of the developing world there are well developed and sophisticated markets in foreign exchange. With satellite linkages and integrated computer networks enormous volumes of currencies can cross borders within seconds of any change in sentiment about a country or in the relative value of currencies.

Interest rates, exchange rates and prices are all determined by money. The previous chapter explored the relationship between money, interest rates and prices. Given the importance of foreign exchange markets, a full understanding of financial markets demands an understanding of the relationship between exchange rates, prices and interest rates.

In this chapter we introduce exchange rates first by means of the balance of payments accounts. This is followed by a discussion of nominal and real exchange rates, after which we consider exchange rate adjustments in the case of a small open economy.

18.1 Balance of payments accounts

The accounts of the balance of payments record the flows of money between a country and the rest of the world. The accounts are made up of three separate accounts:

- *Current account.* The current account records the flows of money resulting from a country's involvement in the international trade of goods and services. The current account is traditionally divided into the *trading account* and the *services account*:

  1. The trading account records the value of imports and exports of raw materials, capital and intermediate goods and consumer goods.

2. The services account records the value of services traded on international markets. The largest portion of services traded consists of transport and financial services.

- *Capital account.* The capital account of the balance of payments records flows of money into and out of a country which are not related to the trade in goods and services. The capital account records separately so-called long-term and short-term capital movements:

  1. Long-term capital flows. A long-term asset is one where the original contract was for more than a year. From a national point of view this is the most desirable type of capital inflow.
  2. Short-term capital flows. A short-term asset is one which has an original contractual maturity of less than one year. This component of the balance of payments is usually regarded as the more speculative type of capital and is often called 'hot money'.

     It is important, however, to realise that long-term capital can also be moved on short notice. Long-term assets like shares and bonds can be sold on the securities market.

- *Official reserves and liabilities.* This account serves two purposes in the balance of payments. First, it records a country's holding of foreign reserves and gold. Second, it serves as the means of correcting imbalances between inflows and outflows of foreign currencies. For example, if there were no capital flows and a country imports more goods and services than it exports in any one year, the difference will be made up by a decline in the official reserves.

Of course, in the above example it is also possible for the country's exchange rate to depreciate. As indicated in Chapter 3, such a depreciation will raise import prices and lower export prices which, under certain conditions, will curb the volume of imports and boost exports. A country's exchange rate plays an important role in helping it to achieve balance of payments equilibrium.

In what follows we shall draw on various theories of exchange rate determination as a means of presenting a coherent picture of how exchange rates are determined. One of the essential differences between these theories concerns the time horizon. In other words, if there is some relevant disturbance today, how long does it take for the exchange rate to reach equilibrium?

As a means of simplifying the approach we define three time horizons. These coincide with three different approaches to the determination of exchange rates: long term, medium term and short term.

18.2 Exchange rate determination in the long run: the monetary approach

The leading theory of exchange rate determination in the long run is referred to as the monetary approach to the balance of payments. The monetary approach takes as its starting point the concept of *purchasing power parity* (PPP).

According to this theory, the price of a unit of Currency A in terms of Currency B (i.e. the exchange rate) will, in the long run, tend to equal the ratio of the price level in Country B to the price level in Country A. In a world where all goods and services are traded internationally, with no transport costs or barriers to trade, the purchasing power parity theory would presumably hold.

This means that price levels within one country are determined by price levels outside the country. How are these prices transmitted? Through the exchange rate! Suppose, for example, that the USA and British domestic price levels are such that $100 will buy exactly twice as large a basket of goods in the United States as can be bought for £100 in Britain. Purchasing power parity will then imply that the exchange rate must be two sterling pounds per dollar. If a dollar could be exchanged for more than £2, US consumers would all try to turn in their dollars and do their shopping in Britain. Their attempts to do so would immediately drive the price of the dollar back down to £2. Similarly, if a dollar could be purchased for less than £2 the British would try to turn in all their pounds for dollars and shop in the United States. This would quickly push the price of the dollar up to £2.

The PPP (or monetary) approach to exchange rate determination is indicated in Equation 18.1: it shows the exchange rate as being equal to the ratio of the average price levels in two countries.

$$e = P/P_w \qquad\qquad [18.1]$$

where e = exchange rate
     P = domestic prices
     P_w = world prices

In the case of South Africa the exchange rate, e, could mean the rand/dollar exchange rate, for instance $1=R4. The domestic price level, P, is the price level inside the country, for example the South African CPI. P_w is the price level in the rest of the world. For all practical purposes P_w refers to the average CPI, suitably weighted, of South Africa's trading partners.

Imagine a similar good in two different countries. For example, if a computer in South Africa costs R4000 and the equivalent machine costs $1000 in the USA then the exchange rate would be $1= R4. A number of factors can cause deviations from this PPP exchange rate:

- *Transport costs.* The price of South African computers must include the cost of transporting those components made in other countries. This factor is especially important for low-value, high-mass goods like coal, sugar and iron ore.
- *Tariffs.* Where tariffs exist, domestic prices will be higher than their PPP levels.
- *Imperfect markets.* If there are imperfect markets, such as monopoly, prices will again be different from their PPP levels.

Equation 18.1 – the PPP exchange rate – is important in understanding some of the fundamental forces which determine exchange rates. The equation can be used to make two important predictions:

- If the ratio of prices between two countries changes, then, in the long term, the relevant exchange rate will also change. If, for instance, inflation in the USA exceeds that in the rest of the world, the dollar will depreciate. This is precisely what happened to the dollar in the 1970s.
- If the exchange rate suddenly changes due to an unexpected disturbance, domestic prices will adjust. One of the factors which helped to keep UK inflation low during the 1980s was its ability to export North Sea oil and the impact that this had on the value of sterling. In South Africa's case the political and social turmoil of the 1980s resulted in capital flight and a sudden depreciation in the value of the rand. The resultant increase in import prices meant that South Africa experienced its highest inflation ever in 1986.

The monetary approach to the balance of payments is closely associated with the Quantity Theory of Money – as discussed in the previous chapter. Monetarists follow their Classical counterparts in believing that economies are either close to or at full employment. As a result any increase in the money supply leads to an increase in the price level. In turn, this increase in the price level leads to a depreciation of the currency. There are two potential mechanisms through which such a depreciation can occur:

- *The money supply increase leads to increases in domestic prices.* As prices increase people buy more imports, while other countries buy less of the country's exports. There is a fall in demand for the domestic currency and the exchange rate depreciates.
- *Money supply increases lead directly to increased imports.* This causes the currency to depreciate. In turn, imports cost more as do domestically produced exports. These price increases filter through the rest of the economy and become a general price increase.

While PPP and the monetary approach to the balance of payments are matched by forceful economic logic, this approach has not proved of much use in forecasting exchange rate movements. What the monetary approach to the balance of payments has to offer is an explanation of how exchange rates are determined over a relatively long period of time. Probably the major flaw of the PPP is that it does not explain why prices may not adjust instantly and often require a considerable time before adjusting fully. It is therefore not a good indicator of exchange rate determination in the short term. However the major contribution of the monetary approach to the balance of payments is the proposition that prices between countries cannot stay out of alignment for ever; in the long run either the price level or the exchange rate must adjust.

18.3 Medium term – the elasticities approach

The elasticities approach or the current balance approach, as it is sometimes called, is essentially a microeconomic explanation of the determination of exchange rates. It was this approach that formed the basis for our brief discussion of exchange rates in Chapter 3.

The elasticities approach is largely a trade-dominated model and therefore provides an explanation of how exchange rates are determined in the medium term.

In the absence of capital mobility, and given a free floating exchange rate (i.e. with no central bank intervention), the current account would have to be in equilibrium if the foreign exchange market is to clear. The reason is that there would be no other accounts to balance out any disequilibrium in the current account. The way that such a market will clear is that the exchange rate will adjust to the point where the demand for foreign exchange to buy imported goods and services equals the supply that is forthcoming from the sale of exports and other current receipts.

As in Chapter 3, the model proceeds by establishing a trade-dominated explanation of the supply and demand curves for foreign exchange.

Supply of foreign exchange

Foreigners supply foreign exchange to the domestic market for two reasons: to pay for domestic exports and as capital inflows into the domestic economy. It is suggested that the supply of foreign exchange curve is upward sloping because, as the domestic currency depreciates against the foreign currency so domestic exports become cheaper to foreigners. Foreigners therefore buy more domestic exports and supply more foreign exchange. The supply of foreign exchange curve is therefore shown in Fig. 18.1 as an upward sloping curve with respect to the rand/dollar exchange rate.

Demand for foreign exchange

The demand curve for foreign exchange is seen to be inversely related to the value of the dollar in terms of domestic currency, as illustrated in Fig. 18.1. The domestic economy (e.g. South Africans) demands foreign exchange for two reasons – to pay for imports and to repay foreign loans (or invest outside the country). The demand for foreign exchange curve is downward sloping because as the domestic currency depreciates against the foreign currency so imports become more expensive. People therefore buy less imports and demand less foreign exchange.

Determination of the exchange rate

As with any other price-based model (and in the absence of any central bank intervention), the equilibrium exchange rate is determined by the interaction of demand and supply. In Fig. 18.1 the equilibrium exchange rate equals e_1. If, for some reason, the exchange rate was e_2 and not e_1, the supply of dollars will exceed the demand and force down the value of the dollar relative to that of the domestic currency. The opposite will happen in the case of an excess demand for dollars.

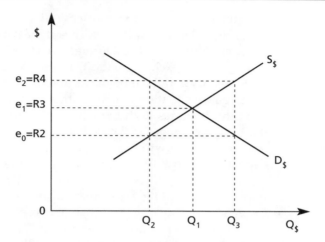

Fig. 18.1 Exchange rate determination – the elasticities approach

Changes in the exchange rate

Any change in the position of either the demand or the supply curve in Fig. 18.1 will bring about a change in the exchange rate. Such changes may occur for at least five reasons:

- *Business cycle changes.* Business cycle changes occur on a fairly regular basis in most economies, and especially in small open economies. Recessions cause people to spend less on both locally produced and imported goods and services. South African exports, for example, consist largely of primary and semiprocessed products destined for the industrialised world. Recessions in industrialised countries reduce the demand for South African exports and may therefore cause a depreciation of the rand. Similarly, an economic upswing in an important trading partner can be transmitted back to the domestic economy through the balance of payments.
- *Change in preferences.* Changes in taste and fashion can sometimes have a major impact on foreign trade and therefore on the exchange rate. This is again true of small open economies, especially those with a narrow export base.

  South Africa with its gold is a prime example. The strong economic growth of the early 1980s, spurred by the high gold price is a far cry from the performance of the South African economy after the gold price had tumbled. It should be realised that changes in the gold price usually result from changes in the preferences of financial institutions and portfolio managers. The high inflationary expectations of the 1970s led to a widespread acquisition of gold. The demise of these expectations in the early 1980s brought about a reversal in gold holdings and consequently brought the gold price down again.
- *Changes in the price of a traded good.* Any relative change in the price of a traded good will bring about a change in the exchange rate. If an individual

country becomes more productive it will be able to sell its exports at a lower price. Exports will increase and the currency will appreciate.

- *Different inflation rates.* Differences in inflation rates will bring about changes in the exchange rate. This also follows from the purchasing power parity theory and the monetary approach to the balance of payments.

  Imagine a situation where South Africa has an annual inflation rate of 10 per cent. It trades with the USA which has, for example, no inflation. If there are no changes in the exchange rate, then by the end of the year South African exports will cost 10 per cent more in the USA while American exports will cost 10 per cent less than their South African equivalents. Demand for South African exports will fall while South Africans will import more from the USA, thus causing the rand to depreciate.

- *Changes in capital flows.* Any change in capital flows into or out of a country will change the position of the demand and supply curves and change the exchange rate. Capital inflows increase the supply of foreign exchange (i.e. move the supply curve to the right) and cause the currency to appreciate. Capital outflows increase the demand for foreign exchange (i.e. move the demand curve to the right) and cause the currency to depreciate.

  The two most important determinants of capital flows are, first, the state of the economy which is important for longer term capital flows and, second, expected future changes in the exchange rate.

18.4 Short term – the asset market approach

Since the early 1980s there have been times when currencies have fluctuated, in what appeared to be some random fashion, around their expected equilibrium. The tendencies for currencies to overshoot or undershoot equilibrium after some shock cannot be explained by any of the other approaches to exchange rate determination. One plausible explanation is that given by the asset market approach.

The major difference between the world of the monetary approach to the balance of payments and today's world is that of speculative capital flows. The monetary approach to the balance of payments emerged during the 1970s and early 1980s. These were the years following the breakdown of the Bretton Woods fixed exchange rate system. Under the Bretton Woods system most countries had in place some system of exchange control. Where there were capital flows these were long term in nature. The breakdown of Bretton Woods and the growing globalisation of international capital markets saw the gradual abolition of exchange controls. Today's industrialised countries have hardly any form of exchange control.

The demise of exchange controls, together with international capital markets which now operate globally for 24 hours a day, have led to the development of enormous markets in speculative capital. Large quantities of money can be moved in or out of a country within seconds of any change in the world's perception of its future. The impact of such movements is seen in the behaviour of exchange rates. Domestic currencies can appreciate or depreciate rapidly depending on the size and duration of short-term capital flows. Sometimes the sheer mass of these funds can result in changes in the exchange rate which are well out of line with the underlying (PPP) exchange rate trend.

The asset market approach assumes that capital flows are more important than flows of goods in determining exchange rates. The approach takes as its starting point the fact that monies (especially interest yielding securities) are held as assets and that the willingness of people to hold these assets is determined by the relative prices of a range of available financial assets.

In the absence of exchange controls, interest rates across countries will be governed by two major factors:

- *Different levels of risk attached to investing in particular countries.*
- *Expectations of future changes in the exchange rate.* Consider the case of an Italian who buys rand-denominated securities. The Italian is concerned not only with the interest rate of the security but also with the likely future value of the rand. If the rand is expected to depreciate, for example, the Italian would want South Africa to pay a higher interest rate in order to offset the expected loss to him resulting from the depreciation.

This second factor is capable of explaining how currencies can overshoot or undershoot. To illustrate, consider the following interest parity equation:

$$i = i_w + (e^* - e)/e \qquad\qquad [18.2]$$

where i = domestic interest rates
 i_w = international interest rates
 e^* = expected future exchange rate
 e = current exchange rate

Equation 18.2 states that domestic interest rates are equal to international interest rates plus the expected percentage change in the exchange rate. For example, if international interest rates are 5 per cent and the domestic currency is expected to depreciate by 2 per cent, the domestic interest rate must equal 7 per cent.

We can also use Equation 18.2 to explain how a currency might over- and undershoot. Imagine a situation in which the domestic money supply increases unexpectedly. The immediate effect is that domestic interest rates fall. Now, since foreign investors know that prices will eventually rise by the amount of the change in the money supply, they also know that the currency will depreciate. Because of the expected depreciation, investors will demand a higher interest rate than before in order to continue holding the domestic currency.

However, as shown above, domestic interest rates are falling not rising.

What will now happen is something of a speculative run on the currency as investors start selling it. As a result the currency will depreciate to below its long-term equilibrium from where it may well be expected to appreciate again. Now investors will be prepared to hold the currency again as the expected appreciation will offset their lower interest returns.

What has happened is that the currency is said to undershoot its equilibrium level. In a reverse situation, for example, after a tightening of monetary policy, the currency can overshoot its long-term equilibrium level.

18.5 Exchange rates, interest rates and prices

If we bring together our earlier equation for the real interest rate (see Equation [17.2]) and the interest parity equation (Equation 18.2), we can determine how interest rates, inflation, and exchange rates are connected. Remember that the real interest rate is given by:

$$i = r + P^*$$

or

$$r = i - P^*$$

where, as before, r is the real interest rate, i the nominal interest rate and P^* is expected inflation.

Next we assume that real interest rates are the same in two countries, e.g. South Africa and the USA, that is,

$$r_R = r_\$$$

Under these conditions the only difference between the nominal interest rates is expected inflation which can be expressed as:

$$i_R - i_\$ = P^*_R - P^*_\$ \qquad [18.3]$$

When this is substituted into the interest parity equation [18.2] the resultant equation summarises the link between interest, inflation, and exchange rates:

$$i_R - i_\$ = P^*_R - P^*_\$ = (e^* - e)/e \qquad [18.4]$$

What this expression states is that real interest rates are equalised between countries when nominal interest rates incorporate differences in inflationary expectations. These inflationary expectations determine the expected future exchange rate. This means, in simple terms, that inflationary expectations and the expected future exchange rate are determined concurrently.

In the real world the relationships shown in Equation 18.4 are determined simultaneously as interest rates, inflationary expectations and exchange rates are collectively affected by new events and information.

18.6 Real exchange rate

One of the important relationships that has emerged in this chapter is the one between prices and exchange rates. At this point it is appropriate to outline more fully a concept called the real exchange rate.

> **The real exchange rate.** *The real exchange rate is a measure of the nominal exchange rate adjusted for differences in the inflation rate between countries. The nominal exchange rate is the commonly quoted exchange rate. It is what we have until now simply called the exchange rate.*

The real exchange rate is determined by deflating the nominal exchange rate by the inflationary differential which exists between two countries. The real (R/\$) exchange rate is defined as in Equation 18.5:

$$e_r = eP_w/P \qquad\qquad [18.5]$$

where e_r = real exchange rate
e = nominal exchange rate
P_w = world prices
P = domestic prices

Importance of the real exchange rate

The real exchange rate is important because it is a determinant of a country's international competitiveness.

It is a commonly held notion that a depreciation in the nominal exchange rate causes the country to become internationally more competitive because the prices of its goods have fallen. Yet it has been shown above that a depreciation of the nominal exchange rate will lead to a domestic price increase. From Equation 18.5, if the price increase is equal to the exchange rate depreciation, i.e. the increase in e, there will be no change in the real exchange rate and, therefore, in the country's international competitiveness.

International competitiveness thus depends on a depreciation of the real rather than nominal exchange rate; that is, on an increase in e_r. What this means in practice is that a nominal exchange rate depreciation must be greater than the resultant increase in prices. In other words, for international competitiveness to improve it is the real exchange rate which must depreciate.

CASE EXAMPLE

Real exchange rate in South Africa

The course of the real exchange rate in South Africa for the years 1979–95 is presented in Fig. 18.2. The two sets of data refer to the nominal and real effective exchange rates. An effective rate is a trade weighted exchange rate.

▶

Case example continued

In this case it is the value of the rand against a basket of foreign currencies where the basket is made up of South Africa's trading partners and the weighting determined by the importance of each in South Africa's total international trade. In other words, the data presented in Fig. 18.2 represent the best indicators of actual nominal and real exchange rates in South Africa.

A number of important features are immediately evident:

● The turbulent times South Africa experienced during the 1980s are well reflected in both the nominal and real exchange rates.
● Both the nominal and real exchange rates appreciated up to 1980; that is, both e and e_r decreased. From this point on the nominal rate depreciated more or less consistently while the real exchange rate did not.
● The real exchange rate depreciated rapidly between 1984 and 1986, being pulled down by the falling nominal rate.
● Since late 1989 the real rate appears to have stabilised.
● Due to real exchange rate effects South Africa's international competitiveness is greater now than it was during the early 1980s.

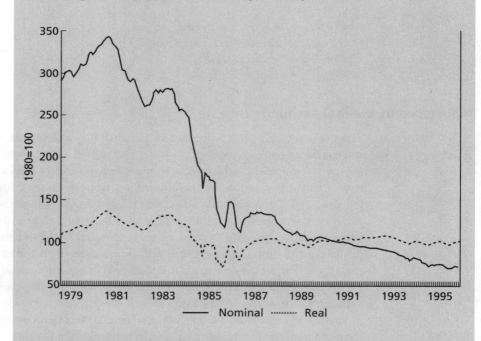

Fig. 18.2 Effective rand exchange rate

18.7 Exchange rate adjustment to equilibrium

In this final section we discuss the process by which an economy might adjust to equilibrium following some monetary shock. In order to do this we return to our Pacific island and consider an increase in the money supply in the light of the theory outlined above.

There are two changes which have occurred on the island since our last visit:

- The first is that the island has been 'discovered' by the world and has started to trade with a number of very large islands which are physically so close to it that transport costs are negligible.
- The second is that the Custodian (central bank) has been actively encouraging a foreign exchange market between cowrie shells and the dollar, and has been borrowing offshore.

We consider the impact of each of these changes separately.

International trade but no foreign capital flows

Again we allow the money supply on the island to increase. Remember that when the island was a closed economy money supply increases led directly to price increases. What will happen when the supply of money increases and the island trades with the rest of the world? Once again interest rates begin to fall as the real money supply increases. Do prices start to increase? For goods and services which can be traded there is no reason why they should, at least in the short term.

Why do prices not increase in the face of increases in the money supply and therefore increases in demand? Because as soon as prices threaten to rise people will import goods from the other large islands which are close by. If goods can be imported rapidly in the face of an increase in the money supply, domestic prices will remain stable.

Prices do eventually increase but not directly as in the closed economy case. The increase in imports causes the exchange rate to depreciate, and it is this depreciation which is responsible for subsequent price increases.

As the currency depreciates so the domestic price of imports increases, and so too does the price of domestically produced exports. Why should the price of domestically produced exports increase within the country? If the producers of exports themselves do not increase prices there is room for arbitrage where goods are purchased on the island and sold offshore. As more and more goods are exported so the domestic price is driven up until the local price equals the international price.

In short, inflationary shocks in open economies, especially small open economies, are often transmitted via the balance of payments. Any factor which causes a currency to depreciate will result in domestic price increases. Likewise countries with appreciating currencies are likely to have more stable prices.

International trade and international capital flows

In this case the island not only trades with the rest of the world but also has an active foreign exchange market. Once again we allow the money supply on the island to increase.

Now there is a number of possible courses of adjustment. These depend largely on the sophistication of the financial markets on the island, the extent to which exchange controls exist and are effective, and the extent to which the theoretical underpinnings are valid.

On the one extreme is the country with efficient foreign exchange markets, no exchange control, no major economic disturbances, and where expectations are formed rationally – as, for example, in the major industrialised countries. Here the likely effect of a money supply increase is the one outlined under the asset market approach. Interest rates will fall, the currency will depreciate and undershoot its true value. It will then begin to appreciate. Prices will increase over the entire period.

At the other extreme is the country with a small and inefficient foreign exchange market and exchange control. In this case the adjustment will take place through the current account of the balance of payments, as outlined in section 18.4.

Summary

- The balance of payments (BOP) accounts record all the moneys which have come into a country over a period of time (usually a year) and all the moneys which have left it. The BOP accounts are made up of three separate accounts. These are the current account, the capital account and the changes in reserves account. The current account measures the movements of moneys due to trade in goods and services. The capital account measures moneys which have come into or gone out of a country for non-trade reasons. The bulk of these flows are for investment purposes. A distinction is made between long term and short term capital flows. The changes in reserves account is the balancing account in the balance of payments. If there is a surplus on both current and capital accounts (and in the absence of a change in the value of the currency), this surplus is accumulated as foreign reserves. The reverse happens if there is a balance of payments deficit.

- Exchange rates indicate the value of one currency relative to some other currency. A variety of forces work to determine the exchange rate. These forces are best understood if we regard them as long term, medium and short term forces. There are three theories that explain these different forces, i.e. the monetary approach for the long term, the elasticities approach for the medium term, and the asset market approach for the short term.

- The monetary approach attempts to explain movements in exchange rates over the long term, and assumes purchasing power parity. Purchasing power parity suggests that in a world with international trade similar goods around the world will have similar prices. If similar goods do not have similar prices people will trade in these goods until prices adjust. The implication of this approach is that an exchange rate is nothing more than the ratio of the domestic price level divided by the price level of the country's trading partners.

● The elasticities approach attempts to explain movements in exchange rates over the medium term, and takes as its starting point the demand for and supply of foreign exchange resulting from trade and capital flows. It is in essence a microeconomic analysis. This approach suggests that any factor which brings about a change in the demand or supply of foreign currency will bring about a change in the exchange rate. Examples of such factors include business cycle changes, changes in preferences, changes in the prices of traded goods, different inflation rates (as per the monetary approach) and changes in capital flows.

● With the general abolition of exchange controls in most countries during the early 1980s some currencies fluctuated in an apparently random fashion around their expected equilibrium level. The asset market approach is one attempt to explain these fluctuations. In order to attract foreign capital, interest rates in a country must be equal to interest rates in the rest of the world plus the future expected change in the exchange rate. If the exchange rate is expected to depreciate domestic interest rates must be higher than world rates in order to compensate foreigners for the capital loss which they will incur when the domestic currency depreciates. Similarly if the currency is expected to appreciate then domestic interest rates will be lower than interest rates in other countries. Now, imagine that there is an increase in the domestic money supply. This has the short term effect of lowering domestic interest rates, while it may also eventually lead to a depreciation of the currency due to increased imports and threatening inflation. Yet in order to compensate foreigners for the likely depreciation, interest rates should actually rise. The consequence is that foreigners take their funds out of the country so that the currency actually depreciates immediately. Thus the depreciation now has to be great enough so that in the future the currency will again appreciate to offset the lower interest rates. Here the currency is said to undershoot its equilibrium level. Similarly if money supply is reduced then the currency may overshoot its long term equilibrium.

● There is an important link between the nominal exchange rate and the domestic price level. When currencies depreciate domestic prices are likely to increase. When currencies appreciate domestic prices are likely to fall. Hence it is important when discussing changes in the nominal exchange rate also to consider the resultant price effects. A measure which considers both of these simultaneously is the real exchange rate.

Questions for review

1. Imagine an economy which is in some stable long-run equilibrium situation. There is suddenly an unexpected increase in the money supply. What is the likely effect on prices, real GDP, nominal interest rates, real interest rates, the nominal exchange rate and the real exchange rate? (There is no central bank.)

2. There is a sudden and unexpected increase in the money supply. What is the likely response of the nominal exchange rate in the short, medium and long run?

3. There is a common perception that a depreciation in the value of the domestic currency will make local exports more competitive and hence stimulate the domestic economy. Demonstrate why, for this to happen, there has to be a depreciation in the real exchange rate, and that changes in the nominal exchange rate cannot guarantee an increase in the competitiveness of exports.

4. Why is it that in small open economies the slightest suspicion of a small currency depreciation can lead to a very large currency depreciation?

PART VI

Macroeconomic policy

In Chapters 19 to 22 we turn our attention to several important issues pertaining to the conduct of macroeconomic policy. These issues are all related to the theoretical models discussed in previous chapters, and particularly to the macroeconomic problems implied by those models.

CHAPTER 19

Introduction: macroeconomic problems

Macroeconomic policy is primarily aimed at addressing the problems of unemployment, inflation and cyclical instability. Its overall aim is to create a business environment that is conducive to achieving and sustaining economic growth under conditions of certainty.

Before discussing specific policy measures, however, it is necessary to say something about each of the above problems. This is done in the following sections where the focus falls on definitional matters as well as the relevant theoretical underpinnings.

19.1 Unemployment

An unemployed person is someone who is actively searching for a job but unable to find one within a specified time period. The rate of unemployment is defined as the number of unemployed job-seekers divided by the total number of employed and unemployed persons. The unemployment rate is conventionally measured in terms of particular registration procedures, or by means of representative samples drawn from the economically active portion of the population on a regular basis.

Official estimates of unemployment do not usually reveal the actual number of job-seekers, or the working conditions of employed persons. They may, for example, exclude people who are working on a part-time or temporary basis, or whose work is unrelated to their formal qualifications and working experience. In developing nations in particular, the official rate may exclude many potential job-seekers who eke out an existence in the traditional agricultural sector and the urban informal sector. Nevertheless, official estimates of the unemployment rate do at least provide a reasonably accurate indication of the unemployment rate of the economy insofar as they tend to vary inversely with cyclical fluctuations in economic activity.

Broadly speaking, economists distinguish between three types of unemployment, namely cyclical, structural and frictional unemployment.

Cyclical unemployment

Cyclical unemployment arises from periodic downswings in the business cycle. Such downswings may be initiated, for example, by autonomous decreases in consumption, investment, or exports, and reinforced by an attendant degree of wage rigidity. While the issue of wage rigidity has attracted a good deal of attention in the literature, it generally refers to the inability of wages to adjust in a downward direction. When this occurs, any decrease in the demand for labour must perforce give rise to an excess supply of labour, or cyclical unemployment.

As discussed in several earlier chapters, there are several reasons why wages may be 'sticky':

- In some sectors wage levels may be fixed, either by government in the form of minimum wage legislation or by trade union monopoly power.
- Wage rigidity may result from the fact that workers are subject to a money illusion, insofar as they are unaware of changes in the prevailing price level in the economy. Thus, the supply of labour is based on an expected real wage which adjusts only slowly to changes in the actual price (and real wage) level. Since a cyclical decrease in actual prices will not affect expected real wages in the short term, labour may refuse to accept a drop in their nominal wage which will force firms to retrench some workers in order to maintain profitability.
- Wage rigidity can also be explained in terms of the existence of explicit and implicit contracts. Many firms may be contractually obliged to keep wages and prices constant. Others might prefer not to employ workers below a certain minimum wage in order to prevent their turnover rate and the attendant costs associated with search and on-the-job training from rising.

In all these cases an autonomous decrease in aggregate demand will give rise to the emergence of cyclical unemployment.

In Fig. 19.1, for example, the economy is assumed to be in an initial equilibrium at point A, with price equal to OP_2 and real income OY_f. The short-run aggregate supply curve, $SRAS_1$, is determined by the prevailing nominal

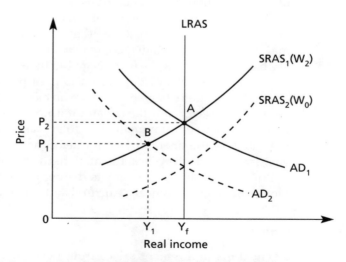

Fig. 19.1 A decrease in demand leading to cyclical unemployment

wage rate, W_2. A demand contraction now shifts the aggregate demand curve from AD_1 to AD_2. With no change in nominal wages, and hence in the short-run aggregate supply curve, the equilibrium will move to point B indicating a decrease in output to OY_1 and a commensurate drop in employment. The difference between OY_f and OY_1 can be regarded as a proxy for the extent of cyclical unemployment in the economy. It is evident that a fall in nominal wages, or a downward shift in the aggregate short-run supply curve to $SRAS_2$, would have enabled the economy to maintain its full employment level of output, OY_f.

Structural unemployment

The second type of unemployment mentioned above is structural unemployment which, unlike cyclical unemployment, is not sensitive to changes in aggregate demand. It refers to a situation in which the skills profile of unemployed persons does not match the skills demanded by employers, or where the unemployed find themselves in a different geographical location from where the job vacancies exist. Structural or 'mismatch' unemployment may result from changes in the composition of demand and supply, technological progress, and from various discriminatory practices in the labour market.

Frictional unemployment

The third form of unemployment, namely frictional unemployment, can exist in a situation where there is no skill or locational mismatch. Frictional unemployment refers to an economically rational process of job search where people *voluntarily* remain unemployed while they seek out and weigh up suitable job vacancies. Frictional unemployment thus includes people in the process of searching for jobs which do exist but where complete information concerning these jobs is lacking.

Structural and frictional unemployment together constitute what economists term the natural rate of unemployment. The 'natural rate' may be defined as that rate of unemployment consistent with overall equilibrium in the labour market; in other words, the rate of unemployment to which the economy automatically gravitates in the long run. While there is much disagreement among economists over the size and composition of the natural rate, and about its responsiveness to changes in aggregate demand, it has become a focal point in recent debates on the efficacy of macroeconomic policy.

CASE EXAMPLE

Unemployment in South Africa and Zimbabwe

Bhorat and Leibbrandt recently came up with a novel way of estimating the extent of unemployment in South Africa. They distinguished between a so-called 'strict' and an 'expanded' definition of 'the unemployed', where *both* definitions included the following two important categories: (i) those members of the labour force who were not in paid employment or self-employed,

▶

Case example
continued

and (ii) those who were available for paid employment or self-employment during the seven days preceding the interview. The 'strict' definition also included: (iii) those who took specific steps during the four weeks preceding the interview to find paid employment or self-employment; while the 'expanded' definition included a different additional category, i.e. (iiia) those who had the *desire* to take up paid employment or self-employment.

Based on CSS data, they found the 'strict' unemployment rate to be 20.3 per cent in 1995, and the 'expanded' rate to be 32.6 per cent in the same year. The latter estimate, based on the 'expanded' definition, would seem to be the more appropriate of the two as it captures the important category of 'discouraged' work seekers. These are people who want to work but who have become too discouraged to actively search for a job. They would consider the probability of finding a job too low to justify the costs and effort involved in searching for it.

As far as Zimbabwe is concerned, it is estimated that 40 per cent of its labour force is currently unemployed. Of those fortunate enough to be working, only 2 million, or 58 per cent, work in the formal sector, while 1.5 million, or 42 per cent, work in the informal sector. This means that only about 35 per cent of the available labour force are fortunate enough to be working in the formal sector, while the rest – 65 per cent – are either unemployed or busy trying to make ends meet in the informal sector.

Source: Bhorat, H. and Leibbrandt, M., 'Understanding unemployment', in Baskin, R. (ed), *Against the current: labour and economic policy in South Africa*, Johannesburg: Ravan Press, 1996

19.2 Inflation

Inflation is customarily defined as a persistent rise in the general level of prices. Thus, inflation refers to the rate of increase in the general price level, and not to a high level of prices *per se* or to a one-off increase in the price level. Generally, inflation is measured in terms of price indexes such as the *consumer price index* and the *producer price index*, both of which are published in the South African Reserve Bank's *Quarterly Bulletin of Statistics.* In South Africa the consumer price index, or CPI, is based on a representative household's basket of goods and services which is adjusted from time to time. Although the rate of increase in the level of prices, as measured in terms of an appropriate price index, is an acceptable estimate of inflation, to the economist inflation in strict terms refers to the persistent decrease in the quantity and quality of goods and services that can be purchased with a rand.

Since the early 1970s, inflation in South Africa has shown a tendency to accelerate. Indeed, from 1974 onwards South Africans have experienced double-digit inflation of varying degrees of severity. This contrasts rather starkly with an annual inflation rate of 3.5 per cent in the 1950s and 2.7 per cent in the 1960s. Moreover, during the 1980s the nature of the rate of increase in the general price level appeared to have changed. Specifically, the rate of inflation did not seem to correlate with the level of economic activity; prices did not fall significantly during periods of recession nor rise during boom periods. This situation is referred to as the phenomenon of *stagflation*, or the coexistence of high rates of inflation together with low levels of economic growth, and the consequent under utilisation of productive capacity and high levels of unemployment. It is only since 1992 that inflation has returned to single digit figures.

The complex nature of inflation, both in South Africa and abroad, defies ready explanation. Economists do not agree on its causes, processes or consequences, and this disagreement has led to a proliferation of theories. One method of organising the large number of theories purporting to deal with inflation is to differentiate between *inertial* or *core inflation*, *demand–pull inflation*, and *cost–push inflation*.

A characteristic feature of inflation in modern times is its tendency to proceed at some historical rate. Consumers, firms and workers expect the inflation rate to continue at its present level, and consequently enter into contracts and other informal arrangements on the basis of this anticipated or *core rate of inflation*. As long as expectations of a given rate of inflation prevail, they can become self-fulfilling.

While notions of an inertial or core rate of inflation can explain its persistence over time, they obviously cannot account for fluctuations in the inflation rate. In order to understand why the rate of inflation changes through time, it is thus necessary to look at theories which can explain these changes.

Changes in the rate of inflation have traditionally been explained in terms of either demand–pull factors or cost–push factors:

- *Demand–pull theories of inflation* all rest on the same basic proposition: if aggregate demand exceeds aggregate supply, then the general level of prices in an economy will rise to accommodate this excess demand, e.g. the increase in price that will result from an outward shift in the aggregate demand curve, AD_1, shown in Fig. 19.1. Thus the cause of an increase in inflation resides in the demand side of the macroeconomy. Despite some disagreement on the nature of the equilibrating forces involved, Keynesians, monetarists and exponents of the rational expectations school are in general accord on demand–pull inflation. However, since inflationary episodes in the real world often occur in the absence of high levels of aggregate demand, it is clear that demand–pull theories of inflation do not provide a comprehensive explanation of inflation.

- *Cost–push theories of inflation* attempt to account for persistent increases in the general level of prices which occur as a result of increases in production costs; that is, when costs rather than demand factors push up prices. Cost–push theories all assume a degree of monopoly power in one or more of the major markets of the macroeconomy. Thus one line of reasoning sees trade unions as causing wage–push inflation where real wages increase faster than productivity growth. Similarly, high degrees of economic concentration in the business sector are claimed to result in profit–push inflation. The interplay of monopoly power in labour and output markets is often viewed as the primary cause of wage–price spirals and, consequently, of changes in the core rate of inflation.

Although the traditional distinction between demand–pull and cost–push factors may be helpful in identifying the root causes of inflation, in practice and in theory the distinction often becomes blurred. Cost–push inflation cannot be divorced from the demand side of the economy, and indeed depends for its continued existence on accommodating increases in the money supply. Likewise, demand–pull inflation cannot exist unless accompanied by induced increases in the costs of production.

19.3 Cyclical instability

One of the characteristic features of a modern, market-orientated economy is that it tends to oscillate over time between periods of economic upswing and recession. South Africa too has experienced considerable fluctuations in economic activity. While the 1950s and 1960s were characterised by rapid economic growth, interspersed only by one major downswing in 1957, the 1970s saw two dramatic economic booms – in 1973 and 1978–81 – and a strong downswing in 1976. After another major downswing in 1982, the country experienced several smaller fluctuations during subsequent years.

There is little agreement among economists over the chief sources of instability in a modern economy. Keynesian economists maintain that free market economies are inherently unstable because of the existence of contracts and because private consumers and producers do not usually have the information necessary to anticipate and act upon exogenous disturbances in a world of uncertainty. Such disturbances may push the economy into a state of perpetual disequilibrium, thus necessitating an activist policy to return it to its equilibrium path.

Monetarists, on the other hand, argue that the private economy is basically stable if allowed to operate in a free and unfettered environment. The relative stability of private spending stems from the permanent income hypothesis, according to which private consumption expenditure is assumed to be a function of long-run or permanent income, rather than short-run fluctuations in current income. The chief source of instability is the government itself whose interventionist policies precipitate a temporary deviation from the natural level of real output. Thus, monetarists advocate adherence to a money supply rule whereby the supply of money is allowed to increase at a rate commensurate with the growth of productivity in the economy.

The above debate is, in the final analysis, an empirical matter which depends on the nature of people's expectations about the future. While many economists believe that these expectations adjust only gradually and imperfectly, being based on past rates of inflation, supporters of the rational expectations school believe that people are able to anticipate fully the consequences of government policy and incorporate them into their current wage and price contracts. Monetary and fiscal policies will thus have no effect on the real level of output and employment.

19.4 Conclusion

The economics profession is characterised by widespread disagreement among its members, and the preceding pages appear to confirm this. Economists do not even agree about the relative importance and fundamental causes of the various macroeconomic problems. Some even question whether unemployment and cyclical instability should be viewed as a matter of concern in the first place. These differences evidently reflect a more fundamental difference of opinion about the speed with which markets adjust to changing demand and supply conditions, and about the role of government in the economy.

Each of the problems discussed here appears to be highly complex in the sense that each may result from both cyclical and structural changes in the economy. It can therefore be expected that the relevant solutions will be similarly complex. In the chapters that follow we shall consider several macroeconomic policies which may *all* apply, to varying degrees and at different times, to *each* of the above problems. Coming to grips with the unemployment problem, for example, may require not only an appropriate mix of monetary, fiscal and exchange rate policies, but also a longer term growth-enhancing policy aimed at exploiting export markets, promoting technological advancement and providing the necessary skills. These policies are discussed in the remaining chapters of this book.

Summary

- Unemployment refers to a situation in which work-seekers are unable to find wage employment within a specified time period. The so-called 'expanded' definition of unemployment also includes people who have the desire to work but have become too discouraged actively to search for a job.

- Cyclical unemployment results from a cyclical downswing in the economy, coupled with an attendant degree of wage rigidity. It can be eliminated either by expansionary macroeconomic policies or by a flexible wage policy.

- Structural or 'mismatch' unemployment exists when vacancies cannot be filled by the unemployed, either because of a skills mismatch or because of the distances involved and the fact that unemployed persons may not be aware of the existence of suitable vacancies. The solution to structural unemployment requires a range of policies aimed at training and retraining the unemployed, improving their mobility, and providing them with the necessary information.

- Frictional unemployment refers to a situation in which people are voluntarily unemployed while searching for or weighing up suitable job vacancies.

- Inflation is defined as a persistent rise in the average price level, as reflected in changes in the consumer price index (CPI). It is customary to distinguish between demand-pull inflation – caused by persistent increases in aggregate demand – and cost-push inflation – caused by persistent cost increases at given levels of productivity (i.e. inward shifts in the aggregate supply function).

● Cyclical instability refers to the oscillating nature of modern economies, according to which they may experience successive periods of economic upswing and recession. Keynesians believe that the problem of instability is due to the existence of contracts and a lack of information on the part of consumers and producers; while monetarists lay the blame at the door of governments whose interventionist policies precipitate a temporary deviation from the 'natural' level of real output and employment.

Questions for review

1. Distinguish between cyclical and structural unemployment and comment on the relevant policy implications.

2. Can inflation be avoided simply by controlling the growth of the money supply – e.g. by adhering to a 'money supply rule'?

3. Should governments attempt to achieve cyclical stability?

CHAPTER 20

Fiscal policy

Fiscal policy remains a source of much economic debate. The disagreements range from normative issues such as the appropriate role of government in the economy to disagreement on important theoretical issues. These include arguments about whether or not changes in government expenditure will have any effect on the economy and whether there is any difference in the impact of tax-financed increases in government expenditure compared to deficit-financed increases. In addition, the monetary impact of a fiscal deficit remains high on the list of theoretical disputes.

Fiscal policy has had a chequered history. The rise of fiscal policy has its roots in Keynes' *General Theory* published in 1936. In the industrialised countries fiscal policy came into its own during the 1940s and 1950s. At the time, the emphasis was on the expenditure side of government, and taxes were rarely changed for fiscal policy reasons.

The Keynesian euphoria was not to last. The 1950s already saw the re-emergence of monetary policy as an important policy instrument and the recognition that a fiscal–monetary mix was a more appropriate policy approach. Subsequently the Vietnam war, the breakdown of the Bretton Woods system, the oil price increases, and the demise of the Phillips curve all contributed to throw macroeconomics into disarray. Today, theoretical macroeconomics and its implications for fiscal policy remain hotly contested areas where there is no single, unified body of theory.

Before discussing the practical aspects of fiscal policy, in sections 20.5 to 20.7, we first focus on a number of important theoretical issues. These are discretionary fiscal policy, built-in stabilisers and the budget deficit.

20.1 Discretionary fiscal policy: the multipliers

Discretionary fiscal policy is the vanguard of orthodox Keynesian economics. It involves a discrete change in government expenditure and/or taxes with a view to bringing about changes in economic activity.

Discretionary fiscal policy became very popular during the 1950s and 1960s in some of the industrialised countries. However, it is today generally regarded with some disfavour. Now the general consensus is that, given the problems of discretionary fiscal policy, it should be reserved only for dire economic emergencies.

Traditional fiscal policy relies for its success on two fundamental propositions, namely the existence of multipliers, and the belief that budget deficits are expansionary.

At a theoretical level there are distinct and distinguishable multipliers which come into play as a result of fiscal changes. When there is an increase in government expenditure or a decrease in taxes, there will be an increase in GDP which is greater than the original change in expenditure or taxes.

These multipliers are usually referred to as the Keynesian *expenditure multiplier*, the *tax multiplier* and the *balanced budget multiplier*. The most important of these – the expenditure multiplier – was detailed in Chapter 12. It was shown that a given change in exogenous expenditure will give rise to a multiplied increase in national income. The extent of this increase depended on the marginal propensity to consume and, for an open economy, the propensity to import. The expenditure multipliers are, as before, given by:

$$1/(1 - MPC) \quad \text{for a closed economy}$$
$$1/[1 - (MPC - MPM)] \text{ for an open economy}$$

Introducing taxes

One of the central tenets of the Keynesian expenditure model is that equal changes in taxes and in government expenditure can have different impacts on national income. In coming to grips with the tax multiplier it is useful to distinguish between a lump sum tax and income taxes. Income taxes are, of course, taxes on income. Lump sum taxes include:

- all forms of licensing (car, television, business, hawker);
- all poll taxes (being taxed simply because you are alive) and death duties;
- all taxes on property and assets (municipal rates, wealth taxes, land taxes).

In order to understand the derivation of the tax multiplier, it is necessary to return to our familiar aggregate expenditure model. The basic model is restated in Equation 20.1 (net exports are omitted for the sake of simplicity):

$$Y = C + I + G \qquad [20.1]$$
$$C = a + bY_d \qquad [20.2]$$
$$Y_d = Y - T \qquad [20.3]$$
$$T = T_o + tY \qquad [20.4]$$

where: Y_d = disposable income
T = total taxes
T_o = lump sum taxes
t = rate of income tax

Equation 20.2 is the statement for the short-term consumption function which we explored in Chapter 12. Note that the only difference between 20.2 and the equation used in Chapter 12 is that previously consumption was a function of national income. As we are now introducing taxes, consumption is a function of after-tax income, or disposable income.

To derive the relevant expenditure and tax multipliers we now substitute Equations 20.2, 20.3 and 20.4 into Equation 20.1. The result is seen in Equation 20.5 below:

$$Y = a + b(Y - T_0 - tY) + I + G \qquad [20.5]$$

By simplifying and rearranging terms we can change Equation 20.5 into 20.6:

$$Y = (a - bT_0 + I + G)/(1 - b(1 - t)) \qquad [20.6]$$

We are now in a position to extract the expenditure multiplier, suitably adjusted for the inclusion of income taxes:

$$1/[1 - b(1 - t)] \qquad [20.7]$$

In other words, a given increase in G or I will raise income by a multiple of $1/[1-b(1-t)]$. We may also note that the corresponding expenditure multiplier for an open economy is given by $1/[1 - b(1 - t) + m(1 - t)]$.

The lump sum tax multiplier is given by:

$$-b/[1 - b(1 - t)] \qquad [20.8]$$

which means that a given increase in lump sum taxes, T_0, will cause income to decrease by a multiple of $-b/[1-b(1-t)]$. It is also worth noting that an increase in the income tax rate will be reflected in a corresponding change in t.

Balanced budget multiplier

Following from the equations above, Keynesian economists have suggested that it is possible for the government budget to have an expansionary effect on the economy, even when the government balances its budget. This is shown in its simplest form for a closed economy where lump sum taxes are the only form of tax. Under these circumstances our tax function becomes:

$$T = T_0 \qquad [20.9]$$

the expenditure multiplier:

$$1/(1 - b) \qquad [20.10]$$

and the lump sum tax multiplier:

$$-b/(1 - b) \qquad [20.11]$$

Let the government now run a balanced budget by raising T_0 and G by exactly the same amount. The net multiplier effect is simply given by the difference between Equations 20.10 and 20.11:

$$(1/(1-b)) - (-b/(1-b))$$

or:

$$(1-b)/(1-b) = 1 \qquad [20.12]$$

The result says that the balanced budget multiplier, in a pure Keynesian world, is equal to one. In other words, the final impact of a government budget which is in balance is that it will increase national income by an amount equal to the value of the budget.

Expansionary impact of a budget deficit

Even if the multipliers are small, Keynesians argue that fiscal policy financed through debt issues can be expansionary. This works in two steps:

- Government expenditure can be increased without an offsetting increase in taxes. This is done by selling government bonds to the public.
- As people are now holding more government stock than before they will feel wealthier, i.e. they own more assets; and as they feel wealthier they will consume more.

Today most economists believe that government expenditure financed through debt issues is likely to be more expansionary than tax-financed expenditure. Those critical of this Keynesian view argue their case in two ways. First, the increased supply of bonds in the capital market will increase interest rates and so 'crowd out' private investment. Second, increases in public debt today mean increases in taxes tomorrow to pay for the debt. Rational taxpayers will increase their savings today in anticipation of the future tax hikes. Both these effects are contractionary, and if they are sufficiently contractionary they can entirely offset the expansionary impact of the original fiscal change.

20.2 Problems with discretionary fiscal policy

There are several problems associated with the over enthusiastic use of discretionary fiscal policy.

Timing

There can be considerable time delays between the beginning of an economic disturbance (e.g. an economic downturn) and the impact of a change in fiscal policy. As a result fiscal policy may end up being pro-cyclical rather than counter-cyclical. In other words, a fiscal policy change may affect the economy only after the initial problem has disappeared. This could mean that the expansionary impact of fiscal policy on the economy occurs during an upswing rather than downswing phase of the business cycle, or that a contractionary fiscal policy is only felt during a recession.

Economists usually distinguish between several kinds of delays, the most important of which are the recognition, administration and implementation lags.

- *Recognition lags* occur when there are delays between changes in economic circumstances and the actual recognition of these changes. Such lags are largely the result of delays in reporting procedures. The determination of national income is the result of the activities of large numbers of individual firms. A true picture of the state of the economy can only emerge when a substantial number of these firms have reported their own individual positions. Delays of more than a year are possible here.
- *Administration lags* refer to the time delay which can occur between an economic problem being recognised and administrative actions taken to correct the problem. The government budget is the most important policy instrument in the conduct of fiscal policy. The actual budgeting process is usually spread over two years. In the first year budgets are prepared for the forthcoming government budget which, in South Africa, is usually presented in March each year. In the second year of the process the budgets, and the funds allocated, are administered. As it is very difficult for this process to take account of economic shocks there can be considerable delays between recognising that a problem exists and action being taken to correct it. The most rapid form of fiscal response is through the use of relief aid – drought, poverty and disaster relief.
- The *implementation lag* refers to the delay between action taken to correct some economic shock and the impact of that action on the economy. Here the type of fiscal response will determine the extent of the lag. Should a sensitive government respond to an adverse economic shock by doubling the salaries of university lecturers, the funds will quickly find their way into the economy and correct for the shock. An alternative response, like the building of a dam, will take far longer to work its way through the economy.

Business uncertainty

Sudden and unexpected changes in fiscal policy, either on the expenditure or the revenue side, may create uncertainty among business persons causing them to drastically revise their business plans. Such uncertainty may well undermine investment and economic growth.

One of the least desirable aspects of the conduct of fiscal policy in South Africa has in fact been such changes, and their consequent impact on business confidence. Examples include sudden and large changes in import surcharges, import duties, and in investment and depreciation allowances.

Expenditure inflexibility

Discretionary fiscal policy must rely on flexibility in government expenditure and taxes for its success. Such flexibility is not always that evident in the real world. As far as individuals are concerned, lower taxes and more benefits provided by government are clearly desirable, but higher taxes and fewer benefits will meet far more resistance. The result is a political 'ratchet effect' where expenditure can be increased easily but decreased only with great difficulty, while taxes are more easily decreased than increased.

The macroeconomic impact of budget deficits

Discretionary fiscal policy usually implies that government expenditure exceeds tax revenue. Where expenditure exceeds taxes, government incurs a budget deficit, and when taxes exceed expenditure a fiscal surplus exists.

The chief concern here is that the possible unintended side effects of an increase in the budget deficit may outweigh the beneficial effects of the initial policy response. We shall return to this issue in section 20.4.

20.3 Built-in stabilisers

There are parts of government expenditure and taxes which change automatically as a result of changes in the state of the economy. Those which are counter-cyclical – move against the trend in the business cycle – work as a stabilising force in the economy.

On the expenditure side of the fiscal budget there are three types of stabilisers. These are unemployment benefits, relief payments and subsidies to business. In a recession such expenditures will automatically increase (in the absence of offsetting discretionary changes), while in times of economic upswing they will automatically decline. This is shown as the function G in Fig. 20.1 where there is an inverse relationship between changes in GDP and changes in government expenditure.

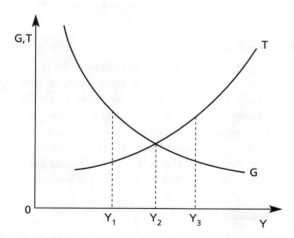

Fig. 20.1 Built-in stabilisers

On the tax side of the budget the existence of a progressive tax system has a similar stabilising effect. A progressive tax system is one in which the percentage of income paid in the form of taxes varies according to the level of income. For example, a person who earns R30 000 might have to pay 10 per cent of that income to the government, or a total of R3000 in income taxes, while someone earning R60 000 might pay 15 per cent, or a total of R9000.

When the economy therefore enters a recession and incomes fall, people will move into lower tax brackets and pay proportionately less tax. In times of economic prosperity income taxes increase rapidly as people move into higher and higher tax brackets.

If we now bring together the separate stabilising effects of expenditure and taxes we can appreciate the full stabilising effect of the structure of government expenditure and taxes. This is also shown in Fig. 20.1. What is apparent from the figure is the impact that different levels of income have on the structure of the government budget. There are three possible positions:

- If the level of national income is OY_2, government expenditure equals tax revenue and the government runs a balanced budget. Depending on the size of the multiplier, and the marginal tax in particular, a balanced budget may well have an expansionary effect on the economy.
- For levels of income below OY_2, such as OY_1, government expenditure exceeds tax revenue and the government runs a budget deficit. We have argued above that budget deficits are generally expansionary, and it is this very effect that will help to boost income beyond OY_1. In other words, the built-in stabilisers automatically help to bring the economy out of a recession.
- Levels of income in excess of OY_2, such as OY_3, have the reverse effect on the economy. At a level of income of OY_3, taxes exceed revenue and the government runs a budget surplus. This will have the effect of reducing national income and stabilising the upswing in the business cycle. Again the multipliers are important.

The combination of these two effects means that in a recession government expenditure automatically increases while revenue falls, both of which have a stimulating effect on the economy and reduce the severity of the recession. The reverse happens during economic upswings and as a result there is some constraint on the rampant economy. Figure 20.2 shows the position for South Africa. Here an inverse relationship between the budget deficit and the rate of change in GDP exists for most of the periods indicated.

Limitations to built-in stabilisers

While built-in stabilisers are theoretically appealing, and the evidence in Fig. 20.2 appears to point to their existence in practice, their overall impact is nevertheless limited:

- The stabilisers can only really work effectively if the government budget varies between surpluses and deficits. Surpluses must also be 'sterilised'

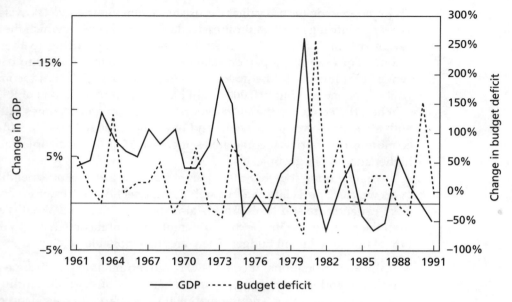

Fig. 20.2 Change in GDP and the budget deficit

(i.e. removed from the economy) and used to fund deficits during times of recession. The efficacy of built-in stabilisers is seriously undermined by the existence of a so-called structural budget deficit, i.e. one which exists irrespective of whether there are economic upswings or downswings.

- Inflation pushes people into higher tax brackets as nominal incomes increase. As a result real disposable income falls and consumption expenditure decreases. Unless tax brackets are reduced on an annual basis to counter such bracket creep, budget policy will gradually become more contractionary.

- Inflation also reduces the real value of government benefits. Therefore, unless government makes a discrete decision to increase the nominal value of unemployment benefits and the like, budget policy again becomes more contractionary.

The result is that built-in stabilisers now become subject to the discretionary decisions of government.

20.4 Budget deficits and the public debt

A budget deficit is like sin. To most of the public it is morally wrong, very difficult to avoid, not always easy to identify, and susceptible to considerable bias in measurement. To the body politic, and perhaps also to many economists, the apparent unifying reality is that every dollar of deficit – of a person, business or government – adds a dollar to debt. And debt is bad!

(Eisner, R., 'Which Budget Deficit? Some Issues of Measurement and their Implications', AEA Paper and Proceedings, Vol. 74, No. 2, 1984)

This section explores the validity of Eisner's comments, and it does so by outlining the meaning and implications of the budget deficit and the public debt.

> *The budget deficit. The budget deficit is the difference between government expenditure and revenue before borrowing. If revenue exceeds expenditure, a budget surplus exists. It is very rare for countries to achieve a budget surplus, with the exception being the United Kingdom, Japan and Botswana, all of which experienced it only for short periods of time. Some countries, notably the USA, have incurred high budget deficits in recent years.*

> *The public debt. A continuous budget deficit accumulates to what is known as the public debt. The public debt is held by banks and other financial institutions, such as the life assurance companies, the general public and the Reserve Bank. Many countries also fund their budget deficits by borrowing directly offshore.*

The bulk of government borrowing is made through the sale of long-dated stock. The length to maturity can vary between one and thirty years and often exceeds ten years. South African government stock is sold largely on tender. The Treasury announces the day of the tender and the amount of stock to be sold. The allocation of the stock is then made to the highest bidders. The major advantage of this system is that the government is fairly certain of securing the needed finance, although it is uncertain about the price. In recent years the Treasury has also been selling stock at a discount without annual interest payments.

Governments also use short-term financial paper to finance lags between government expenditure and tax payments. A large part of the annual taxes are paid only twice a year while expenditure is continuous. The Treasury finances this cash flow shortage by the sale of Treasury Bills (usually short-term stock of 91 days' duration).

Why do governments incur budget deficits?

Governments incur budget deficits for a multiplicity of reasons – social, economic and political. In essence budget deficits occur as a result of the mismatch between government expenditure and taxes. Consider Fig. 20.1 again. Imagine that the economy represented there is operating at full capacity at a level of national income equal to OY_1. Levels of income beyond OY_1 cannot be reached in the short term. This means that the government budget will remain in deficit irrespective of the state of the economy. At the time of writing this is exactly the situation faced by the USA. The solution is simple, although rather painful – either expenditure must be cut or taxes must be raised. Either way certain individuals will be made less well-off.

Budget deficits are not always bad. There are two economically acceptable reasons for governments to run budget deficits:

- Budget deficits may be justified on the grounds of their built-in stabilising effect, as discussed above. For such policies to be acceptable, however, they should produce deficits in recessions and also generate budget surpluses in times of prosperity.

- Like private firms and even non-profit enterprises, governments borrow in order to finance expenditure of a capital nature. The intention here is that capital expenditures will boost future revenues and enable the government to finance the future repayment of the loan. Where governments provide physical infrastructure or invest in human capital they do so in the hope that it will raise future tax revenues and help to pay off the debt.

Two caveats need to be emphasised here:

- There is disagreement about whether expenditure on human capital, such as education and health services, can legitimately be financed through deficit financing. On the one hand, it is suggested that expenditure on human capital is an ongoing expense, i.e. current consumption. It should therefore be financed from tax revenue and not loans. Others argue that expenditure on human capital, especially education, is for the benefit of people in the future. Rather than pay for their own education, pupils and scholars should be financed through government borrowing and taxed only when they start producing income.

- Many people believe that the market is capable of making the best use of scarce factors of production. Government has a greater capacity than the market to make mistakes and therefore waste resources. As a result there are many people who suggest that government activity should be kept to the bare minimum. They would certainly not support governments building roads, bridges or schools because they believe the private sector can do so more efficiently.

Macroeconomic impact of budget deficits

The macroeconomic impact of the budget deficit is essentially threefold:

- It may stimulate private consumption and production if the economy is operating below its full capacity level of output. The extent to which this happens will depend on what happens to interest rates and the price level.

- Budget deficits may force up interest rates and so 'crowd out' private investment. The reason why increased borrowing may raise interest rates concerns the inverse relationship that exists between bond prices and interest rates (in the capital markets). As the government issues more bonds on the market, their prices will fall and interest rates will increase. Private investors may consequently decide to reduce capital investments and instead buy bonds and other financial assets to benefit from the higher interest rates offered in the money and capital markets.

- Budget deficits might also increase the money supply, but this will depend on how they are financed. It can be shown that if the Treasury borrows from the general public there will be little or no impact on the money supply. After all, the money exchanged for government bonds is transmitted back into the economy in the form of government capital expenditure. Of course, if people use (long-term) savings to buy government bonds, the resultant increase in government expenditure may well raise money supply via the familiar money multiplier. In this case idle money balances, i.e. savings, would have been activated for transactions purposes.

When governments borrow from the banking sector, which they often do, there is likely to be a net increase in the money supply. The reason is that banks often count short-term government bonds as part of their reserves. If they therefore convert long-term investments into short-term bonds, they are able to issue more loans to the public and activate the money creation process.

Long-term concerns about public debt

Apart from the immediate macroeconomic impact of the budget deficit, there are also many concerns about the year-on-year accumulation of the public debt:

- Concern about the 'burden of the debt'. Here it is suggested that resources are being consumed today, while the responsibility to pay is being passed on to future generations. This becomes a serious problem if the budget deficit is being used to fund government consumption expenditure. Where it is used to fund projects that will boost future economic growth, it can be argued that expenditure is being incurred now for the benefit of people in the future. It seems only fair that these people should be expected to contribute to such benefits.

- Concern about the 'service burden of the debt'. As the public debt grows so the interest cost of maintaining that debt will also grow. The concern lies with the interest cost of the debt and the fact that current resources are being used up to maintain the debt. This could have serious implications for the balance of payments in countries where the public debt is held mostly by foreigners, such as the USA. In countries like the United Kingdom and South Africa most public debt is held domestically.

- For those countries with large service costs of domestically held debt the concern is with the disincentive effects of increasing taxes in order to finance the service charges. Taxes on assets or income can reduce savings and the incentive to work, and undermine long-term economic growth. If the debt becomes very large relative to GDP, high tax rates may be required to meet the debt interest burden.

- The government may be unwilling or unable to raise tax rates beyond a certain point, either because of the disincentive effects or because qualified people and businesses may leave the country. A sufficiently large debt may thus lead to large deficits which the government can finance only by borrowing or printing money. Since borrowing merely compounds the problem, eventually the temptation to print money on a massive scale may become irresistible.

20.5 Fiscal policy in South Africa: government expenditure

Government expenditure, taxes and the public debt are contentious issues in most economies. Unlike many other areas of policy, these issues affect individuals on a day-to-day basis. Budget policy is the subject of much debate among the general public and the popular media. Some of the more common perceptions, and sometimes misconceptions, which are levelled at the conduct of budget policy in South Africa are:

- The government is very large relative to the size of the economy.
- Government expenditure has been growing at an almost uncontrollable rate.
- South African taxes are very high.
- Public debt is out of control.
- Government expenditure is inflationary.
- The budget deficit is inflationary.
- The budget deficit causes interest rates to increase and therefore 'crowds out' private investment.

These issues are discussed in the remaining sections of this chapter.

Figure 20.3 presents the total of central government expenditure and taxes as a percentage of GDP for the years 1960–95. The trends shown there provide a reasonably accurate measure of 'general government' involvement in the economy as they include the transfers made to the provinces and homelands. Three features are apparent:

- There has been a considerable increase in the size of government relative to the size of the economy. This ratio was under 20 per cent during the early 1960s and by 1994 had risen to nearly 36 per cent of GDP.

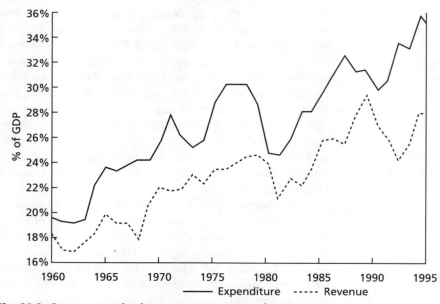

Fig. 20.3 Government budget as a percentage of GDP

- There has been an apparent acceleration in this ratio since the early 1980s.
- Tax revenue has been consistently less than total expenditure, resulting in a cumulative budget deficit (public debt).

Growth in government expenditure

The apparent acceleration in the ratio of government expenditure to GDP since 1980 does give some cause for concern and has certainly been noted in the press. This trend must however be seen in perspective. The main reason why the ratio increased during the 1980s was not because government expenditure increased dramatically but because the economy was in recession for much of the decade. This is supported by the data presented in Fig. 20.4.

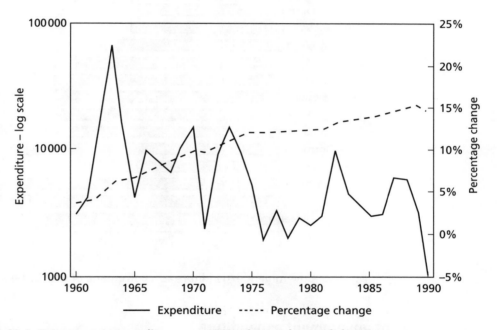

Fig. 20.4 Government expenditure – at 1980 prices and annual change

Figure 20.4 presents the values of government expenditure and the rates of change in this expenditure for the years 1960–90. Both data sets are in real 1980 prices and the value of expenditure is presented in log form. From this data it is evident that, if anything, the rate of growth in government expenditure has slowed and not increased. In 1990 government expenditure actually decreased, in real terms, relative to the previous year.

Comparative size of government

It is instructive to compare the size of government in South Africa with that in other countries. This is done in Fig. 20.5.

While the selection of countries and the suitability of data are always a bit contentious, the data does suggest that South Africa is not that far out of line with the countries shown in Fig. 20.5. What has been argued by some commentators, with some justification, is that the size of government in South Africa does not compare favourably with that of other countries at a similar stage of development. These countries include Mexico (with a ratio of 18.4 per cent), Venezuela (23.1 per cent), Uruguay (27.5 per cent), Brazil (36.0 per cent), and Argentina (15.5 per cent).

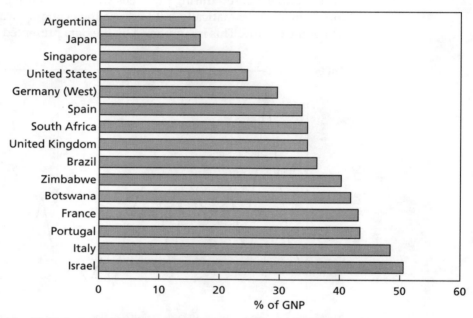

Fig. 20.5 Government expenditure as a percentage of GNP in 1990

Composition of government expenditure

The composition of government expenditure can be shown in a variety of ways for a variety of reasons. In Fig. 20.6 government expenditure has been categorised along functional lines. The diagram shows that the three major areas of government expenditure are social services (education, health, social welfare, housing), public order (defence, police, prisons, justice), and interest payments (on the public debt).

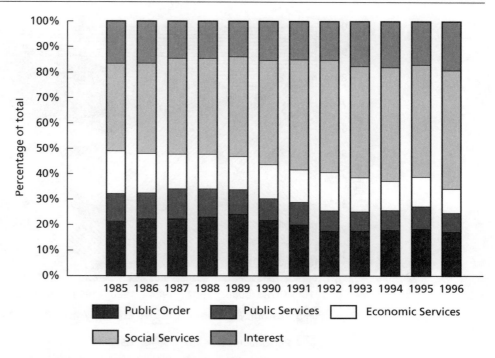

Fig. 20.6 Government expenditure by function

20.6 Fiscal policy in South Africa: government revenue

In countries without large budget deficits the long-term trend in government expenditure is similar to that of taxes. But with or without a large or growing budget deficit, both the rates of taxation and the composition of tax revenue play an important role in the macroeconomic performance of a country.

Figure 20.7 presents the composition of government tax revenue for the years 1976–95. The data shows a very pronounced change in the composition of tax revenue with taxes on individuals increasing relative to other forms of taxes. As far as the latter is concerned, the figure indicates that the share of customs and excise revenue fell off during the 1980s – reflecting more the recession and exchange rate depreciation than a decrease in individual tariffs. Taxes on gold mines have fallen to negligible proportions, and at the time of writing several marginal mines are being subsidised. Of all the non-personal taxes the only one which saw little change was company tax revenue.

The result is that individuals now carry more of the tax burden than ever before. This burden consists of personal income taxes and VAT. Since the inception of a consumption based tax in 1976 two factors have contributed to its increasing share of total tax revenue: increases in the rate of the tax, and increases in the prices of goods as a result of inflation. Inflation is also the major driving force behind the increase in the contribution of personal income

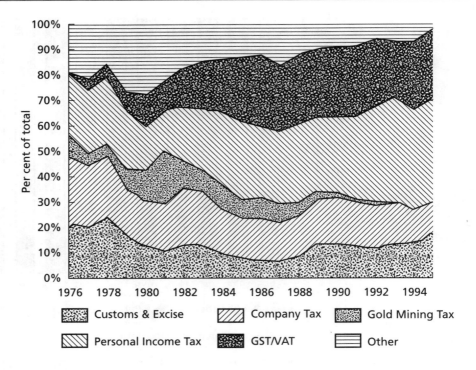

Fig. 20.7 Composition of tax revenue

taxes. Given the structure of the income tax system in South Africa, increases in nominal income push people into higher tax brackets – the so-called *fiscal drag* or *bracket creep* phenomenon.

High taxes often have a so-called *disincentive effect* on labour supply. When individuals have to pay higher taxes they may decide to work fewer hours, or work less intensively than before, in which case labour productivity is bound to fall. Alternatively they may decide to use their savings to pay for the higher taxes, in which case aggregate savings and private investment expenditure will fall. Companies may also cut back on their capital projects or leave the country altogether in search of a tax free haven. In all these cases the country's ability to produce wealth is compromised.

20.7 Fiscal policy in South Africa: government borrowing and the public debt

Every year in the run-up to the tabling of the government budget in parliament the financial press becomes very passionate about the size and conduct of the budget deficit. The impression given is that the budget deficit is out of control and is the main driving force behind South Africa's inflation.

In both cases, nothing could be further from the truth. Of all the aspects of budget policy in South Africa, it is the management of the budget deficit which has probably been the most conservative.

Size of the budget deficit

Figure 20.8 illustrates the budget deficit relative to government expenditure and GDP for the years 1960–95. Two features are immediately apparent:

- The budget deficit has varied enormously relative to GDP and government expenditure.
- The long-term trend in these ratios has been increasing, but at a very low rate.

Little concern need exist about the observed variability of the budget deficit. This variability can be an advantage rather than a disadvantage. It will be noticed that increases in the budget deficit coincided with years in which the country experienced economic downswings, while decreases in the deficit took place during periods of economic upturns. What is being seen here is the operation of the built-in stabilisers. As a result the changes in Fig. 20.8 coincide with the changes shown in Fig. 20.2.

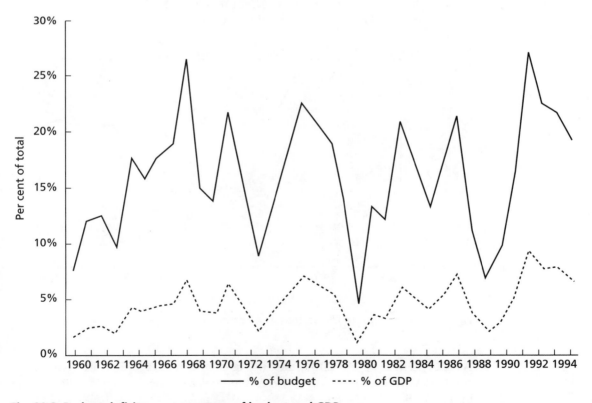

Fig. 20.8 Budget deficit as a percentage of budget and GDP

Size of the public debt

The commonly held notion that budget deficits imply a growing public debt is not necessarily true in the case of South Africa. Since 1965 the value of public debt has, in fact, been falling marginally. Figure 20.9 shows two different measures of the value of public debt relative to the value of GDP. The par value of debt is the face value of outstanding debt. This is the value of debt which is most commonly reported in the financial press.

Yet it is not the par value of debt which impacts on the capital markets (and therefore supposedly pushes up interest rates and crowds out private investment). Rather it is the market value of that debt. The difference between the par value of debt and the market value is determined by the time to maturity and the coupon rate.

From Fig. 20.9 it is clear that the long-term trend in the value of government debt has been downwards, at least until 1990. Since 1981 public debt – both the par and market value – relative to GDP has remained more or less constant.

Financing the budget deficit

At the time of writing, South Africa has weathered ten years of an international debt crisis in the form of the debt repayment schedule. The conduct of the public debt, however, has had little or no affect on the foreign debt crisis.

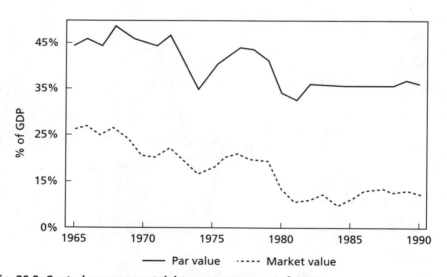

Fig. 20.9 Central government debt as a percentage of GDP

As is evident from Fig. 20.10, the bulk of public debt is funded from domestic sources. With the exception of 1991, there has been no foreign funding of the budget deficit since 1986.

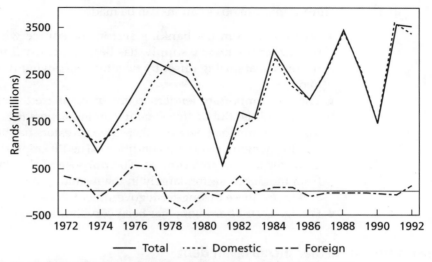

Fig. 20.10 Budget deficit – foreign and domestic debt (1980 = 100)

There are four major sources of funding of the budget deficit. These are the banking sector which includes the Reserve Bank, the private non-monetary sector (i.e. individuals and corporations other than banks), the Public Investment Commissioners, and the foreign sector. The composition of and trend in the financing of the budget deficit are presented in Fig. 20.11.

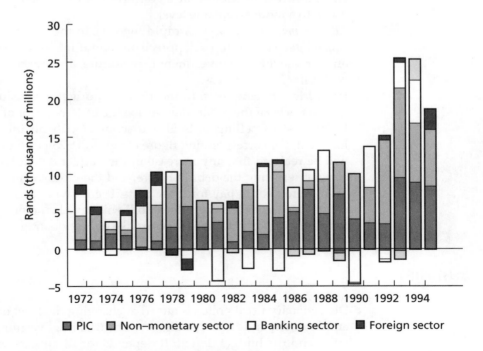

Fig. 20.11 Financing the budget deficit (1980 = 100)

Three important observations can be made:

- Borrowing from the banking sector, the source which is most likely to impact on the money supply, has been generally limited with borrowing in some years being offset by negative borrowing (i.e. repayment of debt) in others.
- The most important lenders to government are the private non-monetary sector and the Public Investment Commissioners (PIC). The distribution of the borrowing load between these two investors has been variable – largely due to changing economic conditions. The PIC represent the statutory fund manager for the government. The purpose of the PIC is to receive funds from the public sector, largely in the form of public servant pension funds, and invest these in long-term government stock.
- Foreign sector borrowing has been very limited.

Constraints on further increases in debt

There are, of course, several reasons why a government should not allow its budget deficit to get out of hand. We mention three of the more important ones:

- *Future expected economic growth.* To ensure that a country does not fall into a 'debt trap', the rate of growth of the budget deficit should not exceed that of GDP. Prudence suggests that a budget deficit should not exceed 3 per cent of GDP. In 1996, the South African budget deficit was 5 per cent of GDP, but it does seem that a concerted effort is being made to bring it down to a more acceptable level.
- *Adverse market responses.* A rapid increase in the budget deficit may well cause interest rates to rise appreciably, and if markets are sensitive to such an increase, private investment expenditure, and hence economic growth, will suffer in the process.
- *High debt servicing costs.* In the 1991/92 budget, provision was made for total services of the public debt to a value of 16 per cent of the total budget. If the cost of selling bills at a discount (with no interest payable) is included, the corresponding figure comes to 18.25 per cent of the budget. It will be realised that any increase in the budget deficit will lead to higher costs of servicing the debt in future, and therefore to either higher taxes or even more debt to pay for these costs. It goes without saying that governments faced with a rising interest bill will have less money left with which to finance important public services like education, training and health.

Summary

- Discretionary fiscal policy is aimed at changing the level of real output and employment and involves discrete changes in government expenditure, taxes and the budget deficit. It depends for its success on the size of the multiplier, and hence on the marginal propensity to consume and the tax rate, and on whether increased government expenditure is financed by taxes or new debt issues.

- Discretionary fiscal policy is hampered by long time delays (including recognition, administration and implementation lags), business uncertainty and inflexibility as regards government expenditure.

- Built-in stabilisers refer to those expenditure items and taxes that change in a counter-cyclical manner and serve as an automatic stabilising force in the economy. Unemployment benefits, relief payments and subsidies all increase during recessionary times, and automatically decrease when the economy experiences an upswing. Likewise, progressive income taxes have a similar stabilising effect on the economy.

- The efficacy of built-in stabilisers is seriously undermined by the existence of a so-called structural deficit, and by the effects of inflation on real disposable income, including the real value of government benefits.

- The budget or fiscal deficit is the difference between government expenditure and revenue before borrowing. The main reason why governments incur deficits is that, like private firms, they borrow to finance their capital investments, e.g. roads, harbours and school buildings. These investments will boost the well-being of future generations and enable them to help repay the loans.

- While fiscal deficits may boost consumption and production, they may also drive up interest rates and 'crowd out' private investment. When governments issue new bonds on the market their prices will fall and interest rates will rise. Private investors may thus decide to invest in the money and capital markets, rather than in new capital projects. Budget deficits may also increase the money supply, especially if governments borrow from the banking sector or if government borrowing implies a net decrease in the level of savings.

- The size of the public debt is determined by the accumulation of budget deficits over time. A major concern here is the 'burden of the debt', or the fact that the responsibility to pay is passed on to future generations. This becomes a serious problem if governments borrow to finance their current or consumption expenditure, as it implies that future generations will be paying for the consumption of the present generation.

- Another concern is the 'service burden of the debt', i.e. the amount of interest that has to be paid (from current resources) to maintain the debt. A growing debt implies a higher level of interest payments, which in turn requires either higher taxes – with their attendant disincentive effects – or a cut back in other categories of government expenditure.

Questions for review

1. What is fiscal policy? Why is it important?

2. Why, in theory, is the tax multiplier smaller than the expenditure multiplier?

3. What sort of 'real world' factors might make the tax and expenditure multipliers equal?

4. Discretionary fiscal policy was once hailed as the economic salvation for market-based economies. What went wrong?

5. The budget deficit can be financed from one of three sources: domestic borrowing, foreign borrowing and the printing of money. What is the effect on prices, interest rates, the exchange rate and real GDP of each of these methods of financing the budget deficit?

6. Explain why there is an inverse relationship between the budget deficit and the state of the real economy. Is this inverse relationship a good thing or a bad thing?

7. How big (or how small) should government be?

8. In South Africa most taxes are paid by people and relatively few are paid directly by business (see Figure 20.7). What has led to this structure? Does this structure matter? What, if anything, should be done to change the structure of the tax system?

CHAPTER 21

Monetary policy

Monetary policy is primarily aimed at stabilising the economy. Unlike fiscal policy, changes in monetary policy can be instituted more rapidly and in smaller increments. Monetary policy often has fewer side effects than other policy instruments.

Monetary policy consists of attempts by the central bank to control such monetary aggregates as the money supply, as measured by M1, M2, and M3, and short-term interest rates. These aggregates are an important means of influencing aggregate expenditure, employment, the inflation rate and exchange rates.

At the outset it is important to make a distinction between the availability and use of the various monetary policy instruments under different types of monetary regimes. Central banks which attempt to control money supply directly use different instruments and follow different procedures to those which attempt to control money supply indirectly through the use of interest rates. Each of these cases will be considered in turn in this chapter, after which we give a brief assessment of the conduct of monetary policy in South Africa.

21.1 Direct control of the money supply

Several policy instruments are available to central banks when they attempt to control the money supply directly. In essence such controls are aimed at influencing the money base and the money multiplier. Under such a system the central bank sets the reserve requirement and issues currency. The money base is made up of currency and foreign reserves while the money supply is ultimately determined by the willingness of commercial banks to issue loans and the willingness of customers to take up these loans. In theory, when banks are fully loaned up, the only way that the money supply could increase without express central bank intervention would be through an increase in foreign reserves or increased government borrowing at the central bank.

Under such a monetary regime central banks have five policy instruments at their disposal:

- *Changes in reserve requirements.* A change in the reserve requirements of banks impacts directly on the size of the money multiplier and therefore on the money creation process. In Chapter 16 we showed how the reserve requirement eventually determines the size of the money multiplier and thus the amount of loans which banks can issue.

  Because of the money multiplier, a small change in the reserve requirement can result in a large change in the money supply. For example, the change in money supply following a R1000 deposit is R5000 when reserve requirements are 20 per cent, but increases to R10 000 if the reserve requirement is reduced to 10 per cent.

- *Open market operations (OMO)*. Open market operations refer to the buying and selling of government bonds by the central bank as a means of influencing the money base and therefore the money supply. If the central bank wanted to increase the money supply it would conduct an open market purchase. In other words, it would purchase bonds from the banks which would release funds into the market in the form of central bank cheques. Once deposited, these funds will increase the money supply through the money creation process. An open market sale will have the reverse effect on money supply.

- *Changes in the bank rate*. There are times when commercial banks are forced to borrow from the central bank. The most likely reason for this is the withdrawal of cash from a bank which is fully loaned up. As this cash forms a reserve against other deposits the bank will now find itself in an illegal position where its reserves do not meet the legal reserve requirement. If the commercial bank cannot find funds anywhere in the market it must either call in loans – a very unpopular option – or approach the central bank for the necessary funds. Here the central bank is acting as the 'lender of last resort'. The interest rate which the central bank charges on these funds is known as the bank rate or discount rate.

- *Direct controls*. Direct controls consist of direct legislative attempts to control the money creation ability of banks. While there have been a variety of these direct controls, in South Africa the most common one has been the institution of credit ceilings.

Credit ceilings are an attempt to limit directly the ability of commercial banks to create money by restricting the quantity of loans which they can issue, irrespective of their reserves. While credit ceilings may well restrict the quantity of loans issued, they do not necessarily restrict the growth in the money supply. The reason is that a so-called 'grey money' market usually develops, where private non-banking institutions begin to borrow and lend among themselves, and entirely circumvent the banking system. While banks may not be able to create money, other financial institutions certainly are.

The central bank may also force banks to hold certain liquid assets against their deposits. These assets usually include government bonds of differing maturity. If banks are forced to use some of their deposits to buy low yielding assets such as government bonds, they will offer a lower interest to their depositors and charge their debtors a higher interest rate. They do so to protect their own profit margins. Liquid asset regulations thus render banks' intermediation services more expensive.

The imposition of such liquid assets provides opportunities for intermediation by other agents who are not constrained in the same way as banks; or alternatively deals can be arranged directly between borrowers and lenders. Disintermediation thus enables lending activity to continue largely as before with little or no impact on the money supply. However, since only bank-mediated deals are included in the official money supply figures, the control techniques succeed in reducing measured money supply growth, and by this criterion appear to have worked.

- *Moral 'suasion'*. Moral 'suasion', or moral persuasion, refers to the practice by which the governors of the central banks put pressure on bank managers to conduct their business in some particular way. The real impact of moral suasion is difficult to measure.

21.2 Interest rate control

Interest rate control is the monetary policy regime currently used in most countries, including South Africa. When a central bank chooses to set interest rates the objective is still to control money supply, but indirectly through changes in the cost of borrowing rather than directly through controls over the actual amount of money in existence. Under these circumstances there is really only one effective monetary instrument available – changes in the discount or bank rate.

If the central bank wishes to set interest rates in the economy it must have some control over interest rates within the banking system. The way it has chosen to do this is by keeping the banking system constantly in debt to the central bank and charging an interest rate for this indebtedness. The central bank does this by means of open market operations. If liquidity in the banking system increases the central bank will conduct an open market sale as a means of reducing liquidity. Conversely, if liquidity decreases commercial banks have to use the central bank as the 'lender of last resort'. Commercial banks borrow through the *accommodation window* and pay the appropriate *discount rate*. The amount the commercial banks borrow is called the 'money market shortage'. Today the discount rate paid is called the *Bank Rate*.

Under this type of monetary policy the central bank is really acting as a wholesaler of money with the deposit-taking institutions acting as retailers. Money is effectively purchased by the banks at the discount rate and loaned to borrowers at the 'market rate'.

The conduct of monetary policy is now relatively straightforward. If money supply growth is too high the central bank will increase the discount rate. This will force commercial banks to raise their own interest rates in order to protect their profit margins. Higher interest rates discourage borrowing which results in fewer deposits and a fall in the money supply. Similarly if money supply growth is too low interest rates will be dropped which will encourage more borrowing from the banks.

Possibly the best way of illustrating the difference between a fixed money supply policy and the control of interest rates is to consider what happens when there is an autonomous increase in deposits. Such an increase can come about either as a result of central bank open-market purchases or because of an inflow of foreign reserves resulting from a trade or capital account surplus.

Under a direct control regime the central bank can raise the reserve requirement or sell bonds to the banks in order to curb the growth of the money supply. With interest rate control, however, the banking system can choose between using the deposit to issue new loans and therefore creating money, or repaying previous central bank accommodation.

Its first choice will be to lend the money out and boost its profits. The problem is, however, that no-one will want to borrow the money. Everyone who wished to borrow at the prevailing interest rate had already done so. In the absence of a lower interest rate there will be no increase in demand for loans. While the commercial bank could reduce its own interest rate, such a reduction could only be marginal before it becomes more profitable to repay previous accommodation than issuing new loans at the lower rate. As a result the only increase in the money supply will be the first deposit.

21.3 Conduct of monetary policy in South Africa

During the 1970s the conduct of monetary policy in South Africa followed international practices. It was thought that the money supply could be controlled by means of regulatory measures like credit ceilings and liquid asset requirements. Banks had to hold particular assets defined as 'liquid' (e.g. treasury bills and Land Bank bills) up to a specified minimum proportion of their deposits. The belief was that the limited supply of liquid assets would serve to limit bank lending, money growth and inflation.

The direct method of monetary control has now been discredited, in line with experiences overseas. At the beginning of the 1980s, credit ceilings in South Africa were dismantled and liquid asset requirements progressively reduced, so as not to be a significant constraint on bank activity. The monetary authorities expressed a general dislike for regulatory interference in financial markets.

Since the implementation of the recommendations of the De Kock commission in the early eighties, the Reserve Bank has used interest rate control as its main monetary policy tool. Monetary policy can thus be gauged by the levels of interest rates, the most representative of which, over this time, was the BA rate (discussed in Chapter 15). Figure 21.1 provides data on the BA rate and the inflation rate and can be used to assess the success and failure of monetary policy over the last three decades. The relationship between interest rates and inflation is an important one. If inflation exceeds the interest rate, for example, the real interest rate will be negative which in effect means that borrowers are being paid to borrow. In such a situation the central bank would have lost control over the money supply.

Three distinct periods can be identified:

- In the years leading up to 1972 real interest rates were positive and inflation was low. There was obvious success with monetary policy.
- Between 1972 and mid-1980 real interest rates were negative and inflation accelerated. This was the time of credit ceilings and liquid asset requirements.

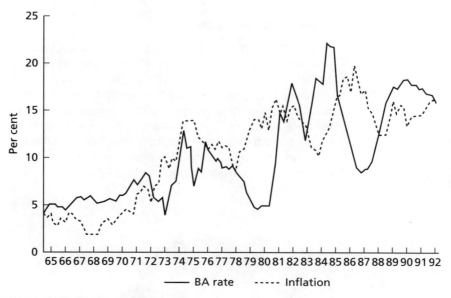

Fig. 21.1 The BA rate and inflation

It is no coincidence that 1972 is also the year in which the Bretton Woods system of fixed exchange rates came to an end. It will be seen in the following chapter that fixed exchange rates severely limit the ability of the monetary authorities to control the money supply and interest rates.

- The final period is marked by a switch to interest rate control. There were two sharp increases in interest rates during the first half of the 1980s. Between 1980 and 1981 the BA rate increased from about 5 to 17 per cent. After a short drop it increased again, this time from 12 to 22 per cent during 1983–4. The first of these increases marked the abandonment of direct monetary policy controls in favour of interest rate control, and for the first time since the early 1970s real interest rates became positive. The second was the reaction of the Reserve Bank to the continued increase in inflation.

By August 1984, the prime overdraft rate had reached 25 per cent – its highest level ever – indicating a high point in the Reserve Bank's fight against inflation. It would be fair to say, however, that these rates were more onerous than was really necessary at the time. They were one of the major causes of the economic downturn during the mid-1980s, and also encouraged many South African companies to borrow on a short-term basis abroad, thus precipitating or at least contributing to the subsequent foreign debt crisis.

The economic stabilisation objective of monetary policy came to the fore during 1986–7. Interest rates were reduced as a means of stimulating the economy (the BA rate fell to 9 per cent), but inflation remained high at 17 per cent. Between 1988 and the time of writing it appears that the dominant concern of monetary policy had moved away from stimulating the economy to that of fighting inflation again. Interest rates have exceeded inflation since 1988.

CASE EXAMPLE

Money supply targets

Since 1986 the Reserve Bank has been announcing specific money supply targets. These targets are specified in terms of floors and ceilings between which the Reserve Bank wishes the money supply to grow.

Money supply targets are a very useful means of assessing the likely future trend in interest rates. If actual money supply growth exceeds the target ceiling then it is very likely that interest rates will rise. Alternatively, should money growth be below the target floor interest rates are likely to weaken.

The money supply target floors and ceilings, as well as the actual changes in money supply, are presented in Fig. 21.2 for the years 1986–96.

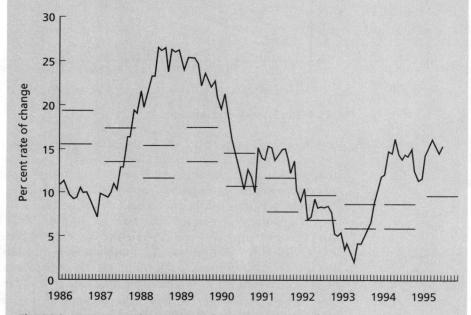

Fig. 21.2 Money supply targets and actual money supply

Two features are worth noting:

- The Reserve Bank has had great difficulty, and limited success, in ensuring that the actual money supply growth coincides with its money supply targets.
- A comparison of Figs 21.1 and 21.2 also confirms the inverse relationship between the money supply and interest rates.

Summary

- Monetary policy consists of actions aimed at changing the money supply and/or interest rates in such a way as to avoid undue fluctuations in the level of income and prices. In times of economic upswing and threatening inflation, for example, the central bank may try to curb the growth of the money supply and/or raise interest rates in an attempt to limit spending and prevent prices from rising.

- The money supply (as measured by M1, M2 and M3) can be controlled in several ways. These include changes in the reserve requirements of commercial banks, which have a direct impact on the size of the money multiplier and therefore on the money creation process; open market operation, which affect the monetary base in the economy; changes in the bank rate, which determine the extent to which commercial banks borrow from the central bank; direct controls such as credit ceilings and the imposition of certain liquid asset requirements; and 'moral suasion' on the part of the central bank.

- Central banks may choose to control interest rates, or the cost of borrowing, and thus exert an indirect influence on the money supply. This is done by keeping the banking sector constantly in debt to the central bank – e.g. by conducting open market operations through the 'accommodation window' – and charging an interest rate – the bank rate – for such indebtedness. Commercial banks will thus adjust their own interest rates in accordance with changes in the bank rate.

- Monetary policy in South Africa has fluctuated between direct control of the money supply and the control of interest rates, and has recently also included attempts to set certain money supply targets. These targets are important as they give some indication of the likely future trend in interest rates.

Questions for review

1. What is monetary policy? Why is it important?

2. When central banks conduct monetary policy, they can choose between controlling the money supply or controlling interest rates. They cannot do both. Explain why this is the case.

3. When a central bank attempts to control money supply directly it will use one set of monetary policy tools. When it attempts to control money supply through interest rate control it will use a different set of policy tools. Explain what these tools are and how they are used.

4. What factors does the Reserve Bank take into account when it chooses a particular Bank Rate? What would make it change the Bank Rate?

CHAPTER 22

Exchange rate policy

Monetary policy depends for its success on the state of the balance of payments and the exchange rate system in use. In this chapter we therefore focus on two broad areas of balance of payments policy. The first is an examination of three possible exchange rate systems and their implications for policy. The second examines the conduct of balance of payments policy in South Africa and the dual exchange rate system.

22.1 Exchange rate systems and policy

Prior to the demise of the Bretton Woods system of fixed exchange rates in 1972, central banks had no choice but to maintain a fixed exchange rate. Today central banks have a choice between fixed or flexible rates. While most countries have opted for free exchange rates, certain less developed countries, especially those with no foreign exchange markets to speak of, have chosen to peg their rate to that of their largest trading partner. South Africa made this choice at times during the 1970s when the rand was linked to the dollar and later to sterling.

The choice of an exchange rate system is fundamental to the conduct of macroeconomic policy. Simply put, when exchange rates are fixed, there is no domestic autonomy in the conduct of monetary policy. Under these circumstances, monetary policy in a small open economy is dictated by the actions of the world's major central banks. Under a more flexible exchange rate regime, however, countries do retain a degree of control over domestic monetary policy.

There are essentially three possible exchange rate systems. Each of these, and its policy implications, are outlined below.

Flexible exchange rates

A flexible exchange rate system is one where the value of a currency is allowed to respond to market forces without any interference by central banks or other authorities. The determination of flexible exchange rates was at the centre of discussion in Chapter 18 and is not taken any further here.

Fixed exchange rates

A fixed exchange rate system is one in which member countries agree to fix the relative values of their currencies and to make changes only under certain specified conditions. Historically there have been two important fixed exchange rate systems. The first of these was the Gold Standard which ended with the Great Depression of 1929. The second was the Bretton Woods system which operated between 1944 and 1972. Today the only important fixed exchange rate system in operation is the European Monetary System (EMS).

The great virtue of fixed exchange rate systems is that they remove the uncertainty from international trade and encourage long-term investments in such trade. As such they maximise the gains from trade.

However, under a fixed exchange rate system the government is forced to defend the value of its currency should it threaten to move away from the fixed rate. This is illustrated in Fig. 22.1. The situation presented is one in which the domestic currency is pegged to the dollar at an exchange rate of e_1. With the supply curve given as S_1, the fixed exchange rate coincides with the market-determined exchange rate only when the demand curve for foreign exchange is D_1. Should the demand curve for foreign exchange move from D_1 to D_2, there will be pressure for the currency to depreciate relative to the dollar. In order to prevent such a depreciation the central bank has to buy domestic currency on the foreign exchange market by using foreign reserves and/or gold to the value of $OQ_2 - OQ_1$.

Defending the value of a currency is not difficult so long as the exchange rate moves around the pre-determined fixed exchange rate. This means that when the currency is defended the loss of reserves can be offset by an increase in reserves when the currency strengthens. But a fixed exchange rate system becomes problematic when some long-term structural change moves the economy permanently away from the pre-determined fixed exchange rate. Under these circumstances the continued defence of the currency will only lead to a total loss of foreign reserves. The only solution then is a one-off devaluation of the currency.

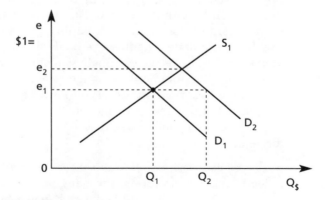

Fig. 22.1 Fixed exchange rates

Managed floating

A managed float, as implied by the title, is an exchange rate system in which the currency is allowed to fluctuate as the market changes but where the central bank intervenes to smooth out short-term fluctuations in the exchange rate. In terms of Fig. 22.1, for example, the central bank may intervene to defend the value of its currency if it believes that the depreciation from e_1 to e_2 is only temporary. Rather than exposing the domestic economy to unnecessary shocks, the central bank will defend the exchange rate at e_1. However, if the central bank believes that the depreciation is likely to endure for a long period of time, there will be little point in defending the currency.

As the short-term effect of a currency appreciation is to make exports less competitive and imports more so, central banks may also intervene to prevent excessive currency appreciation. Under these circumstances the central bank would use domestic currency and buy foreign currency.

22.2 Exchange rate policy in South Africa

Balance of payments and exchange rates only became important policy instruments after the breakdown of the Bretton Woods system in 1972. Previously world trade and exchange had been conducted on the basis of fixed exchange rates. It is not surprising that the implications of flexible exchange rates were not well appreciated by theoreticians or policy makers. This lack of knowledge, combined with the often insular economic outlook of some of the industrialised countries, especially the USA, has seen dramatic swings in world currency markets since the early 1970s.

In South Africa the conduct of exchange rate policy has also had its ups and downs since 1972 when the authorities were faced with the challenge of flexible exchange rates. Their initial response was in fact to maintain a predominantly fixed exchange rate. During the early years after the end of Bretton Woods the rand was initially pegged to sterling and then to the USA dollar, even though these currencies were themselves floating against other currencies. In these years the volatility of the major currencies proved to be highly problematic. The Reserve Bank also experimented with independent managed floating as well as floating against a 'basket' of currencies. Since the early 1980s the dominant exchange rate policy has been one of free floating with some Reserve Bank intervention to even out fluctuations around the long-term trend of the exchange rate.

There are essentially three reasons why the Reserve Bank intervenes in the foreign exchange market:

- *To even out short-term fluctuations in the exchange rate.* These can result from leads and lags in foreign exchange transactions that have nothing to do with the long-term trend of the exchange rate.
- *To control inflation.* It has been shown above that depreciations in the nominal exchange rate will raise import prices and production costs, thus

contributing to general price rises. If these depreciations can be held in check so too can price increases.

- *To maintain a constant real exchange rate*. Without a stable real exchange rate it is virtually impossible to plan export ventures with any degree of certainty.

One of the single most important economic shocks ever experienced by the South African economy was the capital flight from the country and collapse of the rand during the early 1980s – see Fig. 22.2. Domestic violence, political intransigence, inflationary expectations and a poor economic outlook were all responsible for the turbulence in the value of the currency.

The nominal effective exchange rate has depreciated almost consistently since the end of 1989. Political uncertainty and the ongoing violence in the run-up to the election were responsible for the decline in the nominal effective rate. The nominal effective rate did however stabilise during 1995 and even showed some appreciation.

It is important to note that these changes in the nominal effective rate more than compensated for the inflationary differentials between South Africa and its trading partners. In consequence the real exchange rate also depreciated during the first quarter of 1994 and made South African exports more competitive on world markets. Such changes do put inflationary pressures on the economy through the balance of payments. On average the real effective exchange rate has remained largely constant since mid-1993. This is in line with Reserve Bank policy.

Until recently South Africa laboured under a severe balance of payments constraint. The SARB's 1994 Annual Economic Report showed that the overall cumulative balance of payments surplus of R7.9 billion built up over the four-year period to 1992 was neutralised completely in 1993 when net gold and other foreign reserves decreased by R10.3 billion. This deterioration in the overall balance of payments position was principally caused by a large exit of capital unrelated to reserves, which wiped out the surplus balance on the current account. At the time the net surplus on the current account was positive, and necessarily so (in order to finance the depletion of foreign reserve levels). In 1993, the current account surplus was R5.9 billion (that is 1.5 per cent of GDP).

As is evident from Fig. 22.3, South Africa's balance of payments position has undergone a rapid transformation since the political changes of 1994. Between 1984 and 1994 very large capital outflows occurred as a result of the political uncertainty in South Africa and poor foreign perception about the future of the country. The debt standstill and the subsequent debt repayment schedule forced a deficit on the capital account. Of necessity, and to prevent the further collapse of the rand, the current account was in surplus for the ten-year period 1984 to 1994.

In recent years a number of factors have contributed to rapid export growth. These include:

- The opening up of new offshore markets.
- The easing, and then lifting, of sanctions and other types of politically motivated constraints on trade.

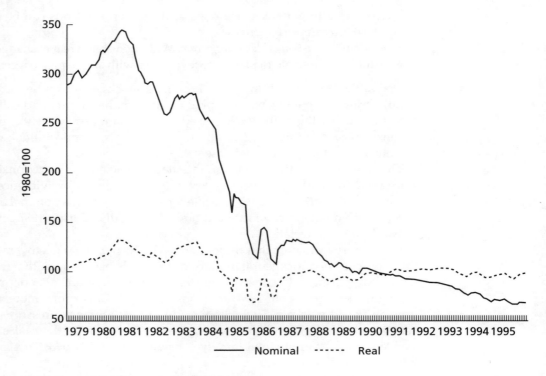

Fig. 22.2 Effective rand exchange rate

- The promotion of export growth under the general export incentive scheme (GEIS). Under the agreement of the Uruguay Round of GATT, GEIS has recently had to be abolished.
- The signing of a variety of new trade agreements.
- Low levels of domestic demand which encouraged producers to seek out new export markets.
- The depreciation of the nominal effective rand exchange rate and, in 1993, the depreciation of the real effective rand exchange rate. As always, it is the real effective exchange rate which is responsible for an exchange rate related change in the international competitiveness of local products.
- The coming on stream of a number of manufacturing enterprises aimed specifically at the export market.
- These trends were reinforced in the third quarter of 1995 by a 21 per cent increase in the volume of net gold exports

(Source: *South African Reserve Bank Quarterly Bulletin*, December 1995, pp. 11–12)

The positive effect on the balance of payments of the increase in exports has been offset by an increase in imports. The most important of these were imports of mineral products, machinery and electrical equipment. In addition, there has been a sharp increase in 'net service and transfer payments'. In the third quarter of 1995 this amounted to R16 billion. The two factors largely responsible for this were an increase in dividends on foreign investment and an increase in the number of South Africans travelling abroad.

In contrast to these changes on the current account, the capital account was in surplus from 1994 to the beginning of 1996. Capital inflows in the first three quarters of 1995 amounted to R13.8 billion. Capital inflows between the third quarter of 1994 and the third quarter of 1995 amounted to R22.8 billion. What is particularly encouraging about these capital inflows is that they are mainly long-term capital inflows and are being invested in the private sector.

At the beginning of 1996 three factors prompted foreign investors to move part of their capital out of South Africa. These factors included a scare about the health of the President, the appointment of a new Minister of Finance, and a series of country-wide strikes. The rand lost well over 20 per cent of its value in three months and the effect on the capital and current accounts is clear from Fig. 22.3.

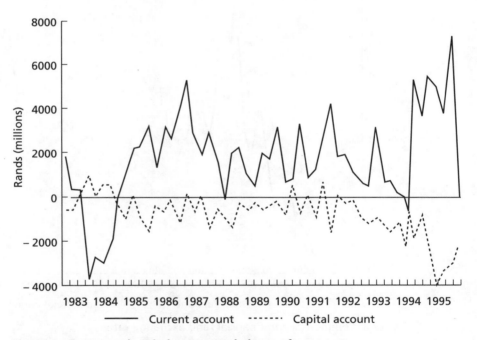

Fig. 22.3 Current and capital accounts – balance of payments

One of the notable events to effect the balance of payments was the abolition of the financial rand at the beginning of 1995. The dual exchange rate system – commercial rands for trade and financial rands for foreign investment – was introduced (for the second time) in 1985. The value of the commercial and financial rands relative to the dollar are presented in Fig. 22.4. A number of features are immediately apparent from this figure:

- The continued depreciation of the commercial rand relative to the US dollar and the increased depreciation during the run-up to the elections.
- The often large variation between the commercial and financial rand exchange rates.
- The extreme volatility of the financial rand exchange rate. This volatility reflected foreign perceptions of South African domestic conditions. The usual measure of these perceptions was the financial rand discount to the commercial rand. This is illustrated in Fig. 22.4. In the first week of April 1994 the financial rand traded at an exchange rate of R5.58 per dollar – its lowest level since 1979 – before appreciating to R4.74 by the end of May. The financial rand was abolished in February 1995 when it was worth R3.90 against the dollar.

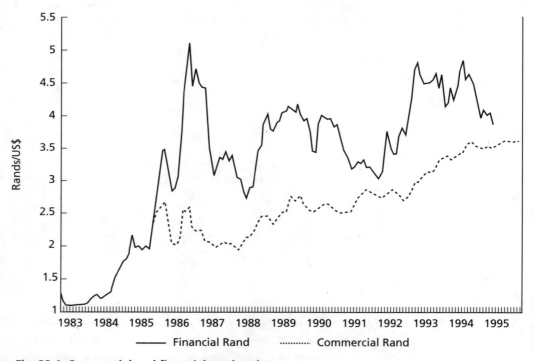

Fig. 22.4 Commercial and financial rand exchange rates

22.3 Exchange control

During the Bretton Woods era exchange control was in place in many countries of the world, including the industrialised ones. While exchange control is still widely used in developing countries, it has been gradually phased out in the wealthier countries as the threat of capital flight disappeared.

South Africa has had exchange controls in place since World War II and intensified them in 1961 following a massive capital outflow after political violence broke out in Sharpville. The controls that were imposed at the time limited the movement of capital out of the country by both residents and non-residents. Residents were able to take out limited funds while non-residents had to use the so-called blocked rand mechanism. The latter was aimed at insulating the balance of payments from rapid capital flows as blocked rands could not be purchased by residents. Blocked rands effectively worked as a pool of investment currency traded between foreigners, with a separate price or exchange rate applying to such transactions. The blocked rand mechanism remained in place, with few changes, until 1983. Over this time blocked rands came to be called securities rands and since 1979, financial rands.

Following the recommendations of the De Kock Commission the financial rand was abolished in 1983. The De Kock Commission saw this abolition as desirable in that it would help develop an active and competitive spot and forward foreign exchange market. The financial rand was reinstated in 1985 as a result of the capital outflow and debt standstill that followed the escalation of social unrest during the mid-1980s. It was finally abolished in 1995.

Today the only exchange control which remains in South Africa is a restriction on the amount of foreign exchange that residents may take out of the country. As from 1 July 1997, South African residents are allowed to invest a maximum of R200 000 in foreign countries. While this limit applies to both individuals and companies, the latter can get permission from the Reserve Bank to exceed this limit, especially if it is deemed to contribute to the country's foreign trade.

The major advantage of this type of exchange control is that it helps to limit the damage to an already battered currency. The biggest disadvantage of exchange control in today's world is that it is an important signal that South Africa is still not able to open its doors fully to the rest of the world. And until it does, the country is unlikely to become a fully fledged 'emerging market' (see accompanying case example).

CASE EXAMPLE

Emerging markets

Interest in emerging markets as an investment area offering high returns and opportunities for diversification is on the increase. Evidence of this is the doubling of estimated gross portfolio equity flows to emerging markets, from $6.2 billion in 1989 to $7.6 billion in 1991, reaching $13.2 billion by 1993 (World Bank 1994). Investment successes in emerging markets in South East Asia, Latin America and Eastern Europe have stimulated interest in other markets.

Africa is a potential emerging market, one which the Calvert Group terms 'the ultimate emerging market opportunity – unknown, embryonic and filled with unrealized potential' (Calvert, 1996). Africa has much to offer – it is the second largest continent in the world, it has a key geographical position, it

▶

**Case example
continued**

has a potential market of 600 million people, a vast natural resource base and 14 established stock markets. Within Africa, South Africa represents a prime investment opportunity, since it has the growth potential of an emerging market while offering a degree of market sophistication unrivalled in the rest of Africa. The Johannesburg Stock Exchange lists more than 650 companies, with a combined market capitalisation in excess of $240 billion.

In the post-war years the USA represented an exciting emerging market, as industry rode a wave of success derived from servicing the needs of a burgeoning middle class. With political change (including the end of the Cold War and consequently the East-West battle for Africa), and structural reform in many countries, a similar trend is expected to emerge in Africa. Emerging markets offer the growth potential of rapidly increasing consumer demand and diversification opportunities, since emerging market economies rarely move in tandem with developed markets. On the downside, emerging markets tend to be volatile and often carry increased risk of political or social instability. It is also not simply economic fundamentals which determine security prices – the structure of the market, the type of information supplied to traders, the ease of trading and the degree of regulation influence liquidity, trading costs and volatility. Thus market structure is a key determinant of success or failure in emerging markets.

The Calvert Group provides the following classification:

Pre-emerging markets	Emerging markets	Growth markets	Mature markets
South Africa	Korea	Japan	UK
Botswana	Chile	Spain	USA
Kenya	Turkey	Hong Kong	Germany
India	Mexico	France	France
Morocco			
Zimbabwe			
China			
Egypt			
Nigeria			
Tunisia			

Summary

- Monetary and fiscal policies depend for their success on the state of the balance of payments and the exchange rate system in use. Governments, and central banks in particular, basically have to choose between fixed and flexible exchange rates.

- Under a fixed exchange rate regime there is a great deal of certainty about imports, exports and foreign investment, and individuals and companies may more readily engage in such activities than they would under a system of free exchange rates. But governments may also have to defend their currencies against persistent changes in the underlying supply and demand conditions. A dramatic increase in the demand for foreign exchange may either threaten the foreign reserve position of the central bank, and thus reduce the country's ability to import goods and services; or it may force the government to introduce tight monetary and fiscal policies aimed at curbing domestic spending and imports.

- Under a flexible exchange rate system the domestic currency is free to respond to market forces without any interference on the part of the central bank. While free exchange rates do introduce a degree of uncertainty in the market, they also provide an automatic means of protecting the foreign reserves of a country. They also leave the government free to use monetary and fiscal policies for domestic purposes.

- Under a managed float the central bank will intervene in the forex market to smooth out short term fluctuations in the exchange rate. The extent of such intervention will depend on whether the fluctuation is considered to be temporary, in which case the central bank may well intervene to stabilise the currency; or whether it is deemed a permanent change, in which case it may allow gradual adjustments in the value of the currency in order to effect the desired change in exports, imports and capital flows.

- Most countries have adopted fixed and free exchange rate systems at different times while in South Africa the authorities have also imposed strict controls on the ability of residents and foreigners to move capital in and out of the country. These controls have gradually been relaxed over the past few years, and it is probably fair to say that the country is now on the point of assuming the status of an 'emerging' market.

Questions for review

1. What is balance of payments policy? Why is it important?

2. Show how the conduct of monetary policy is influenced by the choice of exchange rate policy. Use the two extremes of fixed and fully flexible exchange rates to illustrate your answer.

3. How does a central bank use its foreign reserves to protect the value of the domestic currency? When should it and when should it not try to protect the value of its currency? How long can one protect a currency?

4. What were the forces which worked on the balance of payments accounts between 1985 and 1996?

5. Should South Africa abolish all remaining exchange control? What would be the likely consequences?

PART VII

Structural adjustment, poverty and the role of government

CHAPTER 23

Structural adjustment and the small open economy

(with A. Mendelson)

Small open economies (SOEs) trade extensively with the rest of the world, and because of their small size, are predominantly price-takers on world markets. These factors present a number of problems quite distinct from those faced by advanced industrialised countries.

As Adam Smith observed, the degree of specialisation is limited by the extent of the market. SOEs, faced with low levels of domestic demand, are unable to develop highly diversified structures of production, and are thus compelled to trade with the rest of the world. This renders these countries extremely sensitive to changes in the world economy; for example, a recession in North America and Western Europe will reduce the demand for imports in these regions, causing the exports of SOEs to fall.

Furthermore, the fact that many SOEs derive much of their export revenue from primary commodities renders them extremely vulnerable to fluctuations in prices and quantities caused by changing supply and demand conditions. Such problems are greatly magnified when a country relies on a single commodity for the bulk of its export earnings, as is the case with Brazil (coffee), Ghana (cocoa), Nigeria (petroleum), Zambia (copper) and many others.

To compound these problems, most SOEs are subject to a so-called balance of payments (BOP) constraint; net capital outflows, or negligible inflows, severely limit a country's ability to finance necessary imports, thus undermining growth and impairing its ability to meet important social and economic objectives.

In this chapter we shall expand on some of these themes, examining the acute problems many SOEs have faced in the last two decades, considering the relative merits of various policy options designed to deal with these crises, and analysing the often controversial roles played by the International Monetary Fund (IMF) and World Bank in their attempts to assist SOEs with their BOP and structural problems.

23.1 The balance of payments constraint

It is a truism to say that the balance of payments of a country must always be in balance. Any imbalance in the current account must be offset by changes in the capital account (net foreign debt and net foreign investment) or by changes in the foreign exchange reserves.

Consider the case of an advanced industrialised country for which the current account of the balance of payments is initially in balance. Income growth stimulates the demand for imports, which creates a current account deficit, often loosely referred to as a balance of payments deficit. However, growth also has the effect of attracting capital inflows, drawn by high expected returns, which creates an offsetting surplus on the capital account.

However, as indicated above many small open economies experience net capital outflows as a result of the reluctance of foreigners to undertake direct investment and the inability of these countries to raise capital from international commercial banks. The resultant shortage of foreign exchange acts as a significant brake on growth, since imports, and hence aggregate demand, must be restrained in the interests of achieving a current account surplus to counterbalance the capital account deficit. The implications of such measures will be examined in section 23.3.

23.2 Small open economies in the 1980s

The 1980s were a particularly difficult period for many SOEs, with a series of exogenous shocks and injudicious policy decisions creating BOP and debt crises in a large number of these countries. Many are still struggling to recover from these crises.

The causes of this widespread predicament include:

- *The second oil crisis of 1979–80* which saw oil prices double, due to the restriction of output by the Organisation of Petroleum Exporting Countries (OPEC). As the demand for oil was relatively inelastic, at least in the short run, these price hikes caused a significant worsening of the trade balances of all oil-importing countries, including the SOEs. Many countries also experienced higher inflation as oil was a key input in industries across the board, either directly in the production process, or indirectly, in the form of increased transport costs.
- *Significant increases in real interest rates in the United States and Western Europe* in 1980–1 which were aimed at combating domestic inflation. As a side effect of these policies, interest payments of indebted SOEs rose considerably, increasing capital outflows from these countries. The US dollar also began to appreciate significantly in the early 1980s, due largely to capital inflows attracted by the United States' high real interest rates. This development increased the cost of servicing dollar-denominated debt, which comprised the bulk of SOEs' foreign borrowing.
- *Recessionary conditions in the advanced industrial nations* which dampened demand for the exports of many SOEs.
- *Misguided economic policies* on the part of the SOEs. Many pursued overly expansionary fiscal and monetary policies, causing inflation and economic distortions. In many cases this led to capital flight from the affected countries, further tightening the balance of payments constraint.

Although these events had a profound negative impact on SOEs around the world, Sub-Saharan Africa was unquestionably the worst affected. Domestic economic policies were often wildly expansionary, causing massive inflation and distortions. While such policies may seem irrational, they must be understood within the broader socio-political context. Many African governments lack the legitimacy conferred by the democratic process, and thus need to enlist the support of various strategic groups in order to govern effectively. Thus, while huge public sector wage increases may be incomprehensible from a narrow economic perspective, they may in fact make perfect sense from a political point of view. For many governments, economic stability may simply not be one of their immediate priorities, and the pursuit of legitimacy through profligacy may significantly add to a country's economic woes.

Table 23.1 charts the current account balance of a selected group of countries between 1975 and 1990. This clearly illustrates the problems of persistent disequilibria and large fluctuations in the trade balances of these countries. The case of Mexico illustrates how closely a country's fortunes can be linked to commodity prices (in Mexico's case, oil). The rise in oil prices in the early 1980s transformed a persistent BOP deficit into a surplus, which was reversed by the oil price fall of 1985–6.

Japan and the United States are included for the sake of comparison. Much concern has been expressed at the size of the United States' trade deficit and Japan's surplus. These flows are significant, and have considerable implications for the two countries; the fact that these flows are dwarfed by those experienced by many SOEs illustrates the magnitude of the problems faced by the latter.

Table 23.1 Current account balance as a percentage of GDP

	Zambia	Nigeria	Kenya	Argentina	Brazil	Mexico	Japan	USA
1975	−29.5	0.2	−8.6	−3.3	−5.7	−4.4	−0.1	1.4
1976	−5	−0.8	−4.6	1.7	−4.3	−3.7	0.7	0.5
1977	−9.2	−1.9	−0.8	2.7	−2.9	−2.2	1.6	−0.5
1978	−11.4	−6.6	−13.9	4.3	−3.5	−3	1.7	−0.5
1979	0.1	2.4	−9.3	−1	−4.7	−3.9	−0.8	0.2
1980	−14	5.7	−13.8	−8.4	−5.5	−5.5	−0.9	0.3
1981	−19.1	−7.4	−9.9	−8.2	−4.5	−6.4	0.5	0.5
1982	−15.3	−9.4	−5.5	−4.1	−5.8	−3.7	0.7	0.1
1983	−9.3	−5.5	−2.7	−3.8	−3.4	3.6	1.9	−0.9
1984	−6	0.2	−3.9	−3.2	0	2.3	2.9	−2.4
1985	−17.9	3.2	−3.6	−1.4	−0.1	0.2	3.8	−2.7
1986	−22.4	0.9	−2.6	−3.6	−2	−1.4	4.4	−3.1
1987	−12.4	−0.2	−8	−5.3	−0.5	2.6	3.7	−3.3
1988	−9.8	−0.7	−8.4	−1.7	1.3	−1.5	2.9	−2.4
1989	−6.7	3	−10.4	−2.2	0.2	−2	2.1	−1.8
1990	−15.7	6.3	−7.8	1.7	−0.6	−2.7	1.4	−1.3

Source: World Bank World Tables 1992

The cumulative effect of all these problems has been a precipitous decline in per capita incomes in several SOEs, especially those in Sub-Saharan Africa, as shown in Table 23.2. This is in stark contrast to the experience of the advanced industrialised countries and the world as a whole.

Table 23.2 Gross National Income per capita (1987 US dollars)

	1970	1975	1980	1985	1990
Sub-Saharan Africa	320	360	410	360	320
Nigeria	230	360	500	350	290
Zambia	710	350	300	230	260
Kenya	320	350	380	330	380
Malawi	410	340	300	240	230
Latin America	1340	1610	1880	1870	1630
Argentina	2690	2840	2990	2380	2170
Brazil	1170	1680	2000	1830	1820
Mexico	1310	1530	1920	1800	1750
Japan	11820	13480	15730	18260	22770
USA	14000	14730	16200	17700	19500
World	2830	2990	3240	3370	3650

Source: World Bank World Tables 1992

23.3 Policy options: exchange rate depreciation

Faced with a current account deficit, the government of an SOE has various policy options to choose from:

- currency depreciation
- direct controls
- structural adjustment
- running down of foreign exchange reserves
- borrowing.

The last two measures may be appropriate when the disequilibrium is transitory, but are obviously less appropriate when the disequilibrium reflects fundamental structural problems, as they cannot be continued indefinitely. Thus, when dealing with a persistent BOP crisis, a government must avail itself of one of, or a combination of, the first three measures, which are examined in this and the next two sections.

A currency depreciation or devaluation increases the price of foreign goods and services relative to those produced domestically. This promotes an *expenditure switch* as both locals and foreigners switch towards domestic products, thereby increasing exports and reducing imports, with a consequent improvement in the trade balance.

Alas, economic policy-making is seldom that simple. There are a number of reasons why a devaluation may be ineffective or unattractive.

The J-curve

Due to the existence of contracts and other factors promoting short-run inflexibility, the volume of exports and imports may not immediately adjust in the wake of a devaluation. If exports are denominated in domestic currency, and imports are denominated in foreign currency, then, in the period before quantities adjust, the foreign currency value of exports falls, while that of imports remains constant, thus causing an initial worsening of the trade balance. This process can also be viewed in terms of domestic currency prices: the domestic price of exports remains constant, while that of imports rises.

The above phenomenon is only temporary – quantities adjust over time in response to the change in relative prices, resulting in an increase in exports and a decrease in imports, thus improving the trade balance. Figure 23.1 illustrates the evolution of the trade balance over time, which approximates the letter J (hence 'J-curve').

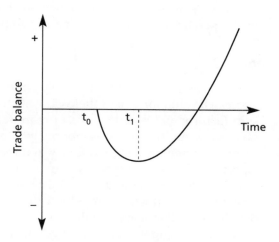

Fig. 23.1 The J-curve

It would be wrong to view this perverse effect as a short-run aberration of little consequence; since the balance of payments must always be in balance, the temporary worsening of the trade balance must be accompanied by a capital account surplus or a decrease in foreign exchange reserves, neither of which may be feasible.

However, this effect is not felt by the majority of SOEs, since the bulk of their exports are denominated in US dollars or other major currencies. In practice, it transpires that the J-curve is of greater relevance to larger, more advanced countries, which have a greater tendency to denominate their exports in their domestic currencies.

Elasticity pessimism

Remember that a depreciation decreases the price of exports and increases the price of imports. Ideally this would promote an expenditure switch from foreign to domestic goods, thus improving the country's trade balance. However, the impact of such a depreciation on the trade balance depends crucially on the price elasticities of the world demand for exports and of the domestic demand for imports. If both are inelastic, quantities demanded will respond sluggishly to the devaluation, and since exports are now cheaper and imports more expensive, the trade balance will actually deteriorate.

The bulk of imports of SOEs normally comprises essentials such as food and investment goods, and thus demand for them tends to be rather price-inelastic. With the theories of perfect and monopolistic competition in mind, one might assume that, because of their small size relative to the world economy, the demand curve faced by a typical SOE for its exports would be highly (or infinitely) elastic. However, many SOEs, despite their size, supply a large proportion of world output of one or two commodities, and are thus no longer price-takers. This implies that their exports may well be price-inelastic.

Thus one may conclude that, in theory, unfavourable elasticities may cause a currency depreciation to worsen the trade balance. The likelihood of this occurring in practice needs to be investigated empirically on a case-by-case basis.

Cost–push inflation

In many cases, SOEs rely extensively on imports for raw materials and capital goods. Devaluation raises the cost of such essential imports, and could thus significantly increase the costs of manufacturing firms. Such firms tend to possess some degree of monopoly power, due to the often concentrated nature of manufacturing industries in these countries. These firms are thus in a position to pass cost increases on to consumers in the form of higher prices. This may in turn lead to demands for higher wages, which the firms can again pass on to consumers by raising prices, thus laying the foundations for a debilitating inflationary spiral.

While the arguments for devaluation are often seductively simple, we have seen that there are a number of significant caveats. Devaluation may be a powerful instrument for improving the trade balance under the right circumstances, but it can by no means be regarded as a panacea for all that ails a country's balance of payments.

23.4 Policy options: direct controls

Direct controls over imports and foreign exchange allotments are popular in many SOEs as a means of resolving balance of payments difficulties. They can take many forms, including quantity restrictions on imports, import licences and foreign exchange rationing.

Such measures have the advantage of being immediately effective, and can be applied selectively, allowing the government to simultaneously achieve other policy objectives; for example, quantity restrictions may be imposed on selected goods in order to simultaneously improve the current account and protect domestic firms against foreign competition.

However, direct controls have a number of disadvantages:

- Selective intervention distorts relative prices, which may generate serious inefficiencies. Thus, direct controls require careful, meticulous planning, which may be beyond the capabilities of many SOEs, due to the paucity of data and policy-making expertise.
- Direct controls tend to be administratively complex, which may well necessitate expansion of the civil service with all its attendant cost implications.
- Even if the above-mentioned problems could be satisfactorily addressed, a major deficiency of direct controls is that they would have to be maintained indefinitely in the absence of adjustment or a change in external conditions.

23.5 Policy options: structural adjustment

At some stage, an SOE faced with a persistent current account deficit will have to address the structural factors causing the imbalance. Excessive demand for imports can be combated at a macroeconomic level by dampening aggregate demand, and hence imports, or by increasing the economy's productive capacity.

Demand-side policies

These policies consist of various forms of monetary and fiscal policy aimed at curbing aggregate demand, reducing national income and hence imports. Such policies must be applied with the necessary circumspection, since reducing national income could have grave welfare implications. Reducing aggregate demand can lead to a significant increase in unemployment if not correctly calibrated. In addition, one of the simplest ways in which a government can reduce aggregate demand is to reduce public sector spending. Since many forms of recurrent expenditure, such as social security payments and public sector wages, are politically sensitive, the brunt of spending cuts are borne by infrastructural investment projects and social expenditure on marginalised groups with little political influence. The neglect of investment will in all likelihood undermine a country's growth rate and thwart its attempts to expand productive capacity.

A further problem is that contractionary monetary policy may actually be inflationary – higher interest rates increase the financing costs of firms, which may then pass these cost increases on to the consumer. This factor is particularly significant in the vast majority of SOEs with non-existent or nascent stock markets, which forces firms to rely heavily on debt finance.

The consequences of such perverse results are illustrated in Fig. 23.2. Suppose that the economy is initially at point A. The country is experiencing inflation, and hence a current account deficit, as domestically produced goods become more expensive than foreign goods, precipitating an expenditure switch in favour of imports.

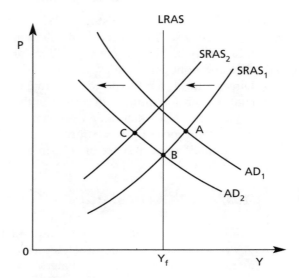

Fig. 23.2 The effect of a contractionary monetary policy

Now suppose that the government implements a contractionary monetary policy in order to dampen aggregate demand. The aggregate demand curve therefore shifts inwards from AD$_1$ to AD$_2$. *Ceteris paribus*, the economy should now move to point B, with inflation and hence the current account deficit eliminated. However, because of increased financing costs, the aggregate supply curve shifts upwards, from SRAS$_1$ to SRAS$_2$, and the economy settles at point C, rather than B. Thus the government's policies have effected little or no reduction in the general price level, while plunging the economy into recession. This example well illustrates the dangers inherent in attempts to manipulate aggregate demand.

Finally it must be recalled that the bulk of most SOEs' imports consist of essentials such as food, raw materials and machinery, and thus, while demand management policies may well effect an improvement in the current account of the balance of payments, the curtailment of such imports may well have large negative effects on consumption, production and investment.

Supply-side policies

Economic policy may also be aimed at promoting investment in productive capacity, thereby shifting the long-run aggregate supply (LRAS) curve rightwards. This is typically achieved by creating a climate conducive to investment, and specific policy measures include infrastructural development, tax incentives for investment and relaxation of bureaucratic controls.

Compared to demand-side policies, such measures involve little risk, and have the advantage of promoting, rather than retarding, growth. The main drawback of supply-side policies is the lengthy time lags before such policies have the desired impact on investment and income, and hence on the balance of payments. Thus, most adjustment programmes would have to include some elements of demand management, in order to reduce the current account deficit in the short run, until the supply-side measures take effect.

23.6 The International Monetary Fund and World Bank

We have seen above that SOEs undergoing balance of payments crises generally have a number of short- and long-term policy options, each of which entails a number of potential problems. In this section we examine the roles played by the International Monetary Fund (IMF) and the World Bank, both of which attempt to render assistance to countries undergoing temporary BOP crises or longer term adjustment.

The IMF and the International Bank for Reconstruction and Development (universally known as the World Bank) were created in 1944. The IMF is primarily responsible for *balance of payments finance*, providing short-term loans to countries experiencing BOP crises, while the World Bank is primarily responsible for *development finance*, providing loans for investment projects and economic adjustment. Both organisations espouse a predominantly free market ethos in their dealings with SOEs, generally favouring liberalisation over regulation, in accordance with the views of their major stakeholders, the advanced capitalist economies.

The IMF

The IMF is charged with overseeing the international monetary order, promoting exchange rate stability and the expansion of world trade, and most importantly, providing bridging finance to members with balance of payments disequilibria, in order to ease the balance of payments constraint and enhance policy flexibility.

All members receive a quota, in proportion to the size of their economies and their participation in world trade. Members pay an annual subscription to the Fund equal to their quotas, which determine the distribution of voting rights.

IMF support can take on a number of different forms, depending on a country's needs and its level of indebtedness to the Fund:

- *Special Drawing Rights (SDRs)*. SDRs are a form of money created by the IMF, and accepted as an international currency by member nations. SDRs are allocated to members in line with their quotas. Members may draw these at will, with the sole condition that those who do so should pay interest to those who hold excess SDRs.

- *The credit tranches.* There are several of these tranches, the most important and controversial of which is the so-called upper credit tranche. Here the IMF provides credit support to a member country only if it can satisfy a number of conditions. The member must enter into a *Standby Arrangement* with the IMF which commits it to pursuing a stabilisation programme agreed upon with the Fund. The IMF's practice of attaching preconditions and performance targets to its loans is known as *conditionality*, which has been the target of much criticism. *Conditionality* focuses on the control of key macroeconomic variables, such as money supply, inflation and public sector spending, with the aim of stabilising the balance of payments in a relatively short period, largely through demand management. The manner in which these targets are met is left to the nation concerned; the IMF refrains from micro- or sectoral-level conditions.

- *Extended and supplementary facilities* are designed for those countries which require support over a longer period than that covered by conventional Standby Arrangements (which generally require repayment over five years). Conditionality is the same as for the upper credit tranches.

- *The compensatory finance facility* is designed to assist countries experiencing *temporary* balance of payments problems due to fluctuations in primary commodity prices or quantities. No significant conditionality is attached.

The conditionality debate

As indicated above, IMF conditionality is a most controversial issue. Some critics are deeply sceptical of the motives of the advanced capitalist economies, which effectively shape Fund policy, while others question the competence, judgement and priorities of the Fund.

The IMF uses conditionality for the twin purposes of assisting members to solve their BOP problems and ensuring repayment. Few critics indeed would argue in favour of unconditional finance, and thus the central question relates to the form that conditionality should take.

Leaving purely ideological critiques aside, there are three main criticisms of conditionality as presently practised. First, some critics argue that the IMF fails to consider that the sources of current account disequilibria are often external to the SOE. This critique is informed by the belief that the imposition of conditionality wrongly implies the failure of a country's economic policy.

The Fund, on the other hand, sees the issue of endogenous versus exogenous sources of disequilibria as largely irrelevant, choosing rather to focus on whether the crisis is likely to be of a temporary or permanent nature; after all, external shocks may necessitate adjustment just as surely as endogenously generated disequilibria.

Second, it is often charged that the control of inflation assumes a disproportionately important position in IMF stabilisation programmes. However, it must be remembered that unless exchange rates are completely free to adjust and reflect inflation differentials, as they seldom are in SOEs, bringing inflation down to the level of an SOE's trading partners is necessary to avoid an expenditure switch in favour of imports.

Third, critics allege that the IMF's stabilisation programmes often fail to consider the limited capacity for adjustment of many SOEs, characterised as they are by pervasive structural rigidities, low real wages, legitimacy-starved governments and limited domestic proficiency in terms of policy formulation and implementation. This is undoubtedly a serious problem, with no obvious short-term solution.

The role of the World Bank

The World Bank has been providing *project finance* for large-scale investment projects in less developed countries since its inception. In 1980, it introduced *structural adjustment lending* to provide bridging finance for countries undertaking often painful medium-term adjustment. Conditionality is similar to that of the IMF, although it especially tends to emphasise the reform of public sector expenditure and institutions.

Obviously, the work of the IMF and World Bank often overlap; for example, countries would often need a programme of structural adjustment to resolve or avoid BOP crises. In recognition of this need the two organisations now coordinate policy to a large degree, and the World Bank often insists on the country having an existing standby arrangement with the IMF before approving a structural adjustment loan.

Both organisations have become more flexible in recent years, showing a greater willingness to tailor their policy prescriptions and conditionality to the circumstances of the borrower. For example, Mexico took out a structural adjustment loan in 1986, and managed to negotiate repayments linked to the price of oil, Mexico's principal export; this represented a significant departure from previous practice. Naturally, such developments are extremely welcome, and should imply that the relationships between the World Bank and IMF on the one hand, and many SOEs on the other, become less antagonistic than in the past, with the emphasis on both sides shifting from doctrine to pragmatism.

CASE EXAMPLE

Structural adjustment in Africa

The objective of structural adjustment is to establish market-friendly incentives to encourage capital accumulation and efficient resource allocation. For sustainable growth, macroeconomic stability coupled with agricultural and private sector development is necessary. In the African countries which have undertaken, and sustained, policy reform, adjustment seems to be bringing rewards. Although the approaches adopted, and the successes, have varied considerably, of 29 countries studied by the World Bank, the six with the most improvement in macroeconomic policies have reaped the largest benefits in terms of economic performance. In general, African countries have had more success in macroeconomic, trade and argricultural reform, than in reforming the public and financial sectors, or securing significant improvements in education, health and infrastructure.

CASE EXAMPLE

Structural adjustment – Zambia

Following the succession to power of Frederick Chiluba, economic reforms have been initiated which have restored hope in Zambia's future. Among these reforms have been trade liberalisation, a reduction in subsidies, the lifting of foreign exchange controls, a reduction in the budget deficit, a lowering of the inflation rate from 189 per cent in 1993 to under 45 per cent in 1995, and most significantly, privatisation of industry (including copper). Adherence to the structural adjustment guidelines of the IMF and the World Bank has enabled the government to make use of financial assistance from these institutions.

Zambia is the world's fourth largest producer of copper, yet mismanagement, low prices and reliance on expensive machinery have brought the industry to the brink of collapse. The Chiluba government seeks to revitalise the industry through privatisation, despite the repercussions for the 50 000-strong labour force of the nationally controlled mines. The move to privatise has attracted foreign investment in the mining sector (including South African conglomerate, Anglo American).

The new government has focused on developing agriculture, to exploit Zambia's enviable agricultural potential, and reduce dependence on mining. In the past, the bulk of spending on agriculture was to cover losses by inefficient parastatals (public enterprises or state owned enterprises). The new government has encouraged large-scale farming, and has attracted foreign investors with a range of incentives, such as tax allowances, duty free imports of capital equipment and repatriation of profit. The new policies have led to an increase in the area under cultivation, the growing of new crops, including crops for export, and a greater role being played by the private sector. Priority has also been given to infrastructure development, with opportunities for joint ventures between the public and private sectors.

Critical problems have yet to be overcome: corruption in government, one of the world's highest per capita external debts, and regional conflict which severely disrupts exports.

CASE EXAMPLE

Structural adjustment – Ghana

Ghana has had one of the more successful adjustment programmes in Sub-Saharan Africa. Since 1984 Ghanaian economic performance has improved substantially: real GDP growth has averaged 5 per cent per annum, a reasonable fiscal balance has been achieved and its balance of payments has strengthened. The bulk of growth, however, has come from the service sector, while agriculture, although the largest sector, has contributed only 5 per cent.

A gradual economic recovery programme was embarked on in 1983. Among the most successful policies implemented in the first stage was a devaluation of the currency, from cedi 2.75 to the dollar in 1983 to cedi 90 to the dollar by 1986. Fiscal discipline was another key element. Revenue as a percentage of GDP was increased through tax reforms which sought to broaden the tax base

▶

Case example continued

and lower personal tax rates. This increased revenue collection allowed for greater spending on social services and infrastructure development.

Trade reform has included foreign exchange liberalisation, and the removal of quotas and price controls. Efforts were made to promote exports by removing export duties and introducing tax rebates based on export sales, but progress has been hampered by continuing state control of marketing and logistical services.

Despite major financial sector reforms (*inter alia* restructuring the financial position of commercial banks, deregulation of interest rates, and the abolition of credit ceilings), the financial system remains precarious. Savings are low which constrains lending, and non-bank intermediation is still dominated by public enterprises.

With about two-thirds of formal sector employment accounted for by the public sector, labour market reform has been minimal: since 1983 real public sector wages have increased 20 times that of the growth in real GDP per capita. Adjustment has also been slow in agriculture and in the public sector. The civil service remains one of the largest in Africa, and parastatals maintain a presence in virtually every economic sector.

23.7 Conclusion

In this chapter we have focused on the balance of payments and structural economic problems facing many small open economies (SOEs) in the world today. Apart from operating under a so-called balance of payments constraint, most SOEs are not sufficiently diversified and rely too much on the exports of one or more primary commodities. This renders them vulnerable to cyclical and structural changes in the rest of the world. None of the policy options reviewed here – i.e. currency depreciation, direct controls and structural adjustment – are painless, and the conditions on which IMF and WB assistance is based appear to be particularly severe.

Of course, there is no quick-fix solution to these structural problems, or more generally to the problem of poverty, and in the next chapter we look at possible long-term solutions.

Summary

- The typical small open economy (SOE) operates under a severe balance of payments constraint: it cannot expand its domestic economy for too long, and thereby run a current account deficit, because it cannot rely on getting a net capital inflow on the capital account. The shortage of foreign exchange thus acts as a brake on growth.

- The governments of SOEs have several policy options to choose from, but none of them can be said to be costless. A currency depreciation may well boost exports and curb imports, but could also give rise to imported inflation and raise the domestic value of the country's foreign debt.

- The imposition of direct controls on imports and foreign exchange holdings has an immediate effect on the balance of payments, but also distorts relative prices and is costly to administer.

- A third option is 'structural adjustment', according to which an attempt is made to dampen aggregate demand, and hence imports, e.g. through stricter fiscal and monetary policies, while at the same time expanding productive capacity in the local economy. But cutting back state expenditure is a politically sensitive issue, and perhaps even morally indefensible, and may also thwart the government's attempt to expand productive capacity. Likewise, contractionary monetary policy will boost the ranks of the unemployed and, due to higher financing costs, may also contribute to inflationary pressures in the economy.

- Supply-side policies include tax cuts, infrastructual investments and a relaxation of bureaucratic controls, and are aimed at expanding productive capacity. While these policies involve little risk, they do take a long time to have the desired effect on investment and real income, and hence on the balance of payments.

- Both the IMF and the World Bank provide assistance to countries experiencing temporary balance of payments crises. But such assistance does not come free, and the IMF in particular usually requires the recipient country to adhere to a carefully thought out structural adjustment programme.

- IMF conditionality has been severely criticised from several quarters, e.g. that it fails to recognise that the source of the problem is often external to a recipient country, or that the country has only a limited capacity for structural adjustment. Nonetheless, both the IMF and the WB have recently become more sensitive to the needs of recipient countries.

Questions for review

1. Discuss some of the structural economic problems experienced by small open economies (SOEs).

2. Does exchange rate depreciation provide a solution to the balance of payments constraint under which SOEs are operating?

3. What do you understand by 'structural adjustments'? Should IMF assistance be conditional?

CHAPTER 24

Poverty, growth and the role of government

Some two-thirds of the world's population are poor – either in the absolute sense of the word, or in the sense that their average incomes are much lower than those of the rich. The problem of poverty is generally conceived of as a struggle to make ends meet – which it certainly is. But it also refers to the huge income inequalities that exist between different countries and among people of the same country. Getting one's macroeconomic house in order (with or without IMF assistance) is one thing, but coming to grips with poverty is quite another. In the sections that follow we shall elaborate on this point and look at the nature of the problem itself, after which we consider some of the relevant policy implications.

24.1 GDP as a measure of poverty

It has become something of a convention to measure a country's economic performance in terms of the level and growth of its real per capita income. Thus, if nominal GDP increased by 13 per cent, the average price level by 10 per cent, and population by 2.5 per cent, then the level of per capita income would have risen by only 0.5 per cent. While there are significant differences in per capita income levels between the countries of the world, such discrepancies do not necessarily provide a basis for differentiating between rich and poor countries. Indeed, it is often claimed that the level of per capita income of a country represents an inadequate, if not misleading, measure of its true standard of living.

Statistical problems

In the *first* place, there are numerous statistical problems associated with the measurement of real per capita income. Apart from such standard problems as the choice of a suitable base year and deflator, some price rises may not be inflationary as they merely reflect costly improvements in the *quality* of the goods or services in question. In addition, population censuses are notoriously inaccurate, and in developing countries in particular there is much evidence of under-counting having occurred during past censuses. Thus, if the accuracy of census data should improve over time, as it usually does, it must follow that growth rates based on such data will represent an over-estimation of the true rate of population growth.

Subsistent sector

Secondly, published data often refer only to those sectors of an economy in which money transactions are taking place on a regular basis. Thus, official estimates may exclude parts of the informal sector, and also the subsistent agricultural sector which, in many developing countries, constitutes a significant sector of economic activity. The typical subsistent producer is either the chief consumer of his or her own produce, or enters into barter transactions with other producers. Now, if the monetised sector gradually encroaches upon the subsistent sector, as might be reasonably expected, it is very likely that growth estimates based on the former sector alone will be biased in an upward direction.

For example, consider an economy in which the real value of output produced in its monetised and subsistent sectors is R80 million and R20 million, respectively. If during the ensuing period production in the monetised sector increased by R8 million, the national accountant might conclude that the economy has experienced growth of 10 per cent, i.e. R8 million/R80 million. Of course, the correct denominator to use would be the real value of total production, i.e. R100 million, whence the growth rate would be estimated at 8 per cent only. However, it is also possible that a portion of the (reported) increase in output, say R4 million, was due to commercialisation of the subsistent sector, according to which money was being introduced as a medium of exchange in transactions that were previously conducted on a barter basis. In this case, the *real* value of output in the economy as a whole would have risen from R100 million to R104 million only, or at a rate of 4 per cent, rather than 10 per cent.

Prices of non-traded goods

A *third* problem arises from the practice whereby comparisons are made between the per capita income levels of countries on the basis of their official exchange rates *vis-à-vis* the US dollar. Returning to our earlier island example, if the official exchange rate of the rupee in Utopia was $1 = R20, then it would imply that $1 represents the same real standard of living in the USA as does R20 in Utopia.

There are at least two reasons why such an inference may not be valid. First, the rupee may be overvalued in terms of the US dollar due to a desire on the part of Utopia's monetary authorities to keep import prices low. This could be done by fixing the exchange rate at an unrealistically high level, or by buying and selling foreign exchange in such a way as to maintain an artificially high exchange rate. Thus, if the official exchange rate was fixed at $1 = R20, while supply and demand conditions dictated a real rate of $1 = R30, it must follow that the official (dollar) value of Utopia's income will exceed its real market value by 50 per cent.

Moreover, exchange rates may fail to reflect differences in the composition of demand and in the prices of non-traded goods between countries. It is often claimed that non-traded goods are cheaper relative to traded goods in developing countries than they are in industrially advanced countries. We may illustrate this point by once again referring to the rate of exchange between the US dollar and the Utopian rupee. Table 24.1 gives a breakdown of household expenditure on two goods, one a non-traded or domestic good, D, and the other a traded good, T, for each of the two countries. The typical household in Utopia uses its total (weekly) income of R600 to purchase 20 units of D and 10 units of T each week, while its American counterpart spends its weekly income on acquiring 20 units of D and 40 units of T.

Table 24.1 Household expenditure per week

	UTOPIA			USA	
Good	Unit price	Expenses	Good	Unit price	Expenses
20 D	R20	R400	20 D	$2	$40
10 T	R20	R200	40 T	$1	$40
Total exp/income:		R600	Total exp/income:		$80

Now, using the official exchange rate of $1 = R20, one would conclude that average household income in Utopia is $30 per week, as compared to $80 in the USA. But here one is assuming that $1 can buy the same quantity of D in the USA as can R20 in Utopia, which is patently not the case. Clearly, the dollar value of 20 units of D in Utopia is equal to $40 – not $20 – and thus the dollar value of total household expenditure (and income) in Utopia is simply 20D + 10T = $40 + $10 = $50. It follows that Utopia's income will be underestimated if no account is taken of the fact that non-traded goods of the same quality are cheaper in Utopia than in the USA.

Failure to account for these price differentials may result in a distorted picture of real living standards in developing countries. In the case of Kenya, for example, it has been shown that elimination of this bias could raise the dollar value of its GDP by almost 100 per cent.

24.2 Inequality

The *fourth* and possibly most serious shortcoming of using per capita GDP as an index of poverty is its failure to provide any indication of the distribution of income within a country. The latter is generally viewed as a matter of public concern, especially in developing countries where the degree of income inequality is significantly higher than in industrially advanced countries.

The problem of inequality can be usefully explained with the aid of the familiar Lorenz curve. We have already used this curve when we measured the size distribution of firms in an industry in Chapter 6 – the same principles apply here. In Fig. 24.1 (a), for example, we measure the percentage of total households, cumulated from the lowest to the highest income bracket, on the horizontal axis. Likewise, the percentage of total income earned is indicated along the vertical axis. As in the case of the size distribution of firms, the diagonal from bottom left to top right indicates a perfectly equal distribution. It therefore provides a bench-mark against which to measure inequality in the size distribution of income. The higher the degree of income inequality, the more the Lorenz curve will be bowed toward the lower right-hand corner of the diagram.

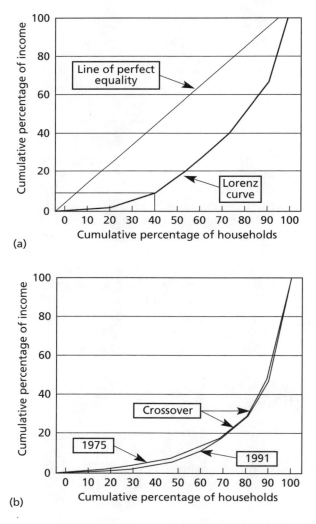

Fig. 24.1 (a) Lorenz curve; (b) Lorenz curve for South Africa: all population groups

We can now use the Gini coefficient to measure the extent of income inequality in the size distribution of income. This is done in Fig. 24.1(b) for South Africa, where Lorenz curves for the years 1975 and 1991 are indicated. It can be seen that the Gini coefficient for all population groups remained more or less unchanged between 1975 and 1991 (at 0.68). However, the shares of total personal income accruing to African, Coloured and Asian households – not shown in the diagram – did in fact increase over the period 1980 to 1991, while the share accruing to White households declined. In 1991 the income shares were as follows: 27.6 per cent for Africans, 61.2 per cent for Whites, 7.3 per cent for Coloureds and 3.9 per cent for Asians.

More recently, the Gini coefficient for South Africa has shown a marginal decrease – to about 0.65 in 1993. But the latter figure is still one of the highest in the world, and is much higher than those reported for the selection of countries shown in Table 24.1.

Table 24.1 Gini coefficient: selected international comparison

Developing country	Gini	Developed country	Gini
South Africa	0.65	Portugal	0.41
Brazil	0.61	Australia	0.40
Cote d'Ivoire	0.55	USA	0.38
Turkey	0.51	New Zealand	0.38
Malaysia	0.48	France	0.35
Philippines	0.45	Canada	0.34
Hong Kong	0.45	Israel	0.33
Singapore	0.42	United Kingdom	0.32
India	0.42	Sweden	0.32
Pakistan	0.36	West Germany	0.30
Korea	0.36	Japan	0.28
Taiwan	0.27	The Netherlands	0.27
Average:	0.46	Average:	0.34

It is also of interest to note that almost 50 per cent of the South African population is currently living below the so-called Minimum Living Level (MLL). To eliminate this poverty completely would require an income transfer to the poor of almost R8000 million, or alternatively, an economy growing at 5 per cent per year continuously over a period of 24 years.

24.3 Reasons for inequality

There are presumably many factors that could contribute to the problem of inequality in developing countries. Some would argue that the free market system tends to reward those who already 'have' and discriminate against the 'have-nots'. Others would blame it on a lack of economic growth, pointing to the fact that rising levels of per capita income usually go hand in hand with an improvement in the personal distribution of income. We shall focus here on a few of the more important reasons, before turning our attention to possible solutions.

The distribution of wealth

A person's income – which is a flow concept – is partly determined by his or her wealth – a stock concept. The latter consists of many kinds of assets, the most important of which are fixed property, equity, government stock and life insurance. Wealth generates income in the form of interest payments and dividends, and also through the sale of assets. It also determines the *ability* to generate income, insofar as it can be used as collateral for the purpose of borrowing funds.

The degree of inequality in the distribution of wealth is generally much greater than that associated with the personal distribution of income. This implies that the distribution of income earned from wealth is much more unequal than the distribution of income earned from work. And it follows that an unequal distribution of wealth may be partly responsible for the high degrees of inequality in the distribution of total income in many developing countries.

Factor demand and marginal productivity

We have already examined the determination of wages according to the marginal productivity theory of factor demand. We found that, *ceteris paribus*, the greater a worker's productivity, the higher will be his or her wage, and hence income. All factors influencing the productivity of workers will therefore have an impact on the distribution of income. The distribution of natural abilities, character traits, education and training all help to explain the degree of inequality in the size distribution of income.

Age distribution

An individual's income usually varies considerably over his or her lifetime. As work experience is gained, the individual's earning power increases. In professions such as law and medicine, networks of contacts and clientele established over time significantly enhance the individual's income. Because earning power tends to vary with age, a changing age structure will cause the distribution of income to change over time, *ceteris paribus*.

Market power

The exercise of market power is certainly a factor affecting income inequality. Some unions and professional bodies have adopted policies to limit the supplies of their productive services, thus raising the incomes of those who are admitted to the market. Legislation which requires registration of legal and medical practitioners and licences for the provision of other services restrict the supply of these services. In our analysis of the product markets we found that the possession of market power leads to greater profits. The exercise of monopoly power may ensure monopoly profits almost indefinitely: thus market power may influence the distribution of income.

Preferences, luck and opportunity

Even if all individuals were born with identical talents and abilities and given equal access to education and training, the income distribution would still not be perfectly equal. Differences in preferences with regard to risk, leisure and other factors will lead to differences in income.

Being in the right place at the right time, or luck, is also a source of income differences. In a similar vein, opportunity or lack of it can have the same effect. Discrimination, or selective access to opportunities such as training, education or jobs, may act to increase the inequality in the distribution of income. Restricted access, on the basis of criteria other than merit, will lead to inequality in the distribution of income. Such inequality is considered inequitable, and calls for a redistribution of income often draw on this cause of income inequality.

24.4 New growth theory and the relief of poverty

What can be done about the problem of poverty? Can it be eradicated altogether? Or can it at least be reduced to manageable proportions? Well, it has been done before! Today's advanced countries were once poor, and it is worth noting that many of the Southeast and East Asian countries, including Thailand, Malaysia, Indonesia and the traditional four 'tigers', were also once poor. Their per capita income levels were lower than those of most African countries in the early 1960s. Yet 30 years later they are all much better off, with some of them now counted among the rich countries of the world.

What these countries had in common is the fact that they had all experienced long periods of sustained economic growth. Not only did this growth raise levels of per capita income by considerable margins, but it also brought about a more equitable distribution of income.

Growth and redistribution

The relationship between growth and distribution has a long history in economics. Traditionally it was held that economic growth required an adequate volume of savings, and since savings propensities among the rich exceeded those of the poor, savings in turn depended on there being a sufficient degree of inequality in the distribution of income. Countries were thus faced with an unenviable choice: they could either go for growth first, ignoring the distributional problem, and eventually redistribute the fruits of that growth;

or they could go for a policy of restribution but forfeit the chance of achieving economic growth.

The alternative view – and the one currently holding sway – is that such a trade-off need not necessarily exist. Developing countries can thus achieve the twin objectives of economic growth and an equitable distribution of income simultaneously; or at least achieve the latter objective at a relatively small cost in terms of growth foregone. This view has much in common with the growing body of literature known as 'new growth theory'. The theory examines the dynamics underlying investment and technological progress, and suggests ways in which governments can foster growth and innovation by appropriate interventions.

New growth theory (NGT)

The Classical and neo-Classical schools viewed investment, or additions to the capital stock, as a primary source of economic growth – the *deus ex machina*. According to NGT, however, this is an oversimplification of what is really a very complex process. They adopt a much broader definition of 'capital', and focus attention on the role played by each of the components of capital in fostering economic growth.

In addition to privately owned physical capital (e.g. office buildings, factories and luxury homes), 'capital' also includes the following three important components:

- the existing physical ('material') infrastructure (e.g. roads, street lighting and sewerage systems);
- accumulated human capital acquired ('intentionally') through education, training and health care;
- the stock of technical know-how acquired through learning-by-doing and research and development (R&D).

The main thrust of NGT is that additions to any of the components of capital may yield increasing returns because they create externalities that benefit a range of sectors and industries in the economy.

Consider a firm that invests in R&D to create a new invention or innovation. Such an investment is potentially profitable only because the company can expect to secure a degree of monopoly power over its invention or innovation. This is typically attained through patents or non-disclosure of information, which allow the firm to gain a (temporary) advantage over its rivals. However, the firm is seldom able to appropriate all of the benefits of its innovation, since some form of technological spillover inevitably occurs. This creates positive externalities, in the sense that the R&D of one firm creates benefits for others, both locally and abroad.

Similar arguments apply to the other components of capital. Investment in the physical infrastructure creates (pecuniary) externalities by lowering production costs and boosting returns in the private sector. Likewise, investment in human capital generates knowledge and skills which are often transferred free of charge to third parties. As we saw in Chapter 9, skills gained at one firm are easily transferred to other firms.

Each of the components of capital can be influenced by government through appropriate policy intervention; and in the present instance, the case for such intervention is the standard one based on market failure (see Chapter 7). Since the marginal private benefit of investments in physical infrastructure, human capital and R&D is lower than the marginal social benefit, the untrammelled operation of the market will lead to an under-provision of these services. NGT thus provides a strong justification for government intervention in these areas because it will create favourable conditions for private sector investment and economic growth.

Two caveats

There are at least two caveats worth mentioning here. First, it is not at all clear which policies will create an optimal flow of externalities, or which services should be given priority. Should one go for education or health? Or for urban road-building projects or agricultural extension services? Where should the next million rand be spent? On pre-primary, primary or secondary education? Or on primary or specialist health care? Or on training specialist economists?

There are no simple answers here and, as always, economists are in more than two minds about these issues (which, perhaps, rules out the 'specialist economists' option mentioned above!). But looking at Southeast Asian countries again, it would seem that their focus on pre-primary and primary education, science training and preventative health care did render high returns.

A second caveat concerns the question of whether a 'new' growth strategy should or could address the problem of the 'poorest of the poor'. New growth theorists themselves would argue that government-induced external effects will not materialise if there are no takers, or if potential beneficiaries are too poor to fully internalise them. Private entrepreneurs in poor countries may not have the means with which to start or expand their own businesses and thus avail themselves of physical and social services provided by the government. As far as NGT is concerned, governments should not operate in a vacuum but focus their efforts on those communities (including the poor) where they can expect to earn the highest returns.

24.5 Entitlements and capabilities

The latter argument need not imply that a concern for the poorest of the poor is in any way misplaced. After all, governments may wish to maximise something other than economic growth, as conventionally defined. As Amartya Sen has reminded us, national income should not be considered an end in itself, nor even a particularly efficient means if it fails to reduce poverty. He produced evidence to show that the growth rate of GDP per capita moved in opposite directions to average life expectancy in both the UK during the first six decades of this century and in China after Mao. It is thus not GDP growth *per se* that determines the duration and quality of life, but rather people's 'command over health services'.

The level or growth of GDP is at best a means towards an end, and Sen believes that public policy should focus on people's 'entitlements', or the alternative commodity bundles that they can acquire, which will in turn help them to develop 'capabilities'. The latter refers to what people can or cannot do, e.g. whether they can read and write, become educated and well-nourished, and whether they can ultimately pursue profitable opportunities.

According to Sen, development policies should provide the means – services, access and funding – that will enable the poor to expand their capabilities. Sen's argument comes very close to saying that governments should redistribute resources to the poorest of the poor, irrespective of the consequences for GDP growth. While such a focus is unlikely to promote economic growth, and may well forestall it, it will at least improve the income-earning capacity of the poorest members of society.

24.6 A final caveat: government failure

A final caveat concerns the question of whether governments in developing countries can deliver the proverbial goods – as outlined in the previous sections.

Just like markets can fail, so can governments. We have all experienced 'government failure' of one kind or another – standing in long queues at the post office, getting no response to complaints about rates and taxes, waiting endlessly for passports, visas and ID documents . . . the list goes on and on. But when economists talk of government failure they mean something different. To them it refers to the maximising behaviour of politicians, bureaucrats and government officials.

Politicians and bureaucrats are no different from ordinary consumers and producers. They too want to maximise utility. Politicians can be viewed as 'rational' entrepreneurs who pursue vote maximising strategies in order to secure and retain political office. This often means that they will try to please as many voters as possible, by meeting their different public needs, and in the process contribute to an over-supply of public goods.

We can illustrate this point by means of our familiar island example. Imagine a politician standing for election on the island of Famine and supporting three unrelated public programmes, e.g. a subsidy scheme for the fishing industry, a primary schools project, and drought relief for the farming community. The subsidy scheme will naturally draw strong support from the fishing community, while the primary schools and drought relief programmes will be strongly supported by the parents of young children and farmers, respectively. But the parents of young children are unlikely to feel strongly about the subsidy scheme or the drought relief programme, and may even oppose them; and similarly for the fishing and farming communities. A *majority* of voters will thus oppose *each* of the three programmes, or at least feel indifferent about it.

The politician, of course, will have an incentive to lobby each of the three constituent groups – by promising to meet each of their separate needs (and down-playing the cost implications) – and can count on each one's support because each group will feel very strongly about its own preferred programme. Clearly, our politician does not have to please a majority of voters on any one of the three programmes, and will no doubt defeat any politician opposing them.

Now, the net effect for the island economy is essentially twofold. Firstly, one can expect a preponderance of relatively unpopular public projects, i.e. projects that do not necessarily enjoy majority support. Secondly, one can expect an aggregate over-supply of public goods on the island. Eventually, of course, Faminers will discover that their taxes are too high and, if they know what's good for them, perhaps get rid of the politician.

Another source of government failure concerns the maximising behaviour of bureaucrats. Unlike private firms, bureaucrats do not maximise profit but instead receive annual budget allocations from the legislature. These allocations are usually based on their own estimates of the costs involved in supplying public goods. Bureaucrats therefore do not face any market test. Instead, they are interested in the size of their own bureaucratic empires, and hence in the size of their budget allocations. Why? Because this will help them to earn higher salaries and enhance their reputation in the broader community. William Niskanen was one of the first economists to argue that the material well-being and reputation of bureaucrats are positively related to the size of their budgets.

There is no simple solution to the problem of bureaucratic failure. Tightening control of budgetary procedures comes at its own costs, while any attempt to shift responsibility up or down the administrative hierarchy may simply amount to a reshuffling of bureaucratic deck-chairs. Utilising the services of outside consultants is also not costless, while changing the incentive structure – e.g. by making salary increases contingent upon budget cuts – may only meet with partial success. Perhaps the only solution is an unattainable one: public administrators should have the interest of the *public* at heart!

24.7 Conclusion

Governments have an important role to play in the economy – not only in the macroeconomic sense of helping to smooth fluctuations in national income, but also in promoting economic growth and looking after the interests of the poorest of the poor. According to new growth theory, governments are required to focus investments in human capital and the infrastructure in those communities, including the poor, where they will earn the highest returns. Alternatively, if they were to concentrate their efforts on the poorest of poor communities, they may have to forfeit economic growth but would still develop the capabilities of people who have the greatest need for them. Of course, none of this will materialise if government programmes fail to get beyond the eager hands of politicians and those responsible for administering and implementing them.

Summary

- The problem of poverty is a pervasive one, but its measurement leaves much to be desired. There are several problems associated with the use of per capita GDP as a measure of a country's poverty.

- Apart from numerous statistical problems, published data do not as a rule adequately account for the subsistent sector. A further problem relates to the use of the US dollar when comparing standards of living in different countries. Official exchange rates may be overvalued (or undervalued), while they also do not usually reflect differences in the composition of demand and in the prices of non-traded goods between countries.

- A major shortcoming is the fact that per capita GDP does not provide any indication of the *distribution* of income in developing countries – arguably the most important indicator of a country's well-being. The extent of income inequality can be measured by means of the Gini coefficient, which has been found to be relatively high in developing countries, including South Africa.

- Income inequality in developing countries closely mirrors the distribution of physical and human capital, and as such can be attributed to differences in opportunity and luck, and in people's ability to avail themselves of the benefits associated with education and training.

- An important question facing developing countries is whether they can achieve the twin objectives of a higher growth rate and a more equitable distribution of income simultaneously. According to new growth theory (NGT) this may well be possible if governments promote technological advancement and invest in the physical and social infrastructure of the country.

- Adopting a broad definition of 'capital', which includes the infrastructure and accumulated human capital, NGT believes that additions to these components of capital will yield increasing returns because they create externalities that benefit a range of sectors and industries in the economy. Thus governments are required to focus their investments in human capital and the infrastructure in those communities, including the poor, where they will earn the highest returns.

- Such a strategy may not address the problem of the 'poorest of the poor', and it may therefore be necessary to redirect policy to the development of 'capabilities' among the poorest sections of the population. This may well retard growth, at least temporarily, but it will improve the distribution of income.

- Irrespective of which strategy is adopted, and good intentions notwithstanding, there is every chance that government policies will fail to deliver the proverbial goods. Government officials are not under the same pressure to perform as their counterparts in the private sector, and often pursue their own goals rather than those of the general public. Building administrative empires is a case in point, and usually comes at a high opportunity cost.

Questions for review

1. Does the per capita GDP of a country provide an accurate indication of its state of development?

2. The poverty problem is often seen as being synonymous with an unequal distribution of income. What are the main reasons for inequality in developing countries?

3. Is there a trade-off between the objectives of a higher rate of economic growth and a more equitable distribution of income? Discuss with reference to the body of literature known as new growth theory.

4. What do you understand by 'government failure'?

INDEX